A-LEVEL ENGLISH

COURSE COMPANION

Rosemary Coxon BA
Second in English Department, St. Crispin's School, Wokingham, Berkshire

Michael Baker MA
English Teacher, Northfleet Grammar School

Charles Letts & Co Ltd
London, Edinburgh & New York

First published 1983
by Charles Letts & Co Ltd
Diary House, Borough Road, London SE1 1DW

Revised 1986, 1988

© R. Coxon and M. Baker 1983, 1986, 1988

British Library Cataloguing in Publication Data
Coxon, Rosemary
    A-level English: course companion. –
    3rd ed. – (Letts study aids).
    1. English literature – Examinations, questions, etc.
    I. Title II. Baker, Michael
    820'.76   PR87

ISBN 0 85097 820 3

Printed and bound in Great Britain by
Charles Letts (Scotland) Ltd

Acknowledgements

The authors wish to record their gratitude and thanks to Dr A Wheater, Mr BW Caws and Mr DF Mackenzie for material help with the text of the book and to Peter McClure for the excellent Plot Diagram of *The Way of the World* on p. 58.

The authors and publishers are grateful to the following for permission to quote copyright material (page numbers refer to this book unless stated):

AD Peters & Co Ltd (extract from *Brideshead Revisited* by Evelyn Waugh, reprinted by permission of AD Peters & Co Ltd, p. 130); Laurence Pollinger Ltd and the Estate of Frieda Lawrence Ravagli (extract from *The Rainbow* by DH Lawrence, p. 131); Malcolm Bradbury and Martin Secker & Warburg Ltd (extracts from *The History Man* by Malcolm Bradbury, pp. 132 and 136); Penguin Books Ltd (extract from *Madame Bovary* by Flaubert, trans. Alan Russell, pp. 75-76 (Penguin ed.), Penguin Classics, 1950, Copyright © the Estate of Alan Russell, 1950, reprinted by permission of Penguin Books Ltd, p. 132); the Estate of the late Sonia Brownell Orwell and Martin Secker & Warburg Ltd (extract from *Animal Farm* by George Orwell, pp. 134-5); Iris Murdoch and Chatto & Windus Ltd (extract from *The Sandcastle* by Iris Murdoch, p. 137); Weidenfeld & Nicolson Ltd (extract from *The Millstone* by Margaret Drabble, pp. 137-8); David Higham Associates Ltd (extract from *Billy Liar* by Keith Waterhouse, p. 141); Laurie Lee and The Hogarth Press Ltd (extract from *Cider with Rosie* by Laurie Lee, p. 143); Literary Estate of Virginia Woolf and The Hogarth Press Ltd (extract from *To the Lighthouse* by Virginia Woolf, p. 133); Edward Arnold (extract from *A Passage to India* by EM Forster, pp. 133-4); The Society of Authors on behalf of the Bernard Shaw Estate (extract from *Man and Superman* by GB Shaw, pp. 104-5); Elaine Greene Ltd (extract from *Death of a Salesman* published in *Collected Plays* by Arthur Miller, Secker & Warburg, *Death of a Salesman* Copyright © 1949 by Arthur Miller, pp. 107-8); Vernon Scanell (*Incendiary*, published in *Collected Poems* by Vernon Scanell, Robson Books, p. 48).

The authors and publishers are also grateful to the following for permission to reproduce photographs and prints (again, page numbers refer to this book):

The National Portrait Gallery for the portraits of *John Keats* p. 14; *Gerard Manley Hopkins* p. 20; *WB Yeats* p. 23; *TS Eliot* p. 26; *Geoffrey Chaucer* p. 30; *John Milton* p. 36; *Ben Jonson* p. 54; *William Shakespeare* p. 66 and *Virginia Woolf* p. 133; The Imperial War Museum for the *Grave of an unknown British soldier* p. 47; Mary Evans Picture Library for prints of *The Elizabethan Playhouse* and *An Elizabethan Apron Stage* p. 52 and for *The Globe* p. 67; The Thorndike Theatre, Leatherhead for stills from productions of *The Provok'd Wife* p. 57; *Arms and the Man* p. 61; *The Importance of Being Earnest* p. 62; *Twelfth Night* p. 68; all designed by Stuart Stanley. We are also grateful to the Thorndike for the photograph from their 1981 production of *Macbeth*. Costume design by Alexandra Bryne. The BBC Hulton Picture Library for *A Winter's Tale* p. 71; *Henry IV* p. 73; *Henry IV* p. 76 and *Measure for Measure* p. 77; Holte Photographics Ltd for *Hamlet* p. 80; British Home Entertainments for *Othello* p. 89; BBC *To The Lighthouse* p. 113; *Wuthering Heights, Tess of the D'Urbervilles* and *Pride and Prejudice* pp 118, 119 and 128 courtesy of Metro Goldwyn Mayer; Peter Brooke *Lord of the Flies* p. 117; still from the film *Secret Agent* p. 113 by courtesy of The Rank Organisation plc; Granada TV *Brideshead Revisited* p. 130; Thorn EMI Elstree Studios Ltd for *Saturday Night, Sunday Morning* and *Billy Liar* p. 140; *Brighton Rock* p. 166 and *Ulysses* p. 167; 20th Century Fox Film Co Ltd for *Jane Eyre* p. 166 and A-R Television PLC for *Richard III* p. 164.

Contents

Part I Introduction and guide to using the book

This book is not a text book, but has been written for English Literature and Language candidates at A Level and for the Scottish Higher Grade examinations. Our main objective has been to provide a book through which the student will gain skill and assurance in the techniques of A-level English and will be able to sit the examination with confidence. It is written by two practising teachers and examiners and has been compiled after carefully analysing the requirements of all the main A-level syllabuses. Our knowledge as examiners and our interpretation of Chief Examiners' Reports help us to provide you, the student, with the techniques and skills to make a success of your examination. You will find a summary of the syllabuses of the different Boards in tabular form and the addresses of the main Examination Boards. This information may need checking from time to time as syllabuses change.

Although you will find reference to a wide variety of texts which appear on A-level syllabuses, this is **not** intended as a study aid to individual books or authors. It is a general guide to **transferable critical and study skills.** You should use the general advice given and **apply suggested methods of approach to your own set books.** You will find that we have used a wide range of approaches to different authors, genres and forms. You will get from this ideas on how to tackle your own study of individual texts. Close commentary, notes, the tracing of themes and diagrammatic aids are all represented.

The difference between GCSE and A-level study

1 There is a great deal more freedom attached to A-level work and students who embark upon A Level direct from GCSE will find it bewildering that they have the responsibility to discipline themselves. Much reading, research and note-taking has to be done in the candidate's own time and many of the least successful A-level candidates have failed to organize their time properly and thus have not prepared themselves adequately for the examination.

2 The A-level examiner will expect more of you in terms of breadth and depth of knowledge as you are only studying three, or at the most four, A-level subjects instead of up to ten or eleven GCSEs. Also, because of your increased maturity and your obvious desire to pursue this subject in depth, the A-level examiner will expect you to apply this knowledge to specific questions which will not be as straightforward as GCSE questions. There is more about this under Point 3.

3 The different approach to A-level questions is apparent in the vocabulary used in the questions. At GCSE the most common directions are 'describe', 'give an account of', 'account for'. At A Level these words can recur, but they are more often replaced by **'assess', 'discuss', 'compare', 'contrast', 'comment on', 'critically examine'** and **'to what extent would you agree with'.** It is a good idea to underline these key words which tell you *how* to answer the question and to ask yourself whether you are being relevant to these key words all the way through your answer. Always bear in mind that A Level demands an increased sophistication in the way you answer the question.

4 Another major difference between GCSE and A-level study is the difficulty of the set texts. Although GCSE literature is by no means 'easy reading', the language of the novels is usually

fairly straightforward, and the Shakespeare and poetry should present little difficulty to the average student if they are thoroughly taught and the student conscientiously prepares him- or herself for the examination.

A-level texts usually offer more scope for appreciation and thought along the lines of themes, imagery, moral or political ideas, symbolism and other such more intellectual considerations. Understanding of a more complex field of interrelationships of character, ideas or language is required. Collections of poems by a single poet, often of a more demanding degree of difficulty, are set, rather than selections from groups of different poets, with a more superficial reference to their subject matter, which is sometimes classified in the anthology rather loosely.

The immediate practical result of all this for the student, is that he or she has to consider the texts, looking more closely for such things and considering them more deeply; he/she may have to find advanced books of criticism or biography on the set author. The former are unfortunately often harder to grasp than the author's work itself; the student will need guidance and help in this. Intense and appreciative reading by a student comparatively widely read already, especially in the works of the set author or his period, is in the end the best preparation. Ability to write on the question well is then rather a matter of an ability to form connections, select relevant material and discuss intelligently the prescribed topic, as well as of mere memory.

The following thoughts will be a useful guide to any student embarking upon an A-level English course after having prepared him- or herself for a GCSE examination.

In general, GCSE tests competence in the appreciation and knowledge of three sections– (i) Shakespeare, and sometimes other drama; (ii) prose works, usually novels and (iii) Poetry. Emphasis is placed on a sensitive and informed response to the text. The standard derives from a requirement that candidates should have sound understanding of the text and thorough knowledge of individual details such as character portraits and features of the language. Where references to other matters are made or unusual words used, candidates are expected to be able to explain them.

When a context passage is introduced, the questions concern what light the passage throws on the character, what it reveals about the character's feelings, what the candidate finds worthy of note in the situation, characters or speech of the passage. Relevance is required and vigilance to select all the evidence present.

This type of question is unlikely at A Level. The philosophy behind A-level questions on set passages is, 'you have been trained to write about passages like these; you have had experience in appreciation; now do it'. There is little further guidance except in A-level language comprehension papers (see p. 155). All the writing is left to the candidate who must therefore be well practised in analysing unseen or seen passages. Useful advice on this can be found in the chapters on Practical Criticism. A study of these chapters should give the candidate certain ideas of technique and terminology which have to be acquired.

GCSE asks for evidence of knowledge of incidents and facts concerning the story, characters and language of the printed passage or whole text. A Level tests the ability to organize and select from one's knowledge. What you must not do is reproduce it uncritically or in narrative sequence. An A-level candidate must try to adjust his or her thinking to the actual requirements of a question that turns on ideas and implications deriving from the book.

Although GCSE candidates are required to **think** as well as remember, they are usually only asked to apply directly and immediately to their knowledge as a source for the relevant material, not to use it for evaluations or discussions of any controversial or debatable nature. For A-level work a higher degree of appreciation, critical awareness and subtlety in marshalling the points of discussion is expected.

At GCSE the books or authors chosen need only be sufficiently known and understood on a basic level, not necessarily commented upon or appreciated in any depth. A Level will presume a knowledge of good criticism, whether written for sixth formers or more advanced; biographical background which throws light on the work, and literary history, all of which can be valuable in an A-level essay. Also at A Level there is room for intelligent comparison or contrast with other works, not specifically prescribed for study, by the same or related authors. What is not prescribed at A Level can often be enlisted to support essays on what is. One need only have knowledge of the texts alone at GCSE. Revision aids for the texts are helpful, but often summarize or give simplified 'synopses' of the texts or paraphrases of poems and are too simplistic for much use at A Level.

A-level English examination technique

Far from being an easy option, A-level English is a difficult subject. It will test intellectual ability and maturity. Maturity of judgement and maturity of emotion are called for. Literature must not just be **read,** it must be **studied.** This means that you must consider not only *what* the writer has achieved, but *how* he or she has achieved it. You must try to **understand** the author's intentions and to respond intellectually and imaginatively to the written word.

Knowledge of what happens in the text and a few thoughts on the characters is not enough. You must also have a close, first-hand knowledge of your texts–second-hand knowledge, i.e., critics and 'crib' notes–can be useful to support first-hand knowledge, but is no substitute for it. Critics are helpful, providing that you understand what they are saying. Half-understanding leads to gibberish in the examination. Have your own thoughts and your own opinions, but make certain they are based on close study and careful thought (see pp. 156-9).

NOTE-TAKING

Annotate your set books freely and conscientiously. Look up any difficult words in a glossary or in the notes at the back of the book. This particularly applies to books where the language is difficult, like Shakespeare, Chaucer and Milton. Make brief notes of what your teacher says in lesson or lecture time and read them through in your own time, making sure that you fully understand them.

If you make notes from any other source i.e., a novel by the same author or a critical work on a set book, make sure that you record the author and title. Sometimes the page number is also useful for future reference.

Do not lose yourself in detail. Keep the main issues and the important questions clear. This is particularly important in the study of Chaucer and Shakespeare, where the language is often a barrier to understanding.

ANSWERING THE QUESTION

Learn to construct an **argument.** A-level questions will not ask you 'what happened'. They will ask you to 'discuss' an issue or give your opinion. Underline the key words in the question and make sure you do 'discuss' or 'compare' 'or contrast' all the way through.

Be **RELEVANT.** Learn to use the text to support your argument; give it some thought before you start and then keep it clear and concise. English examiners are very used to dealing with waffle and object to answers which are ill-prepared and irrelevant.

Never try to bend a question to suit the answer you wish to write. However brilliant an essay you may have written for your teacher during the year, you must answer the question asked otherwise the examiner's red pen will be drawn through your brilliantly written but irrelevant essay.

During an A-level course, take some pride in your own writing. Try to develop an appropriate style which is neither too pompous nor too colloquial. If you have something to say, say it as neatly and effectively as possible. If you have nothing to say, then do not write anything until you have.

Long, memorized chunks of quotations are neither necessary nor helpful. This advice applies to exams of traditional character, but obviously more will be expected of you if you are allowed to take books into the exam. Your aim should be to know the works you are studying so well that you can refer to any section to support the points you are making. Close reference is usually enough–no one expects you to memorize a novel! Complete accuracy in direct quotation is, of course, necessary if you are using the quotation as a detailed illustration of style.

Learn to write to a particular length. An A-level paper of three hours with four questions gives you about 40 minutes per question, allowing for reading and planning. This is about 500 words. Learn to say what you have to say within specified limits. This will help to stop the woolly, wandering approach that examiners so often meet.

Finally, take pleasure in the subject. It is a great privilege to be given time to explore the great writers. Read around your texts, on such themes as biography and social history, but always come back to the texts as the centre of your study. Increasing familiarity will bring increased understanding, and increased understanding greater confidence. This will be reflected in the examination. In this way you will have the double reward of pleasure and success.

THE INTRODUCTION OF COURSEWORK AND OPEN TEXT EXAMINATIONS INTO A-LEVEL SYLLABUSES

Most of the A-level examination boards are now introducing an optional or compulsory coursework element into their syllabuses. The AEB 660 A-level syllabus has for many years had a coursework component and, with the introduction of coursework into GCSE English, coursework at A level is a natural progression. It provides the candidate with more preparation time since less emphasis is placed on memorizing the set books. However, a more genuine exploration of the texts and appreciation of literature is required, along with evidence of relevant wider reading. Obviously, the standard and amount of preparation expected will be greater than that expected under normal examination conditions. Candidates may now be allowed to take annotated texts into the examination room with them. However, candidates must ensure that they annotate their texts thoroughly and know their books extremely well, otherwise they will waste valuable time trying to find the relevant passages. A different technique is needed for both coursework and open text examinations which students may find helpful to discuss with their teachers.

A NOTE ON CRITICAL TERMINOLOGY

A-level students are often uncertain how to make the best use of critical books written on their prescribed texts or authors. We have therefore given guidance on this in the book (p. 156). The use of critical terminology can be another stumbling block for the student.

Technical critical terms are like a workman's tools, in that if handled well, they carry out a task expertly and swiftly, but if mishandled, or especially if the wrong tools are chosen, the results are disastrous. It is not enough that terms should be learnt; they should also be seen working in good critical language, and used in one's own criticism until by experience their use is exact and appropriate. It is best not to use a word from the bank of critical terminology unless its use is natural and well-tested.

Some terms have special and obvious applications, such as the names of various verse forms and metres. Others have a wider application outside the world of literary criticism and you must be careful to use properly words such as 'satire' and 'didactic' when applying them within a critical literary context.

On p. 169 of this book there is a Glossary. You should use this to discover the meaning of terms new to you and to check that you understand fully the meaning of terms with which you are already familiar.

The examination system

1 The rôle of the Chief Examiners and Moderators

In general, the procedure is as follows, though each board may do things a slightly different way. The examination papers are set many months before the actual date of the examination by a Chief Examiner, sometimes assisted by a team of setters. The wording of the questions is checked by a Moderator who must ensure that the questions comply in every way with the requirements of the examination. Marking schemes for each question are also prepared when the question paper is set and this again is re-checked by a Moderator who can suggest changes when necessary. Further checking may be carried out by a sub-committee before the paper is printed.

2 The rôle of the Assistant Examiner

The English papers are marked by a panel of Assistant Examiners who are normally A-level English teachers themselves. Each examiner marks several hundred papers in the three weeks which follow the examination and no examiner is allowed to mark the work of a candidate he or she may have taught. Examiners only know the candidates by the names and numbers on the examination papers; they probably have no knowledge of their schools or the part of the country in which they live. Examiners rarely mark all papers of one candidate. Paper I will go to one examiner, Paper 2 to another and so on.

In our experience as A-level Examiners, after we have received the examination papers and marking schemes and before the marking begins, all the examiners attend a standardization meeting with the Chief Examiner. At this meeting each question is discussed in detail and after much debate the standards are fixed and marks allocated. Photocopies of scripts are marked by examiners at the meeting to check that all are using the same standard before the marking programme begins.

As we mark our scripts we send samples of our marking to one of the Chief Examiners for checking and further random samplings of scripts are carried out to ensure that all Assistants are marking to the correct standard.

3 The Award Stage

The office staff at the Board's Headquarters check the scripts in detail to ensure that marks have been added correctly and that correct marks are recorded on computer sheets.

'The Award Stage' follows where a Panel of Awarders assisted by the Chief Examiner studies the examination papers and marking schemes to decide the standard of answer required for each grade. At this stage, too, scripts on the border line between two grades may be reconsidered.

Any candidate who is dissatisfied with his or her grade may appeal to the Board and the work of this candidate will be checked again. A fee is usually paid in this case by the school or the candidate to the Board to cover the cost of the administrative work involved.

If any candidate wishes to be given special consideration in view of handicap or disability this must be communicated to the Board who will try to deal as fairly as possible with each candidate.

SYLLABUS REQUIREMENTS

The following list includes the requirements of Examining Boards during the 1980s. For the sake of brevity, most syllabuses have been summarized and candidates are strongly recommended to read the full syllabus before embarking on the course.

IT IS ALWAYS ADVISABLE TO CHECK THOROUGHLY FOR CHANGES AS SYLLABUSES ALTER FROM TIME TO TIME.

A-level Syllabuses

AEB SYLLABUS I (623)

Paper I (2½ hours) (100 marks)

It will be assumed that the candidate includes daily and weekly newspapers and suitable periodicals in his general reading.

(a) An essay on one of a number of subjects which may include:
 (i) current movements and events.
 (ii) social, scientific technical and economic topics of general interest.
 (iii) literary and artistic topics.
The majority of the subjects offered will require balanced discussion but some topics will provide opportunity for thoughtful, narrative or descriptive treatment. Candidates will be advised to devote about 1½ hours to this part of the paper.

(b) A test of skills of summary writing which may include:
 (i) the recognition of relevant ideas.
 (ii) note and minute taking.
(iii) incorporating selected material in a written piece of continuous idiomatic English.
Questions may also be included on the context of the passage for summary.

Paper II (3 hours) (100 marks)

This paper contains a compulsory exercise in comprehension and calls for a study of modern writing including novels, short stories and plays as well as non-fiction. A range of books is offered giving information and expressing views on aspects of modern life and including critical writing on literature. Candidates should offer **three** of the set books, at least one to be chosen from each section. An alternative question on the use of modern English will also be set. The candidate is expected to be able to apply standards of effective communication, to speeches, letters, reports, advertisements and newspaper comment. Suitable radio programmes, television and films may be useful.

The following books have been prescribed for 1988 examinations:

Section I	(a) G W Turner *Stylistics* (Pelican)
	(b) James Reeves *The Critical Sense* (Heinemann)
	(c) Brian Friel *Translations* (Faber)
Section II	(d) John Fowles *The French Lieutenant's Woman* (Granada)
	(e) Thomas Keneally *Schindler's Ark* (Coronet)
	(f) Angus Wilson *Anglo-Saxon Attitudes* (Granada)

Paper III (3 hours) (100 marks)

Candidates are required to offer four books, two from Section I and two from Section II. A detailed knowledge of the matter and form of the content of the chosen books will be expected, but **context questions will not be asked.** A knowledge of the general history of English literature will not be required, but a grasp of the historical background will be regarded as necessary.

AEB SYLLABUS II (652)

Three written papers, two of 3 hours and one of 2½ hours.

Paper I Shakespeare and Chaucer (3 hours) (100 marks)

The paper is divided into four sections, and candidates are required to attempt one question from each section. The first section consists solely of a question on the texts set for detailed study. Candidates are required to paraphrase into modern English prose a passage from Chaucer, and to comment on a passage from Shakespeare, including comment on style.

Paper II (3 hours) (100 marks)

Four authors. One essay to be chosen from each of the three sections and one from any section (4 essays in all).

Paper III Practical Criticism (2½ hours) (100 marks)

Two questions will be set, one calling for a comparison of passages, the other dealing with a single passage.

AEB SYLLABUS III (660)

Two open book written papers, each of 3¼ hours, together with a coursework folder including an extended essay.

The aim is to encourage an enjoyment and appreciation of English Literature based on an informed personal response and to extend this appreciation where it has already been acquired.

Paper I Comprehension, Practical Criticism and Prescribed Poetry Anthology (3¼ hours) (120 marks)

Paper II (3¼ hours) (120 marks)

Section A	Shakespeare
Section B	Poetry
Section C	Plays
Section D	Novels

COURSEWORK (120 marks)

Separate notes for guidance to teachers on the production, assembly and marking of coursework folders are available on application to The Secretary General (A1) at the Board's offices.

CAMBRIDGE SYLLABUS (9000)

Paper I Critical appreciation and comment (2½ hours)

Answer two questions on critical appreciation of prose or poetry passages.

Paper II Shakespeare (2½ hours)

Context question and 2 other essay questions.

Paper III Chaucer plus other major authors (2½ hours)

Context question plus 2 other essay questions. Must write on Chaucer passage in Part I plus one other passage (50 minutes). Choose one other text in Part II (3 texts altogether).

Paper IV Literature 1760–1832 (2½ hours)

Answer four questions, including not more than one on any one text.

Paper V Literature of Victorian Age (2½ hours)

Answer four questions, including not more than one on any one text.

Paper VI Literature since 1900 (2½ hours)

Answer four questions, at least two of which must be taken from Section I. Do not do more than one question from each text.

Paper VII Renaissance period (2½ hours)

Answer four questions, at least one of which must be taken from Section I.

CAMBRIDGE ALTERNATIVE SYLLABUS 9001

Paper I Comment and Appreciation (2½ hours)

Either answer two questions from Section A (questions 1–3)
or answer one question from Section A and two questions chosen freely from Sections B and C (i.e. questions 4–12)

Paper II Shakespeare (2½ hours)

Answer Section A and any two questions from Sections B and C.

Section A context questions, choose two of the passages (only one from any one play) and answer the questions.

Paper 5 Plain texts (3 hours)

Answer three sections chosen from at least two sections.

JMB A-LEVEL ENGLISH SYLLABUS

Three papers

Paper I   3 hours 40% of total marks
Paper II   Alternative A 3 hours 40% of total marks
            Alternative B 3 hours 40% of total marks
Paper III   2 hours 20% of total marks

The abilities to be tested

Within the general context, the examination attempts to assess:
(a) The candidates' understanding of the books studied.
(b) His response to literature and why he responds as he does.
(c) Practical criticism of poetry and prose.
(d) Evidence of wide reading.
(e) Ability to write clearly on literary subjects and to comment precisely on use of language.
An optional test in creative writing is provided to develop the ability to write originally.

Paper I (3 hours) 40% of marks

Divided into three sections, Section A (extracts from the plays of Shakespeare), Section B (essays on the plays of Shakespeare) and Section C (prescribed poets). Candidates are required to answer either Question 1 or Question 2 from Section A together with two other questions from Section B and one question from Section C.

Section A 10% of marks

Question 1 Two context questions from Shakespeare's three prescribed plays, with questions designed to test the candidates' detailed knowledge of the text. Candidates must choose two of the three plays.
Question 2 Choose one play of Shakespeare and answer questions on a long passage from the play, commenting on the dramatic and literary aspects of it.

Section B 20% of marks

Question 3 Two alternative essays on one play.
Question 4 Two alternative essays on second play.
Question 5 Two alternative essays on third play.

Section C 10% of total marks

Questions 6, 7, 8 and 9. Alternative questions on each of four short prescribed works by major poets.

Paper II 40% of total marks

Two alternative papers:

Alternative A consists of two alternative questions on each of 16 prescribed texts of authors from Chaucer to the present day, excluding Shakespeare. Candidates must answer four questions.

Alternative B two sections – one on study of period
                                – one on topic or theme
6–8 texts prescribed on each section, candidates required to answer on one section only, answer four questions in all and show evidence of study of minimum of four texts. Three alternative general questions will be set.

Paper III 20% of total marks

Two compulsory questions designed to test candidates' ability to use their critical powers on unseen passages of verse and prose.

LONDON UNIVERSITY A-LEVEL ENGLISH 170

Scheme of Examination

Candidates will be required to take three papers of three hours each, equally weighted.
Paper I   Comprehension and Appreciation
Paper IR   Varieties of English
Paper II   Prescribed texts
Paper III   Prescribed texts
or Paper IIIR Prescribed texts

Paper I

Candidates will be required to answer **two** questions on unseen passages of verse **or** prose **or** drama, one of which is compulsory, designed to test the ability to understand their meaning and to show appreciation of their literary form and content.

Paper IR

Candidates will be required to demonstrate some awareness and understanding of: the nature of language variety and change; the sound and sentence patterns of present-day English; factors affecting the styles and uses of English – social, regional, situational, historical; the differences between a descriptive and prescriptive attitude to language usage, and between notions of 'correct' and 'appropriate' language use; how to make a simple descriptive analysis of a text, or a contrastive analysis of two or more texts, in order to relate their linguistic features to their function and context of situation.

Candidates will be required to answer questions on passages of English which may include transcripts of speech and extracts from both literary and non-literary texts.

Paper II

The emphasis on this paper is on the close reading of individual works of English Literature.
Eight texts are selected
Section A Shakespeare: two texts.
Section B Poetry: Chaucer and two other texts.
Section C Other works: three texts, a twentieth-century work may be included. Candidates will
                  be required to answer **four** questions, each on a separate text, including at least **one**
                  on Shakespeare (Section A) and **one** on Poetry (Section B). Some questions may be
                  based on substantial extracts from the prescribed works.

Paper III

The emphasis in this paper is on the study of a group of works to complement the study of individual works in Paper II.

Three topics will be prescribed in each examination (Sections A, B, C). Six texts will be prescribed in each Section, questions will be set on the individual text, or more generally on several texts. Candidates will be asked to answer **four** questions chosen from any part of the paper. A further section, a selection of African and Caribbean texts, is available as a special alternative paper.

Specially Approved Syllabuses

Candidates may replace Paper III by an extended essay or course work on work of their own choice (Mode 3). Criteria for this examination must be obtained from the Secretary to the Board.

OXFORD LOCAL EXAMINATIONS A-LEVEL ENGLISH LITERATURE

Eight papers are set as follows:
9803/1 Compulsory paper on Shakespeare (1½ hours, maximum mark 40)
9803/2 Compulsory paper on Major Authors (2¼ hours, maximum mark 60)
9803/3 Period 1550–1680 (3 hours, maximum mark 100)
9803/4 Period 1660–1790 (3 hours, maximum mark 100)
9803/5 Period 1790–1832 (3 hours, maximum mark 100)
9803/6 Period 1832–1896 (3 hours, maximum mark 100)
9803/7 Period 1896–present day (3 hours, maximum mark 100)
9803/8 Poetry, Prose and Drama (3 hours, maximum mark 100)

Paper 1 Shakespeare

Questions are to be answered on one of two alternative extracts from the prescribed play. In addition, two essay questions are set, of which one must be attempted. No alternative Shakespeare play is set.

Paper 2 Major Authors

In Section A two extracts are printed from each of three texts which include one Chaucer text, one book of Milton's *Paradise Lost*, and one major novel. Candidates must answer on one of the extracts from one of the texts. In Section B candidates must attempt essay questions on two of the prescribed texts. One of the essays must be on the novel.

Papers 3–7

These papers are period papers in which candidates are expected to show a general knowledge of the social and literary history of the period, with special reference to the works named. A passage of appreciation is set for each of two texts, and candidates must attempt one of these. They must also answer three essay questions.

Paper 8 Poetry, Prose and Drama

For this paper candidates are required to attempt the 'unseen' appreciation of verse or prose in Question 1 and one question set from each of *three* sections of Poetry, Prose and Drama.

OXFORD AND CAMBRIDGE SCHOOLS EXAMINATIONS BOARD A-LEVEL ENGLISH LITERATURE (9620)

The following papers will be set:

Paper I (3 hours)

Two plays of Shakespeare.

Paper II (3 hours)

Chaucer and one other author. Question 1 will ask for an explanation of the meaning of certain phrases only and for answers to specific critical questions about the passages chosen.

Paper III (2½ hours)

English Literature from 16th–20th century. Three groups of books will be prescribed: one group of poetry, one of plays, one of a novel or short stories. Questions will be set on each book. Candidates should have an adequate knowledge of any **four** books either in the same group or in different groups.

Paper IV

Deals mainly with comments and appreciation.
Candidates offering English at 'A' level must take Papers I, II, and III.

NORTHERN IRELAND SCHOOLS GCE COUNCIL A-LEVEL ENGLISH

The examination will consist of three 3-hour papers.
Papers I and II will be designed to assess the quality of the candidate's understanding of and response to set texts of moderate difficulty.

Paper I

One context question and one essay question will be set on each of the prescribed Shakespeare plays. Candidates must answer **one** context question on one play and **one** essay question on the other play.

Paper II

Four essay questions on four of ten or more set texts, of all periods, including poetry, prose and drama.

Paper III

Literary criticism of passages of prose, poetry or drama, testing the candidates' comprehension of the given material and their response to it.

SOUTHERN UNIVERSITIES A-LEVEL ENGLISH (9005) ENGLISH LITERATURE

The examination will comprise three papers.

Paper I Poetry, Prose and Drama (3 hours)

Section A Poetry Candidates should bring to the examination a copy of the Poetry text (texts) they have studied – Section A; it (they) must be as printed, without added notes.

Section B Drama

Section C Prose In Sections A, B and C, an alternative question is set on each book.

Section D This will consist of questions that will test reading of literature related to the texts prescribed in Sections A, B and C. Candidates must answer four questions from at least three of the Sections A, B, C and D.

Paper II Special Authors (3 hours)

Candidates will be required to answer a compulsory question requiring detailed knowledge of the texts and three other essay questions, one on each of the chosen texts.

Candidates will be well advised to read other works by the authors chosen for study and to interest themselves in their relevant literary and historical background.

Paper III Comprehension and Appreciation (2 hours)

This paper will test the comprehension and appreciation of a passage of verse and a passage of prose.

WELSH JOINT EDUCATION COMMITTEE, ENGLISH LITERATURE A-LEVEL (0014)

Candidates will be required to take three papers:
A1   3 hours   40% of the marks
A2   3 hours   40% of the marks
A3   2½ hours   20% of the marks
Candidates will be judged on:
(a) Their knowledge of the content of the books and, where appropriate, of the personal and historical circumstances in which they are written.
(b) Their understanding, extending from simple factual comprehension to a broader conception of the nature and significance of literary texts.
(c) Their ability to recognize and describe literary effects and to comment precisely on the use of language.
(d) Their capacity to make judgements of value based on close reading.
(e) Their ability to see a literary work in its historical context as well as that of the present day.
(f) Their ability to write organized and cogent essays on literary subjects.

Paper A1

Requires the study of **three** texts, one in each of the three main literary genres, and the ability to undertake close analysis of textual features. One play by Shakespeare will be prescribed; there will be a choice between works by two poets and two novelists. Candidates will be required to answer **four** questions: two on the prescribed play by Shakespeare, one on the poetry text studied and one on the novel studied.

Paper A2

Requires the study of **four** texts chosen from a list of approximately twelve texts. Texts will not be grouped by a period or genre.

Centres may submit proposals for replacing Paper A2 by components of internal assessment. Guidelines for coursework submissions are available from the WJEC.

Candidates will be required to answer **four** questions. Alternative questions will be set on each of the texts; where appropriate extracts may be printed.

Paper A3

Tests candidates' ability to use their critical powers on unseen passages of poetry, prose and drama.

Candidates will be required to answer two questions requiring the critical appreciation of unseen passages. Three questions will be set:

Question 1 will be based either on a single poem or on two poems to compare and contrast.

Question 2 will be based on a single passage of prose or on two passages of prose to compare and contrast.

Question 3 will be based either on a single excerpt from a play or on two excerpts to compare and contrast. Candidates will be expected to comment on the dramatic and theatrical qualities as well as on the literary qualities of the excerpt(s).

In all three questions the context or background will be provided where this is appropriate.

AS-level Syllabuses

These syllabuses are designed to appeal to students who can profit from a course in English Literature that is as demanding in its standards as an Advanced Level syllabus but has a much reduced content. The syllabus is intended to provide a contrasting area of interest for those not wishing to specialize in English (for example, students of science and mathematics) and to complement the study of other subjects in the field of humanities.

Aims

The aims of the syllabus are:

(a) to offer students the opportunity to extend their experience of English language and literature;

(b) to encourage attentive and sensitive reading;

(c) to develop students' capacity to respond imaginatively to what they read;

(d) to encourage students to make, articulate, and support independent opinions and informed judgments.

Assessment objectives

The examination will assess a candidate's ability to:

(a) demonstrate knowledge and understanding of a range of literary texts;

(b) communicate a sensitive and informed personal response to what is read;

(c) recognize, appreciate and comment on the varied ways in which writers handle language, content and structure;

(d) appreciate the terms and requirements of the questions and write organized and cogent responses to them.

The following syllabuses give all the information available at present.

UNIVERSITY OF OXFORD DELEGACY OF LOCAL EXAMINATIONS AS-LEVEL ENGLISH

Candidates must attempt two written papers.

Paper 1 – Commentary

This paper will be of 1¼ hours duration, carry 25% of the total marks and will consist of two questions, of which candidates must choose one.

Question 1 will consist of a passage or passages on a topic of general literary or cultural interest and may include extracts from works of criticism. Questions may be asked on content, language, argument and attitude.

Question 2 will consist of a passage or passages (either prose or poetry, or both) for critical appreciation; and may, or may not, ask specific questions.

It is intended that the precise form and nature of the questioning in both parts may vary from year to year, according to the character of the pieces selected.

Paper 2 – Poetry, Prose and Drama

This paper will be of 2½ hours duration and carry 75% of the total marks. Three questions are to be answered.

A range of texts from the 16th century to the present day is offered, giving a balanced coverage of the genres of poetry, prose and drama. The texts will be drawn from those prescribed for Paper 8 of the 9803 syllabus; where these do not include a Shakespeare text, one such text will always be offered in addition to the other texts and on the same optional footing.

A choice of two questions will be set on each text; candidates must answer *one* question on each of *three* texts, drawn from at least *two* sections of the paper (Poetry, Prose, Drama).

JOINT MATRICULATION BOARD. AS-LEVEL ENGLISH

Paper I (50% of the total marks) (2½ hours)

The paper will offer source material in the form of selected pieces of writing linked by a common theme drawn from various sources, not necessarily literary in form. Candidates will be provided with a copy of the source material two weeks in advance of the examination. An appreciation of style or register will be required in response to some of the material. Other questions will be related to the common theme, allowing a range of response from analytical essays to the writing of individually creative and imaginative pieces.

Either

Paper II (50% of the total marks) (2½ hours)

Two alternative papers are available.

Alternative A will consist of two sections. Section 1 will be identical with Paper II Alternative A of English Literature (Advanced) and the same questions will be set for both examinations. Section 2 will consist of two alternative questions on each of the three Shakespeare plays prescribed for Paper I of English Literature (Advanced); the questions will be different from those set in Paper I of English Literature (Advanced) and will be essay questions or questions based on one passage from the prescribed play requiring candidates to comment on dramatic and literary aspects of the passage and to relate these to the rest of the play. Candidates will be required to answer three questions, of which at least two must be taken from Section 1.

Alternative B will be identical with Paper II Alternative B of English Literature (Advanced) and the same questions will be set for both examinations. Candidates will be required to answer three questions from their chosen section and to show evidence of the study of a minimum of three texts.

Or

Internal assessment of coursework

Entries from external candidates will not be accepted for this option.

Each candidate will be required to submit a folder containing four pieces of work chosen from work done during the course.

CAMBRIDGE, OXFORD AND SOUTHERN SCHOOL EXAMINATIONS COUNCIL AS-LEVEL ENGLISH LITERATURE

Paper 1 (Compulsory) (40% of marks) (2 hours)

Critical Appreciation

One passage will be set from each of the three genres, Prose, Poetry and Drama. Candidates will be required to answer on any *two*. The prose passage will be taken from a work of literature but may be imaginative, discursive or argumentative in nature. Candidates will not be obliged to compare passages, though the opportunity to do so will be provided. Examiners will not presuppose specialized knowledge of any particular period.

Either

Paper 2 Set texts (60% of marks) (3 hours)

This will be divided into three sections, Prose, Poetry and Drama. Each section will contain three questions on each of three texts, at least one of which will be from the twentieth century. One of the questions on each prose text will involve an imaginative response to the text; one of the questions on each work of drama will involve a consideration of stagecraft. Candidates will be instructed to answer only one such question in each section.

Candidates will be able to range freely over the paper, confining themselves, if they wish, to one genre. Three questions should be answered in all and a detailed knowledge of three different set texts should be shown.

Or

Coursework (60% of marks)

Centres will submit a scheme of work covering a minimum of three texts either of their own choice or taken from the set texts. It will therefore be possible for those Centres wishing to do so to use three texts from those set on their A-level syllabus, or to link the work in some other way with that of their A-level classes. An indication of proposed units of work and marks allocation will be required. This work will be submitted in an individual folder for each candidate, school assessed and externally moderated.

WELSH JOINT EDUCATION COMMITTEE AS-LEVEL ENGLISH

Paper 1 (50% of marks) (3 hours)

Candidates will be required to answer *three* questions: one from Section A on a prescribed play (20%); one from Section B on a prescribed prose work (20%); and in Section C to respond to an 'unseen' poem (10%).

Section A

Either	*King Lear*–Shakespeare
or	*Death of a Salesman*–Miller
or	*Jumpers*–Stoppard

Section B

Either	*Emma*–Austen
or	*The French Lieutenant's Woman*–Fowles
or	*Staying On*–Scott

Copies of the prose and drama texts studied *must* be taken into the examination room. Particular editions are not prescribed, but in the case of the Shakespeare play a good modern annotated edition should be used. Personal annotation of the text is permitted; however, candidates will be reminded in the question paper of the importance of answering the question set.

Section C

A poem or poems will be set for appreciation and comment.

Coursework (50% of marks)

Candidates will normally be required to submit *four* pieces of work, each of between 1,000– 2,000 words. In certain circumstances, and with the approval of the Chief Examiner, these requirements may be varied; e.g. if a set of poems is being submitted as one of the pieces of work; if the scope and length of an extended piece of writing warrants its inclusion in place of two pieces.

Pieces will be selected from work undertaken during the AS-level course as representing the best achievement by the candidate. All of the work within a candidate's folder must come within either the category of 'textual work' or the category of 'non-textual work' as outlined below:

(a) *Textual work*

Study of poetry is likely to feature in candidates' coursework submissions in view of the preparation needed for Section C of the written paper. However, there are no genre restrictions in this category. Drama is taken to include radio, TV and film.

In the case of literary texts there must be evidence of the study of two 'texts'. Work may be of a comparative nature, rather than being restricted to single texts. Work on texts listed for Paper 1 may not be submitted in the year of examination for which those texts are prescribed. As well as anthologies of poetry, collections of short-stories or one-act plays are acceptable.

In the case of other media it is not possible to make generally applicable requirements about the nature and volume of the texts studied. Instead, some examples of assignments and folders that would be acceptable are given in Coursework Guidelines. A single topic or 'text' must not be the basis for more than two assignments.

(b) *Non-textual work*

At least *two* of the three main literary genres must be reflected in a candidate's folder if this option is chosen. Unless a poem is of some length (e.g. 50 lines or more) a group of poems will count as a single piece of work. An explanation of the genesis of the writing and an evaluation of its success should normally form part of the work to be assessed. However, if this is not appropriate, then it is essential that the circumstances of production are clearly indicated.

UNIVERSITY OF LONDON AS-LEVEL ENGLISH

Paper 1 Teacher-assessed coursework

Extended Studies (30%)

A folder of work of some 3,000–3,500 words comprising one or more pieces of work in one of the following fields:
(a) Studies of contemporary fiction and biography
(b) Studies in contemporary journalism
(c) Short story writing

Paper 2 Examination Paper (3 hours)

A. Textual commentary (1½ hours) (35%)

Candidates will be required to answer *one* question asking for some systematic commentary, together with some evaluative response, on passages of various kinds. The passages may include extracts from literary texts and transcripts of speech.

Two alternative questions will be set in the examination.

B. Desk study (1½ hours) (35%)

Candidates will be required to answer *one* question in which a specific writing task will be set on material from two or three sources. This material may include graphical/statistical material.

THE ASSOCIATED EXAMINING BOARD AS-LEVEL ENGLISH (985)

Paper 1 Written Paper–Comprehension and Comment (2½ hours) (50% weighting)

Section A

A compulsory exercise in comprehension.

Section B

Eight books are prescribed giving information and expressing views on aspects of modern life and including critical writing on literature. Two questions are set on each book and candidates must answer one question on each of *two* texts. An alternative question on the use of modern English will also be set.

Paper 2 Coursework (50% weighting)

The folder should be a sample of the student's work during the course and should contain for assessment and moderation:

1. Two pieces illustrating different kinds of summary skills;
2. A detailed study of some aspect of language in use;
3. An essay exhibiting discussion and argument;
4. A reflective, narrative or descriptive piece of writing;
5. An essay on some aspect of English either based on a book or on the candidate's own observations and interest.

Coursework pieces 3, 4 and 5 should not normally exceed 1000 words each. Coursework piece 2 should not normally exceed 2000 words and the two pieces of summary work should not normally exceed 500 words each.

THE ASSOCIATED EXAMINING BOARD AS-LEVEL ENGLISH LITERATURE (986)

Paper 1 Written Paper (3 hours (plus 15 minutes reading time)) (40% weighting)

Section A

Comprehension and practical criticism of either a poem or poems *or* literary prose/drama passages *or* non-literary material. A choice of questions will be offered.

Section B–Plays

Four plays will be set of which *one* will be chosen. *Two* of these plays will be the same as those set for advanced Level English Literature (652) in the same year. Copies of these plays will not be allowed into the examination room. The other *two* plays will be the same as those set for Advanced Level English Literature (660) in the same year. Candidates should take copies of these plays into the examination room in order to answer the questions.

Section C–Novels

Four novels will be set of which *one* will be chosen. *Two* of these novels will be the same as those set for Advanced Level English Literature (652) in the same year. Copies of these novels will not be allowed into the examination room. The other *two* novels will be the same as those set for Advanced Level English Literature (660) in the same year. Candidates should take copies of these novels into the examination room in order to answer the questions.

Paper 2 Coursework (60% weighting)

Candidates will submit:

(a) at least one piece of writing on a Shakespeare play;

(b) two pieces of writing based on *either* at least two poets *or* at least two themes in poetry;

(c) not more than three pieces of writing based on wide reading which should not include any texts used in (a) and (b) in coursework or any of the set texts prescribed for the examination paper.

The average length of each piece of writing should be 1000 words. A review of a theatrical performance of a play seen by the candidate, in which the production is related to the text, will be acceptable as one piece.

Scottish Syllabuses

SCOTTISH EDUCATION BOARD HIGHER GRADE SYLLABUS 1988

There are two alternatives: the old examination-based syllabus, and a new syllabus which permits a Folio of the candidate's coursework to be submitted in addition to two written examination papers. Paper I and part of Paper III of the old syllabus are absorbed by the Folio and there is a change to Paper II.

First syllabus

The papers will test knowledge and skills relating to continuous prose writing, interpretation, language studies and literature. The examination will comprise the following components:

Paper	Format	Time Allocation	Mark Allocation
I	Composition – essay and report	1 hr 40 mins	50
II	Interpretation and Language – short answers	1 hr 30 mins	50
III	Literature – essays	1 hr 50 mins	60
		Total	160

In all parts of the examination candidates will be expected to write legibly, to spell correctly and to punctuate accurately.

Paper I will consist of two questions, both of which must be answered. This paper will carry a total of 50 marks, but the allocation of marks between the two questions may vary slightly from year to year.

Question A (30± marks)

Candidates would normally be expected to devote not more than one hour to this part of the paper. Candidates will be offered a number of themes and will be required to write on one of these. The themes offered will allow candidates to choose from some or all of the following modes: narrative, descriptive, reflective essay; discussion, diary, journal, personal memoir, debate, speech, article, letter. Candidates will be expected to show in their answers that they understand the structuring, language usage, grammatical conventions and punctuation appropriate to the mode of their choice and the manner in which they treat it.

Question B (20± marks)

In this question candidates will have no choice. A body of information will be presented, and the question will test candidates' ability to compose from the given material a passage of continuous formal prose. Candidates will be required to adopt in the answer a tone appropriate to the instructions given in the rubric and to the nature of the material, to evaluate the relative importance of the varied items of information offered and to achieve a suitable structure within the answer. The length of answer required will be indicated.

Paper II will consist of two questions, both of which must be answered. This paper will carry a total of 50 marks, but the allocation of marks between the two questions may vary from year to year as may the order in which the questions are presented.

Question A (40± marks)

This will test candidates' ability to understand in its various aspects a prose passage of moderate difficulty. Candidates' understanding will be tested in any or all of the following: the meaning of words, phrases and sentences; the inter-relation of ideas; the summarizing of ideas; the appropriateness of language; grammatical structure and usage; the conventions of written English. The areas of competence tested may vary from year to year.

Question B (10± marks)

This will test candidates' awareness of the features of different varieties of English, and their ability to observe the ways in which a difference of purpose in the use of language leads to differences in typography, choice of vocabulary, structuring of material, choice of grammatical forms and other related matters.

Paper III will carry a total of 60 marks and will consist of four sections:

Section 1 – Drama
Section 2 – Prose
Section 3 – Poetry
Section 4 – Practical Criticism

Candidates will be required to answer three questions, each question chosen from a different section of the paper. Each question will carry a value of 20 marks. The questions in Section 1, 2 and 3 will generally be so worded that candidates will be able to make their own choice of the text or texts on which to base their answers; but there will be specific invitations to write on Shakespearean drama. Opportunities to write on Scottish literature will always be given. These will be in the form either of specific questions or of general questions to which a knowledge of Scottish literature may be applied. Candidates who have studied literature thematically will be provided with opportunities to use in answers the kind of understanding resulting from such a method.

Answers to questions in sections 1, 2 and 3 will be expected to show some detailed knowledge of the text or texts selected for treatment, the ability to organize that knowledge in the form of description or argument, and the ability to communicate, in an appropriate style, the candidates' own impressions of the works they have chosen to treat. Little formal knowledge of literary history as such or of the technicalities of prose or poetry will be expected in the candidates' answers. However credit will be given for thorough knowledge of the selected texts, awareness of the techniques used, sincerity of personal response, competence in written English, and evidence of wide and independent reading.

Section 4 will consist of a test of practical criticism. This will be based on a poem, a piece of prose or dramatic dialogue. Answers to questions will be expected to show an understanding of the meaning of the text, an appreciation of the manner in which it is written, and the ability to express, in acceptable forms, the candidates' own responses to the text.

Second syllabus

Paper	Form	Time	Marks
Folio	Candidates must submit 6 pieces of writing, two of		30

which will be externally assessed. The remainder will be scanned to ensure that the requirements have been met and that the work is the candidate's own.

Reading and Writing – I	1 hr 35 mins	45

This paper will test candidates' understanding of one or more passages of prose, and will require candidates to write in response to the ideas of the passage(s).

Reading and Writing – II	1 hr 15 mins	25

This paper will require candidates to

(i) respond to questions on one or more literary texts (or extracts therefrom) and

(ii) compose an essay on some aspect of a literary text. (Some of the questions offered will relate to the literary texts or extracts in (i) above.)

The Folio

The folio will be completed by candidates throughout the period of the course. It will consist of six pieces of writing, varying in length but not individually exceeding 1000 words, as specified below:

(i) three pieces (1 of personal writing, 1 of discursive writing, 1 of imaginative writing) showing proficiency in a variety of modes;

(ii) two pieces of extended writing on substantial literary texts;

(iii) one piece on any one of the above modes of writing.

Two pieces of writing from the folio, one from each of (i) and (ii) above should be designated for external marking respectively thus: **Designated piece I** and **Designated piece II.** For the designated pieces the candidate's earlier draft(s) must be included in the folio. The teacher's corrections and any advice given should be clearly indicated on the draft(s).

In (i) above, candidates will be expected to demonstrate the kind of mature thought, reflection or insight which stems from prior reading, discussion and reflection on the topic being written about. Candidates should append to each submitted piece a brief indication of the context for his/her writing. Candidates will also be expected to show in their submissions that they understand the structuring, language usage and grammatical conventions appropriate to the mode of their choice, to the purpose and audience of their writing and to the manner in which it is treated.

In (ii) candidates will be expected to demonstrate a thorough knowledge of the text or texts chosen. They may choose to write about one novel or one play or a collection of short prose works, but if poetry is chosen, a number of poems, by the same author or linked thematically, chronologically or by mode, should be dealt with in considerable detail.

It should be clearly understood that while candidates are encouraged to read widely and discuss their work in preparation for writing their folio pieces, the writing must be their own. Clear cases of plagiarism will be severely penalized.

Reading and Writing – Paper I

This paper will consist of one or more passages, ranging widely in nature from year to year, selected from journalism of various kinds as well as descriptive, narrative, functional and argumentative prose from other sources, including literature. In the case of some journalistic passages and of literature, complete texts may appear. On some occasions passages may be thematically linked.

Candidates will be tested on their ability to read reflectively with care and understanding. Questions will be appropriate to the passage, which implies that not every reading skill will be tested every year. However the skills tested will be extensive, and will be chosen from the following:

The ability to identify key ideas
grasp an argument
evaluate and respond to an argument
identify techniques of style and persuasion
see the significance of particular words, phrases, sentences
summarize ideas
indicate word relationships, inferences and appropriateness of language usage.

In papers where passages are thematically linked, some questions may ask candidates to compare and contrast their ideas, themes, styles and usage.

In addition to these reading tasks there will be a demand for a short piece of writing whose subject matter will stem from the passage(s) for comprehension. The candidate will be expected to use the material in the given passage(s) and develop a personal line of thought about some aspect of it. He may in some years be expected to assume a role which may or may not be close to his own experience. Although this question will not be a formal summary, it will test the candidate's ability to select ideas from the passage(s), draw upon related experience and reading, and find the language and style appropriate for a particular writing purpose. In the assessment of this piece of writing, particular attention will be given to the candidate's control of grammatical structure.

Reading and Writing – Paper II

This paper will consist of:

(i) Section I   – two passages for practical criticism.
These will be of different genres.

(ii) Section II – a number of questions linking the practical criticism passages to the candidate's own reading.

(iii) Section III – a range of questions on drama, prose and poetry.

Candidates will be required to answer **one** question from Section I and **one** question from **either** Section II or Section III.

In Section I the practical criticism questions will be based upon a poem or poems and/or a piece of prose and/or an excerpt of dramatic dialogue. Candidates will be expected to show an understanding of the meaning of the text, an appreciation of the manner in which it is written, and the ability to express in acceptable forms their own responses to the text. In some years the passages for practical criticism may have a thematic link with the passages in Paper I.

In Section II there will be a choice of questions which ask the candidate to relate an aspect of one or other of the texts offered for practical criticism in Section I to a similar aspect of another text, not necessarily of the same genre, in the candidate's own reading.

Section III will consist of questions which will allow the candidates to write about their own reading and study of drama, prose or poetry. Opportunities to write on Scottish Literature will always be given, either in the form of specific questions or of general questions to which a knowledge of Scottish Literature may be applied. Candidates will be expected to show a detailed knowledge of the text or texts studied, the ability to organize that knowledge in the form of a description and/or argument, and the ability to communicate in an appropriate style their own impressions of the works chosen. Credit will be given for awareness of the techniques used, for sincerity of personal response, and for evidence of wide and independent reading.

In all parts of the examination candidates will be expected to write legibly and in an appropriate style, to spell correctly and to punctuate accurately.

SEB 'CERTIFICATE OF SIXTH YEAR STUDIES' 1983 ENGLISH

The Certificate of Sixth Year Studies is designed for only a tiny proportion of the school population. It is rarely a qualification for tertiary education, and unlike Higher and Ordinary levels, only *school* candidates may sit it. Nevertheless we have included the 1983 CSYS syllabus for those interested.

A Dissertation and three papers will be offered, all, though differing in character, of equal value.

Candidates will be examined in the Dissertation, which will be compulsory, and any two of the following Papers I, II and III:

Paper I   – (3 hours)   : Creative Writing
Paper II – (3 hours)   : Literature
Paper III – (3 hours 15 minutes): Practical Criticism

The courses of candidates being prepared for this examination should include provision for the following:

(a) training and practice in the various forms of continuous writing which are likely to be encountered in the examination;

(b) a course of reading, study and discussion designed to establish standards of discrimination and foster powers of judgement;

(c) a course of literary study in some depth in at least two of the following: Drama, Poetry, Prose;

(d) training and practice in the detailed critical examination of texts of literary merit, both in verse and in prose.

Dissertation on a nominated topic

Candidates should make a careful choice of topic in consultation with their teachers. The desire of the Board is to give maximum freedom of choice to candidates, provided that the fields are the study of literature, the study of language, and those studies which relate English to other subjects. (Studies in those other subjects by themselves will not be accepted.) Thus topics might appropriately be found in one of the following categories:

> literary studies: studies relating literature to other arts or disciplines; studies relating literature to its social background; literature and language; language studies, including studies in applied linguistics; local literature and folk-lore wherever these can be studied in depth; aspects of communication.

The Board reserves the right to reject any topic which it considers inadequate for sixth year study and it will advise candidates against topics which in its experience are likely to lead candidates into difficulties. If, however, despite the Board's guidance, a presenting centre, with its greater knowledge of the candidate and his resources, is convinced that the candidate can treat the topic adequately, it should so inform the Board. The dates for submission of topics to the Board each session are normally 16th June, and 1st October, of the relevant year (candidates should check the syllabus).

Candidates who are taking Paper II must not attempt any question which concerns a text central to the Dissertation.

Paper I – Creative Writing

The paper will be divided into two sections. The first section will consist of a number of specific themes drawn from areas of life with which the candidates are likely to be familiar. The themes will require to be treated in poetical, prose or dramatic form. The second section will consist of themes to be treated in prose. The questions will be designed to give the candidates the opportunity to write in a personal way on topics about which they have read and thought with some range and depth. The questions will require candidates to determine their own standpoint on issues of contemporary and abiding interest. To allow the candidates maximum freedom in their answers they may choose to do one question only.

Paper II – Literature

The questions in the Literature paper will seek to give the candidate the opportunity to reveal both that he has been involved personally with the text and that he has learned enough about it by guided study to be personally involved at those deeper levels of experience for which the authors and works have been chosen.

Preparation for the paper should be based on such a number of texts as will give candidates fair opportunities for cross-references and comparisons. At the same time they should be encouraged to demonstrate their detailed knowledge of the texts.

The paper will consist of three sections, viz.: Drama, Poetry and Prose. Candidates will be expected to attempt three questions drawn from more than one section.

The paper will always contain questions on each of the specified authors and on each

Shakespearian text. Questions will also be set that may be answered from the candidates' wider reading. In the Drama section the dramatists will always include Shakespeare.

Paper III – Practical Criticism

The paper will consist of three questions. Candidates will be required to attempt Question 1 and either Question 2 or Question 3. The text for Question 1 will consist of a modern poem the questions upon which will be designed to test the candidates' appreciation of poetic thought, structure, imagery and language. Both Questions 2 and 3 will test the reading of prose which may include prose drama. A question may consist of one passage only or of two or more passages related in some way but differing in the treatment of the material. The prose questions will demand an understanding of the differing purposes, attitudes, resources and techniques found in prose writing. The best preparation for this paper will be a wide-ranging study of literature in which areas of text are studied in close detail in their context.

Question analysis

This is an analysis of the major question divisions on the A-level English literature papers. It should be used as a general guide and candidates are advised not to use this analysis to predict future questions.

Question Analysis A-Level English Language and Literature

Examination Board	AEB I 623/1	AEB II 652/1	Cambridge 9000	Cambridge 9001	Joint Matriculation Board	London 170	Oxford 803	Oxford and Cambridge	Northern Ireland	Scottish	Southern Universities 9005	Welsh
Context Questions Shakespeare Chaucer/Milton		●	●	●	●	●	●	●	●		●	
Explanation of phrases		●	●	●			●	●	●			●
Style, effect and importance		●	●	●	●	●	●	●	●		●	●
Comment on character		●	●	●	●	●	●	●	●		●	●
Paraphrase Chaucer		●	●	●			●	●	●			●
Paraphrase Milton			●	●			●	●	●			●
Essay Question	●	●	●	●	●	●	●	●	●	●	●	●
Discussion of quotation	●	●	●	●	●	●	●	●	●	●	●	●
Main characters	●	●	●	●	●	●	●	●	●	●	●	●
Minor characters	●	●	●	●	●	●	●	●	●	●	●	●
Style and imagery	●	●	●	●	●	●	●	●	●	●	●	●
Comparison of 2 poets	●	●	●	●	●	●	●	●	●	●	●	●
Treatment of themes	●	●	●	●	●	●	●	●	●	●	●	●
Settings	●	●	●	●	●	●	●	●	●	●	●	●
Autobiographical and narrative detail	●	●	●	●	●	●	●	●	●	●	●	●
General historical/literary essays on a period			●	●		●	●		●	●	●	●
Literary Criticism		●	●	●	●	●		●	●	●	●	●
Poetry			●	●	●	●		●	●	●	●	
Prose			●	●	●	●		●	●	●	●	●
Drama			●		●	●		●	●	●		
Language Questions	●										●	
Essay	●										●	
Summary	●										●	
Comprehension	●										●	

Question Analysis of AS-Level English Language and Literature 1989

Examination Board	AEB	COSSEC	Joint Matriculation Board	London	Welsh	Oxford
Literature Papers	●	●	●	●	●	●
Examined work	●	●	●	●	●	●
Appreciation	●	●	●	●	●	●
Comprehension and criticism of poetry	●	●	●	●	●	●
Comprehension and criticism of prose	●	●	●	●		●
Comprehension and criticism of drama extracts	●	●		●		
Essays on prose		●				●
Essays on poetry		●				●
Essays on plays	●+	●			●+	●
Essays on novels	●+	●			●+	●
Essays on themes from material provided			●+	●+		
Coursework (weighting)	60%	60%	50%	30%	50%	
Shakespeare	●	●	●		●	
Poetry appreciation	●	●	●		●	
Essays on prose	●	●	●	●	●	
Essays on own choice of theme and creative work	●	●	●		●	
Language Papers	●	●		●		
Examined work	●	●		●		
On prescribed texts	●+					
Analysis		●		●		
Comprehension	●	●				
Communication, signs	●	●				
Description of printed texts				●		
Language studies				●		
Spoken language analysis		●				
Summary	●	●				
Coursework (weighting)	50%	50%		30%		
Special project	●	●				
Spoken language project	●			●		
Creative work	●	●				
Prescribed writing task		●				
Unprescribed task	●					

Notes 1 Coursework is related either to prescribed texts, or texts of candidates' own choice.
    2 + Texts so marked should be taken into the examination room, annotated by candidate.

EXAMINATION BOARDS

AEB   The Associated Examining Board
Stag Hill House, Guildford, Surrey GU2 5XJ

Cambridge University of Cambridge Local Examinations Syndicate
Syndicate Buildings, 1 Hills Road, Cambridge CB1 2EU

COSSEC As for Cambridge, Oxford and Cambridge
(AS only) or SUJB.

JMB   Joint Matriculation Board
Devas Street, Manchester M15 6EU

London University of London Schools Examinations Board
Stewart House, 32 Russell Square,
London WC1B 5DN

NISEC Northern Ireland Schools Examinations Council
Beechill House, 42 Beechill Road, Belfast BT8 4RS

Oxford Oxford Delegacy of Local Examinations
Ewert Place, Summertown, Oxford OX2 7BZ

O and C Oxford and Cambridge Schools Examinations Board
10 Trumpington Street, Cambridge and
Elsfield Way, Oxford

SEB   Scottish Examinations Board
Ironmills Road, Dalkeith, Midlothian EH22 1BR

SUJB   Southern Universities' Joint Board for School Examinations
Cotham Road, Bristol BS6 6DD

WJEC   Welsh Joint Education Committee
245 Western Avenue, Cardiff CF5 2YX

Part II Poetry

INTRODUCTION

School students see plays and read novels, but, like many of their parents and teachers, never read poetry in their free time. Further, they do not hear it read today, except with varying success at school. It inevitably becomes more neglected even in the last outposts of our former literary culture, possibly still taken seriously only because A-level English syllabuses devote about a third of their attention to it.

With the invasion and flood of other, more immediately satisfying, art forms much prejudice and many erroneous ideas about poetry have grown up. There is no indication that poetry can be appreciated with any less ease than the novel or drama and no Examining Board seems inclined to be influenced by its relative unpopularity. Discovering poetry can be one of the great pleasures of A-level English.

Special nature of poetry

Many would claim that the peculiar pleasure of poetry does not derive primarily from its thought. Nevertheless, a grasp of the ideas of a poem may simplify the reader's appreciation and clear the way to enjoying other more important qualities. In trying to disentangle the 'thought' or 'idea' of a poem we may be in danger of knocking to pieces those elements which are arranged in a pleasing way for their sound, colour and rhythm.

A good poem does not depend for its worth on originality of ideas; it often prefers its ideas to be already well understood by the audience, in order the better to embody them in the most excellent language, that synthesis or pattern of words called a poem. We may feel, understandably, that it is necessary to clarify whatever thought a poem contains, as one of the simplest ways of approaching it. However, it is important not to fall into the trap of neglecting style and language but to work towards a full response to the poem, noting meaning *and* form.

Some poems can be left to speak for themselves. For example, Burns' *O my luve's like a red, red rose* would need little or no analysis of its meaning as it conveys an immediately communicated experience. In contrast, Yeats' *A Nativity*, a shorter poem, cannot be appreciated fully without a knowledge of other poetry and prose by Yeats. It is the business of the A-level student to work towards a 'full response' to a poem, whether it by lyric or epic. On p. 40 in the section on practical criticism of poetry, you will find basic guidelines suggested to help you approach each new poem you encounter.

1 General

In this section we will take the five major 'classes' of poetry set at A level. We will discuss the main areas of difficulty in each group.

1 The metaphysical poets of the seventeenth century, with special reference to Donne
2 Augustan poetry with special reference to Pope
3 The Romantic School
4 The Victorian poets with special reference to Tennyson, Browning and Hopkins
5 Twentieth–century poetry with special reference to Yeats and Eliot.

1 THE METAPHYSICAL POETS OF THE SEVENTEENTH CENTURY

In poetry selections set at A level, as few as two and as many as seven of the metaphysicals may be represented. Donne is often set alone, and single selections from Herbert or Marvell are also sometimes set. In any case the student can generally expect Donne, Herbert, Vaughan and Marvell to be favoured in any choice from the metaphysical poets.

Definitions

Definitions of metaphysical poetry or other significant material in the introductions to anthologies or single poet selections are always worth reading with a view to preparing material for your answers. Examination questions often rely upon the ideas in such introductions and you can use them as critical clues and leads. For example, you could consider the following definition, thinking of illustrations from the poems you are studying: 'The essence of a metaphysical poem is a vivid imagining of a moment of experience or of a situation out of which the need to argue, or persuade or define, arises.'

If questions on the style or language are set, they are likely to hinge on that aspect which gives this type of poetry its title – metaphysical. You should understand thoroughly this term, know the characteristics of the metaphysical conceit and have plenty of examples ready. The term 'metaphysical' was established in this connection by Dr Johnson. He was referring to Donne's habit of drawing images from all the sources of knowledge: scientific, theological and philosophical.

Dr Johnson disapproved of the school, referring to the poets' 'heterogeneous' images 'violently yoked together' (*Lives of the Poets* 1779–81). You should ask yourself whether the imagery in the poems you are studying is, in your opinion, unjustifiably extreme, far-fetched or immoderate. You should prepare examples of types of imagery, showing how and where they are used in the poems.

A typical example of questions relating to the 'metaphysical' label, what it means, and how far one or more of these poets conform to any definition, is:

'From three poems in your selection show how they represent the main characteristics of metaphysical poetry.' Perhaps the question itself may select one or two of the characteristics, thus: 'Metaphysical poetry is concerned with the lack of coherence and certainty in this world. Discuss', or: 'The metaphysical poets set out to express and explore ideas and feelings about the complex and changing world in which they lived, and also about their own natures. Of which poet do you think this is most true?'

Themes

The variety of the work of different poets, and that of the work of a single poet, is commonly touched upon in A-level questions. For example, 'Poetry which has much variety must lack sincerity. Discuss.' It would be the business of the essay to demonstrate, while showing a good understanding of the implication of the question, that 'sincerity' in Donne or Marvell for example need not be lacking though attached to poems of a variety of forms, themes, and tones. Donne wholly changes from a man really interested in secular matters and earthly love, to one devoted to divine matters and love of God.

It is useful to prepare material on common themes in the work of the metaphysical poets. A typical short-list you might isolate, with illustrations, may include:

(*a*) Love
(*b*) Nature
(*c*) Sin
(*d*) Hope
(*e*) Grief

Love is especially important in Donne; Nature in Vaughan (where it is used to express God), Marvell and Herrick (where the pastoral convention survives) and Sin, Hope and Grief in Herbert where there is always a Christian context for them.

Sometimes special characteristics of the religious poems are asked for in A-level questions, e.g. their vividness, sincerity or the personal nature of most of them. If Donne's sonnet *Batter my heart, Three Person'd God* is studied in depth it will yield a good deal in answer to such generalized questions: its passionate tone and its appeal to God as though he were a great but familiar man. (Herbert also addresses God like a friend or a lover.) The close line of argument and bold but consistent imagery may be noted, and the firm, decisive final line. Last lines make an interesting study if compared with first lines, in poems by Donne and Herbert.

The theme of love in Donne

When studying Donne's commonly set *Songs and Sonnets* and *Elegies,* you should make a special analysis of every facet of their treatment of the beloved. There is a wide range of devices – arguments, celebrations, complaints, use of 'wit' (of which Donne is said to be 'the monarch'), despair, jokes and playfulness. Dryden said of Donne, 'He affects the metaphysics not only in his satires, but in his amorous verses, where nature only should reign, and perplexes the minds of the fair sex with nice speculations of philosophy.' (*Discourse of the Origin and Progress of Satire,* 1629.)

The loved one seems at times merely to be the occasion for a string of extraordinary 'conceits'; one poem *(The Indifferent)* begins jauntily:
'I can love both faire and browne'
and so on listing other types – so long as 'she be not true.' It proceeds with the idea that fidelity in love is a vice; and Venus, having heard that two or three lovers are daring to grow constant, goes off to let them know that,
'since you will be true
You shall be true to them, who're false to you.'
Fantastical and Wildean as this may appear, there is a serious point, passionately held even if disguised by Donne. The passion is expressed in the detail, the elaborations:
'Will it not serve your turn to do, as did your mothers?'
The point is his favourite theme of 'no woman can be true', so brilliantly expressed in direct terms in *Song (Goe and catche a falling starre).*

Love's Growth

1 I SCARCE believe my love to be so pure
    As I had thought it was,
    Because it doth endure
  Vicissitude, and season, as the grass;
5 Methinks I lied all winter, when I swore,
  My love was infinite, if spring make it more.
  But if this medicine, love, which cures all sorrow
  With more, not only be no quintessence,
  But mixt of all stuffs, paining soul, or sense,
10 And of the Sun his working vigour borrow,
  Love's not so pure, and abstract, as they use
  To say, which have no Mistress but their Muse,
  But as all else, being elemented too,
  Love sometimes would contemplate, sometimes do.

15 And yet no greater, but more eminent,
    Love by the Spring is grown;
    As, in the firmament,
  Stars by the Sun are not enlarg'd, but shown.
  Gentle love deeds, as blossoms on a bough,
20 From love's awakened root do bud out now.
  If, as in water stirr'd more circles be
  Produc'd by one, love such additions take,
  Those like so many spheres, but one heaven make,
  For, they are all concentric unto thee;
25 And though each spring do add to love new heat,
  As princes do in times of action get
  New taxes, and remit them not in peace,
  No winter shall abate the spring's increase.

John Donne (1572-1631)

Love's Growth as an example of Donne's general manner

The poem *Love's Growth* offers the simple proposition that in spring love grows, a theme dear to the hearts of medieval people, although they would not have much appreciated Donne's handling of it. Donne begins by affecting surprise that what he thought was already infinitely great in winter, actually grows further in spring, like the grass – he must have 'lied' in winter! He continues almost as an aside, that since love is not therefore an ultimate substance incapable of change, but a mixture that is given energy by the sun, it is not such a pure abstraction as poets (whose only mistress is their Muse) like to suppose. Since love has material substance it will at times be passive, and at other times, active. Returning to the main subject, he reflects that love does not become any bigger, but becomes more evident, in the way that stars are revealed by the sun (the reflected light of the planets), not enlarged by it. Then (in a couplet, 19–20, like one from a Shakespeare song), he compares love's deeds to blossom in the spring, opening from the 'awakened root'. Love increases as rings in water do, when the water is 'stirred', making many 'spheres' but still one universe ('heaven'), all concentric to love itself. Donne concludes with an image not taken from nature: each spring causes an increase in love, just as princes raise new taxes in wartime. Princes do not cancel the source of expanded revenue when peace comes, and no winter reduces spring's growth.

The proposition is teased out in a mock-serious way, sustained by a series of images that surprise and yet compel acquiescence in their validity, indeed their choice is psychologically right even if on the surface incongruous. It is like hearing a brilliantly persuasive lawyer prove a point with frequent recourse to metaphor and simile, with this difference: a real lawyer really needs to establish a conclusion and so will not break up the direct flow of his argument till he has made his point; the poet has already won his point by declaring it; he now appears to argue it, but it is merely for the sake of a display of wit as he does so; this does not appear to hold up or break up the process of proving the point, because it is already accepted.

Further than this, the images are actually integral to the argument; the beginning or middle do not exist for the end, any part exists for any other. Thus in other poems the point or series of points, may emerge as the poem proceeds, by way of the images; images and meaning become fused. As Donne writes in another context:

> '. . . Nor must wit
> Be colleague to religion, but be it'.

A good example of this is *The Extasie (The Ecstasy)* where the propositions in some cases simply cannot be extricated from the images that make them. Donne first establishes that two lovers sitting on 'a pregnant bank of violets', are so in sympathy that their souls may join in one, and the idea proceeds with the usual variations, vivid pictures in their own right, till at last he moves serenely in the idea and can draw further conclusions:

> 'This Extasie doth unperplex
> (Wee said) and tell us what we love,
> Wee see by this, it was not sex
> Wee see, we saw not what did move;'

The new soul, formed by the mixture of the lovers' souls, stands outside them (a literal 'ex-stasis'), and as the new whole is greater than the sum of its two parts, it can tell new truths: they can now see what moved their love, and it was not mere 'sex' or the needs of the flesh; it can perform new services:

> 'When love, with one another so
> Interinanimates two soules
> That abler soule which thence doth flow
> Defects of loneliness controules.'

Donne has brought us to the point where we must accept this exactly as it is meant; it is still a picture and therefore presumably a sort of metaphor, but now we are living in it, and even if you disagree with the first proposition, by this time you must be either believing it for the sake of the poem, or every line becomes an insuperable problem.

Notice how in quatrains Donne likes to use an adverbial clause structure for an antithesis that fills the verse; the movement is almost identical with those quoted above in this from *A Valediction; forbidding mourning'*:

> 'But we by a love, so much refin'd,
> That our selves know not what it is,
> Inter-assured of the mind,
> Care lesse, eyes, lips and hands to misse.'

It was a technique that Marvell admired and imitated later in the century, and TS Eliot in this one:

> 'The sleek Brazilian jaguar
> Does not in its arboreal gloom
> Distil so rank a feline smell
> As Grishkin in a drawing-room'

(Notice that in the Eliot example (from *Whispers of Immortality*) however, only the second and fourth lines are rhymed.)

Particular themes of Marvell

Marvell's verse shows many of the characteristics of metaphysical poetry already discussed, particularly his use of wit and his choice of love as a theme for many of his poems. (On p. 43 there is a critical commentary on one of his 'love' poems.) There are two other areas which are particularly his: poetry in the pastoral tradition and political satire.

Marvell combines an instinctive liking for nature with the ready made use of it as in pastoral poems like those of Spenser and Milton, which themselves owe much to Greek and Roman eclogues. Rustic figures in rural settings may be made the mouthpiece of satire or meditation or even wit in the metaphysical manner. Like Donne, Milton, and to a lesser degree Herbert (although the last named was connected to a great aristocratic family), Marvell was involved in public affairs. His poetry reflects this in satire which was formidable in its time, though less interesting now, and in formal set-pieces in honour of Admiral Blake and Oliver Cromwell, and of Lord Fairfax, his patron, whose daughter he taught and whose great house and garden he describes. There is an interesting contrast, therefore, between the 'private' introspective musings and relationships, and the 'public' man-of-affairs aspects in Marvell's poetry.
(On p. 41 there is a critical commentary on Vaughan's *The Retreate*.)

AUGUSTAN POETRY WITH SPECIAL REFERENCE TO POPE

(We have chosen to concentrate here on Pope, rather than Dryden as his poetry is more commonly set at A Level.)

For many, Pope (1688-1744) stands as the most perfect representative of the Augustans in poetry as does Congreve in drama and Swift in prose. His verse, almost entirely composed in heroic couplets, is the most finished and inspired of any satire using that medium. Poems most often prescribed at A Level are: *The Rape of the Lock, Epistle to Dr Arbuthnot, Eloisa to Abelard,* the first Epistle of *Essay on Man,* the second, third and fourth of the *Moral Essays,* one of the books of *The Dunciad.* Although it is seldom actually set, it is also a good policy to read the *Essay on Criticism.* This will give a good idea of Pope's range, variety, and special strengths. He also produced a translation into couplets of the whole of Homer, but Pope as a translator has not yet featured in A-level syllabuses. It should be noted that *The Rape of the Lock,* our language's greatest example of 'mock heroic' satire, is the poem most commonly set.

Pope's background

Questions on how the Augustan age is reflected in Pope's poetry are common at A Level and you should understand something of the time at which he was writing. As well as studying your set poems, you would benefit by looking at other work by him, such as *The Epistles,* springing directly from the social, artistic, intellectual and political life of the time. A useful background book for the period is Basil Willey's *Eighteenth Century Background* (see p. 160 for full reference).

Pope's satire

A-level questions on Pope's satire usually concentrate on his targets and how he hits them. From this grow branches such as: Is the satire too bitter, angry or personal? What is the mock heroic mode? Illustrate its nature, variety and range.

You should be able to give examples of the range of Pope's satire, including illustrations of the power and effectiveness of some of his character sketches such as 'Atticus and Sporus', or groups of people such as the Grub Street scribblers in *The Dunciad,* with examples of the grotesque, or humorous, methods of satirizing them. There is venom and contempt in some of the lines against those whom Pope particularly disliked, and follies he was most scornful of, but in general it may be seen that, ferocious and cutting as the satire is, the targets are anonymous, generalized, or disguised (if often thinly, note the Atticus–Addison equivalent), and the purpose not animosity or vengeance, but the preservation of moral, aesthetic and social standards. Pope wrote that his satire was published 'in the cause of virtue, to mend people's morals'.

The variety of Pope's satire may be illustrated by his use of

– humour
– serious moral indignation
– bitterness
– prejudice
– contempt
– bawdiness (*The Dunciad*)
– scorn
– personal animosity
– social criticism

You should find illustrations for each mode or for those you consider important in your set poems. For example, you may show Pope's bitterness against aspects of his society by quoting from *The Dunciad:*

> 'The hungry Judges soon the Sentence sign,
> And Wretches hang that Jury men may dine.'

Humour lies everywhere in Pope, and everyone must have his or her favourite illustration, whether subtle or crude:

> 'Or stain her honour, or her new Brocade,
> Forget her Pray'rs or miss a Masquerade.'

> (*The Rape of the Lock*)

The mock heroic mode

The mock heroic joke can be seen in Dryden's work and is developed effectively by Pope. Note Dryden's use of incongruity in this couplet from *Absolem and Achitophel:*

> 'The midwife laid her hand on his thick skull
> With this prophetic blessing: be thou dull'

The mock-heroic mode is adopted to make a trivial subject seem grand and in this way to satirize it.

The Rape of the Lock is acknowledged as the greatest example of the mock-heroic epic, satirizing triviality by treating it in the lofty style of the classical epic. The machinery of interfering gods and goddesses from classical epics are reduced to 'sylphs' and 'gnomes'. The main characteristics of the classical poem are parodied, from broad effects to the smallest details such as verbal mannerisms and formulae. An effect is designed and gained of frivolity and the nonsensicality of the people and activities that are being satirized. The variety and foppery of men and women are shown and, more profoundly, love and honour (the grand themes of classical epic) are debased to flirtation and fatuity.

The non-satiric Pope

A-level questions often ask candidates to assess how far Pope was a satirist only. You need to be familiar with the non-satiric aspects of his work in order to consider this question. You may also be asked whether Pope has the ability as a love poet, and the nature of serious moral purpose in his work. There may be an opportunity on your paper to refer to the earlier pastoral work of *Windsor Forest,* but there is much other material to illustrate his non-satiric side, for example, the literary criticism of *Essay on Criticism,* the philosophy of *Essay on Man* (although all the thought is second-hand, whether from Boileau or Horace or Lord Bolingbroke, Pope's restating of it is valid for discussion of the kinds of his poetry). There is also pure fun without special satiric intent, and, perhaps most important, the poems of compliment to men he approved, such as Richard Boyle, Allen Bathurst or Noble the landscape gardener. A common question on *The Dunciad* and *The Epistle to Dr Arbuthnot* asks what permanent appeal (if any) the poems have now the issues and people written about are almost totally forgotten. In other words, you must be aware of what other qualities the poetry possesses, and whether sins and follies common to every age lurk behind Pope's satirical targets.

Pope's style

Some questions at A Level relate to Pope's style, and particularly whether Pope was a man of genuine imaginative power, or merely of surface brilliance. This entails a full description and appreciation of Pope's style; his mastery of the heroic couplet (described by one critic as an elegant coach and two horses, trotting in perfect time) and his range of language to suit various modes of writing. It also requires attention to the more creative aspects of Pope's writing: his ability to control the structure of *The Rape of the Lock* and *The Dunciad* and the deeper themes in these and other poems; the morality, as well as the satire of more superficial matters, and the originality and appositeness of the imagery. The felicitous balance in Pope of language with content is exemplified as well as expressed in the couplet:

> 'True wit is nature to advantage dress'd
> What oft was thought but ne'er so well expressed'

If *The Essay on Criticism* is included in your prescribed poems, then there may be a question related to Pope's ability in criticism. It is mainly a matter of what the above couplet expresses: well known critical theory very neatly rewritten for the delight as well as the instruction of the early eighteenth-century audience.

The romantic school

Background – What is Romanticism?

The usual limits for this period are from Blake (first poems 1783) to the first volume of Tennyson (1830).

It is notoriously difficult to set limits to the romantic spirit in art, literature, or even poetry. The romantic poets are lumped together for convenience mainly because they lived at the same time, with not more than a generation between them; but also because they were able to benefit by a shift in attitude and literary technique which occurred at the close of the eighteenth century.

This new attitude is complex in origin and nature, but broadly speaking it coincided with a revolutionary fervour, with new value given to the ordinary people of the poorer class, and to dignity and freedom of the individual. There occurred also a revival of interest in romance, especially medieval romance, the supernatural, and the mystery of life.

Romantic sensations, such as the vague love of the mysterious, and yearning for the unknown or the strange, the regard for uncultivated nature, the emphasis on the individual and his liberty, and other similar characteristics of the romantic school, were all present earlier, in varying degrees and forms and in other arts. For example, James Thomson's *Winter* was composed in 1725 and Dyer's *Grongar Hill* published the following year. Three books of Young's *Night Thoughts* were brought out in 1742. Collins' *Odes* were published in 1746.

In music, Haydn's *Seasons* were suggested by Thomson's completed poem of the same name (published 1730) and many of Mozart's tunes and opera airs are equally 'romantic'.

Painters such as Rembrandt in the mid-seventeenth century, but especially Watteau, Fragonard, Chardin whose landscapes anticipated the Impressionists a century later, together with that seventeenth-century pair, Claude and Poussin, all had an incalculable influence on the nature poetry of the eighteenth century. Keats' poetry especially owes much to visual art.

A sense of striving, quest and the urge to discover are strong in romantic writing; the ideal to be won was 'beauty', or the expression by the creative faculty, called 'imagination', of high forms of love (as in Shelley), and 'sublimity'. Such ambitious aims often fell short, turning into romantic self-regard, or solipsism. 'Imagination' tended to take too high a place in man's existence; the virtues of social life were underestimated, and romantic love exaggerated. Stories of sensational magic, or exotic scenes, weakened allegory or more purposeful narrative.

Crabbe

George Crabbe (1754-1832), three years older than Blake, is the oldest of the poets writing during this period. He chose to continue in the old 'heroic couplet' metre, writing verse tales, and became an anachronism, out of the main tradition of the other great romantics. His poetry is still very interesting and occasionally set for A Level. There are two good modern selections: those of John Lucas in the Longman's English series, and of Geoffrey Newbold in the Macmillan's English Classics series. The *Letters and Tales* reveal great powers of observation, both for scenery and psychology of character, with an unerring ability in narrative, an overriding intelligence and a sure sense of dramatic situations.

Blake

In the case of William Blake (1757-1827) the longing for an ideal world is transmuted into that for an innocent past or a glorious future. Blake differed from Wordsworth in that he thought that the human heart was innately evil: man must purge himself to become innocent. For Wordsworth, Nature was Man's *alma mater*: for Blake she was a whore. Both poets saw eighteenth-century England as oppressed by tyranny and loss of human dignity. Machinery and the factory were the symbols of this.

Blake is often represented in the syllabuses by his famous collection *Songs of Innocence and Experience* (1789). His prophetic and mystic side later possessed his mind and work, but he remains the first to attack reason, advance the imagination, and emphasize the importance and purity of man's natural desires which become corrupted by the various oppressions of society. Similar attitudes were taken by Gray (*Ode on a Distant Prospect of Eton College*, 1742) and later on by Wordsworth in his *Ode: Intimations of Immortality*.

Blake's short lyrics contain visionary power and unusually penetrating psychological insight. His gift was for bringing an inventiveness of concepts to bear upon a prophetic purpose – prophetic in the manner of Isaiah, Ezekiel and the later Milton. Indeed a knowledge of the Authorized version of the Bible, and of Milton, is almost indispensable to an understanding of Blake. Scientific historicity had no interest for Blake; on the contrary he actually held history to blame for most of the world's evils. The Bible for him was a great document of the imagination; its truth lay in its vision. It is not what the eye sees that is important, but what the inner eye perceives; hence his easy movement among symbols. When he was a boy he saw a thistle with thistledown as a grey-headed old man.

Blake abhorred the scientific and analytical world of the Royal Society. He considered that the Augustan poets were in league with it, and later poets of refined sensibility, such as Gray and Cowper, too weak to counteract it. He symbolized this repressive world as *The Accuser of Sin*, who persecuted the people of 'Albion'. The elaborate structures of Blake's symbolism and myth-making are hard to appreciate which is why the earlier, lyrical poetry is more popular.

Blake's prophetic poetry is a sustained and major effort to equal Milton and the Biblical prophets, rather than merely to follow their lead as his contemporaries were apt and content to do. Later Wordsworth was endowed with the same energy to forge his own creation in poetry, but he chose the opposite way: to remove completely all symbolism and myth from his work. Wordsworth's central poems such as *Michael* were about ordinary men experiencing events such as anyone might; far different from such as befell his friend Coleridge's *The Ancient Mariner*. But Blake looks back: his difficulties resolve themselves and may be understood in the light of older traditions; Wordsworth looks forward: his energy went into creating modern poetry. It is ironical that Blake should have spoken more directly to modern writers, with their revived interest in symbolism, while Wordsworth, after his Victorian vogue, has come to be disregarded by many.

The Songs of Innocence and Experience are designed as counterparts or contraries: each state (and 'Innocence' thus implies also 'inexperience') comments critically upon the other; pairs of poems are matched, and even printed thus in some editions. Each state embodied in the pairs is a necessary condition of the soul, but inadequate alone.

Blake's use of symbols

When studying Blake's poetry, it is important to acquaint yourself with the main symbols he uses and apply the 'meanings' to the poems in which they occur. You may find it helpful to group symbols as in the examples given below. However, it is important to remember that every poem with its symbols stands alone and that the meaning of symbols may change from poem to poem. A general grouping can only give a rough guide.

Innocence, ignorance or inexperience
Represented by
children, flowers, birds, sheep, fields, dew, Spring

Parental, religious or political oppression
Represented by
priests, forests, clouds, thunder, stone, iron, mills, mountains

Joyful *or* over-possessive sex
Represented by
roses, gold, moonlight, nets, arrows, branches

Creative or heroic energy
Represented by
tigers, lions, eagles, forges, swords, spears, chariots, sun, fire

Wordsworth

William Wordsworth (1770-1850), if not the greatest of the Romantics – a position challenged by Keats alone – produced the most considerable body of great poetry. In 1798 he announced to the world his revolutionary manifesto for a new kind of poetry – the Preface to the *Lyrical Ballads* by himself and Coleridge. This condemned to outer darkness all 'Arbitrary and capricious habits of expression in order to furnish food for fickle tastes and appetites'. Wordsworth's aim in his Lyrical Ballads was to take natural subjects from common life and to find a less obviously 'literary' medium for their expression. When studying Wordsworth it is useful to look at the 'Preface' and pick out a few helpful quotations to illustrate Wordsworth's ideas. (You may not feel these are always put into practice in the poems.) Examination questions on Wordsworth sometimes quote the 'Preface', for example (London 1981).
'"A selection of language really used by men" Is this what Wordsworth used?'

As with most great writers, the parts of Wordsworth's best work fit into a coherent whole; he had something of major significance to communicate, and for thirty years until his powers flagged, he managed to say it in a great many different kinds of poem, in which he effected a fusion of moral feeling and a sense of the greatness and beauty of Nature, by establishing his conviction of the interaction of Nature and human nature.

The air of philosophy in Wordsworth's work led his admirer Coleridge to encourage him to write a philosophic poem, whose 'Prelude' was completed in twelve books, sufficient for such philosophy as Wordsworth had to express in the personal, autobiographical manner; but continued and completed in the nine books and nearly ten thousand lines of *The Excursion*. This poem is a discursive meditation on the same themes as *The Prelude* (not published till after Wordsworth's death), *Tintern Abbey* and the *Ode: Intimations of Immortality*.

Questions on Wordsworth at A Level regularly turn on the morality or the aesthetic qualities of the poems, or the two combined. All his conclusions derive from observed life, especially his own, or that of his sister Dorothy. Philosophy and morality have to be tested against what has been perceived; consequently there is a strong autobiographical element in all his poetry. This is the 'egotistical' half of Keats' phrase describing Wordsworth's remarkably sustained and unified vision: the 'egotistical sublime'. The exploration of his vision of 'Nature' would not have yielded anything of great value had it not been linked with 'human nature' as he observed this in himself and the characters and behaviour of simple working people, especially solitary ones. His 'pantheism' is no more than his conviction that Nature in her sublime as well as her most lowly states (the violet, celandine, bunch of knot grass, meanest flower, daisy, etc.) radiates a power that meets and inter-operates with a corresponding spirit from the observing man: this power is given various names: 'soul', 'glory' or simply 'power'. *Tintern Abbey* shows this belief in its most intense and lyrical form. About the senses of eye and ear, he writes of

'. . . what they half create
And what perceive'

both sides contribute equally to the glory; that which *Ode: Intimations of Immortality* while lamenting its loss, again affirms.

Thus, *There Was a Boy,* is not so much concerned with the outward scene (which Wordsworth could not describe in visual terms so well as, say, Hardy) and far less with the anecdote about the hooting to encourage owls to respond. It is concerned with what happens in the silent listening pauses, when they will not answer: to the Boy's straining ears something better arrives:

'a gentle shock of mild surprise
Has carried far into his heart the voice
Of mountain torrents: or the visible scene
Would enter unawares into his mind. . . .'

Nature, and the lonely solitaries set there, often in some wild, misty or barren setting, or ruined place, form the external contribution to this poet's special vision, the 'impulse' from outside, the way the wind rings into the ears of the climber after ravens' nests. The greatest of all, *Michael,* is set on an uninhabited mountain side and linked with an unfinished and derelict sheepfold. So we are presented with a line of such solitaries: the Leech Gatherer, the deserted wife in her decaying cottage, the shepherd on the misty fells, the Highland lass in her valley reaping, the woman by the grave under a thorn, Ruth, the ghost of Lucy Gray and so on.

The 'inner' contribution is not simply a wise passiveness, but heightened awareness and response, the 'leap' of the heart at a rainbow. Most typically, he conveys the action of memory on scenes, the recreation of perception in the transfiguring heart or 'inward eye'. So we return to the poet's words in 'The Preface':

'the poet possesses an ability of conjuring up in himself passions, which are indeed far from being the same as those produced by real events, yet do more nearly resemble the passions produced by real events, than any thing which, from the motions of their own minds merely other men are accustomed to feel in themselves; whence . . . he has acquired a greater readiness and power in expressing . . . those thoughts, and feelings which . . . arise in him *without immediate external excitement.'* (Our italics.)

This helps to correct any tendency to suppose that Wordsworth's original stimuli (for 'passions', read 'sensations' and for 'events' read 'phenomena') produced unusual or idiosyncratic responses. All his actual experience was normal – we may all have access to his inner life, and may go away the richer for having shared his vision.

Coleridge

The more interesting period of Samuel Taylor Coleridge's life (1772-1834) was linked with Wordsworth and his sister Dorothy. The most fruitful time was that after their first meeting in Nether Stowey, north Somerset, where Coleridge was living. Wordsworth took a house nearby called Alfoxden, and the two poets began a series of conversations during their walks over beautiful Exmoor. The result was *Lyrical Ballads* (1798) containing, with a few other contributions by Coleridge, his remarkable *The Rime of the Ancient Mariner*.

Coleridge was a voluble and fascinating talker; he read very widely and took an interest in almost everything: theology, philosophy, criticism, political theory – all of which he later planned to work up into a major prose work (never completed). The main topics of his discussions with Wordsworth were, 'the power of exciting the sympathy of the reader by a faithful adherence to the truth of nature, and the power of giving the interest of novelty by the modifying colours of imagination'. Wordsworth's concern was for the 'things of every day', to which he was to add the 'charm of novelty' and to direct the mind to the 'loneliness and wonder of the world before us'. Coleridge was to turn his attention to supernatural events, yet so as to 'transfer from our inward nature a human interest and semblance of truth.' This was no doubt designed to bring such poems into congruity with Wordsworth's poems illustrating the truths of human nature.

Thus we find that much of the visual interest of *The Ancient Mariner* turns upon the 'romantic' elements: strange scenery, supernatural events; but the mainspring of the old man's story is firmly attached to processes of human experience, and the poem's 'argument' follows these. So we read a story that involves a sin (he 'cruelly and in contempt of the laws of hospitality' killed a sea-bird), expiatory suffering (he was followed by many and strange judgements), and the power of love and generosity, reestablishing the bond between him and nature. The awful bondage of his guilt, symbolized by the dead albatross round his neck, is broken as soon as he can bless the beautiful water-creatures:

'O happy living things! no tongue
Their beauty might declare:
A spring of love gushed from my heart,
And I blessed them unaware:
Sure my kind saint took pity on me,
And I blessed them unaware.

The selfsame moment I could pray;
And from my neck so free
The Albatross fell off, and sank
Like lead into the sea.'

The supernatural poem *Christabel* was not finished in time for *Lyrical Ballads*. It illustrates, together with *The Ancient Mariner* and *Kubla Khan*, how differently Coleridge's imagination worked from Wordsworth's. Coleridge was not, like Wordsworth, primarily reflective or meditative. Coleridge was a myth-maker, expressing his ideas as symbols which exist as potent images independently of any of their likely 'meanings'. *The Ancient Mariner*, though it is a unique poem in every respect, springs from several easily identifiable sources of which the main one is the medieval ballad, from which Coleridge took his metre and much of the method:

directness, simplicity, swift movement of event, supernatural features and atmosphere, repetition for effect, abrupt transitions from narrative to dialogue and brilliant visual images. The material of the story is largely owed to travel books and accounts of voyages such as those of the Elizabethans and the more recent voyage of Captain James Cook to the edge of the Antarctic icefield. Sultry calms and dangerous storms of course appear in these accounts. Many other more minor sources are traced by Professor John Livingston Lowes in his book *The Road to Xanadu*.

All these contributory elements Coleridge fused and transformed into a wholly new artistic unity. The Mariner's tale is for the wedding guest, who learns something outside the place of the marriage ceremony, about the rupture and reestablishment of the mystic bond between man and his environment. There is wanton killing of the symbolic bird, guardian angel of the boat and its crew, sent specially by the 'Polar Spirit' by whom the killer's penance is appointed. This takes the form of a kind of physical and spiritual paralysis, 'life-in death'. After the penance is removed, the sailor is gradually restored to full health, beginning with the experience of sleep and life-giving rain.

Kubla Khan is a beautiful fragment springing from as mysterious a psychology as that of the other two poems, but more difficult to analyse. The River *Alph* that so destructively bursts out and then vanishes (like the classical river *Alphaeus*) suggests a spiritual or creative energy similar in force to that which runs through the Temple in the Book of Ezekiel in the Bible. A disconcerting change of names and scene, as suggestively disturbing as a dream, takes us to an Abyssinian maid singing of Mount Abora – another type of Paradise. The poet longs to recapture her song – as Wordsworth did that of the 'Solitary Highland Lass', so that he might recreate the 'pleasure dome', and, like Kubla, control the realm of the imagination. But the 'daemon' of poetic inspiration can be powerfully destructive as well as the source of creative power, and is therefore something to be feared. Coleridge himself must have feared it for he did not allow it to break out in his poetry again.

Christabel was founded on ballad-like romance – a story of enchantment and medieval colour, such as Tennyson and Morris were later to find so congenial.

Byron (1788-1824)

Shelley declared that Byron's *Don Juan* was the greatest poem of the age. Today Byron is reckoned to be an 'original' poet in some of his long poems, (the last two cantos of *Childe Harold's Pilgrimage*, *Beppo*, *The Vision of Judgement* and *Don Juan* itself). Without doubt *Don Juan* is one of the best comic poems in English and examination questions often ask candidates to assess its comic power. Even TS Eliot, who wrote that if Byron had distilled his verse there would have been nothing left, admitted that *Don Juan* is an original poem. It is very readable for its wit, colloquial diction, skilful narration and expertly-handled metrics. The poem has precision of statement and description, though no great penetration into human nature or motive. It expresses eloquently a sincere contempt for hypocrisy in the last cantos. The first stanzas of dedication to Robert Southey are 'one of the most exhilarating pieces of abuse in the language' (TS Eliot's words).

Byron was a great admirer of Pope, Scott and Rogers, some of whose virtues he himself displays:

> 'Then roll the brazen thunders of the door,
> Which opens to the thousand happy few
> An earthly paradise of Or Molu.'

The colloquial and narrative technique was established in *Beppo* (1818):

> 'Now Laura, much recovered, or less loth
> To speak, cries 'Beppo! what's your pagan name?
> Bless me! your beard is of amazing growth!'

In this poem also he switched from the Spenserian stanzas of *Childe Harold* to the ottava rima – a metre whose potential for narrative he had discovered from Italian poetry. Ottava rima was better suited to his style and subject matter: the final couplet in particular was often used to give a special 'snap' to the humour or vigour of the stanza.

In *The Vision of Judgement*, written in 1822 during the time of composition of *Don Juan*, Byron perfected his satiric skill and power. He disliked and dispensed with systematic, structured plots:

'I take a vicious and unprincipled character, and lead him through the ranks of society whose high external accomplishments cover and cloak internal and secret vices, and I paint the natural effects of such characters.'

Don Juan follows the fortunes of the hero across Europe, making full use of the author's travel experiences and his reading, which supplied the material for episodes such as the storm in Canto II and the siege of Ismail in Cantos VII and VIII. As in *Childe Harold,* Byron draws upon his own character for the persona of the hero – it has no connection with the traditional Don Juan. The poem, although often referred to as an 'epic', is more akin to the picaresque novels of Sterne and Fielding, being a highly diverse, rambling but effective criticism of society: there is more to be enjoyed in the narrator's comment than the hero's biography. Parts of this, it is true, are justly praised: the 'Haidee' love story of Cantos, II, III and IV contains a tender, and for once unmodified emotion, which is allowed to grow in a free, Eden-like and unmolested environment.

The incidental comment of the author takes the prime place in the poem. The forceful, vivid nature of this comment, its satirical and shocking turns, look back to the best of the eighteenth-century writing, and forward to Browning and Wilde. Much twentieth-century poetic and dramatic satire and wit also is owed to this tradition. Society is asked to reassess some of its perhaps too-complacently held values. Byron had fallen out of favour with society himself, having contravened some of its cherished taboos; he wrote his best poetry while ostracized from it. This may have added the air of indignation and rebellious aggression to some of the satire, but he knew and preserved in all his mockery the difference between immorality, reprehensible behaviour and humbug. His influence, both as a writer and as a character, proved to be very great on the continent of Europe, and a revival of interest in this country with the evaporation of irrelevant controversy about Byron the man, has accompanied a more attentive reading of his later work.

Shelley

(Some knowledge of Shelley's 'romantic' life is useful as a background to an understanding of his poetry.)

Percy Bysshe Shelley (1792-1822) was born into the minor gentry, educated at Eton where he felt very isolated, and at Oxford from where he was expelled for circulating a pamphlet, 'The Necessity of Atheism', to the Heads of the colleges. He eloped with Harriet Westbrook, but left her for Mary Godwin after entering the Godwin circle, with its intense revolutionary, anti-royalist opinions. The couple visited Byron in Switzerland, frequented Leigh Hunt's company at home, and revisited Byron in Venice. The rest of Shelley's life was spent in Italy, and most of his best work was done during this period. He was drowned while out at sea in a small boat alone.

Shelley is famous for what has been called the pure lyric: a short poem celebrating nothing but the poet's own soul, with few or no attendant circumstances. He was very well-read, and at one time thought about taking up metaphysics and politics; failing to come to terms with society, however, he decided to write poetry as a full-time task, but his intellectual interests found their way into the poetry with a seriousness of purpose and even didacticism that may surprise those who think of him as merely a lyricist. He adopted Godwin's views, which were founded on rationalist principles and the importance of individual liberties, but more as a bulwark against his own chaotic imagination, and the philistinism he saw in the world.

Shelley's first poem, *Queen Mab* (1810-1812), was influential in radical circles as it embodied Godwin's ideas, including the primacy of reason and the natural law, and the disgust that the political theorist felt at any situation in which one man could have absolute authority over another.

> 'Power like a devastating pestilence
> Pollutes whatever it touches.'

Shelley, when writing these lines, had not long said goodbye to Dr Keat of Eton. The problem that engaged the poet was the belief that all men were perfectible, but how were they to begin to improve? He held that man was naturally good, but hopelessly oppressed by institutions; education might dispel the evil; good (i.e. 'enlightenment') was a future possibility, evil (darkness), or the conditions that prevailed, seemed absolute; 'Necessity' (not God) governed all things. A saviour might bring good into being: the power to be used was love.

Alastor (1815) is an allegory of Shelley's own case: loneliness, persecution by the spirit of solitude, inflicted on the poet by Alastor, the avenging demon. The lonely young hero wanders through a dream world until he sees a vision of beauty, and spends the rest of his days searching for her. This may be seen to be a model for Keats' *Endymion* and indeed it describes a typically 'romantic' preoccupation.

The Revolt of Islam (1817) is the story of an ideal relationship which extends into a Platonic love for humanity. The struggle between good and evil (which in Shelley is synonymous with hatred and tyranny) is allegorized in Canto I, as between a serpent and an eagle.

Shelley succeeds much better when he next takes a well-known Greek myth, that of Prometheus' punishment by Jupiter for the theft of fire from heaven as a benefit to man. He turns Prometheus into a saviour figure, the salvation being achieved by his release from the unjust bondage. The story as it appears in Aeschylus' tragedy, is presented in Act I of the lyrical drama, *Prometheus Unbound* (1820); Acts II and III are concerned with Jupiter's overthrow, he being the emblem of tyranny and therefore evil; in Act III Prometheus is liberated. Here he represents the aspiring spirit of Man which longs for freedom. Asia, representing love, travels with her sister Panthea to the cave of Demogorgon – Fate stronger than Jupiter himself – to secure Prometheus' liberation. When this is granted, the hour must arrive when Jupiter simply fades out without a struggle. Heracles releases Prometheus who is reunited with Asia, and the whole earth is saved from pain, disease, and the fear of death. Act IV, an afterthought, turns out to be the poem's crowning glory: an ecstatic celebration of freedom and a sustained hymn of joy.

Although Shelley is best known for his short lyrics, outside some half dozen well-anthologized pieces, they do not show him at his best. He is better in the longer poems which are lyrical in essence: *Adonais* (an elegy on Keats), *The Sensitive Plant* (a narrative), *Epipsychidion* (a love story), and *The Witch of Atlas* (a fairy tale). Between these longer and short poems comes a marvellous group of poems in a rapturous tone: *The Cloud, To a Skylark, Lines Written in the Euganean Hills* and *Ode to the West Wind.*

The images in Shelley's lyric poetry are usually only loosely connected with one another, or with the theme: they seem to float free, yet they still manage to convey a coherent effect overall. The exact meaning of many images does not bear close analysis, nor should they receive it. They should be read in the spirit of the entire poem to which they contribute a part of the aura or atmosphere of the poem. In the same way, each stanza of *To a Skylark* bears little or no relation logically to those before and after, yet the poem as a whole has an undeniable effect, and a unity. A notorious image in *Ode to the West Wind,* severely censured by Leavis in *Revaluation* refers to an approaching thundercloud thus:

> 'there are spread
> On the blue surface of thine aery surge,
> Like the bright hair uplifted from the head
>
> Of some fierce Maenad, even from the dim verge
> Of the horizon to the zenith's height,
> The locks of the approaching storm.'

This strange simile is no more inappropriate or badly visualized than any other image in this great poem; it takes its place in the turbulent stream of emotionally grounded images in the stanza and the whole poem: colourful, energetic, and verbally 'right'.

Shelley's last poem, *Triumph of Life* (1822) was unfinished at his death. It begins with a pageant of slaves to life, which includes Rousseau; all were once free. It is easy to see where the poem is leading. Like *Ode to the West Wind,* the poem is composed in terza rima, which clearly Shelley found a congenial metre, but it was a new experiment in English.

When studying Shelley, it is useful to look at his essay 'The Defence of Poetry'. Again, it provides a useful source of stimulating quotation for the examination boards. Shelley regards poetry as subordinate to 'moral or political science' (his early love); it has a mission and a responsibility to 'reform the world' by the power of imagination. Beauty is an absolute, to which all the arts aspire: the poet may come nearest – he may express truth in beauty's form, giving all uncorrupted people pleasure. Not only can poetry do this, but can even initiate law and lay the foundations of society: 'poets are the unacknowledged legislators of the world'. The ambitious idea lends at least part of the peculiar excitement of *Ode to the West Wind.*

Keats

Questions on Keats (1795-1821) at A Level fall into three main categories: questions on the odes; questions on the unfinished epic *Hyperion* and questions asking for discussion of his narrative craft. Keats' letters, prescribed by some boards, are interesting and useful reading for any student studying the poems.

The Odes

In 1811 Wordsworth wrote a sonnet, remembered by Keats when the younger poet came to compose the *Ode on a Grecian Urn,* on a painting by his friend Sir George Beaumont. After describing

> 'the Bark upon the grassy flood
> For ever anchored in her sheltering bay'

the poem concludes:

> (thou) 'Here . . . has given
> To one brief moment caught from fleeting time
> The appropriate calm of blest eternity.'

John Keats (1795–1821)

The theme of transience and permanence which struck Keats in Wordsworth's poem, forms the leading theme in the Odes. This may be followed through in all except *Ode to Psyche.* The crowning ode, *To Autumn,* may be seen as a satisfying, albeit temporary, suspension in the continuing debate between the two states, in this case emblemized by the sequent seasons. A respite is achieved though even here the problem is not entirely solved:

> 'Where are the songs of Spring' Ay, where are they?
> Think not of them . . .'

In *Ode to a Nightingale* the permanent element is the bird's song, and the emphasis is on the beauty of this and its rural setting. The bird is subject to change but does not in the poem appear to be; it is unseen and identified with its eternal song. The real victims are men who

> 'sit and hear each other groan'

Sorrow and despair reign where neither love nor beauty nor joy can last. There are hints that the nightingale's song symbolizes poetry itself especially in the fourth stanza where there is an apparent reference to Edmund Spenser, once Keats' favourite poet.

In *Ode on a Grecian Urn* the dichotomy is seen as being between 'life' (which is transient) and Art (which is permanent). There is a 'teasing' illusion of life about the scene on the urn – but all its thronging, celebratory and amorous activities will never proceed to any conclusion. Permanence exacts its price; the moulded scene will outlast 'breathing passion', the 'high sorrowful' heart and (like the spectre-thin youth of *Ode to a Nightingale*) the fevers men die of. But it is cold and has an aesthetic message that is uncompromising and exclusive, as Keats later showed in *Ode on Melancholy* and *The Fall of Hyperion,* and even the 'Bright star . . .' sonnet. However, if the last two lines of *On a Grecian Urn* are taken as the urn's complete message to us, then the conclusion is coherent. Beauty is the whole story; permanence wins.

> '"Beauty is truth, truth beauty," – that is all
> Ye know on earth, and all ye need to know.'

So far we see that the two states are unreconciled and tragically separate. In the *Nightingale Ode,* permanent song is clearly superior, and it is unqualifiedly sad for the vision to withdraw, as 'Forlorn', the word like a melancholy bell, indicates; in *Ode on a Grecian Urn* permanence is equivocal; art is long, but dead in itself, though beautiful. In the *Ode on Melancholy,* a synthesis is attempted and achieved; the thematic problem is solved by identifying the principle of beauty and therefore joy (even love) with transience itself. This ode, which significantly concludes the set, Keats' greatest achievement, expresses a vision of those beauties so characteristic of art, visions which are incapable of gaining their effect unless perceived as fleeting. Hence 'melancholy', after being associated with passing things: the morning rose, the rainbow in seaspray, an emotionally aroused lover, is then said to occupy the very throne in 'the temple of delight', and the rhetoric of the last stanza achieves authenticity not only by its own argument, but by the treatment of themes in the other Odes. The law of change is pronounced by Oceanus in Book 2 of Hyperion, in terms of beauty – the greater must displace the lesser. Acceptance of all human suffering and instability is implied in 'Bright star', and finally reach a mature statement by Moneta in lines 147–153 of Canto 1 of 'The Fall of Hyperion'. With the evidence of a cancelled first stanza, it becomes clear that Keats began with the simple idea of showing how melancholy is not essentially linked with the trappings of the Gothic horror novel, but lies in the inexorable transience of beauty. The fortunate loss of this stanza prepared the way for a completely satisfying restatement, in stanza 3, the last of the Ode, of one of Keats' most characteristic themes.

Hyperion

There are three dominant divinities in this unfinished epic: Saturn and Hyperion share equally the leading interest of Book I; Saturn controls the debate in Book II, but at the end attention is once more diverted to Hyperion who arrives to

> 'oppose to each malignant hour
> Ethereal presence.'

However he proves to be ineffectual, only revealing the terrible scene more clearly to the fallen gods. When the poem opens, Saturn is revealed alone, dignified and majestic still in defeat; Thea comes to rouse him, reminding him of his past glory, but he is unheeding in his profound sleep, and Thea can only sigh and weep. When he awakes, he reveals his impotence, with 'palsied tongue' and 'aspen malady'. Surely some figure more powerful and active must be the hero of the epic? We are introduced to Hyperion himself—still, indeed, unfallen in his sun-palace, but everything foreshadows disaster for him too:

> 'horrors, portion'd to a giant nerve
> Oft made Hyperion ache'

The palace is full of frightful omens: his servants stand clustered in fearful groups expecting the worst. All this makes Hyperion apprehensive and angry, and he defies that infant thunderer, rebel Jove; challenging him to try and unseat him. However his heroic defiance only makes the lurking Phantoms rise against him more chokingly; he runs to start the new day, but Fate is against him, and he can only stretch himself 'in radiance faint' in the sky. At this the father of the Titans, Coelus or Uranus, speaks to him, and the speech underlines the new situation, but advises him to oppose the rebellion while he is still able to 'move about, an evident God'.

From this, at the close of Book I, it may be inferred that Hyperion is to become the hero of the epic, opposing himself titanically against the already successful rebellion of Jupiter and the Olympians, rather as Satan did against God and His Creation in Milton's *Paradise Lost*.

The great debate in Book II, so clearly modelled on the similar Council in *Paradise Lost* Book II, is stimulated, begun and conducted by Saturn, hailed by Enceladus:

> 'Titans, behold your God!'

Saturn can see no reason why they should be in their plight: nor, being there, why they should accept it and remain there. The speeches that follow are all in response to Saturn's appeal for opinions on what they should now do. One of these speeches, that of Oceanus, predecessor of Neptune, tries to establish a truth they must all accept: that as they superseded Coelus and Gea, who themselves followed Chaos and Darkness, so there must follow a new set of gods, who will exceed them far in 'Beauty', and

> ''tis the eternal law
> That first in beauty should be first in might.'

This principle, fatal for Saturn, Hyperion and all the old crew, is then given sharper point by Clymene who in her speech mentions for the first time who must be considered to be the probable hero of the poem if it had been finished: Apollo, the God destined to take Hyperion's place. She demonstrates the law of greater beauty putting the lesser to flight, in her story of Apollo's music, sounding across the sea from Delos to where she was attempting to make melody from breathing into a seashell. Apollo's was the brilliant music of his lyre, invented by him – a discovery described in Book III. Apollo, and his name reiterated five times in three lines, is therefore well prepared for.

Enceladus, like the ignorant Moloch in *Paradise Lost,* advocates violent resistence in similarly thundering but mindless terms; he serves also to direct attention to Hyperion, but the still-active god shows rather the hopelessness of the situation.

In Book III, which breaks off after only 136 lines, the epic takes the new but anticipated turn. Apollo, described on his island of Delos prior to the time of his deification – the event which closes the poem – clearly assumes the leading role. He is at the centre of the epic's theme: that of the necessity of superiority in Beauty superseding the old, outworn and outclassed regime.

As Hyperion is seen to approach his 'Nemesis', the toppling into the same sad, sunken vale as Saturn, so Apollo is described as learning from Mnemosyne, ('Memory', the mother of the Muses), his imminent apotheosis as Hyperion's successor.

In the story of the poem, therefore, there may be three leading figures or 'heroes'; in the dimension of the theme, there is but one: Apollo.

Keats' narrative skill

Keats, unlike his contemporary Shelley, loved poetry above any other reading, and his early delight in Spenser's *Faerie Queene,* the Tales of Chaucer and the plays of Shakespeare, all made him naturally inclined to try his hand at writing long poems in which he might 'have a little region to wander in where they may pick and choose and in which the images are so numerous that many are forgotten and found new in a second reading: which may be food for a week's stroll in the Summer.'

The earlier attempts are consequently rambling and plotless: *Sleep and Poetry* in the 1817 volume was followed by *Endymion* in 1818. Some sketch for a narrative thread was provided but this is swamped by the discursive descriptions of the arbitrary scenes; 'As I proceeded my steps were all uncertain' the poet says about its composition, and this is the effect the narrative has on the reader. There is an interesting symbolic level, however, and this may be summarized as the pursuit of Beauty by the enamoured soul – a theme like that of Shelley's *Alastor* as noted above.

The poem which formed the transition to the maturity of *The Eve of St Agnes* is *Isabella,* which later Keats, again his own best critic, called 'weak-sided . . . with an amusing sober-sadness about it.' In it however Keats tackles new themes in a new way: human love, tension and enmity, grief. He chose, probably mistakenly, the Byronic 'ottava rima' to be the metre, but lacked Byron's polished use of the final couplet for neat conclusions to the stanza. Published revisions demonstrate that he eliminated many of the vague phrases, imprecisions, sentimentalities and the like. Several remain, as well as the overall 'inexperience of life' and the incongruity of the gruesome story and the gentle ornate descriptive style.

Lamia is a much finer poem: its couplets proceed more steadily and purposefully; the whole is less sentimental, indeed its theme includes the idea of the necessary, if cynical, rejection of sentimental self-delusion. There are some wonderful passages of rich but exact description, with a most economical use of words to evoke an atmosphere; for example, Lycius' entry into Corinth, and the description of Lamia's house, especially the banqueting hall.

The Eve of St Agnes reveals Keats' poetical and narrative powers to the full; the poem is as near perfect as such can be: the setting, moods and technique chime together in an unflawed whole. Effective as *Lamia* is, the purpose of the story is uncertain, and there is not much left for Lycius to do but die, when his lost love turns out to be an enchantress. Keats now was able to embroider a folk legend in just the manner he wished; all his love of Spenser's elaborate descriptiveness, of the high romance and theme of opposed love in *Romeo and Juliet,* and his late wandering about the magnificent architecture of Chichester and Winchester Cathedrals, where he used to take the love letters of his fiancée, Fanny Brawne, to read, all came together in this beautiful poem. Colour, imagery and contrasts are used as motifs in the narrative. Colour is used for love, while in contrast, hardness, gloom or coldness are associated with the hostile castle and its family. The sensuous atmosphere appropriate to the story of secret lovers and elopement, is evoked by similar means, in the setting of Madeline's bedchamber in particular. The strange but extremely sensuous table of fruits, jellies, syrops and spices that Porphyro heaps up, may be best explained by reference to a cancelled stanza (between VI and VII) in which it is made clear that to offer such was part of the legend of St Agnes' Eve that Madeline expected to be carried out. There is no clear reason why this stanza should be omitted, unless perhaps it was thought by the author or publisher likely to offend virginal delicacy by its reference to 'more pleasures . . . Palpable almost'. The gothic, shadowed architecture is linked with the withered, palsy-stricken bedesman, and the olde beldame Angela 'weak in body and in soul.' These and the loud and brilliant company, contrast effectively with the warmth, quietness and soft lighting of the lovers' setting.

The first few stanzas prepare the way for Madeline, reflecting on the legend of that night, her mind far removed from her company. Then Porphyro is introduced, slipping into the castle unseen except by the sympathetic 'pandar' type, Angela. She informs him of Madeline's hopes about the old legend, giving him the idea of introducing himself as the lover who is supposed to be seen as a vision if the due ceremonies are performed. He compels Angela to assist him. The calm beauty of the following scene is introduced by such touches as:

> 'out went the taper as she hurried in;
> Its little smoke, in pallid moonshine died:'

Porphyro, concealed, observes his love go to bed, and the climax of the poem is perfectly positioned, occupying the stanzas XXXI–XXXVI (there are 42 stanzas). After her alarm and doubts, Madeline's fears are set at rest, and she agrees to escape the grim castle with her lover, and flee south to warmth and security. The clandestine departure is as sensuously and swiftly described as the opening event:

> 'Down the wide stairs a darkling way they found.
> A chain-droop'd lamp was flickering by each door:'

In the concluding stanza, the Baron and his unpleasant cronies are plagued by nightmares (the opposite of Madeline's realized dream), and the two decrepit servants each die in his own barren manner.

All the improvements carried out by Keats are particularly illuminating, in the evidence they show of Keats's ability in revision: weak expressions are altered to strong ones; Lax or diffuse images focused into clear and vivid ones. Observe, for example, two initial versions of the second line quoted above:

> 'But here and there a lamp was flickering out'
> 'A drooping lamp was flickering here and there'.

The improvement over these two lines is continued by a sharper realization of the image of the lamps, and the addition of a setting for them.

THE VICTORIAN POETS

Tennyson and Browning are almost exactly contemporary and their lives squarely occupy the nineteenth century from the first decade to the last. Tennyson, Browning and Hopkins occupy the leading positions in examination syllabuses for Victorian poetry.

Tennyson (1809–92)

Questions on Tennyson at A Level often reflect some still-persisting critical doubt about his greatness, suggesting sympathy but not enthusiasm. Here is a selection:
'Consider the variety of subject matter and style' 'Has Tennyson's emotion any intensity?' 'Consider the aspects of Tennyson's narrative skill'

It would be hard to assess the nature of Tennyson's claim to greatness in his poetry from such questions; nor are the editors of selections much more helpful in their introductions; the following questions all receive different answers:

(a) Are Tennyson's moral concerns provincial or outdated, or are they still vital today?

(b) Are his truths 'commonplace' (as Hopkins said), or 'profoundly simple' (Christopher Ricks)?

(c) Is his famed facility in language, and smoothness of texture, merely skilled versification, or is it more?

Tennyson had a huge public in his day, but his contemporary critics and writers were not so sure of him. The popular journals were wholly enthusiastic and reflected the taste of their readers; later a reaction against him joined that against other Victorian idols. Very many of Tennyson's readers would have read his work aloud to each other, and Sir John Betjeman's reading of *Locksley Hall* and *Enoch Arden* over the radio some years ago, reminded us that this could be the best way to experience Tennyson's poetry, and provided a clue to his once huge popularity. You may find it helpful to read aloud the poems you are studying.

It is still not easy to know what to make of a poet who can as readily write:

> 'Sons be welded, each and all
> Into one Imperial whole,
> One with Britain, heart and soul!
> One life, one flag, one fleet, one Throne!
> Britons, hold your own!
> And, God guard all!'

(did the Headmaster declare it in assembly, or the Colonel in the mess?); as, at an advanced age:

> 'Naay, but tha *mun* speak hout to the Baptises here i'the town,
> Fur moast on 'em talks agean tithe, an' I'd like tha to preach 'em down,
> Fur *they've* bin a-preachin'*mea* down, they heve, an I haates 'em now
> Fur they leaved their nasty sins i'*my* pond, an'it poison'd the cow.'

except to say that if one man wrote both, he was clearly a skilled writer who could and did turn his hand to almost any theme, and publish it. This artistic flexibility may obscure the fact that some things did move him more deeply. He was moved by death, for which he found it expedient in his poetry to provide some trappings of Christian doctrine: compare the second stanza with the first, for example, of *God and the Universe*. He was particularly affected by the death of a great friend, Arthur Hallam, in 1833. He was moved by the idea of a stoical advance into a dark and uncertain future. The music of his lines may suggest a process of escape. They sometimes seem to exist only to create an imaginative auditory effect, and not to respond at a deep and perhaps painful level to the subject of their composition.

When, with the most congenial subjects, Tennyson's polished and perfected technique joins with a strong, purposeful voice saying something that matters, even if, as Hopkins complained, nothing fresh or original is said, we have poetry of which it would be churlish to ask more. For example, for the humour of rustic dialogue, the poem from which the Lincolnshire dialect lines from *The Churchwarden and the Curate* above are taken do all that may be expected of such verse anecdotes. In a poem of the same late period, *Crossing the Bar* we have: (at death may there be) . . . . .

> 'such a tide as moving seems asleep,
> Too full for sound and foam
> When that which drew from out the boundless deep
> Turns again home.'

This is fine enough although flawed for the modern sensibility by the Victorian nod to 'my Pilot' (i.e. Christ) who as in Victorian hymnals, following St Paul, may at last be seen 'face to face'. There is a more convincing note of genuine inner struggle in these quatrains:

> 'I falter where I firmly trod,
> And falling with my weight of cares
> Upon the great world's altar-stairs'
> That slope thro' darkness up to God,
>
> I stretch lame hands of faith, and grope
> And gather dust and chaff, and call
> To what I feel is Lord of all,
> And faintly trust the larger hope.'

This is an honest feeling echoed by Hardy in *The Oxen* seventy years later, and referring to the same decade of the nineteenth century.

The lines above are taken from *In Memoriam (LIV)*, Tennyson's long elegy meditated since his friend Hallam's death. He continued with its composition in the forties, after the publishing of the two volumes of 1842 on which his fame was founded. This, with the building up of his Arthurian epic (whose prologue may be seen in *The Epic* before *Morte D'Arthur* in the Poems of 1842) formed Tennyson's major endeavour until he began writing plays in the seventies.

The news of Arthur Hallam's death was the occasion also for the poem *Ulysses*. It may be helpful to enquire into the tone and meaning of this poem, which is often misread. Relevant attendant information is useful but too much importance should not be attached to Tennyson's sources in Homer and Dante; rather more perhaps should be attached to Hallam's death.

The poet took the situation from Tiresias' prophecy to Ulysses, (*Odyssey* XI): that after his wanderings he would not vegetate in Ithaca but row away to another people. Tennyson took details from Carey's blank-verse translation of Dante (*Inferno* XXVI), but the poem owes little else to Homer or Dante. The tone is not one of debilitated life – weariness incorporating a death-wish and unrelieved by strong imagination; nor is it akin to the 'enervated cadence' of the *Lotus Eaters,* in the phrase of one commentator. On the contrary, Ulysses wishes to accomplish some final enterprise before his death which is now due. The grief expressed in the end is more the noble, temporary cry of Elijah (1 Kings 19.4), uncharacteristic and dependent on the circumstances. The cadences are not so much Homeric or Dantesque as Virgilian, in his elegiac moods, and the final impression is that of sombre stoicism in the face of an obscure future and a grim resolution; as in Tennysons's adaptation from Hallam's own lines 'We are not now as we were once'. Dramatically speaking this is true for Ulysses, the grief of Tennyson makes the tone true for himself and the final lines ironical for his friend.

> '. . and tho'
> We are not now that strength which in old days
> Moved earth and heaven; that which we are, we are;
> One equal temper of heroic hearts
> Made weak by time and fates but strong in will
> To strive, to seek, to find, and not to yield.'

Narrative in Tennyson is illustrated by selections from the earlier contributions to the final *Idylls of the King* completed in 1885, especially *'Morte D'Arthur* and *'The Lady of Shalott'.*

Browning (1812-89)

With Robert Browning we meet quite different problems associated with the quite different quality and content of his poetry.

In the first place, it should be stressed that Browning was not smug or complacently optimistic: the too-well-known lines:

'God's in his heaven –
All's right with the world'.

are like much else in this poet's work, another's words and sentiment; the song of an Italian girl, Pippa, as she passes by different men and women. She sings songs that affect their attitudes and opinions, thus influencing them innocently.

Browning's title for a series of collections published nearly every year from 1841 to 1846 was *Bells and Pomegranates,* an allusion to the pattern on the border of a levite or priestly garment, symbolizing for Browning the 'music discoursing, sound with sense, poetry with thought'. It is the discourse, the sense and thought that should most engage the attention of candidates, whatever edition has been prescribed. It is pleasant to hear the bells ring, but the pomegranates have to be sucked dry.

The well-known children's tale, *The Pied Piper of Hamelin,* appears in Volume III, and the almost equally familiar *How They Brought the Good News from Ghent to Aix* in Volume VII; many others deserve to be known as well, e.g. *Soliloquy of the Spanish Cloister* which is the forerunner of those dramatic monologues for which Browning is rightly famous. These are collected in *Men and Women* (1855), and *Dramatis Personae* (1864), the two most commonly used works in prescriptions from Browning. His variety, fertility of imagination and robust energy are shown to the full in these 'personae' or masks of characters put on by Browning for the dramatic purpose of rendering the different characters immediate, life-like and convincing.

The first ten lines of *Mr Sludge, The Medium,* for example, are at once arresting and striking for their vivid characterization; the vitality of the language is astonishing for the period, and the dramatic shock could only be equalled by John Donne, or the beginning of Shakespeare's scenes. No wonder Ezra Pound, the invigorator of twentieth-century Edwardian verse, admired Browning.

This aspect is emphasized in many questions; often quoting one of the editors of editions of his verse, 'Browning could reveal in a flash the motives which make men and women behave as they do. To what extent is this contention borne out in the selection?'

The method of preparing for this type of question is to make a complete note on what the motives of all the characters are, by asking yourself the question, Why do they speak and act as they do? Then pinpoint the lines and phrases which best communicate such motives.

For example in the poem referred to above, which Browning wrote in annoyance at his wife's attraction to spiritualism, we are soon aware that Mr Sludge is the most unrepentant charlatan. In his seance, observe how smoothly the motive for this is expressed after 20 lines:

'Oh Lord! I little thought, sir, yesterday
When your departed mother spoke those words
Of peace through me, and moved you, sir, so much
You gave me – (very kind it was of you)
These shirt-studs – (better take them back again)'

Note also the cringing, sycophantic, fear-ridden tones, illustrating his sly and oily nature – one that preys on the grief of the bereaved through their credulity.

Hopkins (1844–1889)

Gerard Manley Hopkins is in many ways the most congenial poet to the modern sensibility. He is considered by many A-level candidates to be 'difficult' but he need not be so to those prepared to follow Hopkins' own advice and 'open' their ears.

Robert Bridges, Hopkins' friend, fellow poet and constant correspondent, preserved his poetry, as well as at times attempting to rewrite it into Victorian-style stanzas! He prepared the first edition of Hopkins' verse, published in 1918, 29 years after Hopkins' death. It was not until the second edition of 1930 that with the 'moderns' then mostly published, the public could begin to recognize Hopkins' great and original talent.

Bridges wrote of his friend's verse:

'occasional affectations in metaphor . . perversion of human feeling . . . efforts
to force emotion into theological or sectarian channels . . . the unpoetic line –
'His mystery must be instressed stressed' –
. . . the exaggerated Marianism . . . the naked encounter of sensualism and asceticism'.

Bridge's phrase, 'the naked encounter of sensualism and asceticism' refers to *The Golden Echo,* a good test piece for an appreciation of Hopkins. The poem is counterpointed with its companion piece, *The Leaden Echo.*

All this from a *contemporary* poet indicates the reception Hopkins might have expected if he had been read earlier. It also helps to make clear how far the 'modernist' movement of the twenties brought about a revolution in the sophisticated audience's expectations.

Bridges in his preface goes on to refer to the 'oddity and obscurity' of Hopkins, of which the first 'provokes laughter' when he is 'always serious', while the second must prevent his being understood when he 'always has something to say'.

For modern readers used to the practice of Yeats, Eliot, Auden or Dylan Thomas, there is very little to hold them up when approaching Hopkins. If such handicaps still exist, it is best to approach the poet by way of some of the better apprentice-work poems, such as *Heaven Haven* or *The Habit of Perfection;* or good fragments such *Moonless darkness stands between* or the more characteristic *The Woodlark,* and the remarkably interesting narrative style opening to *Epithalamium,* a very late poem scribbled in pencil on University of Ireland candidates' examination paper in 1888. The poem was to have been an Ode on his brother's marriage, but he only got as far as creating a set of emblems and images for the occasion, worked up into a kind of allegory.

These poems will lead you into Hopkins' characteristic manner in his small finished output. Among these also, several poems are comparatively simple and straightforward and help to accustom the ear and mind to the more inaccessible poetry. Thus *Spring and Fall, Pied Beauty* and *Inversnaid* are useful introductions. Among the 48 completed poems each person has his or her favourites, but no one can ignore the sonnets, nor fail to note Hopkins' modifications to the form, good examples being *The Windhover, Felix Randall, Spelt From the Sybil's Leaves* and *To RB.* Two other major poems cannot be passed over by A-level students of Hopkins: *The Wreck of the Deutschland* and *The Leaden Echo and the Golden Echo* referred to above.

The Wreck of the Deutschland, written after a seven year silence on Hopkins' entry into the Catholic Society of Jesus in 1868 – he was converted to Catholicism by Cardinal Newman while at Oxford – was composed at the suggestion of his superior to commemorate the death by drowning in a shipwreck of five nuns, expelled from Germany. We have analysed a stanza of this poem below.

A study of the poems mentioned above should fit the student to answer such A-level questions as:

'Do you agree that Hopkins writes most movingly when he writes most simply?'

Other questions may well refer to his great feeling for natural beauty, for his most observant eye, and fresh, sensuous response which is reminiscent of the best of Keats. Almost every poem illustrates these characteristics, often by way of brilliant images that by a flash of insight reveal and glorify the real scene and experience:

(on stars): 'Flake-doves sent forth at a farmyard scare!'
(on blossom): 'When drop-of-blood-and-foam dapple
         Bloom lights the orchard apple'
(on a clutch of eggs): 'Thrush's eggs look little low heavens'
(on the kestrel): 'Then off, off forth on swing as a skate's heel sweeps smooth on a bow-bend'
(on the sound of waves): 'the tide that ramps against the shore
         with a flood or a fall, low lull-off or all roar'

This last is a good example of Hopkins's management of exact words rather than images, to render an exact impression.

Hopkins' 'difficulties' are sometimes singled out for special treatment in essays. You should decide if you think these are due to 'mangling' of the English language (see Bridge's lack of sympathy), or whether his poetic techniques may be viewed as brilliant handling of the medium, combining choice of vocabulary, rhythm (special notes are needed on 'sprung' rhythm), metre and imagery, for fully justified effects.

We will select two examples from the very many available, as demonstrations of what Hopkins has done with the language of poetry. The first is from *The Wreck of the Deutschland:*

> 'I am soft sift
> In an hour glass – at the wall
> Fast, but mined with a motion, a drift,
> And it crowds and it combs to the fall;
> I steady as a water in a well, to a poise, to a pane,
> But roped with, always, all the way down from the tall
> Fells or flanks of the voel, a vein
> Of the gospel proffer, a pressure, a principle, Christ's gift.'

Gerard Manley Hopkins (1844–1889)

These apparently unrelated images – hour glass, well, waterfall, finishing with a reference to the gospel, may be fully justified by the theme which contains them, and which they creatively illustrate.

In the first place it may be noted how well each image is established, by verbal colour, rhythm and arrangement: the sand crumbling to its vortex in a phrase that echoes the motion; the poised steadiness of the well water, and its link to the long Welsh waterfall – more of a silvery runnel down the stark flank of the mountain ('voel' – Welsh for 'bare hill'). The water looks like a shining rope, which may link God's saving life-line to the spirit of man, a link like the Gospels, giving life by filling spiritual reserves. We have been led to the theme – salvation, not destruction, by water; a fall into sand, the symbol of time – 'hour glass'. (An attendant circumstance here was that the *Deutschland* foundered on the Goodwins, but such details are not necessary to the understanding of such verses.)

The next example is taken from *The Windhover:*

> 'Brute beauty and valour and act, air, pride, plume here
> Buckle! AND the fire that breaks from thee then, a billion
> Times told lovelier, more dangerous, O my Chevalier!'

These lines form the crux of the sonnet: the physical flesh and blood of the hawk, is juxtaposed to its airy grace of movement, its hovering high up; hence the very strong position, sound and image of the crucial word 'Buckle' – the hinge to the meaning, in which the physical and the ethereal aspects of the hawk join, just as they do in the being of Christ, referred to only once as 'chevalier', a word that is still appropriate to a bird already likened to the 'dauphin' of the King of daylight. In either case the bird is princely, the heir to the divinity of heaven. 'Buckle' not only signifies 'join' but connotes 'break' or 'give way' – the humbling of God in Christ to flesh. These meanings produce the splendour, the 'fire' next described as bursting out from its dark coat of ash.

A final word on Hopkins' religion which is ubiquitous in his poetry, and the mainspring of most of it. Hopkins' religious experience was without question genuine, sincere and turbulent. It is quite as evident as his delight in nature. One question on this is:
'We see more of the terror than of the beauty of religion in Hopkins' poetry. Do you agree?'

The reference to the 'terror' may lead the student to the theme and much of the language and imagery of *The Wreck of the Deutschland*; the nuns 'fought with God's cold', and in the introductory stanzas:

> 'Thou has bound bones and veins in me, fastened me flesh,
> And after it almost unmade, what with dread,
> Thy doing . . .'

In *Carrion Comfort,* after a record of a terrible night of doubt,

> 'That night, that year
> of now done darkness I wretch lay wrestling with (my God!) my God.'

To set against these, there is the more typical sense of God's praiseworthiness

> 'Glory be to God for dappled things!'

finishing 'Praise Him'; and

> 'Christ plays in ten thousand places
> Lovely in limbs, and lovely in eyes not his . . .'

THE TWENTIETH CENTURY

The works most often set at A Level from this century, judging by recent papers of all the Boards are:

TS Eliot, 22% (including two widely used selections – Faber's *Selected Poems* and *Four Quartets*)
WB Yeats, 18%
(Anthologies, 11% (especially George MacBeth's *Poetry 1900-65,* and since that edition, *Poetry 1900-75*)

Poets of the First World War, 8%
Louis MacNeice, 10%
Ted Hughes, 8%
Thomas Hardy, 6%
DH Lawrence, 4%
WH Auden, 4%

Philip Larkin, 4%
Dylan Thomas, 2%
Robert Lowell, 2%
AE Houseman, 1%

This rough breakdown is for interest only as the pattern is constantly changing. Other modern poets are introduced each year, a recent example being Seamus Heaney. Some of the low-weighted poets are present because they have appeared in recent syllabuses. In the past there has been more Dylan Thomas and Edwin Muir, Robert Graves and Thom Gunn have all been represented, and no doubt will be again. It is noteworthy that MacBeth has added Hardy to *Poetry 1900 to 1975*, presumably because of his growing reputation as a very good poet of this century. American poets continue to creep into anthologies used in schools, and as single poet selections for examinations, though anthologies of American poets alone are not set and the policy is not consistent. The two leading poets of the century are American and Irish born, though they have joined the main tradition of European if not English poetry. Both Eliot and Yeats however retain many characteristics derived from their background.

Most of the poets listed above have produced prose of high quality in essays and criticism, and in some cases have also been great novelists (Hardy, Lawrence), or good ones (Larkin, Graves) or playwrights (Lawrence, Yeats, Eliot). It need not be emphasized that the prose or drama of prescribed poets is very valuable supportive reading and in some cases greatly enlightens one's understanding of the poetry (Hardy, Yeats, Lawrence, Eliot, Auden, Dylan Thomas, MacNeice's autobiography, Ted Hughes' stories and essays).

Because of the high incidence of Yeats' and Eliot's appearance on the syllabuses, we will consider them separately below, but first we will refer briefly to two poets of the second rank, but still of sufficient merit and interest to warrant a prominent place in present and future A-level work – Auden (1907-1973), and Ted Hughes (1930-   ).

A note on Auden and Hughes

Any poem from, say, the last collection of each of these poets, if contrasted, will illustrate the difference between this pair. In *Archaeology* (Auden's *Thank you Fog*), one of his multitude of manners, he takes a topic and launches into a series of easy, seemingly casual comments, turning it over as if it were a subject for after-dinner conversation; but the three-line stanzas each contain a separate idea, like a string of matched beads, finishing with a sudden insight into the similarity yet dissimilarity between barbaric rites and Christ's crucifixion. Then in a coda, like an after-thought, casually added, he clinches the discourse on *Archaeology* with a moral proposition that is not only worthy of thought but offers a key to the previous, apparently inconsequential string of variations. Such is the geniality of tone, it is difficult to notice that Auden has used ten coined parts of speech – mainly new verbs from adjectives or nouns; two coined phrases and one word (unless 'stumper' is a slang word like 'poser').

Auden continues the tradition of English poetry from Pope to Browning, with fresh access of tone from American poets such as Marianne Moore. Ted Hughes intensifies the sensuous apprehensions explored by Keats, Hopkins, and DH Lawrence to such a degree that it is difficult to conceive how this can be taken further; a poem on catching fish in the style of *Earth Numb* (*Moortown*) could not be improved upon. In place of Auden's urbanity, and deceptive simplicity:

> 'Poets have learned us their myths
> But just how did They take them?'

we have this of Ted Hughes:

> 'As the eyes of incredulity
> Fix their death-exposure of the celandine and the cloud,'

to end the poem with the landing of the fish.

Set in their contexts, the first quotation excites the assent of the reader, with gratitude for the friendly good-humoured tone, the graceful wit; the second excites at a more mysterious level – the sources of the emotions. As in all the best romantic poetry, nothing can be specifically isolated or defined concerning the response to the poems of Wodwo, Crow or Moortown, but it is as valuable as that of one's intelligence. Indeed it is a kind of intelligence of the emotions, when these are ordered and evoked in good poetry of this type. It is a mere falsification to label as 'horror' the emotion aroused by:

> 'The spider clamps the bluefly – whose death panic
> Becomes sudden soulful absorption'
> (Lumb's songs in the Epilogue to 'Gaudete')

And the emotion evoked in:

> 'He saw the stars, fuming away into the black, mushrooms of the nothing forest,
> clouding their spores, the virus of God' –

a single line from *Crow Alights* is similarly transformed, though the next line states Crow's own reaction:

'And he shivered with the horror of Creation'

We may shiver, but more from the imaginative power of verbal creation.

Yeats (1865-1939)

William Butler Yeats (1865–1939)

If Hopkins was received by the modern age as a long-lost father, WB Yeats and TS Eliot may be regarded as the founding fathers of twentieth-century literature and modern poetry.

No poet's output has been so complex, yet so deliberately unified as that of WB Yeats, whose whole life's work in poetry, prose and drama has together expressed that life from youth to old age, and made of it a unity. He has stated that a writer should 'hammer his thought into unity'; he himself set out with remarkable dedication to apply this principle to himself. Thus to read any one, even a major example of his poems, is not such an enriching experience as to read the same poem in the light of all the rest, a piece of a coherent whole much greater than the sum of the parts taken separately. Many of the shorter pieces indeed do not make much sense until read in this context.

To aid this process, Yeats developed a network of symbols, images and areas of reference that interact, and thereby gather power. Beneath all he writes lies the biography: his country and background, especially Galway; his friends and family; Irish mythology and literary or political heroes, and the development of a philosophical theory, which for Yeats, who said, 'I am a very religious man', took the place of orthodoxy.

Irish history and especially current Irish life are most important for Yeats, and not merely, as for Joyce, convenient material for more universal truth. At the same time, as for Joyce's Dublin, so for all the Irish matter in Yeats, readers may see that there are parallels between provincial affairs and personal passions, and those that concern everyone.

Themes

There is a wide scope for choice of themes on Yeats, but some of the most obvious may be selected. For example the thinking which eventually was 'codified' in the prose *A Vision* (1925), even if at first weird or nonsensical to the student, well repays investigation: a great many poems owe their imagery and even explanations to it. A good clear note should be prepared on the theory of millennial cycles and their association with 'Subjective' and 'Objective' eras, these also being linked to sun and moon symbolism. Also an elaborately worked out set of characteristics for the different stages of a millennium related to different types of person, is symbolized by the 28 phases of the moon. In the 'subjective'–'objective' contrast above there is implicated another major area of thought; that of the 'antinomies' or opposites, represented by an inner man and his 'antithetical' mask.

In particular, significant events in the crucial stages of the world's history should be noted, and the places associated with these events, which are of a strongly supernatural kind, as the idea of 'Fate' is apt to be if taken seriously. James Joyce develops another cyclical view of man's progress through the world's history in his last novel, *Finnegans Wake*.

If this approach does not appeal to you, then a far different area may be profitably explored: that of Yeats's friendships. He has written a considerable number of great poems about different men and women whom he knew and loved: Maude Gonne, Major Robert Gregory (the poem in memory of whom contains stanzas recalling other earlier companions), Mabel Beardsley (the sister of the artist Aubrey Beardsley) who died courageously: 'When she meets our gaze her eyes are laughter lit'.

The poem to her, *Upon a Dying Lady,* should be read alongside two letters which contain enlightening comments: those to Lady Augusta Gregory of 8 January and 11 February 1913. Other poems to friends may be added to form a special study of this fruitful theme.

Other themes include: meditations on Eastern mysticism, and the Western philosophy opposed to it; life and art; gaiety in the teeth of tragedy both in art and life; myth and anthropology (as by Eliot, Graves and others, a rediscovery of this source of poetry was furthered by Yeats) – see, for example, *Leda and the Swan* in *The Tower* (1928), *Vacillation* in *The Winding Stair* (1933) and a host of others. Also, there are: magic and the occult, and Irish politics (e.g. *Easter 1916*).

Of course examples of these and other themes are to be found in all combinations in the poetry and by no means separated into compartments; very often one theme serves to illustrate or expand others – they are all parts of Yeats's complex but unified world.

Yeats's interest in magic is common to his people, he met it at the home of George Pollexfen, his maternal uncle in Sligo, whose servant, Mary Battle, possessed the power of 'second sight'. Her vision of horsemen with swords swinging, riding over the slopes of Ben Bulben, was remembered by the poet when he wrote his epitaph at the close of *Under Ben Bulben*. After some experiments with theosophy under Madam Blavatsky and Rosicrucianism, which result in some poems and images, Yeats' interest in spiritual 'second sight' revived when, after his marriage, he found his wife exercised the power of 'automatic writing'. Much more imagery flowed from this, from 1917 on, and the book, *A Vision* was a result of it. This imagery, and much of the esoteric business, had already been seen in some of Yeats' poetry, e.g. *Ego Dominus Tuus* and the prose of *Per Amica Silentia Lunae:* there is no traumatic change between these ideas and the concerns of *The Second Coming* (1921), or *Byzantium* (1933). They are linked with Yeats' developing thought, which is merely given more images and symbols by Mrs Yeats, when the interest returns with great power in poems from his volume *A Full Moon in March* (1935), especially Ribh's 'holy book' in the twelve 'supernatural songs', really meditations on the nature of love and its relationship to sex. The 'gyres' or wheeling of time, return in the last, *Meru,* where man returns or is returned, at last, to 'The desolation of reality'.

From the 'system', the 'Great Year' or double millennia, linked with the 'Great Wheel', or phases of the moon, we may note in particular the revelations that begin and end such eras. Christ came at the close of a subjectively controlled period, and inaugurated its converse, 'fabulous darkness', and that which

> 'Made all Platonic tolerance vain
> And vain the Doric discipline.'

So in our present century, once more the 'gyres' whirl to their close and renewal:

> 'Things fall apart; the centre cannot hold;
> Mere anarchy is loosed upon the world'

and at the mid point, the time of Byzantium's zenith as a city, there is a state of perfect balance and supernatural revelation. Yeats wrote: 'Each age unwinds the threads another age had wound, and it amuses one to remember that before Phidias and his westward moving art, Persia fell, and that when full moon came round again, amid eastward-moving thought, and brought Byzantine glory, Rome fell; and that at the outset of our westward moving Renaissance Byzantium fell; all things dying each other's life, living each other's death'. Some ideas in both *Byzantium* and the late poem *The Statues* will be illustrated by this, as well as *The Gyres,* and many lesser poems such as *Two Songs from a Play.*

By reference to theory from the 'system' of *A Vision,* interesting connections can be established between poems to their mutual advantage, and ours in their appreciation; for example, *Leda and the Swan,* on more available levels a vividly effective and dramatic sonnet, also announces the beginning of an era which closes with the birth of Christ; here *Two Songs from a Play* will lose much of its obscurity; the process reaches a further transition in *The Second Coming.*

Style

Yeats's poetry has three clearly distinguishable styles, depending roughly on whether it is of his early, middle, or late writing periods. The first, sometimes called his 'Celtic Twilight' phase, may be illustrated by poetry and prose to about 1910, and the poems of *The Green Helmet,* and is characterized by dreaminess, vagueness and sensuality. *The Wanderings of Oisin* conveys the manner best, though it is unlikely to be set for A Level as it is too long for inclusion in Selected Poetry; the music may be heard in *The Lake Isle of Innisfree,* or:

> 'Here we will moor our lonely ship
> And wander ever with woven hands,
> Murmuring softly lip to lip,
> Along the grass, along the sands,
> Murmuring how far away are the unquiet lands.'

The middle period, by many regarded as his best, is represented by volumes from *Responsibilities* (1914), to *The Tower* (1928), which contains 20 poems, more than half of them great ones and most of those as well-known as anything Yeats wrote. The poems are mostly characterized by a new bitterness, but expressed in a vigorous, direct and eloquent style. In this period he developed the 'public' utterance so impressive in poems such as *In Memory of Major Robert Gregory* and *A Prayer for My Daughter,* as well as those of *The Tower.* Yeats owned the tower (in Galway) in which he wrote many of these poems, and noted: 'My poems attribute to it most of the meanings attributed in the past to the Tower – whether watch tower or pharos, and to its winding stair those attributed to gyre or whorl.'

His next volume, *The Winding Stair* (1933), and the rest of his books in the thirties until his death, result from a huge burst of creative energy that led him into new paths. The public tone vanished, except in some deliberate revivals such as *The Circus Animals' Desertion* or *The Municipal Gallery Revisited,* and its place was taken by short lines, quatrains, haunting refrains, a new fervour and bluntness, and a final mystic wisdom.

The negativity of mood in *A Man Young and Old,* for example, a long sequence in *The Tower,* is calculatedly answered by the élan of *A Woman Young and Old,* a sequence in the next book. Yeats's themes are restated in new ways and with fresh intensity and lyricism. Above all, an indomitable joy and acceptance is everywhere apparent. Taking one question as a starting point I will illustrate this: 'Gaiety transfiguring all that dread!. Where is the gaiety and dread? Show how these feelings are aroused.' We will consider *Lapis Lazuli,* from which the phrase is taken, and also refer to *The Gyres,* and *The Man and the Echo.*

The Gyres refers to the growing terror of the modern scene (that of the thirties, when Auden also spoke of 'gradual ruin spreading like a stain'):
'Irrational streams of blood are staining earth'; yet, 'We that look on but laugh with tragic joy'. The ideas that lie behind the poetry of Yeats's last period explain this apparent contradiction.

In the first place the very inevitability of 'anarchy', confusion and disaster, as they accompany the process of the end of the era, render their acceptance a matter of philosophical common sense, or at worst stoicism. The inexorability of the catastrophe is akin to that of a great tragedy, and it is no accident that tragic heroes are several times alluded to. Power cannot be received nor life regenerated, before the old has died. The command 'rejoice' becomes an almost divine one:

> 'Out of cavern comes a voice,
> And all it knows is that one word "Rejoice"!'

Lapis Lazuli opens with reference to war; ostensibly the outbreak of World War Two, but with reminiscence of the First World War (Zeppelin and Kaiser Wilhelm), and reference to the Battle of the Boyne, where in 1690 Protestants under William of Orange, and their howitzers, slaughtered the Catholics.

With these threats 'hysterical women' may well reject what they regard as 'the frivolity of art'; but art creates and survives: the tragic endings of heroes were not spoiled by inappropriate snivelling, but were affirmative and transcending of the curcumstances that caused them.

None of the sculpture of the great Athenian artist Callimachus now survives, but the style he discovered did – there is no cause for grief. Finally we come to the medallion itself; it seems to show a 'tragic scene' in its cracks and discolorations; the Chinamen however seem to escape from and move in the scene; the sky could be full of blossom rather than a blizzard, and their playing now introduces music as a third art (after tragedy and the visual arts of sculpture or intaglio) fully to answer the complaint of the women on its irresponsibility; the triumph of the human spirit survives disaster, and art necessarily demonstrates this: the 'lift' of the spirit Yeats here and elsewhere calls 'gaiety'.

The same idea recurs in *The Man and the Echo;* here the Man addresses questions to a rock-cleft 'christened Alt' near his home town, Sligo. The echo from the rock twice advises him to die, in answer to the questions, but the Man (soon established as the poet himself) considers he is not ready for this, and wonders in his final speech, if we shall 'rejoice' in the final 'great night' of death. But possible 'joy' is overcast again by 'terror' when, in the end, the poet is distracted by the death scream of a rabbit.

The poem is one of Yeats' very last, yet thirty years earlier Yeats could write: 'There is in the creative joy an acceptance of what life brings, because we have understood the beauty of what it brings, or a hatred of death for what it takes away, which assumes within us, through some sympathy perhaps with all other men, an energy so noble, so powerful, that we laugh aloud and mock, in the terror or the sweetness of our exaltation, at death and oblivion.'

Summary of main points

1 Yeats' poems are usually clear and effective when read in the light of all the others, as well as his prose and drama. His entire output constitutes a whole which strengthens and illuminates the separate pieces.

2 The achievement of this unity is assisted by Yeats' use of a 'system' of symbols and of mythologies such as the Irish-Celtic and Greek.

3 Irish political and social history is also an important element, and a unifying influence in Yeats' work.

4 There is a need to be acquainted with Yeats' 'system' as, for example, set out in *A Vision:* the phases of the Moon, the mask and anti-mask, the cyclical 'gyres'; subjectivity and objectivity and the application of all of them to world history and public and private people.

5 Yeats wrote for and about people he knew: their celebration by Yeats often assumes a symbolic character. Knowledge of such persons and the poems written in their honour is an important aspect of the study of Yeats. For example, Maude Gonne, who lies behind the heroine of *Kathleen ni Hoolihan* as well as behind many other poems.

6 Other themes include life and death, art, magic and occultism, the supernatural.

7 Magic and 'The System'. A thread of interest in magic runs through Yeats' life and work, developing from early fascination with Irish superstition to wider application of images used as symbols from his wife's automatic writing. The interest centres on the nature of the relationship between the living and the dead, or perhaps we should say 'the other world'.

8 It is important to note in particular the revelations that occur at the close and new beginning of the cycles of human history.

9 Yeats' work can be seen in three periods:
  (*a*) the early period
  (*b*) the middle period – bitterness
  (*c*) the late period – *The Winding Stair,* 1933 to Yeats' death (1939).

10 The 'gaiety' characteristic of so much of Yeats' late period (see p. 25).

11 It is useful to read Yeats' essay 'JM Synge and the Ireland of his Time' (1910). It shows again the unity of Yeats' thought.

TS Eliot (1888-1965)

Thomas Stearns Eliot (1888–1965)

The Waste Land

This century's greatest poem of horror, despair and boredom, a terrifying vision of the paralysis and spiritual bankruptcy of modern life, is TS Eliot's *The Waste Land*. The immediate background to this poem is the post-war London of the early nineteen-twenties, when it was begun, but there are strong personal springs running into the poem's creation.

Prufrock had been dedicated to a poet, and friend of Eliot, who had been killed in 1915 in the Dardanelles; Mrs. Eliot was receiving treatment for nervous disorders that later resulted in her confinement to a mental hospital; Eliot himself was finding the necessity of working in a bank harder to bear, and there were even other anxieties, such as the effort to found a literary magazine, the death of his father, and the near-impossibility of travelling to see his mother in the USA. He was approaching a psychological collapse, and in such circumstances *The Waste Land* was conceived and begun, continued at Margate where Eliot was sent to rest, and completed at Lausanne by Lake Geneva – the 'waters of Leman' of Part III of the poem.

Personal and intellectual motives therefore combined to give the poem its sombre theme; Eliot assembled a large number of primary and secondary allusions to assist in expressing this, as well as forming part of the structure, and serving as thematic metaphors in very many of the lines; a small selection is explained in Eliot's own notes, most of which are helpful, but some of which are mild leg-pulls.

The most useful and handy guide to this and the other selected poems is BC Southam's *A Student's Guide* (see p. 159), if this is read with the poems open; help also may be obtained from George Williamson's *A Reader's Guide to TS Eliot* (see p. 159), which is a 'poem by poem' analysis; a general introduction to the poems from one or two of the 'profiles' particularly suitable for A-level students is advisable, such as Northrop Frye's in the Writers and Critics series (see p. 159), or TS Pearce's in *Literature in Perspective* (see p. 159).

Eliot had already made use of many allusions in most of the *Poems 1920* collection, but the technique is carried to an extreme in this poem, and not employed again except in a far more subdued and sparing way. The allusions in *The Waste Land,* although they are drawn from an amazing range of historical periods, foreign literatures and different cultures, are all carefully chosen for their power to illuminate the main themes of the poem from different angles, and to aid in the overall structure. The demonstration of erudition is not mere exhibitionism nor as random as it may seem. The diverse 'sources' have been thoroughly assimilated into the poem.

Questions sometimes ask for those passages that are most effective, in the candidate's opinion; or most lyrical, or most descriptive. Before choice is made of such passages the poem should be grasped as a whole, and all its parts seen as taking their fit places.

Thematically *The Waste Land* follows the dramatic monologue *Gerontion* which was to have been its prologue. After some other material had been used in *The Hollow Men,* the thematic sequel to the poem may be appreciated in *Ash Wednesday* (1930). Although there are hints and promises of rain in *The Waste Land,* Part V – 'What the Thunder Said', the land merely waits while it hears the messages of the three thunder claps.

The 'Fisher King' has not yet regenerated his land, and the cities and all else are still disintegrating. *The Hollow Men* is a further vision of living dead, eternally lost. *Ash Wednesday,* with its imagery of fountains springing and gardens, its 'turning' and not turning back, its speaker's invocations to the Virgin Mary, his climbing away from the old sensuous pleasures of the world, redemption of the wasted time (a theme to recur in 'Burnt Norton', the first of *Four Quartets*), takes the theme a stage further: the aridity of *The Waste Land* is transcended, and the calm serenity and beauty of *Ariel Poems* approached.

The allusions, the imagery, and different spokesmen are all methods that Eliot uses to achieve his 'objective correlatives' as he called the process of finding a fit equivalent to his meanings and feelings. Along these lines, one question runs: 'Eliot's poetry attempts to find striking though indirect ways to express personal feeling in impersonal terms. Discuss.' Another: 'These poems are a progress from despair to faith'. Also: 'Eliot looks only for the sordid and depressing. Is this fair comment?'.

Other questions may more specifically refer to *The Love Song of J. Alfred Prufrock,* or *Portrait of a Lady*; for example: 'There is a coldness and shrinking from emotion, a fear of life in Eliot's poetry. How far is this true?' Ideas and images from these poems, together with *Preludes,* and *Rhapsody on a Windy Night,* will give material for such questions as this: 'There is a sense of either elusive beauty or menace in *Selected Poems.* Do you find this so?'. Questions which refer to the content of the poetry may also ask for Eliot's 'social comment', for which the choruses of *The Rock* and the answering 'Workmen' are a good source; or, 'What distinguishes Eliot's early from his later poems?' a question which is tied to changes of style as well as the more obvious progress of the inner philosophy from doubt, disgust, realization and resolution to faith and assurance.

Finally there are the questions more specifically relating to style, and the language. Selective quotation with comment is always important here. It is interesting to note the number of lines in this poetry which are variants of the regular iambic pentameter, and how the verse is a subtle echoing of the metre that is so well established in the ear of the readers of Shakespeare, Chaucer and most English poetry. It is the poetic 'norm' for the verse.

In *Poems 1920* there is a change into tight quatrains similar to those used by seventeeth-century metaphysical poets. Their characteristics are, incisive wit and economy of diction, with reliance on the exactitude of metre and rhyme.

The experiment in *The Waste Land* was to try to achieve the same unity and synthesis in a long poem, whose five parts are literally stuffed with broken 'fragments' from other literature, the knowledge of which is required as background for the reader. If it is known, haunting echoes and reinforcements of sensibility are achieved; if not, then only confusion. The experiment was not repeated, nor by other poets in poems of equivalent status except by Ezra Pound in the *Cantos.*

As an example of how Eliot uses his own reading and other experiences as a field that radiates from and into the parts of the poem, and together harmonize into the whole work; the first section (lines 1-8) of the first part, 'The Burial of the Dead', read simply for itself alone, seems no more than a rather original, fresh picture of spring disturbing the memory of an old lady called Marie, who prefers a cocoon-like existence in winter, reading. She is aristocratic, Lithuanian by birth but a true ('echt') German; she must be looking, talking and reminiscing in Munich. She harks back to the palmy days of the Austro-Hungarian Empire – Emperor Franz-Joseph and his court. So much we may deduce from the text, but does any more knowledge now come to our aid? The author, in view of the later more obscure references, would seem to expect us to know about the old scandal of Mayerling, where the Crown Prince, once the lover of Countess Marie Larisch, shot his latest mistress and then himself; that Marie was a pro-curess for him, even though he had syphilis. We might be aware of all this (there is an excellent opera, *Mayerling,* on the subject), but we would not be expected to know what came to light by chance; that Marie's now forgotten memoirs were read by Eliot, who occasionally visited and talked with this relic of the decayed civilization and culture of Vienna's Empire.

However, we might be expected to have in mind the fresh introduction to Chaucer's Prologue to the *Canterbury Tales* as an ironical contrast to this later April, and to appreciate the ironically counterpointed allusions to the over optimism and pre-war innocence of, e.g. Rupert Brooke's *Grantchester*. Historical, literary and anthropological awareness are what give the lines depth, but more importantly, connect them with the rest of the poem. The mixture of immediate availability and lyricism, with allusive material, varies in quality and degree in the poem; some-times direct quotation takes the place of suggestion; sometimes short phrases are juxtaposed collage-fashion, at others more extended passages are allowed to develop the allusion, such as the opulent opening to Part II, with its echoes of Enobarbus' speech in *Antony and Cleopatra.*

Eliot also begins to develop in *The Waste Land* his mastery of the 'motif' perhaps taking his cue from Wagner's use of 'leitmotif' phrases in his operas. The process is brought to its highest elaboration in *Four Quartets.* For example, the phrase 'Unreal City' referring to London, first appears in Part I of *The Waste Land,* the fourth section. An American appears, and there follow allusions to Carthage, Rome and Paris (the 'Fourmillante cité' of Baudelaire, 'cité pleine de rêves'). The city is the background for most of what follows, until in Part III it again emerges as a leitmotif, linked to the description of the vile merchant Eugenides (ironically named since the name means 'well-born'). Tiresias' central vision of the emotional bankruptcy of city life follows (Henry James' short story *In the Cage* provides more helpful reference here); eighteenth-century satire lies near to this episode (especially with the use of polished pentameters). There follows a hint of possible regeneration, with a further significant reference to Shakespeare's *The Tempest* and an image of the strangely splendid interior of a city church – 'O City city, I can sometimes hear . . .'. The haunting music-imagery ironically contrasts with the immediately preceding gramophone, and the following Thames daughters' songs, (echoing Wagner's Rhinemaidens). These lead to the climax of the poem:

> 'To Carthage then I came'

where the Western Augustine is united to the renunciation-vision of Buddha. In Part V the themes are reorganized for restatement and final coherence:

> 'Falling towers
> Jerusalem Athens Alexandria
> Vienna London
> Unreal'

Most overt allusions were dropped in later poems, and the technique of inner-interrelatedness of imagery was developed through *The Hollow Men* and *Ash Wednesday* to culminate in 'figures in the carpet' of *Four Quartets.* Poems of length are needed for the art to develop its full power.

In *Ash Wednesday* the theme is borne by motifs of this kind, and more use is made, as in *The Hollow Men* of verbal repetition and incantation. For example, the key word 'turn' of line one of *Ash Wednesday,* which gradually establishes its meanings of turning from and turning to; a word which comes to be equated with the Christian doctrine of 'repentance'. It is used eleven times in Part I – then in Part III the word is given imagery: the turnings on a stairway. There are suggestions that the speaker is climbing Mount Purgatory, as the visions of The Earthly Paradise at the top (taken from Dante), are alluded to in the next part (lines 139-140 and following). There are, as in Part I, three turning stages. Finally, in Part VI the original line is repeated with the significant change 'Although I do not hope to turn again' instead of 'Because', for now the speaker is so confident that he will never turn back to the world, or so aware that he cannot, that he can bear to glance back at the poignant beauty of the old life;

> 'For the bent goldenrod and the lost sea smell
> Quickens to recover
> The cry of the quail'

– scenery of New England, where Eliot spent childhood holidays.

Repetitions such as that of 'turn' involve 'Teach us to care and not to care'; trees and flowers; colours; 'rock'; animals; family relation terms.

'"He inhabits our world and thinks in images which are of our world". Is this why Eliot evokes a response today?' This refers mainly to Eliot's 'realism', by which is meant the contemporary world of Eliot, especially its more sordid aspects, such as may be seen everywhere in the four *Preludes* and *Rhapsody on a Windy Night:*

> 'cigarettes in corridors
> And cocktail smells in bars'.

Contemporary imagery of an unpleasant quality falls away after *The Waste Land* together with the increase of attention and orientation to God, and Eliot's endorsement of Dante's statement, 'His will is our peace'. The images then become universalized, timeless and only arresting in their occasional symbolic obscurity, one notorious example being the 'leopards' of Part II of *Ash Wednesday*. Study of these lines will result in satisfactory answers to such questions as: 'Examine the effectiveness of the imagery in at least two poems of Eliot,' and; '"The allusiveness and difficulty of Eliot's poetry which so agitated his early readers looks more and more like a tiresome affectation." Do you agree?' Disagreement is more likely to produce a good answer than agreement. Even if Eliot fails in some of *Poems 1920* and *The Waste Land,* it is wholly reasonable to expect any audience even without all of Eliot's own background knowledge to appreciate such poetry, as he is unquestionably serious and sincere in his endeavour. *The Waste Land* has been discussed above, but we might take for examination here one of the most allusion-ridden poems of the 1920 volume; *Burbank with a Baedecker; Bleistein with a Cigar,* which Eliot himself singled out as having a serious purpose.

Just as in the *Waste Land,* there is at work an organizing and selecting intelligence which aligns all the diverse fragments into one whole theme, so there is also in each of these short poems of 1920. Also 'Sweeney', or Sweeney-like types (Bleistein is an example), and rapacious Jews, appear in most of them.

Even before 'Burbank' begins there are six different allusions strung together in the long epigraph, each one a direct quotation; most are obscure but all relevant to the poem's idea which is to convey an impression of a corrupted and corrupting city, which was once noble and splendid, but has become immoral to the point of danger to unsuspecting travellers. As in the cities named in *The Waste Land,* Venice represents all cities, and the modern world in general. The allusions do not interfere with the poem itself, but illuminate it as it were by outside light if anyone cares to make them operative. Within the poem there are at least fifteen allusions in the thirty-two lines, but these are all woven smoothly and unobtrusively into the texture; some of the references are more obvious, some less, as in *The Waste Land,* which lends a sort of perspective in allusive imagery to the poem. As in the epigraph, all are connected by the various lights they cast upon Venice.

'Casting light' is too passive a phrase; in fact the various imagery creatively shapes the theme. For example, the lion in the last stanza, carries connotations of magnificence and power in general, and Britain's past glory in particular, to set over the specific allusion to the lion of St Mark's Venice, emblem of the old Republic, a reminder of its days of glory, when painted by Canaletto. Time degrades the mighty things of the world, until they become a snare for later wanderers, whether innocent Americans abroad, ape-like philistines or aristocratic financiers.

Summary of main points

1 *The Waste Land:*

   a) The circumstances of its composition.
   b) The peculiar form and style of the poem.

2 Eliot's allusiveness: its purpose and justification.

3 The place of *The Waste Land* in Eliot's oeuvre: its thematic links with *Gerontion* and *Ash Wednesday*.

4 Eliot's search for apt images to express his concerns: his use of 'voices', and notorious employment of sordid images and situations.

5 Questions relating to the early poetry: the theme of evasion or moral failure or weakness; moral decay.

6 Eliot's social concern: neglected churches and the state of the true 'church'; leaderless masses (*The Rock*).

7 Eliot's change of poetic method and style as these accompany the transitions into new themes: a steady progress from doubt and despair through conversion to serene faith and meditative Christian philosophy.

8 Eliot's style: free verse and the tight stanza.

9 The variety and degrees of Eliot's stylistic method especially of *The Waste Land.* Recurrent images as 'motifs', e.g. that of 'the city'.

10 Later abandoning of allusiveness: inter-relation of imagery and 'motif' increased in *The Hollow Men* and *Ash Wednesday,* culminating in the 'figure in the carpet' complexity of *Four Quartets.*

11 For example, use of motif 'turn' in *Ash Wednesday.*

12 Eliot's concentration on the more unpleasant aspects of contemporary life in his references and imagery: its decrease after *The Waste Land* and the growth of Eliot's religious faith.

13 Eliot's serious purpose in his most allusive poems, e.g. *Burbank with a Baedecker.* This poem is analysed closely in order to show the justification for the presence of the plethora of allusions.

Chaucer

Our literature begins with Chaucer, and it is a divine start. There are some fine things in late Middle English literature, notably *Sir Gawain and the Green Knight, Pearl,* Langland's *Piers the Ploughman* and a collection of fresh old ballads and lyrics, but they pale into insignificance beside the great work of Chaucer. His creative genius was seemingly boundless, his learning huge, especially where this country's literature so much needed it – in other European literatures, ancient and recent. The Classics, the great Italians of the emergent Renaissance, the French – he was acquainted in their own languages with them all and probably met several, such as Petrarch in Padua.

Chaucer thus enjoys rightly special status in all the boards' syllabuses, with Milton as a close second, outside Shakespeare. He is still read with the highest pleasure and appreciation in spite of the slight difficulties of the dialect barrier. To be more precise, the dialect is the one he has handed down to us – the London and East Anglian – not even his own native Kentish – but the intervening six hundred years have removed or altered the meaning of many words, and slightly affected grammar and syntax too. All this is nothing like to the extent many students fear when they look at the page. There is a more English tone and rhythm to *The Canterbury Tales* than to *Paradise Lost.*

Geoffrey Chaucer (1344 – 1400)

BIOGRAPHICAL BACKGROUND

To counteract the sense of 'strangeness' many candidates feel when encountering Chaucer at A Level, it is often helpful if they begin by making themselves familiar with his background. To this end, a brief outline of his life is given below.

Geoffrey Chaucer was born in or near 1344. He is first heard of by us when he was a page in the household of Elizabeth, Countess of Ulster, wife of Duke Lionel, Edward III's third son. This was at Hatfield, in Yorkshire. John Chaucer, his father, was a relatively wealthy man with property in Ipswich and London, deputy butler to the Kings, a vintner and collector of wool duties.

When Chaucer was about 15, he was in France as a squire, on a military operation in which he was taken prisoner. The king paid £16 towards his ransom. He probably (according to a reasonably sound tradition), then studied law at the Inner Temple – he was said to have been fined two shillings for a street fight with a friar. In his early twenties he was back in royal service as a Squire, a kind of elevated valet. French would have been the accepted language; the Queen, Philippa of Hainault, was a Frenchwoman. When 25 he accompanied John of Gaunt (the King's fourth son, and with the death of the Black Prince, probably the most powerful man after the King), on a raid in Picardy. In the previous year, 1368 and also the following year of 1370 he was on missions abroad, probably France.

Then in 1372 Chaucer went on a more important, and for his vocation as a poet, very significant journey to Italy. The purpose of the visit was to negotiate with the Doge of Genoa a port of entry in England for Genoese merchants. He went to Florence on the King's business and probably other places – he is reported to have met Petrach in Padua. Italian literature from then on took its place as a major influence on Chaucer's developing art: the whole of *Troilus and Criseyde* and several Tales owe their origins to Boccaccio, whom he might also have visited.

After this Chaucer moved from Westminster to the City, where he became Controller of Customs of Wool Skins and Hides in the Port of London. His connection with John of Gaunt's household was particularly strong, as his wife's sister became the Duke's third wife, in 1396, after being his mistress from about 1372. Chaucer probably had known John of Gaunt since boyhood, from the time of his service at Hatfield. They were more or less the same age. John of Gaunt's first wife, Blanche, had died in 1368, and Chaucer wrote his first major poem, *The Boke of the Duchesse,* in her honour, shortly afterwards. As John was extremely attached to Blanche, the poem was clearly designed to please him.

In 1382 he was made Controller of the Petty Customs on wines and other goods, and in 1385 on Wool; he was made a JP and member of Parliament as a Knight of the Shire of Kent.

From 1374 he lived in a house over Aldgate, in the east wall of the City. There he read and wrote, after his day's work at the Wool-Wharf near the Tower.

In 1386 he lost his job in a general change of favour under the new young King Richard II, John of Gaunt's nephew. John of Gaunt was out of the country and new men were in favour, opposed to the king's powerful uncle. Then Chaucer's wife died, and the poet began to devote himself and the rest of his life to organizing and completing *The Canterbury Tales.* In 1389 Richard II decided to favour the poet, making him Clerk of the King's Works; responsible, that is, for the building and repair of all the King's properties (the Tower of London, Westminster Palace and eight royal manors). He performed this duty for two years, and then received the sinecure of a forestry officer for North Petherton in Somerset. He was over 50, and virtually in retirement. The last year of his life was spent in a new house close to Westminster Abbey, there he died on 25 October 1400, and was buried in the 'Poet's Corner' in the Abbey.

THE CANTERBURY TALES

Apart from *The Canterbury Tales* only *Troilus and Criseyde* is sometimes set at A Level. This is because Chaucer's last work is his best, and there is plenty of superlative material to choose from. Space for more than a minor proportion is limited, usually to one story and its prologue set as a choice, against other major authors, usually including Milton and one or two others. Also most of the best stories are of a convenient overall length, though at times they are cut. The *Knight's Tale* is one of the best but is over two thousand lines long; the *Physician's, Prioress'* and *Manciple's* Tales are too short; the *Miller's, Reeve's* and *Summoner's* are as good as any but are sometimes neglected because of their scurrility.

The parts most often selected for study are: the *General Prologue;* the *Pardoner's Prologue* and *Tale;* the *Wife of Bath's Prologue* and *Tale;* the *Nun's Priest's Tale* (known as 'The Cock and the Fox'); the *Franklin's Tale.* Rather less often set are: the *Man of Law's Tale;* the *Clerk of Oxford's Tale* ('Patient Griselda'), and part of the *Knight's Tale.* Others are never set at all: the two prose tales (even though one excellent one is delivered by the author), the *Monk's, Cook's, Shipman's* and the rest.

The various Boards differ in one method of approach: that of either setting merely essay questions, or a printed passage to turn into clear modern English, and perhaps an essay as well. Usually with Chaucer a fair breadth of choice is given, either to choose one of two passages, or to prepare for and so choose a different major author, not only in the sections containing the 'passage' type of question but in those with essay questions. Oxford is the most traditional in setting only three authors, Chaucer, Milton and one other (so far a great novel), from which two must be chosen.

THE GENERAL PROLOGUE

The *Canterbury Tales* is not the first work to link a sequence of stories by bringing together a group of different characters as the tellers – Boccaccio's *Decameron* has the ladies of Florence exchanging a hundred stories to pass the time in a local villa while the Plague rages in the city below. Nor is Chaucer the first to introduce himself as a persona and participant in a dramatic poem: Dante does so in his *Divine Comedy*. Both these works were well known to Chaucer; the *Canterbury Tales,* however, was the first work in literature to give all the speakers a single purpose within a carefully organized diversity of occupation, character and dress:

> 'whiche they weren and of what degree
> And eek in what array that they were inne.'

Organization

The *General Prologue* which thus presents the tellers of the Tales is carefully organized. In the introductory section, which ends at line 42, Chaucer with great economy gives the setting: the time of the year, with strong associations of rebirth and renewal, life and joy; a time, in short, in which men and women stir themselves; and whoever they might be, whatever they might do, first turn to unite in a common enterprise of pilgrimage, to worship at a famous shrine. They gather in Southwark at the Tabard Inn, kept by a known Londoner, Harry Bailley; walk along a known path through North Kent to Canterbury, on a well-known annual pilgrimage, and on the road exchange stories according to a set of simple rules set by their host and judge, Bailley. All this is perfectly realistic, as are the characters themselves, and the experience of telling and hearing such stories, most of which were very well known either from other literature or the common stock of folk story. The art appears in almost casual details such as calling March a month of 'drought' (only by classical literary convention considered to be such), or rhetorical devices such as referring to spring by zodiacal allusions ushered in with a classical Greek breeze. Then there are broader designs, such as the careful selection of people; representative types of laymen and clerics, good folk and bad, low born or gentlefolk. But the 'fellowship' of all is established at the outset, and Chaucer's plan to make each pilgrim tell two stories on the way, and two more returning, is put into Bailley's proposal for the competition at the end of the Prologue. This would have made 116 tales from the 29 pilgrims (assuming that there is only one Nun's priest and not three). In fact we get only 20 completed and two uncompleted stories, as well as two, the Monk's and Chaucer's own, which the host cuts short. There obviously was also to have been a link between each, provided by conversation between the host and the pilgrims, or between themselves, but several of these 'links' are missing and the order of the whole therefore in doubt.

Nearly half the number of lines of description are given to the religious figures: Friar, Parson, Pardoner, Summoner, Monk, Prioress and Clerk. Among these as well as the other group there are good and bad traits. In the order of their description, there are effective placings for contrast or for useful groupings. For example, the Miller, Manciple, Reeve, Summoner and Pardoner are all rogues in various respects, but the Manciple is a cunning operator by contrast to the more extroverted ruffians he is placed between. Similarly of the first three related types the Knight rightly takes first place. Then the Prioress should preced the Monk, who in turn takes precedence over the Friar. The professional men are divided by the five Gildmen from more workaday types. The last two, the Summoner and Pardoner, are a pair of unholy friends; the Pardoner by his position at the end (his Tale is also the last one, as indeed, the Knight's is the first) is rendered more memorable.

Although all the characters are realistically presented to the reader, and the details of their descriptions confer a vivid life to each, even though some are quite short, these types are not mere commonplace people: each one is heightened in some way – in fact, in as literary a creation as any in Shakespeare or Dickens. The Knight is especially 'worthy' and honourable; the Squire a young brightly singing lover, the Prioress a fastidious aristocrat and so on. Characteristic traits such as the Pardoner's hypocrisy are strongly highlighted. The evidence of characters in their various fields is often asked for in A-level questions. There are also various details which reveal the characters as living people, for example the Friar's 'wanton' (affected) lisping, the Miller's big nostrils, and the Wife of Bath's scarlet stockings and partial deafness.

The General Prologue is wonderful in itself, but even more impressive as an integral part of the Tales which follow: there are very interesting relationships between the characters as sketched in the Prologue, and their subsequent tales.

Note on satire

The expert economy of Chaucer's satirical hints in many of his short descriptions of the pilgrims in the *General Prologue* is to be noted in any study of his text. As usual, Chaucer likes to use humorous or sly innuendo; at times the reader is left to make his own deductions from styles of dress, equipment, horses or even facial appearance. The Prioress is a masterpiece in this manner, but we will illustrate it by four lines on The Man of Law:

> 'So greet a purchasour was nowher noon,
> Al was fee symple to him in effect,
> . . . Nowher so bisy a man as he ther nas
> And yet he semed bisier than he was.'

The first line hints, under the guise of praise, that the sergeant, using his wealth, snapped up property; the second suggests that he perhaps fraudulently converted partly-bought interests into outright possession, probably to anticipate legal moves to deprive him of it; the fourth line suggests that he put on an act to impress his clients.

COMMON QUESTIONS ON THE TALES

The following areas of Chaucer's art are commonly touched upon in A-level questions:

1 narrative skills
2 scene painting and character sketching ability
3 creation of dramatic interest
4 realism in dialogue
5 maintenance of plot interest

For example on the *Wife of Bath's Tale,* there are commonly questions on the status of the *Prologue:* whether it is a tale in its own right, or theoretically linked to the tale that follows; whether the Wife expresses her feminism in both, and how; the role of the 'sermon' embedded in the conclusion; the humour and fairytale element; the marriage-debate advanced by probing the question of who should hold the 'maistrie' or sovereignty (The Middle Ages, following St Paul, assumed this should be the husband; we today accept equality of partnership; Chaucer was thinking it through – see also the *Franklin's* and *Clerk's* tales).

After the 'sermon' on virtue, which is more to be praised in a woman than youth, beauty or money (even than all three together), the knight comes up with the solution to the problem of choice, by answering in the fashion most dear to the Wife of Bath's heart:

> 'I put me in your wise governaunce –
> Cheseth yourself. . . .'

whereupon, without waiting to claim the kiss she demands, the wrinkled hag becomes for him youth, beauty, money *and* virtue – such are the rewards for relinquishing 'sovereignty'; 'May Jesus shorten the lives of those husbands who won't be governed by their wives!'

The opposite point of view is absurdly exaggerated by the Clerk of Oxford in his tale: Chaucer's 'Envoy' sets this right in terms which the Wife of Bath herself might have used. Her bawdy vein is sufficiently indicated by the number of omitted lines in the school texts of her prologue: the last lines of her description in the *General Prologue* run:

> 'Of remedies of love she knew perchaunce
> For she koude of that art the olde daunce.'

This is borne out by her references to the popular medieval love story of Eloise and Abelard (not referred to elsewhere by Chaucer), and her familiarity with Ovid's *Art of Love*. The history of her five husbands, taken by her from her twelfth to her fortieth year, is racily told, and in it her feminism is illustrated best: Chaucer drew upon anti-feminist sources, such as St Jerome's Epistle against the libertine monk Jovinian. By mishandling Jerome's anti-feminist views, Jankin is made to give more credibility to feminism.

Questions on other tales follow these general lines. Some single out the use of irony in

Chaucer's writing. It is usually linked with humour and innuendo. Because of this it is sometimes considered to be 'gentle' irony, but this is a misnomer for its understated, modest subtlety. Chaucer always had high regard for the intelligence of his audience: he seldom laboured his points except for the purpose of character representation.

The Franklin's Tale

In the *Franklin's Tale* the themes are the presentation of love and marriage and their precise relationship (does the lover change his role after marriage?); the nature of 'trouthe', or the making and keeping of one's solemn word; the relationship between this and 'gentillesse' or courteous, high-born, magnanimous behaviour; honesty and loyalty in personal relationships; the nature of and relationship between appearance and reality, and the part magic has to play in this; the interplay of realism and the fabulous.

The characters are: Aurelius, the lover of the virtuous wife (Dorigen), of an honourable knight (Arveragus), who has to depart on a lengthy campaign. This is the classic situation of Courtly Love. In Courtly Love convention the lady yields to her favoured lover after a lengthy 'game' whose rules were almost as standard as those of tennis. In this story she has no intention of giving way, but falling initially into a flirtatious sideline of the code – the setting of 'conditions', she is trapped and has to yield. The black art of magic is used against her, or rather on behalf of Aurelius.

Character questions are asked: how complex is Aurelius; how sympathetic and attractive is Dorigen to the reader; how we respond to her dilemma. We may note how initial 'types' representing ideals, develop into realistic people.

For example, Aurelius at first is represented as a conventional type: the courtier-lover. The terms he employs to express his love are all well-known conventions: his mind is full of 'misery', his lady ignorant or passive; at last she may show some tiny sign of 'pity' for his 'penance' (in other words, a 'come on' sign). This would be a pure act of undeserved 'grace'. He can only 'complain' in troubadour-like songs of his passion. He despairs, he is repulsed and death seems to stare at him. He prays to Apollo and Luna. He swoons and is in more misery than ever, but still corresponding to his models. Love is now referred to as 'a disease'; Aurelius takes to his sick-bed and goes into a decline. His brother sees the only cure is to win Dorigen, and the magician is employed.

Greater realism begins to develop when Aurelius first admits his love to Dorigen: she had never been aware of it: that in itself is original. When she does grasp the truth it is with genuine and convincing astonishment:

> 'She gan to looke upon Aurelius:
> 'Is this youre wil,' quod she, 'and sey ye thus'
> 'Nevere erst,' quod she, 'ne wiste I what ye mente.'

From this point on the interview is handled with growing realism and genuineness of response. The characters become aware of each other, and we become aware of them through their eyes.

Some questions on the Franklin's language refer to the disclaimer in his prologue: he is a plain man, he says, of 'rude speech'. But not only does he use the most artful rhetoric in the prologue, he also employs many devices of rhetoric in his tale, which he affectedly calls a 'Breton Lay'. In fact it is a free retelling of a traditional medieval story. It is indeed set in Brittany with remarkably accurate circumstantial detail, but no Breton lays had such realism of setting.

Rhetoric is a medieval art, very highly esteemed and carefully taught, in which the theme of a communication is amplified and varied by a system of linguistic devices, 'figures of speech' so called. Such an art, however well applied, cannot create fine poetry, but fine poetry can be immensely embellished by the skilful employment of the art.

Thus even while the Franklin is asserting himself to be a man of plain speech, he is using classical allusions, repetition, circumlocution, punning, double simile and indeed the disclaimer itself is a rhetorical colour, a sort of false modesty. This, when followed at once by a style that ostentatiously demonstrates the opposite truth, shows the Franklin to be a man who, while he aspires to 'gentillesse' does not possess it. Not long before, he has betrayed envy of the Squire, contrasting him with his own rake-hell of a son.

In the Tale we find rhetorical digressions that are meant to point up the theme; 'sententiae', anaphora or initial-word repetitions (lines 474-7), and most remarkable of all, the long series of 'exempla' (lines 695-784), delivered by Dorigen to demonstrate that many other women in the past have died rather than lose their virginity. She gives 22 examples. As in the Wife of Bath's Tale the source of many of these is Jerome's Epistle against Jovinian, written to extol virginity, as opposed to marriage.

The list is so absurdly long, it was probably designed by Chaucer as another grotesque exaggeration of the point – most of the later exempla are irrelevant or ridiculous, as if delivered by someone on the verge of hysteria. If this were so it would certainly be dramatically in keeping with Dorigen's state at this time. The defence of virginity is on the verge of vapourizing.

HINTS ON 'TRANSLATION'

When 'translating' Chaucer, the first thing is to establish the most exact modern equivalent to the very different words, and then suitable modern phrases for the outdated expressions that still bear some recognisable meaning. In the example below, 'lye' illustrates the first, 'up peril of my lyf' the second. The first operation depends on careful preparation of the text with the glossary and notes, the second more on a weighing of what is being expressed, and rendering the meaning rather than the words. Glossaries are not much help, only other prose translations may supply deficiences here. It is not advisable though to try to learn other translations wholesale, the way students sometimes will with a Latin text.

In writing the final modern version, care should be taken *not* to translate line-by-line if meanings continue to subsequent lines. The right method is to translate by unit of meaning, whether this ends with a full stop, semi-colon or dash; *not* normally a comma even at the line-end. Sentences should be grammatical and well-constructed; slang should be avoided. Any taint of archaism or false romanticism should be avoided, such as poetic inversions of word order.

Here is a short extract from a recent paper to demonstrate some of this; it should also serve to remind you that Chaucer is essentially an English, not a foreign poet. Nor is he so remote in the past that he cannot speak to us in living language and with still fresh thought. Reading his verse aloud often resolves specious difficulties. Try 'translating' the following passage yourself, before looking at the version below.

> 'Taak fyr, and ber it in the derkeste hous
> Betwix this and the mount of Kaukasous,
> And lat men shette the dores and go thenne;
> Yet wole the fyr as faire lye and brenne
> As twenty thousand men myghte it beholde:
> His office natureel ay wol it holde,
> Up peril of my lyf, til that it dye.'

> 'Take some fire, carry it into the darkest house between here and the Caucasus, and then shut the door and leave; the fire will still blaze and burn as well as if twenty thousand men could see it; I may dare swear that its very nature is always to do what it must, until it dies.'

It is fair to expect A-level students to show their competence to modernize Chaucer. Perhaps the exercise offends those who dislike interfering with poetry, weakening it to no good purpose, but if this objection were pushed too far Neville Coghill's admirable and monumental translation into couplets (Penguin Books) might be called a travesty. The justifiable hope is that after the exercise one may read Chaucer in the original with the same delight and ease experienced in reading Spenser.

We would advise a student to try learning a good passage of between 35 and 40 lines by heart, and reciting them aloud. Apparent obscurities fall into natural, satisfying music. For example two fine openings are suitable: the first 18 lines of the *General Prologue,* and the first 25 lines of the *Wife of Bath's Tale.*

It is not necessary to try to fill up every line into a decasyllabic count; although Chaucer, influenced by French poetry, might have been aiming for metrical 'correctness', we are not now so obsessed with this; many modern poems are deliberately unpolished for greater strength and rhythmic interest. It is still possible that Chaucer did the same service for his music. The flexible and varying narrative and tones of different speaking characters in the Tales are more aptly conveyed by light-stress variations. Thus:

> 'Citees, Burghes, Castels, hye toures'

is ancephalous and possibly robbed of the fifth foot's light stress; it might practically be read as:

> 'Cities, boroughs, castles, high towers'

which the modern ear might prefer to some expletive syllable as in 'lofty towers'. Should the editor (or printer of the examination paper) print the 'e' of 'hye' as a dotted 'e', it is thought in that case to be sounded lightly, and render the line metrically 'regular'. It is true that French poetry prefers to retain sounded final 'e's' for this reason, and Chaucer may be extending this practice to English.

The essay questions deal with such matters as the content of the tale, including its elements of suspense, surprise, climax, revelation, complication, character interactions, passages of argument, preaching, philosophizing, rhetorical amplifications such as sententiae (moral generalizations) and exempla (illustrations by reference to related incidents), digressions and the relevance of all these to the theme.

Milton

TYPES OF QUESTION SET

When passages of Milton, usually from 25 to 30 lines, are printed on the paper, the procedure for questions on them varies. The Welsh Board asks for specific questions under the passage to be answered: candidates are asked to explain phrases and groups of lines, or imagery and allusions; the context may be asked for, and deductions drawn from the passage. The SWB prints the passage together with others from Shakespeare and Chaucer, asking for only one to be considered in terms set for them all – 'Write critical comment; explain anything not readily understood today; give the significance of the passage in its relationship to the whole work.' The choice is wide and a virtually free hand is given to the candidate. The NIEB sets questions on 16 set texts, including one on Milton, asking for comment on four of them.

The Oxford Board gives a smaller choice – either the Chaucer or the Milton or a major novel, where the choice is two of the three, the questions on the Milton are more precise: 'Explain or give the meaning of the italicised words and phrases; say what you find most noteworthy in its style and thought. (The context is not required)'. Three phrases are printed in italics; twelve marks are allowed overall, about one ninth of this paper.

AEB stipulates that Milton may be chosen instead of Shakespeare: the choice is two books from six authors who include Shakespeare and Milton. Oxford and Cambridge Board sets a compulsory Chaucer passage with questions beneath, an essay on the same text, and then a choice of one from three passages including a Milton, and later a similar choice from essays on the three texts from which the passages were chosen. In this case the Milton included *Lycidas* and *Comus,* or *Samson Agonistes.* Questions are set beneath the passages from Milton, asking for specific issues to be explained and for discussion of the context, or other detailed matters.

John Milton (1608–1674)

From this it may be observed that on the whole Milton has held his place in papers which deal with authors of special importance: these always include Chaucer and Shakespeare plus one or two others – a great novel or poet, for example, a Dickens or a Hardy novel, or poems of Keats or TS Eliot.

Whether the passages are from books of *Paradise Lost,* or from the greater of the earlier poems, the questions expect a close knowledge of the text, an ability to explain allusions and obscurities of diction, and a general appreciation of the content. Oxford also asks for the style to be discussed.

BIOGRAPHICAL NOTE

John Milton was born in 1608 in London, and educated at St Paul's School and Christ's College, Cambridge, after which he spent six further years educating himself on carefully planned lines. During this period he wrote *Comus* (1634) and *Lycidas* (1637). He then spent a year and a half in Italy. He embarked on a decade of political pamphleteering, supporting the Puritan faction against the bishops, and defending the execution of Charles I (1649), in *Defence of the English People,* on behalf of Oliver Cromwell, in 1651. The next year he went blind.

Upon the Restoration of the Monarchy in the person of Charles II (1660), Milton was imprisoned in the Tower for several weeks. He now devoted himself to the composition of the epic which has secured his immortality, *Paradise Lost,* published in 1667. Four years later *Paradise Regained* followed, and *Samson Agonistes,* his only play, based on Greek classical models, was also published, but may have been written much earlier. In 1674 he died at his home in Chalfont St Giles.

PARADISE LOST

The books most regularly set at A Level are 1 and 2, 4, and 9 and 10. It is ideal though not *essential* at A Level to read through in order all the other books, perhaps in the summer vacation, to place the set book in its proper context. No balanced view of this extraordinarily well-constructed epic can be gained by reading only one book, or that and some prose summary of the others. The poem's structure, like that of its models (the *Iliad* and the *Aeneid*), gives it a well-proportioned shape that can only be appreciated by reading the whole for oneself. Homer and Virgil have always suffered from piecemeal study: the obstacle of the language even necessitated losing the sense of the single book's structure and form. Although Milton's language is very Latinate, it still may be read easily enough to avoid this sort of barbarism. We suggest that when reading the non-prescribed books as background, you should suspend reference to critical apparatus and explanations. Much of the sense of shape is owed to the continuous flow of thought and sound, the organized music of which is injured by constant turning to notes.

Useful background reading

Among the best introductory criticism of *Paradise Lost,* is Addison's set of *Spectator* essays on the poem for new readers. It is recommendatory criticism at its best; the quotations he selects are all worth memorizing for use in examination questions. It is simple, direct appreciation given at a time when the reputation of the poem was at its height.

In this century, an equally inspiring and more penetrating critical introduction to the poem was provided by CS Lewis: *Preface to Paradise Lost,* written at a time when the poem needed defending against powerful critical attacks.

Among the critical editions provided for schools and colleges, the oldest still in regular use is EMW Tillyard's editions of Books 1, 2, 9 and 10 (1960). Tillyard is the author of standard criticism published before the war. The introduction to these texts is clear, useful and simple; the notes quite adequate for the student's ordinary purposes.

Two later editions are more detailed and elaborate, and designed more for the A-level and University student. The 'Macmillan' edition of the whole poem began publication in 1970, each book annotated and introduced by a different scholar. A biographical outline is followed by an introduction that is sufficiently thorough; the text has notes printed on the facing page, according to the latest practice for Shakespeare. These are full and detailed when appropriate. Appendices contain further useful notes, sources (e.g. the first three chapters of *Genesis* are given) and a reading list which is the only one available of any practical use in any of these three editions.

The last, most recent edition is JB Broadbent's (author of *Some Graver Subject,* 1960), *Cambridge Milton for School and Colleges.* This series has a separately published 'Introduction' to the whole, and has been brought out as one volume per pair of books, thus, six in all. The most notable features of this series are its originality of approach, and detailed analyses of the texts, a combination of vigour and good scholarship. Notes are at the the foot of the page, now known to be an inferior method because of the ugliness of the appearance, and the difficulty of tracking each one down. However nothing by way of notes is left to chance: almost complete ignorance is assumed, rightly. In the intriguing Appendices themes such as 'Light', 'God', 'Free Will and Predestination', 'The Son and Redemption' and so on are discussed, and there is evidently an amazingly wide reference to other literature related in theme or ideas. The bibliography to each part is too specialized; one has to turn to the one appended to the 'Introduction'. The editor is surely right in his insistence on the stimulation of thought as well as the absorbing of information. Milton's own arguments, debates, provocative theological comment and entire conception of God's ways to Man, demand our own like response, of agreement or disagreement. As Mr Broadbent says, we ignore at our peril the adventures of ideas in wider fields, even if, as the Report of the Welsh Committee of the Schools Council said in their paper, *Sixth Form Examining Methods,* these adventures push beyond the bounds of examination requirements!

Common themes in examination questions on Paradise Lost

The principal matters that the questions on Milton devote themselves to are as follows:
1 the ways in which the book set may be part of an epic – the nature of a classical epic and how Milton's conforms to these characteristics; what the epic characteristics contribute to the book;
2 who the hero is – surely not Satan? Following from this is the question of how Satan appears to have heroic stature – applicable especially to Books 1 and 2, but to achieve a sense of proportion in this matter it is necessary to read the rest.
Other questions include:
3 Milton's sources for his allusions and how he makes use of them;
4 what is the nature of Milton's "sublimity", and what this term means (often used to describe *Paradise Lost);*
5 what ideas and desires are expressed and how powerfully, by Satan and his friends in Hell; what they really suffer – physical, mental or spiritual torment; how they manage to convey the impression of being newly-fallen angels; how the confrontation between Satan, and Sin and Death proceeds;
6 what qualities Milton's verse has; the range of description and imagery, and the appropriateness of these to the book's theme – these last subjects particularly require quotations.

These questions crop up in different guises regularly, and between them cover much of what Books 1 and 2 are about. One unusually straightforward question and perhaps untypical, merely asked the candidates to summarize the main arguments of the various fallen angels and Satan in their Book 2 debate. At A Level this sort of summary is usually the basis of answers rather than the answer itself.

Questions that apply to Book 4 include: 'Discuss Milton's power to make us believe in Paradise; how Satan is presented to the reader; how ideal nature and ideal humanity are linked; the contrasts in style and the effect of these; how Adam and Eve are presented to us: for this see, for instance, the lines beginning:

> 'Two of far nobler shape erect and tall,
> Godlike erect with native honour clad
> In naked majesty seemed lords of all . . .

For Books 9 and 10 there should be consideration of the following:
1 How well does Milton unfold the tragic themes of these books? How well does he evoke the bliss of Eden?
2 How far is Satan degraded by his obsession?
3 What is Satan's role in Book 9? Can he be the total embodiment of evil now? (Note here the contrast to Satan's heroic stance in Books 1 and 2; after the courageous and amazing voyage past the Gates of Hell, through Chaos to the Universe, we arrive at the story of the Fall, via the narration of his earlier wicked rebellion and battle against God.)
4 What imagination is present in the scenes of Hell? (This applies to the language used as well as the scenes.)
5 In what ways does Milton please our senses and minds by this poetry?
6 How does Milton reconcile his theological interest in the Fall with the demands of dramatic narrative?
7 How far is the Fall the result of 'Man's First Disobedience', and how far due to other sin?

Minor poems

Occasionally, instead of books chosen from *Paradise Lost,* texts are drawn from Milton's earlier or later work. The earlier is best represented by *Comus,* and *Lycidas,* the elegy written for a Cambridge friend, Edward King, drowned in 1637.

Comus

Comus, 'A Mask presented at Ludlow Castle', specially written for performance by the children of the Earl of Bridgwater, the new Lord President of Wales, is more literary than earlier masques by, for example, Ben Jonson. The latter were essentially spectacles, with elaborate machinery (designed by Inigo Jones), dance, costume and music. Milton's contained some of these elements, especially the music written by one of his favourite composers, Henry Lawes, but it went further in its craftsmanlike text, and its fine poetry. It is in fact a dramatic poem. In it the theme of Chastity is debated. The moral is, that virtue and temperance triumph. As in Lycidas, Christian tones and ideas develop from classical elements, which dominated earlier masques.

Lycidas

Lycidas is written in a carefully constructed mode of pastoral convention, the elegaic tone being generalized rather than attached to a personal grief and loss. The real themes are other than specific lament – Milton was anxious to write a significant and recognizably great poem. The scenes expand beyond those of one individual dying in the Irish Sea, into wider realms of time and space.

Passages of effective contrast are juxtaposed and the transitions managed by carefully devised phrases such as:

> 'That strain I heard was of a higher sound', and
> 'Return Alpheus, the dread voice is past', and
> 'Weep no more, woeful Shepherds . . .'

These variations give the poem dramatic interest and structure, assisted by the variations of line length and rhythm. The style is varied to suit the changes of mood: pastoral elements with classical imagery and names are provided with smooth description and picturesque imagery; the moral warnings are given harsher tones, with stern satire; the celebration of Lycidas' salvation and immortality in heaven, an exultant tone:

> 'There entertain him all the Saints above
> In solemn troops, and sweet Societies
> That sing, and singing in their glory move
> And wipe the tears for ever from his eyes.'

One last observation is that the poem contains a basic uncertainty of philosophy. This springs from Milton's adoption on the one hand of pastoral procedures, and the classical machinery of Phoebus, Jove, the inexorability of Fate and the mystery of death. On the other hand, and progressively gathering strength in the poem, is the assumed truth of God's dispensation, and Christ's salvation, where Lycidas is without doubt saved (he was Christian in his own person of Edward King), and in heaven. There would be no need for mourning in the pastoral mode, with its doubts and despondency, if these assurances were established at the beginning, as one may wonder why they were not. Milton's classical learning and interests were in this instance rather at odds with his Christian faith.

Practical criticism of poetry

Practical criticism is a method of revealing to the student-critic the significance of the structure of words which make up a poem. Everyone reacts in different ways to reading a poem but even the right reactions or feelings may be too simple and not further our understanding of the poem a great deal. In order to know how to go further the student needs to know how to tackle the skills of practical criticism. The basic reaction to a poem, 'I like it', 'It doesn't do anything for me,' is too simple a form of criticism. Through practical criticism you can refine and deepen your appreciation of the poet's skills.

When reading a poem, the first thing you should try to do is to get the general meaning or a grasp of the mood the poet is creating. Further readings will strengthen your first impressions. Gradually ideas that seemed obscure will appear clear. The relevance of particular words or images will manifest themselves. You should have a knowledge of the technical skills of manipulating rhythm, structure and language, and it is through this knowledge that a deeper understanding of the poem will come.

The 'meaning' of the poem has to come from the arrangement of chosen words on paper and the kind of arrangement or pattern the poet has given them. How a poet like Keats, Siegfried Sassoon, Ted Hughes or TS Eliot writes is his own distinctive trademark. A poem is a personal communication with words chosen to suit a variety of purposes and the words so chosen have to be comprehended if we are to get from the poem as much meaning as the poet intended. Each poet agonizes over the correct choice of words and nothing happens by accident. Therefore the student must treat the poem as a deliberate artistic creation with a plan behind it and not a random happening.

Each reader brings to the poem his or her own store of knowledge, his or her own preferences, perceptiveness and degree of response to words. A poem is like a looking-glass where everyone sees his or her own reflection. Probably we respond best to poems written in our own time which contain words whose meanings we are familiar with. For your criticism to be worthwhile you should be familiar with the cultural background. There is no substitute for wide reading among the best authors as a way to acquire sensitivity.

One of the aspects of poetry we are seeking to understand is meaning. We cannot find the total meaning without getting inside the head of the poet. The tone of the words and the choice of words should give you, the reader, the total significance of the meaning. We must also look at the sounds of the words and the effect they have on us. A third source of consideration is the grammatical arrangement of words into a meaningful pattern. If your judgements are to arouse the approval of your teacher and the person who marks your examination paper you must learn to look carefully and methodically at what poets do.

METHOD OF TACKLING A POEM

1 *Get the meaning clear*

At the first reading concentrate on understanding the poem. Try to establish the theme of the poem, the kind of experience the poet is dealing with and the sequence of thoughts or images which are communicated to you. You may find when you read the poem again that you will discover more meaning than you had originally settled for and this may cause you to alter your ideas of the content and meaning of the poem.

2 *Rhythm and metre*

Read the poem out loud to yourself with the kinds of emphasis and pauses intended by the poet. Through this, you are likely to become aware of some of the uses of sound and grammatical structures utilized in the poem's construction. Use the parts of this book on rhythm and metre which will help you.

3 *Use of literary devices* e.g. figures of speech, vocabulary

All these devices are used deliberately and contribute to the total significance of the poem. Decide and comment on what you find distinctive and why the poet uses the literary devices he or she has chosen. Use the parts of this book on literary devices which will help you.

4 *Themes or experiences communicated*

Discuss, in conclusion, not just the meaning of the poem, but whether it is making any comment on the poet's attitude to life in general and give your opinion on the value of the poem's themes.

COMMENTARIES

Below there are detailed commentaries on two seventeenth-century poems. Each has been prepared by an A-level examiner to guide you through the poems and show you how full a commentary on a poem, under ideal circumstances, can be.

The next two poems (on pp. 45–46) provide commentaries and questions for you to answer. Read the 'Method of tackling a poem' and the commentary before attempting the questions. The last poem *Incendiary* (p. 48) will provide no help, but you should feel confident by this time to tackle the questions without a commentary.

> *The Retreate*
> Happy those early dayes! when I
> Shin'd in my Angell-infancy.
> Before I understood this place
> Appointed for my second race,
> 5 Or taught my soul to fancy ought
> But a white, Celestiall thought,
> When yet I had not walkt above
> A mile, or two, from my first love,
> And looking back (at that short space,)
> 10 Could see a glimpse of his bright-face;
> When on some *gilded Cloud,* or *flowre*
> My gazing soul would dwell an houre,
> And in those weaker glories spy
> Some shadows of eternity;
> 15 Before I taught my tongue to wound
> My Conscience with a sinfull sound,
> Or had the black art to dispence
> A sev'rall sinne to ev'ry sence,
> But felt through all this fleshly dresse
> 20 Bright *shootes* of everlastingness.
>   O how I long to travell back
> And tread again that ancient track!
> That I might once more reach that plaine
> Where first I left my glorious traine,
> 25 From whence th' Inlightned spirit sees
> That shady City of Palme trees;
> But (ah!) my soul with too much stay
> Is drunk, and staggers in the way.
> Some men a forward motion love,
> 30 But I by backward steps would move,
> And when this dust falls to the urn
> In that state I came return.

(Henry Vaughan)

Texts from Helen Gardner's *Metaphysical Poets* (Penguin)

Commentary on The Retreate

So-called 'metaphysical' poetry is often thought of as fiendishly clever and difficult. A reading of Vaughan's *The Retreate* should help to reassure you that this is not always the case.

Let us begin by establishing what the poem is *not* about. What we are about to say may seem elementary, but it is a fact that, faced with an unprepared poem in an examination, candidates will often pick up a word or phrase that catches their eye and go on to build upon it a whole shaky edifice of misinterpretation. Beware, therefore, of 'my first love' (line 8), and 'his bright face' (line 10). A candidate in a bit of a panic might jump to the conclusion that this is a poem in which a woman recalls an earlier love affair. However, this can hardly be squared with line 2; love affairs, however precocious, do not begin in 'infancy'. An attentive reading of the poem will confirm that it is not to do with love between human beings.

It seems, in fact, to be about a journey which began in childhood with walking 'a mile or two' (line 8); now, as a man, the poet feels he has long since taken the wrong direction and would like to retrace his steps back to the starting point (lines 21–30). The journey is evidently life itself, as is confirmed by 'race' (line 4). Our forefathers were apt to use the word (usually without any idea of competition) as a metaphor for life. You may be able to call to mind examples from popular hymns (e.g. 'Fight the good fight . .'), or remember how Goldsmith gives it a humorous twist in his *Elegy on the Death of a Mad Dog:*

> '. . still a godly race he ran
> Whene'er he went to pray.'

but we have not yet worked out the full meaning of *The Retreate*. The poet calls life his 'second race'. What, then, was the first? He is evidently concerned with the life of his soul, or spirit, as his frequent use of these words testifies (lines 5, 12, 25, 27). Does he believe in reincarnation? Lines 15–18 indicate clearly that he thinks of life in this world as corrupting our childhood innocence. We learn to wound our consciences with evil speaking, and to gratify all our senses with sinful pleasures. It seems unlikely that from recollections of such a life could spring the radiance of childhood at the start of a second life on earth. It must therefore be that he supposes his soul to have come into this world from another kind of existence, and being a devout man of his age, naturally envisages it as the traditional Christian 'heaven', pervaded by the glory of God, or rather, perhaps, the presence of Christ: for Christ would seem to be the more likely object of the kind of devotion expressed in 'my first love'.

The picture he gives of his childhood can now be more fully understood. He sees himself shining like an angel in those happy early days – and however smug we may find this statement, we must accept that Vaughan did not make it in a spirit of self-congratulation, but rather as a record of fact. The glory of God still shone around and upon him, his innocent thoughts were all of heaven (line 6), he saw hints of the eternal world he had so recently left in the appearances of nature (lines 11–14), and felt his earthly body irradiated by what we can best call intimations of immortality.

These last words are part of the title of one of Wordsworth's most famous poems. If you do not already know it, it would be an excellent exercise to read his *Ode: Intimations of Immortality from Recollections of Early Childhood* and compare it with *The Retreate*.

Down to line 20 the poet has used imagery rather unobtrusively, but in lines 21–28 he develops an extended metaphor. Probably with an impression of the lands of the Bible at the back of his mind, he pictures himself as a traveller who has strayed away from his caravan (the 'train' of l. 24) when its destination was already in sight, and is staggering back, weary with wandering, in the hope of rejoining it. Note how suggestive the details are: the 'track' of line 22 may be 'ancient' because many have trodden it before him, but 'ancient' also makes us think of someone trying to rediscover his half-obliterated footprints; the 'inlightened spirit' sees the New Jerusalem as a keen-eyed traveller might discern his goal in the distance; the 'shady City of Palme trees' is an Eastern City like, perhaps, Damascus in former days, whose palm-shaded streets are welcome to those who have journeyed across the scorching 'plaine', a symbol of the spiritual desert of earthly life.

The style of the poem is by no means extravagant or elaborate. The imagery is used to convey meaning, not indulged in for its own sake in order to demonstrate the poet's inventiveness. Indeed, setting aside the extended metaphor just discussed, most of it is basically traditional, e.g. the body thought of as the 'fleshy dresse' of the soul, the comparison of life to a journey or pilgrimage, death and burial referred to in decorous classical terms – Vaughan did not really expect to be cremated and inurned in the high Roman fashion! At one point it is decidedly homely, when the wearied soul is compared with a staggering drunkard (lines 27–28).

The syntax and the sentence structure are straightforward. The metre is very much a favourite maid-of-all work for seventeenth-century poets, the so-called 'octosyllabic' couplet, consisting basically of four iambic feet to a line, with each pair of lines making complete, or nearly complete sense in itself. Apart from a few inevitable archaisms, the vocabulary of the poem should present little difficulty to a modern reader.

On the other hand, do not assume that Vaughan's easy-seeming verse is, in fact, easy to write. Try to write a few similar couplets yourself, and you will understand why Pope says 'True ease in writing comes from art, not chance.' Vaughan's unpretentious poetic craftsmanship may be seen, for instance, in the way he constructs his couplets so that the first line almost invariably 'runs on' into the second, thus permitting a certain freedom of movement within the strict framework of the closed couplet. Notice how, by using a trochaic foot at the beginning of lines 1 and 2 he emphasises the key words, 'happy' and 'shin'd', and how he achieves an effect of finality by making a strong pause after 'came' in the last line. No one with an ear to hear could read the line otherwise. True poets do not do this kind of thing deliberately, of course; they do it instinctively. Poetry is not composed with a slide rule and a set of tables.

Above all, Vaughan has the knack of creating memorable phrases – 'a white, Celestiall thought' (contrasting simply but effectively with 'the black art' of line 17: 'white' for innocence, 'black' for 'evil' – the black art being witchcraft), or 'bright shootes of everlastingnesse'. Consider the line, 'That shady City of Palme trees'. It is perhaps the palms which are shady rather than the city, but would it be an improvement to rewrite the line as 'That city shaded by palm trees'? Metrically, that would be perfectly acceptable; it would also be prosaic.

Nevertheless, despite the accessibility of the poem to an attentive twentieth-century reader, there are some associations that we tend to miss. When we have worked through the poem, we can understand why it is called *The Retreate*: because in it Vaughan is expressing his desire to go back in order to recapture his childhood innocence and his feeling that 'Heaven lay about him in his infancy' (Wordsworth's words, again!) We can respond to the tone of intense yearning in which he speaks of death as the way back to his lost paradise. To Vaughan's Bible-reading age, however, 'In that state I came return', coupled with the previous glorification of childhood, would have evoked an immediate and precise recollection of the beginning of St Matthew, Ch. 18, where Jesus is described as setting a little child in the midst of the disciples, and saying to them 'Except ye be converted, and become as little children, ye shall not enter into the kingdom of heaven.'

The Definition of Love

My Love is of a birth as rare
As 'tis for object strange and high:
It was begotten by despair
Upon Impossibility.

5 Magnanimous Despair alone
Could show me so divine a thing,
Where feeble hope could ne'r have flown
But vainly flapt its Tinsel Wing.

And yet I quickly might arrive
10 Where my extended Soul is fixt,
But Fate does iron wedges drive,
And alwaies crouds it self betwixt.

For Fate with jealous Eye does see
Two perfect Loves; nor lets them close:
15 Their union would her ruine be,
And her Tyrannick pow'r, depose.

And therefore her Decrees of Steel
Us as the distant poles have plac'd,
(Though loves whole World on us doth wheel)
20 Not by themselves to be embrac'd.

Unless the giddy heaven fall,
And Earth some new Convulsion tear;
And, us to joyn, the World should all
Be cramp'd into a *Planisphere*.[1]

25 As Lines so Loves *oblique* may well
Themselves in every Angle greet:
But ours so truly *Paralel,*
Though infinite can never meet.

Therefore the Love which us doth bind,
30 But Fate so enviously debarrs,
Is the Conjunction of the Mind,
And Opposition of the Stars.

(Andrew Marvell)

[1] flat two-dimensional projection of the two hemispheres to show appearance of heavens

Text from Helen Gardner's *Metaphysical Poets* (Penguin)

Commentary on The Definition of Love

Marvell's poem, consecrated to human love, which ranks equal with religion as a subject for metaphysical poetry, provides a striking contrast with Vaughan's in manner as well as in content.

Its theme of hopeless, star-crossed love is familiar and easily recognized, and its argument not difficult to follow in outline. The poet claims a special distinction or pre-eminence for his love precisely because it is, and must for ever be ungratified. In lines 9–10 there is a hint that the lady, if she were free to do so, would requite his passion, but Fate intervenes and forbids what would be a perfect union – why or how, we are never told. Only if the world were turned upside down in some cataclysm could the lovers ever be united. They are destined, therefore, to remain united in mind but eternally separated in body by a greater power than they can contradict.

The verse form of the poem, too, requires no elaborate commentary. It is in simple quatrains of alternately rhyming lines of equal length, the individual lines having four iambic feet, just as in *The Retreate,* the principal point of difference being that in Marvell the unit of sense is the quatrain, not the couplet. Like Vaughan, he is using a verse form familiar in English poetry with the same deceptively easy-seeming fluency.

The distinctive feature of the poem, of course, is its accumulation of ingenious and elaborate imagery. It opens with a cluster of personified abstractions: his love has two unusual and distinguished parents, Despair and Impossibility, as is only fit, considering the 'strange and high' quality of its object. (Is this a conventional compliment to the lady, or a more specific, if veiled allusion to her superior rank?) Only Despair, described as 'magnanimous', i.e. generous, could have directed his affections to 'so divine a thing' – could have made him love a goddess. Hope could never have flown so high on its 'Tinsel wing': we are led to picture Hope as a glittering but feeble insect. In effect, in lines 1–8, Marvell formulates a paradox: Despair inspires him to higher ambitions than Hope could ever do.

Nevertheless, he continues, he could quickly gain possession of the person of the lady to whom his soul, having gone forth out of his body, is already 'fixt', i.e., attached (note the delicate circumlocution of the language here), did not Fate, like an officious or bullying meddler, 'croud', i.e. thrust itself between to separate them. Alternatively, Fate is thought of as parting them by driving 'Iron wedges' between them, of the kind quarrymen and stonemasons use to split rock: the image suggests both the solidity of the bond and the force employed to break it. Similarly, a little later, the strength of Fate is conveyed in 'her Decrees of Steel' (line 17). The fanciful, as opposed to the practical reason for Fate's hostility is given in lines 13–16: she rules the world as a tyrant, and the union of two lovers she has forbidden to marry would overthrow her despotic power. (The political image must have come naturally to Marvell, who lived through the period of the Civil War and held a public appointment under Cromwell.)

In lines 17–24 the poet develops an elaborate image based on geography and astronomy – a true 'conceit', as this kind of unexpected, ingenious and detailed comparison is usually called. The lovers have been placed by Fate at the opposite poles of the world of love – poles apart, in fact; and just as the North and South Poles of the world's axis can never meet, no more can they, though the whole world of love revolves around them – unless, indeed, there were to be a universal collapse into chaos in which the spinning ('giddy') heavens should fall and the earth be torn apart by some new convulsion. (There was a good deal of speculation in the seventeenth century about the possible floods, eruptions, and the like which Earth might have suffered in its earlier history.)

In short, (lines 23–24) the lovers could only be joined if the whole round world, here completely conflated with the world of love, were to be 'cramp'd into a Planisphere' i.e. reduced to a flat two-dimensional projection of the two hemispheres, so arranged that the two poles are brought together. (Do not be alarmed by this complex and highly technical image. Where such an allusion appears in an appreciation paper, the examiners would feel bound to give an explanatory note. If you were being examined on a prescribed poem, of course, you would be expected to know what was meant.)

Having thus, with typical metaphysical panache, elevated his frustrated love to the cosmic scale, Marvell descends, in lines 25–29, to the merely geometrical. As two straight lines which are oblique to each other converge to form an angle, so may those lovers converge who are naturally drawn together and encounter no opposition; but he and his lady are like parallel lines which, though produced to infinity, never meet. The very long-windedness of this explanation reveals the compression of Marvell's style.

Finally, in lines 29–32, the poet introduces the language of astrology. The lovers are joined in soul like planets in 'conjunction', i.e., in the same sign of the zodiac, but their stars are in 'opposition'.

Looking back, we can now see that there is more depth of meaning in the title than at first appears. Marvell is not just 'defining' love in the modern sense of the word; the love the poem deals with is, in any case, untypical, as he is at pains to point out. 'Definition' seems to be used rather with the meaning of 'fixing boundaries'. Perhaps the title might be best rendered in modern English as 'The Limitation of Love'; for the lovers, Fate has 'set a bourn how far to be belov'd.'

The poem we have considered may be seen as essentially a literary exercise, taking up the well-worn theme of unrequited or hopeless love and tricking it out with the kind of decoration the taste of the day approved. It may be a conscious imitation of Donne's earlier and more celebrated poem, *A Valediction: forbidding mourning,* which is also about lovers parted (at least for a time), employs the same verse-form, and is equally profuse in learned, 'scientific' images. Certainly, to some readers, it may seem to have more of art than of nature. For all that, it is possible that it has some relationship to such known facts in Marvell's life as that he lived through the Civil War, when many family and personal links were broken up by political discord – Milton's first marriage is a case in point –, was for a time tutor to Lord Fairfax's daughter, and seems never to have married. If he was disappointed in love, he might well, as a clever young man, have found relief in composing a highly wrought and sophisticated poem in which he positively glories in the hopelessness of his aspirations.

Speculation and reference to biographical background, though often tempting must be kept under control. You may allow yourself a *little,* but your first and main concern must always be with the text, and with what may fairly be deduced from it.

The Darkling Thrush

I leant upon a coppice gate
When Frost was spectre-grey,
And Winter's dregs made desolate
The weakening eye of day.
The tangled bine-stems scored the sky
Like strings of broken lyres,
And all mankind that haunted nigh
Had sought their household fires.

The land's sharp features seemed to be
The Century's corpse outleant,
His crypt the cloudy canopy,
The wind his death-lament
The ancient pulse of germ and birth
Was shrunken hard and dry,
And every spirit upon earth
Seemed fervourless as I.

At once a voice arose among
The bleak twigs overhead
In a full-hearted evensong
Of joy illimited;
An aged thrush, frail, gaunt and small,
In blast-beruffled plume,
Had chosen thus to fling his soul
Upon the growing gloom.

So little cause for carolings
Of such ecstatic sound
Was written on terrestrial things
Afar or nigh around,
That I could think there trembled through
His happy good-night air
Some blessed Hope, whereof he knew
And I was unaware.

(Thomas Hardy)

Commentary on the poem

This poem expresses the desolation of a late afternoon in mid-winter, with whose grim aspect the poet's own mood is in complete harmony. The first verse describes the isolation of the writer, who is portrayed as a solitary human being, chilled and dreary like the winter and the frost.

In the second verse, the grim reality of the poem is reinforced by the widening of the scene. Hardy compares the whole landscape with the dead body of the century, bare with the sharpness of death. The earth lies under the cloudy skies and the wind is in mourning for the passing of the century. The vitality of life seems numbed and the deadness of the world is matched by the apathetic and uncommunicative state of the poet's mind.

The third stanza introduces a new element, for the song of the thrush bursts into the gloom of the evening: his joy contrasts sadly with the barren scene. However, the poet feels that the scene is so desolate that the thrush's outburst is from an inspiration known only to him and hidden from the pessimistic poet.

The poet brings to the theme of the thrush in the winter time a universal significance. The end of the year makes most men feel pessimistic. The poet wonders whether the creator of the universe has any interest in the life of any human being, and it is a typical belief of Hardy's that he feels the weather is a cruelly ironical background against which man plays his part.

The pattern of the metre is flexible; although the rhyme scheme is rigid, thus underlining the firmness of purpose in the passage, there is considerable use of run-on lines, especially in verse three and four, where the feelings run more freely.

The use of figures of speech 'spectre-grey', 'the weakening eye of day', 'like strings of broken lyres' intensify the gloomy scene of the first stanza. In the second stanza the use of simile and metaphor makes the poet feel sepulchral like the landscape. Note also the alliterative use of 'dregs made desolate', 'Century's corpse', 'crypt the cloudy canopy'. The corpse of the old dead century seems to be leaning uneasily outwards, a ghastly reminder of the passage of time and the inevitability of death.

The final impression of the poem may be seen as a sombre one. If readers have some knowledge of the novels of Thomas Hardy, such as *Tess of the D'Urbervilles,* they will realize that a pessimistic attitude to life is common in his work. However, it is reasonable to conclude that the poet recognizes that the thrush has an intuitive sense of joy and 'blessed hope' which he himself lacks, but *may* be immanent in the universe.

Questions

1 What impression of

(*a*) the landscape

(*b*) the weather

(*c*) the thrush

is created in the poem.

Include use of vocabulary and figures of speech in your answer.

2 What does the poem show of Hardy's pessimistic view of life.

Dulce et Decorum Est

Bent double, like old beggars under sacks,
Knock-kneed, coughing like hags, we cursed through sludge,
Till on the haunting flares we turned our backs
And towards our distant rest began to trudge.
5 Men marched asleep. Many lost their boots
But limped on, blood-shod. All went lame: all blind.
Drunk with fatigue; deaf even to the hoots
Of tired, outstripped Five-Nines that dropped behind.

'Gas! Gas! Quick, boys!' – An ecstasy of fumbling,
10 Fitting the clumsy helmets just in time;
But someone still was yelling out and stumbling
And floundering like a man in fire or lime . . .
Dim, through the misty panes and thick green light,
As under a green sea, I saw him drowning.

15 In all my dreams, before my helpless sight,
He plunges at me, guttering, choking, drowning.

If in some smothering dreams you too could pace
Behind the wagon that we flung him in,
And watch the white eyes writhing in his face,
20 His hanging face, like a devil's sick of sin;
If you could hear, at every jolt, the blood
come gargling from the froth-corrupted lungs,

> Obscene as cancer, bitter as the cud
> Of vile, incurable sores on innocent tongues, –
> 25 My friend, you would not tell with such high zest
> To children ardent for some desperate glory,
> The old lie 'Dulce et decorum est
> Pro Patria mori'.

(Wilfred Owen)

Commentary on the poem

This powerful and bitter poem tells of exhausted troops returning to their quarters and subjected to a gas attack during the First World War. The poem takes a specific incident, but is generally concerned with the horror and squalor of war. In simple terms the story of the poem is as follows: while trudging back from the front line, there is a gas attack. One soldier is too late in putting on his mask and is gassed. Those who saw him will never forget his suffering and we realize how falsely heroic and patriotic is the idea 'Dulce et Decorum est Pro Patria mori' – 'It is good and fitting to die for your native land'. The poet has to make the cruelty, suffering and squalor of war as tangible as possible for us to accept the irony of men dying for their country.

When dealing with the criticism of a poem, one could either talk separately of meaning, figures of speech, imagery and so on, or deal with all of these within each stanza of the poem. I have chosen the latter method for this poem.

In the first stanza the first two lines reflect the humiliation of the soldiers as they crawl back to their positions. They are described as 'like hags', women deprived of all humanity like the witches in 'Macbeth'. Other phrases which show how sick and ill the men feel are: 'bent double', 'like old beggars', 'Knock-kneed' and 'coughing'. They 'cursed' as they marched as it is only by cursing that they can make their way through the mud. The paradoxical statement 'Men marched asleep' emphazises the exhaustion of the troops. The metaphorical use of 'blood-shod', shows their feet were bare and extremely painful. The soldiers can no longer feel anything; they are 'lame', 'blind', 'drunk', 'deaf'. They cannot even hear the noise of the shells dropping behind them.

If the mood of the first stanza is of extreme tiredness, the second verse shocks us into wake-fulness with 'Gas! Gas! Quick boys!' There is sudden violent movement contrasted with the heavy, weary movement of the first verse. The word 'ecstasy' is paradoxically used; it usually means extreme pleasure and supreme happiness. Here the excitement is that of life and death; 'fitting the helmets just in time'. 'Fumbling' and 'clumsy' describes the finger movements of the weary soldiers as they struggle with their helmet straps.

Then comes probably the most effective simile of the passage; the description of the soldier who cannot fix his mask in time

> 'But someone still was yelling out and stumbling
> And floundering like a man in fire or lime . . .'

Grave of Unknown British Soldier, Western Front 1916 (*Imperial War Museum*)

Owen uses this comparison to get over the effect of the gas made of something we know in which we can visualize the man drowning. This image of drowning is highly suitable because the man is gasping for air as though drowning and of course we are looking at him through the green semi-transparent window of the gas mask which makes the whole world look as though it is being viewed from under the water.

The next short stanza shows how the poet's dreams have been haunted by this dying figure. The use of four violent verbs, 'plunges', 'guttering', 'choking' and 'drowning' harshly tell us of the cruel torture and death the man has suffered.

Having involved the poet in the suffering brought about by the cruel fighting of the First World War, Owen now brings the reader into the poem and forces him to face the situation Owen had to face. When the gassed soldier is thrown onto the wagon the words Owen uses are evocative of his agony; 'writhing', 'blood-gargling from his lungs', 'his hanging face' and the four comparisons used, 'like a devil's sick of sin', 'froth-corrupted', 'obscene as cancer',

> 'bitter as the cud
> Of vile, incurable sores on innocent tongues,'

are reminiscent of the disease imagery of *Hamlet* in evoking disgust and repulsion. The suggestion is that even the devil would be sick of this sight.

The restrained tone of the ending of the poem proves Owen's point that it is a lie that it is sweet and fitting to die for your country. The reader now realizes the full bitterness and irony of the tone Owen adopts in telling how stupid people are who still believe such a sentiment.

Questions

1 Comment on the parts of the poem which mention the conditions of the battlefield, the men's fatigue and loss of senses.

2 Explain the following expressions:

(*a*) 'like old beggars under sacks' (line 1)
(*b*) 'blood-shod' (line 6)
(*c*) 'ecstasy of fumbling' (line 9)
(*d*) 'floundering like a man in fire or lime' (line 12)
(*e*) 'misty panes' (line 13)
(*f*) 'thick, green light' (line 13)
(*g*) 'his hanging face, like a devil's sick of sin' (line 20)
(*h*) 'Bitter as the cud
       of vile, incurable sores on innocent tongues' (line 23/34)
(*i*) 'The old lie: Dulce et Decorum Est Pro Patria mori' (line 27/28)

3 Comment on the ironical tone of the whole of the poem. Why would you call it an anti-war poem.

Incendiary

That one small boy with a face like pallid cheese
And burnt-out little eyes could make a blaze
As brazen, fierce and huge, as red and gold
And zany yellow as the one that spoiled
5 Three thousand guineas' worth of property
And crops at Godwin's Farm on Saturday
Is frightening, as fact and metaphor:
An ordinary match intended for
The lighting of a pipe or kitchen fire
10 Misused may set a whole menagerie
Of flame-fanged tigers roaring hungrily.
And frightening, too, that one small boy should set
The sky on fire and choke the stars to heat
Such skinny limbs and such a little heart
15 Which would have been content with one warm kiss
Had there been anyone to offer this.

(Vernon Scannell)

Questions

1 What two different aspects of the boy's character are presented in the poem?
2 Comment on the use of figures of speech, vocabulary, colour and sentence structure in lines 1–6.

3 In lines 8–16 our attitude to the boy softens. What devices does the poet use to enable him to make us feel like this?

4 Write a detailed description of the rhyme scheme of the poem.

5 What judgement on society, the boy and his family would the poet seem to be asking us to make?

6 Comment on the following expressions

(*1*) 'burnt-out little eyes' (line 2)

(*2*) 'as fact and metaphor' (line 7)

(*3*) 'menagerie' (line 10)

(*4*) 'choice' (line 13)

(*5*) 'one *warm* kiss' (line 15)

COMPARING UNSEEN POEMS

Often in practical criticism papers, two or three poems with similar themes are chosen for the candidate to compare and contrast. This type of answer involves careful planning as you have to cross-reference between one poem and another. However, you can still treat each poem under the headings given in 'Method of tackling a poem' (p. 40), but remember *NOT* to write your commentary under headings. It is perfectly permissible to say which poem you prefer, as long as you support your opinion with detailed reference to and quotation from the poem.

We have given you three famous poems on Autumn to consider. Choose two of the three and try to compare and contrast them as though you had been asked to do this in an examination. You could look back on the commentary on *The Darkling Thrush* to see how Hardy deals with the seasonal description in the poem. This may help you to discuss these three poets' treatment of Autumn weather. No other guidance should be necessary at this stage, but ask yourself all the time whether you are comparing the two poems and *not* just writing separate commentaries on each one.

To Autumn

Season of mists and mellow fruitfulness!
Close bosom-friend of the maturing sun;
Conspiring with him how to load and bless
With fruit the vines that round the thatch-eaves run;
To bend with apples the mossed cottage-trees,
And fill all fruit with ripeness to the core;
To swell the gourd, and plump the hazel shells
With a sweet kernel; to set budding more,
And still more, later flowers for the bees,
Until they think warm days will never cease,
For Summer has o'er-brimm'd their clammy cells.

Who hath not seen thee oft amid thy store?
Sometimes whoever seeks abroad may find
Thee sitting careless on a granary floor,
Thy hair soft-lifted by the winnowing wind;
Or on a half-reaped furrow sound asleep,
Drowsed with the fume of poppies, while thy hook
Spares the next swath and all its twined flowers;
And sometime like a gleaner thou dost keep
Steady thy laden head across a brook;
Or by a cider-press, with patient look,
Thou watchest the last oozings, hours by hours.

Where are the songs of Spring? Ay, where are they?
Think not of them, thou hast thy music too,
While barred clouds bloom the soft-dying day,
And touch the stubble-plains with rosy hue;
Then in a wailful choir, the small gnats mourn
Among the river sallows, borne aloft
Or sinking as the light wind lives or dies;
And full-grown lambs loud bleat from hilly bourn;
Hedge-crickets sing; and now with treble soft
The redbreast whistles from a garden-croft,
And gathering swallows twitter in the skies.

John Keats (1795-1821)

November

The shepherds almost wonder where they dwell,
And the old dog for his right journey stares;
The path leads somewhere, but they cannot tell,
And neighbour meets with neighbour unawares.
The maiden passes close beside her cow,
And wanders on, and thinks her far away;
The ploughman goes unseen behind his plough
And seems to lose his horses half the day.
The lazy mist creeps on in journey slow;
The maidens shout and wonder where they go;
So dull and dark are the November days.
The lazy mist high up the evening curled,
And now the morn quite hides in smoke and haze;
The place we occupy seems all the world.

John Clare (1793-1864)

No!

No sun – no moon!
No morn – no noon –
No dawn – no dusk – no proper time of day –
No sky – no earthly view –
No distance looking blue –
No road – no street – no 't'other side the way' –
No end to any Row –
No indications where the Crescents go –
No top to any steeple –
No recognitions of familiar people –
No courtesies for showing 'em –
No knowing 'em! –
No travelling at all – no locomotion,
No inkling of the way – no notion –
'No go' – by land or ocean –
No mail – no post –
No news from any foreign coast –
No Park – no Ring – no afternoon gentility –
No company – no nobility –
No warmth, no cheerfulness, no healthful ease,
No comfortable feel in any member –
No shade, no shine, no butterflies, no bees,
No fruits, no flowers, no leaves, no birds –
November!

Thomas Hood (1799-1845)

Part III Drama

1 General
2 Studying Shakespeare at A Level
3 Practical Criticism of Drama

INTRODUCTION

Non-Shakespearian drama is usually prescribed for general literature papers, where candidates are not necessarily expected to show quite the same intimate knowledge of texts as that required on the Shakespeare papers (see pp. x–xv). This does NOT mean that merely superficial knowledge is sufficient.

The text should be studied with care, making full use of notes and editorial material in annotated editions. Especially with older plays, you should form some picture of the state of the theatre at that time, what was being written for it, and how the prescribed work fits into the general picture. Try to fix the outline of the plot firmly in your mind, preferably by making *your own* summary. Note the main features of character, and how they are revealed in speech and action; look out for the ways in which atmosphere is created and themes developed. Try to see a production of any play you are studying, otherwise try to listen to a recording. Remember that 'classics' are broadcast from time to time on radio, especially Radio 3, and that such broadcasts are often more complete than television adaptations. (See also pp. 160–64.)

Your preparation should equip you to answer 'general' questions and also passage-based practical criticism questions (see pp. 90–109) in which both close analysis of an extract and ability to relate it to the rest of the play will be required.

1 General

INTRODUCTION

This chapter gives a brief survey of the main areas of drama set at A Level. It will help you to place in context your own set plays. It is always useful to 'read round' a set play, either by looking at other plays by the same author or at others of the same period.

The A-level Examinations Boards concentrate on three periods of drama: Elizabethan and Jacobean; the 'Comedy of manners' (Restoration theatre) and the Modern period. The first and third are the richest fields. The second is almost entirely absorbed by Congreve's *The Way of the World* and Wycherley's *Country Wife*. Very often, also, those later eighteenth-century revivals of the comic spirit of the seventeenth century, Sheridan's *The School for Scandal* (1777) and Goldsmith's *She Stoops to Conquer* (1773) appear on the syllabuses.

ELIZABETHAN AND JACOBEAN DRAMA

Background

In 1576 the first public theatre, called the Theatre, was built near the site of Liverpool Street Station and opened by James Burbage, its principal actor. This theatre achieved immediate popularity, and many more were constructed including the Curtain, the Fortune, the Swan and the most famous of all, the Globe Theatre, built on the South Bank of the Thames near the site of the National Theatre today.

The Elizabethan Playhouse

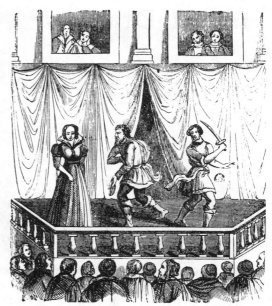

An Elizabethan apron stage

The theatres of Shakespeare's day were divided into private and public theatres. The private theatres were built indoors, usually in large houses and palaces. They were lit by artificial light and the audience sat on benches. The price of seats ranged from 6d to 2/6.

The public theatres were built with roofs that were open to the sky. The performances were always held in the daylight, usually in an afternoon. The seats were far from luxurious and the 'groundlings' sat on stools near the stage. These seats cost 1d. (See also p. 67 for a description of the theatre's structure and design.)

Elizabeth I died in 1603 and James I's accession accompanied the great dramatic phase of the Jacobean drama. This included not only the greatest plays of Shakespeare and Jonson, but also the tragedies of Tourneur (*The Revenger's Tragedy,* 1607, *The Atheist's Tragedy,* 1608); Webster (*The Duchess of Malfi,* 1614, *The White Devil,* 1620); Beaumont and Fletcher (*The Maid's Tragedy,* 1601); Middleton (*The Changeling,* 1622); and the comedies of Dekker (*The Shoemaker's Holiday,* 1599); Beaumont and Fletcher (*The Knight of the Burning Pestle,* 1613), Massinger (*A New Way to Pay Old Debts,* 1625) and Ford (*Tis Pity She's a Whore,* 1627).

It is important to get a feeling for the passion and the realism in staging of the drama of this period. You should make full use of the notes and introduction in individual editions of your set play and consult general 'background' books (see p. 159).

Christopher Marlowe (1564-93)

Of the pre-Shakespearian plays, the most often set are Marlowe's *The Tragical History of Doctor Faustus, The Jew of Malta,* and *Edward II. Tamburlaine the Great,* Marlowe's first play (I produced 1587, II, 1588), is rarely set, though full of great poetry. The main character of the title is so megalomaniac, and the other characters so faceless, that the play is fatally flawed by lack of dramatic tension and interest. It made a great impact in its time, no doubt because of the intensity of the poetry, and the shock effect of Marlowe's famous 'mighty line' (Dr Johnson's description of Marlowe's resounding cadences), then heard for the first time in our theatres.

Dr Faustus (written 1589, printed 1604)

Dr Faustus was, like Tamburlaine, a dominating character whose aspirations the author shared imaginatively, giving them a compelling power. The favourite Renaissance figure of the 'over-reacher' (whose emblem was Icarus), is set in a play which owes much else to medieval morality drama. Marlowe follows in outline the English translation (from the German) of *The History of the Damnable Life and Death of Dr Faustus,* developed from the medieval legend of a man who sold his soul to the Devil. However, Marlowe's conception of Faustus is of a character far more complex than that of the legendary magician.

The hero's monopoly of the play's action, and the great struggle that goes on in him between good and evil, are to be specially noted. Typically for the earlier plays, the supporting characters are given little depth or life of their own. (Compare this with Shakespeare's treatment of his minor characters such as Kent in *King Lear.*) This is often highlighted in examination questions. The following is typical:

'Dr Faustus dominates the action: there is no other developed character in the play.' Do you agree?

(London, 1981)

The dramatic tension in the play owes much to the interior war between man's belief in himself as a superman, and the older faith that sets moral limits to such aspirations. This Renaissance dilemma is to be experienced again in the debate between Satan and Eve in Milton's *Paradise Lost* (Bk IX). As Marlowe's Tamburlaine says

> 'Nature, that fram'd us of four elements
> Warring within our breasts for regiment
> Doth teach us all to have aspiring minds.'

(*Tamb.* Pt 1, Act III, Sc 6)

When studying *Dr Faustus,* it is valuable to give special attention to the extraordinarily anguished scene of the night (final scene) when Faustus must surrender his soul to Satan. The despairing yet still heroic speeches are delivered in the ever-diminishing intervals of the striking clock.

> '(*The clock strikes eleven.*)

> '*Faust.* Ah, Faustus
> Now hast thou but one bare hour to live,
> And then thou must be damn'd perpetually!
> Stand still, you ever-moving spheres of heaven,
> That time may cease and midnight never come;'

This is an intensely tragic scene, emphasizing by contrast the triviality of Faustus' earlier escapades, which themselves culminate in the high lyrical poetry of the address to Helen of Troy

> 'Oh, thou art fairer than the evening air
> Clad in the beauty of a thousand stars;'

The Jew of Malta (*c.* 1590)

With *The Jew of Malta,* in the Senecan tradition of the revenge tragedy, Marlowe takes another step in the right direction of presenting none but immoral characters. Barabas is quite blatantly a bad man—but equalled in villainy by everyone else in the play. The central character, like earlier heroes, is distinct, functional, but lacking in all warm humanity and subtlety.

The role of humour in the play is a common topic for examination questions, for example, '"Primarily comic entertainment". Is this an adequate description of the Jew of Malta?'

(Cambridge, 1980)

You may not feel that the play is in any way comic. You should work out your views on this and note the reactions to the horrors of the play's characters within it. Barabas' servant Ithamore, for example, takes delight in his master's deviousness (Act III)

> '*Itha.* Why, was there ever seen such villany,
> So neatly plotted, and so well perform'd?
> Both held in hand, and flat both beguil'd'

TS Eliot referred to the humour in the play as 'farce' and it is useful to read his opinion in his essay on Marlowe.

Edward II (*c.* 1591–2, see also pp. 91–93)

Edward II draws on a period of history that fascinated Elizabethan audiences: the Plantagenet wars, internal and external, leading to the Tudor supplanting House. It is useful to acquaint yourself with the historical facts and compare them with Marlowe's version. Typically, Marlowe concentrates on his central character, the King, and shows how his ruin springs from his weaknesses.

Note that the striking heroic stanzas and tirades, even the lyricism, of earlier plays have largely disappeared from this stark play.

Webster and Jacobean tragedy

Of the Jacobean tragedies, the two most frequently set at A Level are those of Webster (*c.* 1580–1634). These may represent the gloomy, menacing tragedy of the Jacobean period. The horrors and claustrophobic atmosphere derive partly from the late Roman tragedian Seneca, partly from the changing mood of the audience and King James' love of magic and mystery, partly from the character of the authors. They had observed how much of a success Kyd's melodramatic *The Spanish Tragedy* had been two decades earlier, and how well this vein had been exploited by Shakespeare himself. As taste began to deteriorate and Shakespeare fell silent (*The Tempest* was produced in 1612, a year after *The White Devil*), so Tourneur, Webster and Massinger took over the stage until the Puritans closed it for twenty years.

Sometimes, in critical discussions of Jacobean tragedy, the impression is given that by the end of Elizabeth I's reign audiences had already supped so full of horrors that playwrights felt compelled to go on piling up the atrocities to make any impression at all on blunted sensibilities. This is not altogether true. Considered merely as anthologies of horror, there is not much to choose between *The Duchess of Malfi* and early plays like Kyd's *Spanish Tragedy* or Shakespeare's *Titus Andronicus*. What is different about Jacobean tragedies is not so much any increase in the number, or the essential bloodiness of the murders and maimings, but rather their more refined and ingenious nature, a greater psychological depth, and perhaps above all the more varied and expressive language employed.

Notes on Webster's The White Devil (1612)

Character

The White Devil describes the central and all-pervading character, Vittoria Corombona. Questions set on the play at A Level often concentrate on her. You should explore in detail her relations with the other characters, especially with her lover Brachiano and her brother Marcello. Marcello's character should also be studied carefully.

Like Marlowe's megalomaniacs, Vittoria Corombona will perpetrate any crime to serve her ambitions.

Construction

Editors have commented on how the scenes seem to blaze out of a dark background, so that the impression is not of a whole, but of a series of lurid, imaginatively realized episodes. Two scenes you may find rewarding to examine in particular detail are the trial scene (Act I, Sc. 2) for its revelations of character and the changing directions of the action, and the final scene (Act V, Sc. 6). Here you should assess the effectiveness of the ending and note a common element in Jacobean tragedy – courage in the face of death.

Themes

The White Devil falls into the genre of revenge tragedy (cf. *The Spanish Tragedy*, Kyd, *Hamlet*, Shakespeare). You can trace in it the themes of justice and revenge. You should note also the modifications of ideas on right and wrong throughout the play and the theme of the corruption of the Court life.

(Turn to p. 93 for a commentary on *The Duchess of Malfi*.)

Ben Jonson (?1573–1637)

The comedy of humours

Ben Jonson (1573–1637)

The name of Ben Jonson is always associated with the 'comedy of humours', in which comic effects are achieved by bringing together a collection of eccentric characters, each dominated by a 'humour', i.e., a ruling passion. For Jonson's own definition of 'humour' you should consult the famous lines in the prologue to his play *Every Man Out of His Humour*

'Some one peculiar quality
Doth so possess a man, that it doth draw
All his affects, his spirits, and his powers,
In their confluctions, all to run one way.'

Jonson was by no means the only dramatist of his age to exploit 'humour' on the stage, though he erected it into a theory of comedy. Shakespeare too had his 'humorous' characters; indeed, Hamlet implies that they were among the stock-in-trade of the drama: 'the humorous man shall end his part in peace' (*Hamlet,* Act II, Sc. 2). Note that the 'humorous man' was not a humorist in the popular modern sense; he aroused amusement by his oddity, but did not set out to be amusing.

Jonson's comedies with particular reference to The Alchemist and Bartholomew Fair

Jonson is above all a satirist of the morals and follies of his times. He called comedy 'A thing pleasant and ridiculous and accommodated to the correction of manners.' This is essentially how his comedy should be seen. Despite the large number of topicalities and ephemeral weaknesses that he satirized, there is plenty of recognizable satirical humour. Surly in *The Alchemist* says

'Must needs I cheat myself
With that same foolish vice of honesty?'

Surly should be central to a study of *The Alchemist.* The rest of the characters contain a nest of villains whose brilliant exposure by Jonson was said to have helped clear the streets of London of quacks and imposters. Lovewit, the master tricked by his roguish servants, does not seem much better than they. His attitude is conveyed in the line

'I love a teeming wit as I love nourishment.'

The following questions on *The Alchemist* are typical
Either
(*a*) What effects does Jonson achieve in *The Alchemist* by setting his comedy in contemporary London?
Or
(*b*) Examine the part of Surly in *The Alchemist,* and say how you think Jonson's portrayal fits in with his dramatic purposes.

(Cambridge, 1980)

Bartholomew Fair may be less carefully constructed, but it is full of the keenest most biting satire of which Jonson is capable, full of vigorous invective and City life in all its colourful diversity; the characters have amazing individuality: the Puritan, Zeal-of-the-land Busy; Ursula, the Pig Woman; Justice Overdo; Tom Quarlous and the rest, Littlewit and all, a fine Rabelaisian rout. Here is the comedy of social realism as well as the satire of manners.

Note Jonson's use of names to convey the disposition of humour of his comic characters – Zeal-of-the-land Busy the puritan in *Bartholomew Fair* is an extreme and colourful example. The same device is used in many of Charles Dickens' novels. Like Dickens, Jonson shows great realism in his portrayal of urban life, despite his use of caricature. In *Volpone* the characters generally take their cue from their suggestive names (see p. 97 for a discussion on this play).

The Unities

Jonson was a learned (although largely self-educated) man. He knew more of the ancient Greek and Roman literature than any other dramatist of his time. It is useful to note Jonson's adherence to the classical unities (see Glossary) of·time, place and action – a discipline within which he worked skilfully in his comedies but which did not help him achieve tension in his one tragedy *Sejanus*.

THE COMEDY OF MANNERS

The 'Restoration Drama' or as this is often called, comedy of manners, lasted the fifty years from 1660 to 1710, that is for four reigns in our history. (Charles II, 1660–85; James II, 1685–88; William III (1688-1702) and Mary II, 1688–94; Anne 1702–14.) Its leading exponents were Etherege, Dryden, Wycherley, Congreve, Vanbrugh and Farquhar (see p. 102). Although the drama did not change or develop as markedly as the Elizabethan and Jacobean over a similar period of time, it did run into a general change of public taste by Queen Anne's time – a taste that was adequately guided and expressed by Sir Joseph Addison, whose essays in *The Spectator* began to appear in 1711.

Although Restoration Comedy was a new phenomenon, it had certain links with the 'citizen' drama of Jonson, his use of names to indicate 'humours' or character-traits, above all the satirical drive. The style of the plays however was nearer to that of the comedy of Beaumont and Fletcher, where we also find some of the characteristics of the later drama, such as the 'gallant' – a lover more interested in conquests than marriage (e.g. Mirabel in Fletcher's *The Wild Goose Chase*). Shirley (1596–1666) also wrote plays for the 1630's in which couples similar to those in the 'comedy of manners' are to be found.

With the encouragement of the court newly returned from Paris, and an awareness of the comedies of Molière as they began to appear from 1662, the style of drama as critics now distinguish it began to take shape. The drama concerned itself exclusively with Londoners of the aristocratic class, or played off against country oafs. Ordinary citizens when they appear are often made to appear foolish, or even cuckolded. The gallants, rakes and idle rich are reluctant to marry but are liable to be 'caught' in the end (in which case one assumes they may settle down to a virtuous life). Wives are dissatisfied with husbands, and the dialogue often consists of witty exchanges like verbal fencing matches.

In theory, some of the writers of these comedies, such as Dryden, claimed that it was part of their satirical interest to hold up the rakes and libertines to criticism if not ridicule, but in practice such characters often stole the show and were clearly amusing if not admirable in their behaviour. The later dramatists, Wycherley and Farquhar, tried rather more than Etherege and Congreve to expose the bad behaviour, in keeping with changing opinions. Victorian moral qualms put Restoration Comedy right out of court, and when it returned to the stage in this century there was a certain uneasiness which resulted in its production with finical emphasis on the externals of the age, in order to try and distance the immorality. There was also an unjustifiable tendency to treat the characters as though they were heartless or mere mouthpieces for a stream of wit. Recently there has been a better understanding and presentation of the realism and living qualities of the characters. As Congreve wrote himself in defence of Valentine (*Love for Love*):

> 'He was Prodigal and is shown in the first Act under hard circumstances, which are the effects of his Prodigality. . . . In short, the Character is a mix'd Character: his faults are fewer than his good qualities: and, as the World goes, he may pass well enough for the best character in a Comedy: where even the best must be shewn to have faults, that the best spectators may be warn'd not to think too well of themselves.'

We summarize below the key points to remember about the drama of this period.

General features of the Restoration theatre

(a) It was now an indoor theatre on the contemporary French model, set back behind a proscenium arch with a curtain. Scenery and artificial lighting were employed.

(b) For the first time in England, actresses appeared on the public stage. This gave dramatists wider scope in the writing of women's parts, and no doubt permitted a greater and more persuasive seductiveness in their interpretation. Many of the female roles in Shakespeare's comedies must have been played (by male actors, of course) in a somewhat tomboy-ish fashion, e.g. Rosalind in *As You Like It*.

(c) Even more than in Shakespeare's day, the players depended on Royal and Court patronage. Play-going was a fashionable diversion, much favoured by those members of the upper classes who wished to celebrate their liberation from Puritan rule and by an even larger number of middle-class people seeking to imitate their social superiors. The diarist and civil servant Samuel Pepys was a keen play-goer.

Particular features of Restoration comedies

(a) The plays were almost wholly in prose. In the best of them, the dialogue is splendidly polished and witty.

(b) Some traces of the old 'comedy of humours' survive in the treatment of the more eccentric characters, and in the bestowing of 'characteristic' names on all the people in a play, e.g. Waitwell, a serving man, Fainall, an unscrupulous schemer, Gibbet, a highwayman.

(c) The typical scene of the action is London, and the leading characters are 'persons of quality'. Country life is viewed with exaggerated horror as a desert of unmitigated uncouth boredom. It

Michael Hadley and Nyree Dawn Porter. *The Provok'd Wife*
(Thorndike Theatre)

should be added that the London merchant – the 'City Knight' – is also made a figure of fun, existing only to be robbed of his money and his wife.

(d) The attitude of the upper-class characters – especially, but by no means exclusively, the men – to sex and marriage is cheerfully cynical. The man of fashion devotes his time and energy above all to the pursuit of women, and the women are very willing to be pursued, and frequently overtaken. At the same time they profess a hypocritical concern for keeping up appearances – 'honour' and 'reputation' are words forever in their mouths. Among the men, even a husband who positively loathes his wife is still expected to fly into a fury at the prospect of being made, or reputed, a cuckold. Wives, like pheasants, have to be preserved from poachers.

(e) Almost of equal importance to the fine gentleman is the repair of his generally shaky financial position. Money, and the law in connection with inheritance, dowries, marriage settlements, estates in trust, and so forth, bulk large in almost every play. For the Mirabells and the Aimwells, supreme happiness comes in the form of marriage to a beautiful heiress.

Wycherley – The Country Wife (1675)

Examining two recent and typical questions on Wycherley's *The Country Wife* we can explore some of the moral and social assumptions of Restoration Comedy, touched upon in **(d)** above.

'Wycherley's alleged immorality, in particular his failure to expose Horner's deception, has offended many' (to be discussed).

'"The good characters in *The Country Wife* are dull and colourless; the bad are grotesque but vital". Discuss.'

In this play Pinchwife marries an ignorant woman in order not to be deceived, having had experience of 'whores'. He is duly well deceived, but in view of his motive for marrying, and other characteristics he reveals, no one could be entirely sorry for him. Horner says to him:

'So then, you only marry'd to keep a Whore to yourself.'

He goes on to give a lesson to Pinchwife in better motives for marriage. In the next scene Pinchwife is seen spying on his wife, and in several ways treats her badly in a jealous humour. We can only approve, therefore, of Margery's success in deceiving him.

Horner himself has little difficulty in overcoming the 'honour' (which soon is exposed as a myth) of the various women he seduces by pretending to be a eunuch. He is not really a man to be approved of or condemned by the audience, being more of a dramatic tool used by Wycherley to satirize the society women who are his victims. These are the hypocrites and are strongly condemned. Margery is an exception, but her unfaithfulness is understandable.

In a subplot, the fop Sparkish is the rival to Harcourt, a man of good sense and virtue, for the hand of Pinchwife's sister Alithea. Although the two good characters are not too convincing, they are present as gauges of the moral temperature and do not need to do more than fulfil that role while Wycherley concentrates on the one (Horner), who exposes immorality. Sparkish is similarly exposed as an over-credulous fool.

In view of these considerations, we need not be indignant that the morally reprehensible Horner remains unexposed and unpunished. Present moral sensibility in such matters has tended to draw nearer to that of Wycherley's audience, rather than that of the more 'straitlaced' Queen Anne period: it may be remembered that the Victorians could not accept any Restoration comedy at all, on largely moral grounds. Witty rakes were commonly forgiven moral weaknesses for the sake of their ability to make the contemporary audience – and us – laugh, and as we have pointed out, since Horner is more of a function of the satire than a rounded character, we may trust the playwright's handling of his fate.

The immorality, so called, of the good wife Margery has been explained, and in general the adultery and flirtations between lovers and married people in Restoration comedy, though certainly the product of a comparatively licentious 'upper-class' outlook on life, may stand today within their humorous and satirical contexts as possibly mildly shocking, but not necessarily to be imitated, regarded as the norm, or to be admired by the ordinary man. The same kind of moral anarchy, absorbed by elements of satire and crazy humour, are to be observed today in present drama, the theatre of the absurd or black comedy. We do not now believe that ordinary people will leave the theatre bent on imitating such behaviour, or admiring it. The moral tone of Wycherley and certainly that of later dramatists such as Congreve is close enough to that of, say, Marlowe or Webster, when good is known to be good, and bad, bad. Formerly critics were also demanding why Autolycus of *The Winter's Tale* by Shakespeare did not receive his well-merited prison sentence.

It is however true that characters serving as gauges for virtue, such as Harcourt and Alithea, tend to be overshadowed in vigour and interest by rascals such as Pinchwife or those that fall into (albeit enforced) error, such as his wife.

Congreve – The Way of the World (1700)
(See also p. 100)

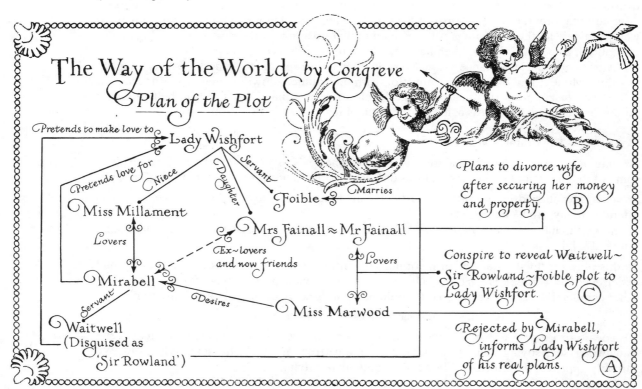

Notes:

(*A*) Warned of Mirabell's true desires; Lady Wishfort witholds her niece's inheritance.

(*B*) This plan fails when Mr Fainall's and Miss Marwood's relationship is discovered; and when deeds are produced which prove that all Mrs Fainall's money has been transferred before her marriage, to Mirabell.

(*C*) Lady Wishfort withdraws her opposition to her neice's marriage to Mirabell, when all Mr Fainall's threats are withdrawn.

Manly Wycherley, the most robust and biting of the Restoration dramatists, was far surpassed by Congreve in plot organization and effectiveness of dialogue. Violence gives way to more subtle satire, and Etherege's admiration of profligacy, to a firmer standard of morality. Congreve's masterpiece is *The Way of the World*, though in his time *Love for Love* was more of a success.

The Way of the World, like many plays of the period, has a highly complex plot. Opposite is a diagrammatic representation of it. You may find it useful to prepare such diagrams as 'aides memoires' for the plays and novels you are studying.

Mirabell, the 'hero' of *The Way of the World*, is a hero with a difference: he is not a saint, because of his past affairs; he takes easily to intrigue, and clearly the loss of his loved one's fortune is important to him – his first concern is to recover it. Yet he has warmth, magnanimity and a fine recklessness in his courtship of Millamant. There is none of the old lust in their relationship: they desire to be justified and their playful intrigues are a form of self-protection. This attitude operates even against each other, as in the wonderful 'proviso' or 'bargain scene' (see p. 100) in which each has to promise the other not to behave as man and wife once they are married, if they are to agree to marry. This is a fairly well-worn convention, but the manner in which Congreve handles it surpasses all other examples. The wit is of the older Comedy of Manners; the serious intention to marry looks forward to the comedy of sentiment (see below).

The style of the play has great variety: it is particularly skilled in giving an individual voice to each character, completely suited to that character, and varying according to circumstances. Here is Lady Wishfort being coy and assuming arch airs with her supposed suitor Sir Rowland, actually Mirabell's servant Waitwell:

> 'You must not attribute my yielding to any sinister appetite, or Indigestion of Widowhood; Nor Impute my Complacency to any Lethargy of Continence – I Hope you do not think me prone to any iteration of Nuptials'

where Malapropism is surpassed by such pretentiousness.

Compare this with the fishwife aspect of Lady Wishfort driving away her maid, Foible, on the discovery of her plot with Waitwell:

> 'Out of my house, out of my house, thou viper, thou serpent, that I have fostered! thou bosom traitress, that I raised from nothing! – be gone, begone, begone, go go! – that I took from washing of old gauze and wearing of dead hair, with a bleak blue nose, over a chafing dish of starved embers, and dining behind a traverse rag in a shop no bigger than a bird-cage, – go, go, starve again, do, do!'

Both these manners are in character and the persons of the play are brought to life by such expert mimicry of speech-tone.

In his dedication to the play, Congreve, after saying that it was not dramatically interesting to portray pure fools, since one can only pity them, goes on, 'This reflection moved me to design some characters, which should appear ridiculous not so much through a natural folly . . . as through an affected wit which at the same time that it is affected, is also false.' This definition only perfectly fits Witwoud, whom, Congreve complains, the audience actually mistook to be genuinely witty. It is interesting here to note Pope's comment, 'Tell me if Congreve's fools be fools indeed.'

(On p. 101 there is a commentary on the important 'bargain' scene where Mirabell proposes to Millamant.)

Goldsmith and Sheridan – The comedy of manners revived

A more sober social morality silenced the genius of Congreve and his fellow dramatists. Perhaps as a reaction against Restoration Comedy, sentiment became more admired than wit, and licentiousness and blasphemy in drama were condemned. There followed a period where the dramatic vogue was for the 'sentimental comedy'. 'Sentiment' at this time implied the solemn and rather pious communication of morality and correct emotion – temperance and wisdom rather than light-hearted gaiety.

The true brilliance of the 'comedy of manners' was revived with Goldsmith and Sheridan and A-level questions sometimes refer to the view that their plays were meant to be 'anti-sentimental'.

Goldsmith describes the sentimental comedy thus, 'the virtues of private life are exhibited, rather than the vices exposed, and the distresses rather than the frailty of mankind'. There are residual elements of the sentimental comedy in his play *She Stoops to Conquer* (1773). This play looks back to Shakespeare's romantic comedy and the exercise of pure humour rather than wit.

In the Prologue to *The Rivals* (1775), Sheridan asks whether we should expect the spirit of Comedy to preach. The reference to the genteel comedy of the time is obvious.

> 'Look on her well – does she seem form'd to teach?
> Should you expect to hear this lady preach?
> Is grey experience suited to her youth?
> Do solemn sentiments become that mouth?'

Sheridan's plays are much closer to the 'comedy of manners' tradition than to the sentimental comedy. He exploited the popular taste of his day for spectacle. *The School of Scandal* (1777) has a succession of well-managed and often spectacular scenes such as the visually effective 'screen' scene, which from the usual reaction of the audience might be called the 'scream' scene.

THE MODERN PERIOD

'I can hardly form an estimate of a play merely by reading it' Chekhov once wrote, and this is probably nowhere more true than in modern plays. Where we do not have to study to understand the language or the social milieu, there is every reason for seeing the play performed and judging its impact in performance.

GB Shaw (1856–1950), with special reference to Saint Joan

Introduction

It is paradoxical that while, from the beginning of the eighteenth to the end of the nineteenth century the theatre grew and prospered as popular entertainment, few of the multitude of plays written during this period have found a place in the first rank of English drama. Certainly, apart from the comedies of Sheridan, they are unlikely to figure in A-level syllabuses.

The appearance of George Bernard Shaw as a new dramatist in the 1890's may be considered – certainly was considered by Shaw himself! – to have saved the English theatre from becoming merely a trivial amusement. Certainly, he dominated the stage during the first 30 years of this century. Shaw's earliest plays reveal a concern with social issues which, although his touch became lighter, he never lost. Indeed, he ostentatiously enjoys parading his didactic intentions; but he persuaded the theatre-goers to absorb, and indeed relish, long discussions of, for example, the 'Irish Question' (in *John Bull's Other Island,* 1904) or medical ethics (in *The Doctor's Dilemma,* 1906) by being enormously entertaining. Strongly outlined characterization, sometimes verging on caricature, highly absurd – not to say farcical – situations, and a splendid fluency and wit distributed impartially among nearly all his characters, ensure that a Shaw play hardly ever fails to hold even a juvenile audience. Moreover, Shaw writes for the reader as well as the spectator; and while he is no poet, his prose has at times, especially in *Saint Joan* (1923) an eloquence that is undeniably poetic in style and feeling.

Several of Shaw's plays appear regularly on A-level syllabuses: *Man and Superman* (see pp. 104–106), *Pygmalion, Arms and the Man* and *Saint Joan.* The last play occurs very frequently and may indeed be his masterpiece, as it combines an intensely serious theme with an adequate historical story for it, excellent dialogue and fine construction. Shaw did not usually trouble much about this last quality; he liked to work through his argument till he was satisfied it was fully aired, and then stop. Shaw himself considered *Back to Methuselah* to be his best play, but this is seldom performed, is very long even to read, and probably appealed to Shaw because it expounds in eloquent terms his final 'gospel': his theory of Creative Evolution and belief in the 'Life Force'.

Shaw's Prefaces

The most obvious way for students to approach the ideas in Shaw's plays is via the Prefaces. Some A-level syllabuses specifically exclude as compulsory study the Preface to a set Shaw play, but they make absorbing reading and are indispensable for those interested in Shaw's ideas.

The Prefaces range far beyond the actual concerns of the plays and to that extent may not be considered directly relevant. However, it is useful to measure the speeches and scenes which crystalize the ideas in the plays, against the points made in the Prefaces. In the Preface to *Major Barbara,* for example, Shaw, having railed against the critics for 'their habit of treating Britain as an intellectual void', attempts to compensate for their 'ignorant credulity' by providing a critique of his own play!

> 'It is this credulity that drives me to help my critics out with *Major Barbara* by telling them what to say about it.'

Nicky Henson and Susan Hampshire – *Arms and the Man* (Thorndike Theatre)

Saint Joan

Every dramatic quality is given masterly expression in *Saint Joan*. Above all it works on the stage. Historical settings for plays of ideas are not out of favour in this century, as other excellent examples fully prove (Bolt's *A Man for All Seasons*; Shaffer's *The Royal Hunt of the Sun*; Eliot's *Murder in the Cathedral* as well as plays by Anouilh and Brecht). As usual with plays historically founded, there is a need to note how far in *Saint Joan* Shaw deviates from and manipulates the actual events: some light can thus be thrown on his special purposes in the theme, and his craftmanship as a playwright. First he had to select the salient episodes from the events of February 1429 to May 1431, and then write appropriate dialogue which also conveys the themes.

No one, not even an historian, can be absolutely sure what historical characters were like; only deductions which do not offend common sense or contradict the evidence may be made. Within his historical framework, Shaw introduces a tremendous variety of characters: English and French, laymen and clerics, the base and noble.

It is sometimes said that Shaw uses his characters merely as mouthpieces for his own ideas. However, *Saint Joan* is a truly dramatic play with characters who are far more than 'dummies' to convey messages. Shaw has a fine sense of dramatic situation and can create a gripping tension of argument in a scene consisting solely of dialogue. An example of this in *Saint Joan* is Act I Sc. 4 – a dialogue between the Earl of Warwick and Bishop Cauchon with occasional explosions by Stogumber.

Sometimes the validity of the Epilogue is questioned and we may ask whether it is fair in modern drama to expect the audicne to accept a living, cheerful ghost, apparently merely for the purpose of rounding off the debate of ideas. But it forms a kind of palinode, like that when Chaucer's Troilus, when killed, returns to shed ironic light on the futility of his sufferings. The justifiable design of Shaw's Epilogue was to establish the permanence of Joan's work and her own immortality. In this way the tragedy is technically almost turned into a comedy: the tone and content of Joan's speeches are as they were: friendly, provincial, simple, full of sense, of a pure integrity, of penetrating vision, above all of irrepressible good humour. The characters each come before Joan and make their excuses, then leave. The ordinary soldier, who gave Joan the cross when she was being burnt at the stake, has the last word which touches on an important theme:

> 'What I say is, you have as good a right to your notions as they (i.e. the captains and bishops and lawyers) have to theirs, and perhaps better.'

Oscar Wilde (1854–1900)

With Wilde, wit, missing for more than a century, returned to the English theatre. In 1892, the same year Shaw's early failure *Widower's Houses* was seen in London, *Lady Windermere's Fan* was produced. That Wilde fully realized how dependent such plays as his are on the qualities of the actors, is revealed by the remark he made in a letter to a newspaper: 'the personality of the actor is often a source of danger in the perfect presentation of a work of art. It may distort. It may lead astray. It may be a discord in the tone or symphony. For anybody can act. Most people in England do nothing else.' He went on, 'The actor's aim is, or should be, to convert his own accidental personality into the real and essential personality of the character he is called upon to personate.'

Whether given superlative actors or not, the thing that made an immediate impact on the audiences of the nineties, and is still fresh now, is the sparkle of the dialogue. Many lines by Wilde are still quoted:

> 'What is a cynic? A man who knows the price of everything and the value of nothing.'
> 'In this world there are two tragedies. One is not getting what one wants, and the other is getting it.'

Margaret Courtnay (as Lady Bracknell) and Barbara Bolton (as Miss Prism), *The Importance of Being Earnest* (Thorndike Theatre).

What makes so many of Wilde's paradoxes arresting is that they are not idle contradictions, but can be justified. In the same way it is an error to suppose that this play and the next two, *A Woman of No Importance* (1893) and *The Importance of Being Earnest* (1895) are mere gossamers of shimmering language spun by lightweight characters. Wilde's characters may sound unserious, even fantastic, but they are founded on types as real as those of the Comedy of Manners and express points of view as worthy of attention. The sustained epigrams should not dazzle us into supposing there is nothing to think about: they would hardly be as effective as they are if they were empty of ideas. The above examples alone demonstrate this, and although Wilde's plots do not work out, as Shaw's are designed to do, a strongly reasoned thesis about the serious concerns of life, they are well enough constructed and true enough to themes of human relationships to be good comedies.

TS Eliot (1888–1965), with special reference to Murder in the Cathedral

In the thirties, after a largely ignored effort by WB Yeats to re-establish poetic drama, Eliot began to produce successful plays in the verse play genre. Two or three of these plays are now classics of the theatre, and *Murder in the Cathedral* is the most commonly set at A Level.

Thomas à Becket is the play's hero, and his heroic status is unusual. Many tragic heroes' deaths are forms of martyrdom, Becket's actually is one, but his willing acceptance of, indeed triumph in his death makes one wonder if he attains tragic dimensions.

The 'Tempters'

The conflict that normally leads to a hero's death is provided in this play by the four 'Tempters' whose rising scale of credibility and power dramatically provides the opportunities for Becket to question his course of action. This action is merely to allow himself to be killed – more, contrary to the fourth temptation; – to allow himself to be made a martyr for the *right* reason, that is, for the good of the Church and the glory of God; not for victory in his quarrel with Henry II, nor for future personal glory.

The fact that Becket was once a very worldly and ambitious man, who owed his elevation entirely to Henry's earlier support, helps to create in Becket a more interesting character when the tempters arrive. Not one offers an entirely idle temptation, although the first is little more than a reminder of luxuries and enjoyment long since given up. The next tempter also derives his allure from the past, but with a more serious proposition: to resume power by restoring the damaged relations with the King. The third tempter offers Becket the opportunity of aligning himself with those powerful elements that oppose the King: the feudal nobility. However, this intriguing against the central power, would entail, apart from its innate immorality, the destruction of the order that Becket believes should prevail in the state. The fourth Tempter creates a dramatic surprise by turning out to be Becket himself, underlining the extremely intimate nature of this temptation. His offer is what Becket secretly dreams of: the glory of martyrdom. He knows that the form of death that threatens him will ensure his veneration in Canterbury through all future ages of Christendom. As with the Third Tempter, Becket is shown a vision of the future that attends upon his acceptance. Even more subtle is the further promise of a certain glorious place in Heaven. There seems to be nothing wrong with this, except what Becket is able to perceive: the motive would be wrong, spiritual pride is masked by the temptation. By being willing to reject this apparently God-willed solution, Becket has it restored to him: the purification of the motive makes the attainment possible.

The Chorus

Many questions on this play understandably select the 'Chorus' for special attention. Eliot has had almost obtrusive recourse to the practice and theory of Greek classical tragedy; for example, the machinery of *The Family Reunion* and the preservation of unities in all his plays. The Chorus appears in *The Family Reunion* by way of choric speaking by all the characters present except the hero (a trick which strangely enough may be dramatically very effective). Eliot employs the device of a Chorus in a manner which exceeds its use in Greek tragedy, where it links episodes by commentary such as might be expected by an articulate spectator. Its reactions guide as well as inform the audience's reactions.

In *Murder in the Cathedral* Eliot makes the Chorus an emotional, excitable group of women-citizens of Canterbury. As such they express far more than comment: they try to sway Becket's behaviour, they mourn his absence, they provide emotion for the brooding menace, and the actual horror. Eliot exercises all his great poetic gift on their lines. One feels Eliot was so thoroughly at home in the medium of choral verse, that rather than assume a subordinate position, they appear in a fully functional role with at least equal status to the dialogue. In Part I the Priests scold them for 'immodest babbling', and later Thomas, more compassionately, tells them to be at peace; but the most remarkable and dramatically effective intervention of the Chorus in the action is when they speak antiphonally, or perhaps operatically, as in a trio, with Priests and Tempters. This emotionally heightened passage follows directly on from more extended observations by the three groups, and is followed by a long choric chant expressing dark horror, and a final speech of clear, calm resolution by Becket, to close Part I.

The Chorus also demonstrates that Becket's martyrdom is already doing for the people what Becket has declared that it should: bringing them back to a recognition of God's ways. They virtually turn the play into a modern morality, as well as underline the 'poetic' side of the drama. They also 'fix' moments of the action in the development of the content and reference; for example to open Part II, they are ironically looking towards a happy Spring after Becket's Christmas sermon: there are signs of hope and regeneration; then there are the three agonized sections while Becket is being murdered; finally a *Te Deum* is chanted by them to return the play to its spiritual plane and historical distancing, after the blunt, stylistically modernized prose of the knights.

Plays of the First and Second World Wars

First World War literature still holds a firm position of popularity and perhaps for that reason the admittedly sometimes brilliant but by no means first rate *Journey's End* by RC Sheriff survives on A-level syllabuses. For its dramatic interest, good construction and accurate 'period' dialogue, Willis Hall's *The Long and the Short and the Tall* makes a fitting companion to Sheriff's play. The earlier play is about the strains between officers in a trench before an attack by the enemy; the later (produced 1958) presents a group of NCOs and men in a hut in the Malayan jungle, at the time of the Japanese breakthrough of the Second World War.

Beckett (1906-)

While the examining boards concentrate on the plays of Shaw, and Eliot's *Murder in the Cathedral,* there are a considerable number of other major dramatists whose plays appear on the syllabuses. Samuel Beckett, otherwise neglected by theatre-goers and readers alike, has been represented by *Waiting for Godot, Endgame* and *Happy Days,* plays which also are French Theatre classics, translated by the author into English. *Krapp's Last Tape, All That Fall, Embers* and others deserve equal attention. Beckett is still living and we will no doubt have to wait some time before he receives the proper recognition.

Beckett concentrates his art most single-mindedly on the mystery of existence, the impossibility of making any rational explanation of time, birth or death, the ineffable nature of such matters, in short the essential incommunicability of much of the would-be material of art. Beckett's characters, or 'surrogates' of one character, are especially obsessed by the point or the pointlessness of death, its curiously unreachable nature; and therefore the absurdity and ennui of life: this takes on the character of a quite meaningless 'wait' for the end. One of the several intense frustrations of both character and creator, is the less than satisfactory nature of the medium, words: these tend to be regarded with contempt as outworn secondhand or even false counters of so-called communication: music or perhaps silence may do better; form, design and arrangements of characters or props on the stage; movements and sound effects, all tend to displace words; when used, words are often employed as elements for verbal games or for resonances beyond denotative meaning. Sometimes, as in *Play* or *Not I,* the words dominate the play, but only as pathetic droning or manic re-enactments of futile pasts. Syntax and sentence structures may be shattered, as in the long speech by the otherwise dumb Lucky (*Waiting for Godot*), where the play is early enough to contain some ordinary satire, in the case of Lucky's speech, of the language of academics. This Beckett had earlier satirized in the 'committee' sequence in *Watt.* However, the real point of the satire is, as usual in Beckett, more to do with the inanity of academic endeavour, in common with any other human enterprise. Man is trapped in an inescapable dilemma in Beckett: only God can authenticate life and death, but God, if he exists, has clearly chosen to pretend that he does not, leaving Man stuck in time and space, sometimes trying to pass the time with all sorts of foolish evasions or delusions. Some critics try to read existentialism, or the 'absurd', or even surrealism, into Beckett's work, but he generally eludes such labels. In such a predicament, Man may either weep or laugh; *Waiting for Godot* is described as a 'tragicomedy', and generally the detail, including much of the dialogue, in Beckett's plays is comic in various modes; the world view is intensely tragic. It is a case of laughing at or in spite of unhappiness, which Arsene, as he was leaving Mr Knott's service in *Watt,* said was the purest sort of laugh.

Pinter

Harold Pinter learned a good deal from Beckett, especially in the musical handling of dialogue, humorous effects such as ironic use of slapstick, and the presentation of only one or two characters in an enigmatic situation. Beckett derived his slapstick humour from the early cinema comedians: Buster Keaton, Charlie Chaplin, Laurel and Hardie and the Marx Brothers, but he was the first to adapt it to high drama. Pinter demonstrates that he can write dialogue in the peculiarly lyrical manner of Beckett:

> *Stanley:* How do I know if I know them until I know their names?
> *Meg:* Well . . . he told me, I remember.
> *Stanley:* Well?
> (She thinks).
> *Meg:* Gold – something.
> *Stanley:* Goldsomething?
> *Meg:* Yes. Gold . . .
> *Stanley:* Yes?
> *Meg:* Goldberg.
> *Stanley:* Goldberg?
> *Meg:* That's right. That was one of them.
> (*Stanley sits at table*).
>   Do you know them?
>
>   (*The Birthday Party, 1958*)

Apart from this brilliant play, and the classic *The Caretaker,* Pinter's *The Homecoming* is now an established choice with A-level boards. Under the deceptive surface of absurd or virtually absurd humour, there is in Pinter's plays an undercurrent of horror, violence, menace or tenseness in relationships to the point of destructive eruption. The incompatibility of the old tramp, Davies, and the sinister Mick, in *The Caretaker,* in which normal, recognizable rascality is set against a weird malevolence, provides both the humour and the tension of this play. Similar tensions and menace are present in most of the other plays, as when Meg announces to Stanley in *The Birthday Party* the arrival of the two men who have come for him, and he first indicates to her his mental unbalance by the way he bangs the drum she has given him for a birthday present. The tension mounts in *The Dumb Waiter* as the two criminals await their orders via the dumb waiter. The eruptions, whether verbal or a stage effect, are all the more shocking because half-expected.

Bolt and Schaffer

Robert Bolt's *A Man For All Seasons* is well established as one of the best modern historical dramas. It concerns Sir Thomas More's resistance of King Henry VIII on the grounds of personal conscience, and his consequent death. Another is *The Royal Hunt of the Sun* by Peter Shaffer, an epic type drama based on the events in Spain and the Inca Empire of Peru between 1529 and 1533, the hero, of course, being Francisco Pizarro. The action turns upon the capture by Pizarro and his pathetically small force of the Inca Sun-king, Atahuallpa. The play is notable for its music, spectacle, narrative by the chorus-like Old Martin – in short for an example of 'total theatre' well carried through. One scene is called 'The Mime of the Great Ascent', another, 'The Mime of the Great Massacre', and the play is full of theatrical interest and relevant action. Dramatic irony is achieved by the Narrator, who from the future, and state of wisdom and understanding, views his idealistic young self, as he blindly follows his 'hero' Pizarro, without fully understanding the nature of warfare or conquest.

Note on other modern playwrights

Of John Osborne's plays, *Look Back in Anger, The Entertainer* and *Epitaph for George Dillon* have all appeared on A-level syllabuses. He excels in the eloquent tirade. Other notable modern playwrights include: David Mercer (*Let's Murder Vivaldi*); John Arden (*Sergeant Musgrave's Dance*); John Whiting (*A Penny For a Song*); Tom Stoppard (*Rosencrantz and Guildenstern Are Dead*); John Mortimer (*The Lunch Hour, A Shot in the Park*); Joe Orton (*Loot, What the Butler Saw*). Orton contains many of the elements of modern theatre: black humour, outrageous wit and irreverence (the tradition of Oscar Wilde), violence and savage protest, often of a satirical nature such as that directed against policemen. He shows in his plays a firm grasp of traditional stagecraft and structure.

Many European dramatists of the first order have injected new life into twentieth century drama, and frequently their best plays are translated and staged in this country; these include Ibsen, Tchekov, Alfred Jarry – the father of Absurd drama, Wedekind, Anouilh, Brecht, Pirandello, Giradoux, Max Frisch and Eugene Ionesco, to name but a few of those I most admire. Most of these playwrights have profoundly influenced the course of modern drama and some have been set in A-level exams. One may add to these the Americans and Irish, whose plays are more commonly set than the translated ones. Eugene O'Neill, the American tragedian (*The Emperor Jones, The Iceman Cometh*); Arthur Miller (*The Crucible, The Death of a Salesman* (see p. 106)), and Tennessee Williams (*The Glass Menagerie*) are all noteworthy. Of the Irish drama, you should note particularly great plays written by John Synge (*The Playboy of the Western World*), Sean O'Casey (*The Plough and the Stars, Juno and the Paycock*) and WB Yeats (*The Words upon the Window-pane, Purgatory*).

Besides the leading dramatists of the age, there is a host of lesser lights, many of whom give great pleasure and good service to the playgoing public. There are comedians, farce writers, thriller writers, tragedians, all of which could be cited in A-level answers as examples of various sorts of drama, if known. The field is very wide and there is no need to be exclusive or narrow while the plays are there to be enjoyed in all our many theatres throughout the country.

2 Studying Shakespeare at A Level

William Shakespeare (1564–1616)

INTRODUCTION

All examination boards include questions on the plays of William Shakespeare (1564-1616). Most syllabuses require candidates to study two plays, and, looking at the papers over a number of years, it is quite clear that there is such a thing as an A-level play. Without doubt, the top ten texts (judging by the number of times they have been set) are: *Antony and Cleopatra, Hamlet, Henry IV pt. 2, King Lear, Macbeth, Much Ado About Nothing, The Tempest, Troilus and Cressida, Twelfth Night* and *The Winter's Tale*. Of these, the current 'chart-toppers' are *Antony and Cleopatra, King Lear* and *The Winter's Tale* (having recently displaced *Hamlet* and *Othello*) and *As You Like It* and *Love's Labours Lost* are now being favoured by a number of boards. There are variations. On two occasions the Oxford Local Examination Board have set *The Sonnets* on its optional paper 2 and the Cambridge Local Examination Boàrd has featured *Coriolanus*. Recently the Joint Matriculation Board has set *King Lear, Antony and Cleopatra* and, more unusually, *Henry V, Measure for Measure,* and *Cymbeline* for study.

What we will try to do in this part of the book, dealing with the study of Shakespeare, is to give you a little general advice, a brief outline of Shakespeare's Theatre, the sources used for the stories of some of Shakespeare's plays and some general comments on Shakespeare's use of imagery. This is only the tip of the iceberg. There is much more for you to find out.

We will continue by giving very practical advice on tackling a two-year course of study of a Shakespeare play and go on to discuss general points on settings, poetry, characterization and so on applicable to any Shakespeare play, but with special reference to *The Winter's Tale, Othello, Henry IV pt. I* and *Measure for Measure*. In conclusion, there is a passage from *Hamlet* to show you how you should handle the difficult Shakespearian language and advice on reading examination questions and writing examination answers. There are also four answers to four questions by anonymous examination candidates with commentaries on each of them.

Using the correct text and the correct notes

Make sure that you are studying the play in a form recommended by the Examination Board, i.e. that you have the correct version of the text prescribed by the recommended publisher.

Read any introductory notes on Shakespeare's life, the Elizabethan Theatre, the verse form Shakespeare uses, the historical background to the play, the sources of the play, the characters, and so on.

Use all the textual notes

These may be at the foot or the side of the page, or at the back of the book. They will be numbered – this is the line reference which you will find alongside the text of the play.

Do not ever be tempted to guess at the meaning of the Shakespearian language. Unless you are very familiar already with the study of Shakespeare's plays you ought to treat it almost like a foreign language at first and use all the 'translation aids' you can. Only when you fully understand the meaning can you 'feel' the poetry of the language.

Annotate your text freely. Your teacher would probably prefer you to do this in pencil! Remember this text will be referred to again and again over the two year period and it is for *your use and your benefit.* Do not be lazy when your teacher is explaining the meaning of words and phrases; WRITE THEM IN. Do *not* rely on 'crib notes'. They are no substitute for detailed study of the text.

The Globe Theatre, London

SHAKESPEARE'S THEATRE

Shakespeare spent most of his working life writing plays for the Globe Theatre, which was situated on the South Bank of the Thames at Southwark. The actors and shareholders included Richard Burbage, the tragic actor; Kemp, the comic actor, and Shakespeare himself who was the resident playwright.

We know very little of the theatre itself; what we do know is conjecture as the historical documentation is practically non-existent. It is thought that it was probably shaped like a cylinder, constructed of wood and plaster and on top of it was what looked like a squat wooden tower. Round the inner wall were three tiers of galleries which extended round the sides of the stage and these were the most expensive seats. The top gallery was covered with a roof of thatch. The platform stage was 40 feet in width and surrounded by the audience on three sides, meaning that most of the audience were exposed. On the fourth side was a room called the Tiring House where the prompter sat and costumes, furniture and properties were kept here. This is where the actors made their entrances and exits between the doors, the alcove and the curtain. It is here that Polonius is stabbed by Hamlet as he hides behind the arras and here where Juliet is discovered supposedly dead in bed by her nurse. Higher still was the place where the trumpeter announced the start of a performance and on the very top was the flag which announced the beginning of a play. It depicted Hercules carrying the Globe.

The audience capacity of the theatre was large, about 2,500. The audience itself was made up of a cross-section of social classes including noblemen, tradesmen, serving men and tourists. The theatre audiences were often criticized as unruly by the Puritans, who were particularly scathing of the women in the audience. The Puritans called these women low and like prostitutes 'plying a convenient trade', but as the Puritans never went inside a theatre, these reports could only be heresay, and there is also much contemporary literature which testifies to the audience's sobriety.

The way the theatres were constructed bore direct relation to the way the plays were performed. There was close contact between the actors and the audience as there was no curtain and the audience could touch the actors. The actor could establish personal contact with the audience and could look the audience in the eye during oration and soliloquies, such as Mark Anthony's oration to the Romans in *Julius Caesar*. The acoustics were very good which made the dialogue easy to hear; essential when a play lasted in full 2½ to 2¾ hours.

PLOT IN SHAKESPEARIAN DRAMA

Shakespeare used a wide range of narrative materials for his plays. For his histories and tragedies he used Roman history, legendary British history and contemporary English and Scottish history. For his comedies he used a rich assortment of prose romances, narrative poems and plays ranging from the Roman dramatist, Plautus, to contemporary dramatists of the sixteenth century.

Shakespeare had an insatiable interest in human nature and experience and people's dilemmas and problems. His range of subject is far greater than any comparable contemporary playwright, for instance, Ben Jonson. Shakespeare does not merely transmit, he also creates and discovers dramatic possibilities. He deepens the existing story and makes it more coherent and makes it more about human behaviour. For instance he took the story *The Moor of Venice* by Giraldi Cinthio, which was rather a trivial sordid tale of jealousy and revenge and transformed it into a major tragedy, *Othello*. He transformed *Romeo and Juliet* from a light romance tragedy to a dramatic narrative. He took the famous story of the Trojan war in *Troilus and Cressida* and enriched it by his dialogue. The play never fails in the theatre, though critics cannot decide whether the play is comedy, tragedy or satire.

The tragedy *Antony and Cleopatra* is taken from Plutarch's life of Anthony, but a lot of the events could not be shown on the stage because of their scale – events like the sea battle of Actium. Instead Shakespeare develops a brilliant technique of short scenes which concentrate on behaviour rather than action.

Shakespeare's dramatic form is characterized by being larger than life. For instance the father, Lear, loses his daughter, Cordelia; brother and sister Sebastian and Viola are reunited (*Twelfth Night*); Hamlet's father is murdered by his brother; Leontes, in *The Winter's Tale*, recovers his lost wife. This sense of pushing things to the extreme until the worst happens

Harriet Reynolds (Maria), Colin Starkey (Sir Andrew Aguecheek), Peter Whitbread (Sir Toby Belch)
Twelfth Night (Thorndike Theatre)

heightens the feeling of tragedy. He also invents characters who have no equivalent in the source; for instance Enobarbus in *Antony and Cleopatra,* Queen Margaret in *Richard III,* Mercutio in *Romeo and Juliet* and Lucio in *Measure for Measure.* These extra characters make a significant contribution to the play. Enobarbus is a spokesman for scepticism, irreverence and humour; qualities which enlist audience participation. He creates a sense of reality in the play. In much the same way Lucio contributes to the plot of *Measure for Measure* and Thersites to the plot of *Troilus and Cressida.*

Shakespeare often combines more than one story or plot into his plays, particularly his comedies. In *Twelfth Night* he combines the story of the girl who adopts male disguise (Viola) and he adds the Malvolio story. Shakespeare felt that he needed two actions that were not incongruous, therefore he keeps linking the two plots. Viola is involved in a duel against Sir Andrew Aguecheek, Malvolio acts as a rival to Orsino for Olivia's hand, Feste, the jester, wanders from one household to the other. Shakespeare's preference for two or more stories gives the plays much of their fascination, as we see the intrigues develop.

IMAGERY IN SHAKESPEARIAN DRAMA

To study Shakespeare's imagery was an accepted critical approach in the first half of the twentieth century. Previous to this there had been very little study of imagery which was surprising, as Shakespeare, of all writers, is much given to using imagery. The revival of interest in the imagery of Shakespeare's plays is simultaneous with the interest in the metaphysical poets and is one way, but not the only way, of analysing his works.

An image should always help the reader to understand the writer's work better by describing something in terms of something else (see Glossary). This can take the form of a metaphor or a simile. A writer always uses imagery to achieve vividness. For example, in *Richard III,* when Hastings is proclaimed a traitor and condemned to immediate death, Shakespeare uses the simile of a sailor about to topple into the sea to convey his feelings of dizziness and vertigo.

> *Hastings*
> 'lives like a drunken sailor on a mast
> Ready with every nod to tumble down
> into the fatal bowels of the deep.'

The image of falling here suggests something essential about Hastings' feelings. It is not always easy to decide what an image is doing. In this case it appeals to our visual sense and conveys Hastings' feelings with precision and speed.

Images, therefore, are word pictures which are essentially visual. In *Macbeth,* many of the speeches of the main characters are densely metaphorical. Lady Macbeth, early on in the play at the murder of Duncan, delivers a speech full of imagery.

> 'Come, thick night,
> And pall thee in the dullest smoke of hell
> That my keen knife see not the wound it make
> Nor heaven peep through the blanket of the dark
> To cry, "Hold" "Hold".'

This speech is full of metaphors, 'pall thee in the dullest smoke of hell', 'my keen knife see not the wound it makes', 'nor heaven peep through the blanket of the dark'. None of these metaphors requires any great effort on our part to picture the processes involved; the metaphors are bold enough. When Macbeth describes the murder of Duncan he talks of

> 'his gashed stabs looked like a breach in nature
> For ruin's wasteful entrance.'

This metaphor evokes the destruction of the entire universe and allows chaos and ruin to rush in and upset the natural order of nature. This violent imagery stimulates us and startles us into thought. It makes us entertain possibilities too remote from our experience and gives the dramatist a degree of control over the feelings of his audience.

Paradox is used in *Measure for Measure,* where Claudio is taken to prison for having unlawful sexual intercourse with an unmarried girl. When Lucio asks why he is in chains, he replies, 'From too much liberty, my Lucio, liberty'. He has been too free, so now he has lost his freedom.

Troilus and Cressida contains a whole stream of metaphors. One example of this is Ulysses' speech on time in which Ulysses tries to describe the way in which time is only interested in present achievements and tries to forget what human beings have achieved.

> 'For time is like a fashionable host
> That slightly shakes his parting guest by the hand
> And with his arms outstretched as he would fly
> Grasps in the comer: welcome ever smiles
> And farewell goes out sighing.'

Imagery criticism is not as important now in literary criticism as it used to be. It is just one of the aspects of the larger study of Shakespeare's language and style. However, it can be very rewarding to read one of the published studies on Shakespeare's imagery such as that by C. Spurgeon (*Shakespeare's Imagery*, 1935).

A SUGGESTED APPROACH TO A TWO-YEAR STUDY OF A SHAKESPEARE PLAY

First Year

Experience the play as a whole before you begin the study to see *how* Shakespeare achieved his effects. The best way, of course, is to see a good production but, failing this, a film or television video. For instance in the Autumn of 1982, two excellent productions of *King Lear* were shown – one at the Royal Shakespeare Theatre at Stratford and one on BBC television. Schools and colleges often have video facilities, so that a tape of a play can be used over and over again. It can also be switched off and discussed, and thus is a most versatile visual aid. A record or tape can be used in a similar way, or you can stage a play-reading with fellow students, but one does miss the visual stimulus. In all of these ways, dramatic experience will precede dramatic analysis. (See also pp. 161-4.)

Then begin by looking at the overall structure of the play and the dramatic movements within the play; for instance the importance of the opening scene, the dramatic excitement, the main issues and protagonists clearly established, the early impressions of character (remembering that characters may well develop during the course of a play), the dramatic climaxes and how Shakespeare handles the build-up and any subsequent anti-climaxes. Such structure can sometimes be rendered in the form of a chart or graph summarizing the narrative sequence of the play and the peaks of the action.

Some knowledge of other Shakepeare plays of a similar kind is useful in Year 1. This can be achieved by play reading in class or video sessions. Similar plays could be linked together – for instance *Macbeth* with *Othello* and *The Tempest* with *The Winter's Tale*.

Then move to study the play noticing some of the topics already mentioned, paying particular attention to *how* things happen as well as to *what* happens. Always refer back to the text to illustrate points. A series of notes with cross references to Act, Scene and Line are very useful here. Short, relevant quotations are better than long, memorized speeches which prove nothing except that they have been memorized.

Second year and revision

Re-work and re-read your notes and essays and re-read the play. *Keep asking yourself questions.* For instance, if you are studying *Othello,* you may ask why is Cassio in the play? Why does Shakespeare give him the kind of character he does? Why does Desdemona go to such lengths to help him?

> 'He hath a daily beauty in his life
> that makes me ugly.'

Is this an important comment by Iago about Cassio? What does it tell us about both men? *Always go back to the text to* answer any of these questions.

Use of critics

Use critics who provide useful background information, but be careful of the way-out opinion designed mainly to show how clever the critic is and to find something new (however outrageous). It is useful to know such criticism exists, but it is dangerous to follow it slavishly and to reproduce it as if it were your own. You may well have only half understood a complicated or tortuous argument.

Go back to the central issues such as the two-play structure of *The Winter's Tale* and ensure that you are thinking clearly about them and that you have appropriate textual references to support your views. Establish your own key words as memory links but, above all, know the play and *do not* try to devise an all-purpose answer suitable for all questions. This leads to the slightly off-focus answer that creates so many problems for examiners. *If you know the play well and understand the basic issues there is nothing that an examiner can ask that you will be unable to answer.*

THE STUDY OF OTHELLO AND THE WINTER'S TALE
(NB, these are general points, applicable to any plays)

Detailed study implies close study, but do not get too involved in textual detail that you lose the wood for the trees. Always see any speech in the context of the play as a whole.
Useful divisions for study (there may be others):

(a) Language – understand the difficulties. Always make sure that you know the basic meaning, using footnotes from the text. The Associated Examining Board and others test this knowledge by the use of italicized phrases in extracts.

(b) Poetry – understand the function of dramatic verse and the nature of the poetry Shakespeare uses. For instance he uses poetry to build up character and the facets of character in *Othello*. In *The Winter's Tale* we see the tortured, broken syntax of the jealousy-ridden Leontes and the different rhythms and imagery in Act IV of the same play. Therefore you need to consider the function of poetry in the plays. Does it interfere with the action in such plays as *Richard II* or *Romeo and Juliet* or does it enhance it?

(c) Dramatic structure – The limitations and opportunities of drama imposing their own restrictions. You should note the particular features of structure for individual plays; for instance the double time scheme and dramatic compression of *Othello*, the two-part structure of *The Winter's Tale* and the usefulness of comparing *The Winter's Tale* with *The Tempest* where the dramatist faces similar problems, but solves them in different ways.

(d) Character – Always, character relates to dramatic function and importance. The 'psychological character study' can be more hindrance than help to a candidate. A play is not a psychological novel though many candidates approach it as if it were. Thus Leontes' immediate jealousy is a dramatic necessity in *The Winter's Tale* and has to be dramatically convincing. The rapidity of Othello's jealousy has to be dramatically as well as psychologically prepared for. Certain traits indicated in Othello's character, position, status and situation make it psychologically credible, but it has to be rapid because of dramatic necessity.

The Winter's Tale (Act II Sc. 3)

(e) Relationship of character to plot – This is linked with section (d) on character but this relationship is of particular importance with such a character as Iago, who begins by controlling the plot, but later becomes controlled by it, in that events move away from him, and also with reference to the character of Cassio. Candidates should always consider the dramatic importance of any character and his role in the play. For instance, why bring Autolycus into *The Winter's Tale?*

(f) How the dramatist creates character – The word 'how' is often ignored in A-level study.

The dramatist creates characters by the following means:

1 the style in which they speak.
2 how they respond to events.
3 if and how they initiate action.
4 what others say about them (bearing in mind the nature and circumstances of those who speak).

and – important – *the relationship between characters* – what such relationships contribute dramatically and what they tell us about each character, e.g. Iago and Emilia, Cassio and Desdemona, Iago and Roderigo as well as the obvious Othello/Desdemona, Iago/Othello relationships, parents/children, Hermione/Paulina and Florizel/Perdita relationships.

Study the permutations of these relationships within a play. The characters will show different aspects in different situations and in different company. But this will always be for a common dramatic purpose.

(g) Theme – A play will be *about* something – but be careful not to over-simplify and force the play into an over-neat box, e.g. *Othello* – jealousy theme, *Macbeth* – ambition, *Hamlet* – delay, *The Winter's Tale* – forgiveness. The plays, of course, contain such themes, but they are more than this. Look for unifying themes, dramatically handled in a play but always go back to the text to see *how* these are worked out in dramatic terms – the interplay of character with character and character with event.

STUDY NOTES ON HENRY IV PT I AND MEASURE FOR MEASURE

First year of study – Henry IV pt I

There are two basic points in the study of Shakespeare, which are applicable to all his plays.

1 The play must be seen as a product of its age, reflecting contemporary ideas, assumptions and so on.
2 It must be judged as drama – poetic drama if you will – and not by other criteria.

(a) Sources

Students must be familiar with the basic historical facts, such as how events are linked with the deposition and death of Richard II. There is no need to go into great detail – any decent edition will supply all that is needful.

Note, however, that this is not a 'plodding' chronicle play, but a product of a creative shaping imagination. The whole Falstaff comedy derived from a few links, Sir John Oldcastle, the Prince's tutor, gossips in his chronicles about the Prince's riotous youth. Shakespeare has also re-shaped 'serious' history to heighten the rivalry between the Prince and Hotspur, making them of an age and bringing them face to face at the Shrewsbury fight. In his tavern scenes Shakespeare conveys the local colour and low life of London at the time.

(b) Events and structure

If you form a clear picture of the sequence of events in the play this should lead to an appreciation of the skill with which comedy and serious matters are balanced, alternated and linked e.g. through the role of the Prince in both worlds, introducing discussions of affairs of state into comic scenes, sending Falstaff to the wars.

(c) Nature of the action

There is plenty of entertaining physical action for the benefit of the simpler spectators – the comic Gadshill robbery, the clowning and play acting at the Boar's Head, the ever popular battle scenes; *but* in fact most of the play's action is on an intellectual plane with debates at a serious level, which are sometimes passionate. Examples of these debates are: the King *v* the Percies, King *v* Prince, Percies between themselves, rebel leaders' summit conference in Act III, Hotspur *v* Blunt and Worcester *v* King. Even the repartee between the Prince and Falstaff is contention of an intellectual kind.

(d) Pattern of relationships

A close study and analysis will reveal a complex and shifting pattern of relationships in which people are seen in many different aspects.

King v Worcester – these are political enemies, but both are essentially the same types – calculating political men.

King v Prince – the King is careful and troubled, but conscience stricken and genuinely concerned for England's welfare and is a worried father. The Prince is seemingly dissipated and careless and not shaping well for the crown.

Ideas of honour – Hotspur is a man of action who has Quixotic notions of honour. The Prince seeks the substance of honour, not outward show. Falstaff presents a negation of honour 'a mere scutcheon' – he perhaps is the realist? He is a corruptor of youth but is also a self-deceiver and is deceived by the Prince, who is outwardly a 'good boy' and apt pupil but is really cold-blooded and master of his relationship, 'I know you all,' and predicts his rejection of Falstaff 'I do, I will'. He is a true son of his father.

Second year of study

A further study, perhaps in the second year, should concentrate on the following areas:

(a) The moral, political and intellectual background. The second-year student should explore more deeply the significance of contemporary history to Shakespeare's age. There was keen contemporary interest in the period between the reigns of Richard II and Henry VII as is found in Hall and Holinshead, Hayward's *History of Henry IV, Mirror for Magistrates,* Daniel's *Civil Wars* and the censoring of Shakespeare's *Richard II.* The Tudor audience believed in the repeated pattern of events and the moral and political lessons to be learned from history. They were very patriotic and had a horror of civil war and social confusion. There is much pre-occupation with the nature of kingship, with the Divine Right of Kings, with sinfulness of rebellion (as inculcated in the 'Book of Homilies' especially 'Against Disobedience and Wilful Rebellion'). The 'Tudor Myth' was the approved version of events in the fifteenth century, in which England's troubles began with the deposition and murder of the legitimate Richard II, thence through divine punishment inflicted on Henry IV by constant plots and rebellions, suspended for the virtuous Henry V, breaking out again in the exaggerated calamities of the Wars of the Roses, culminating in the tyranny of Richard III. His death led to the re-establishment of legitimacy with Henry VII, mandated by heaven to restore social order and good government. The best simple source for all this background is still Tillyard's *Shakespeare's History Plays.*

Good Sir John Falstaff

(*b*) *Its place in a cycle. Henry IV pt I* may now be put into context *as part of a cycle* almost certainly conceived in outline as a whole, though it can be argued that it took shape and definite form in Shakespeare's mind as he wrote. Ideally all four plays (*Richard II* to *Henry V*) should be read: certainly *Henry IV pt II*. Note, though, that while Part I contains many pointers to a continuation, for instance Act IV, sc. 4 and the King's final words, it is still a satisfactory dramatic whole, given unity by the theme of the education of a prince, largely dependent on the Prince/Hotspur rivalry brought to a decisive end at Shrewsbury.

(*c*) *The ironies and resonances* in the play can now be more completely appreciated, for instance King Henry was originally a usurper, but speaks always as a lawful king – 'Thus ever did rebellion find rebuke'. Shakespeare does not make him amiable, though he has a human side, but respects him for his evident desire to preserve the peace and unity of the realm. He is at least King *de facto* and more deserving of support than a crew of magnates who never advance any reason for rebellion outside family and individual grievances and ambition. Consider how an Elizabethan audience's sympathies would be influenced by Act III Sc. 1 with its cool discussion of the division of the Kingdom – the temperature rises when the details are called in question!

(*d*) *Education of a prince* – arguably the main theme. By moving in London low life Hal learns the characters of his future subjects, cultivates tricks of accessibility and the common touch (a Tudor speciality) which serves him well before Agincourt. A certain calculating Machiavellianism in rulers was expected, tacitly applauded, as necessary to their prime duty to maintain order and good government. Note Worcester's lecture to Hotspur in Act III Sc. 1 about losing men's hearts by arrogance and its bearing on the Prince's behaviour.

(*e*) *The characterization* can now be considered in depth and its richness and complexity appreciated especially Falstaff and his many aspects, *miles gloriosus,* fool and jester, butt, wit, adventurer, spirit of unfading youth and serving the Morality play function of a Tempter.

(*f*) *The range and variety of language* – a most important topic, requiring really good first-hand knowledge of the text and the ability to quote accurately, though with relevance and discretion.
Verse
(*i*) Shakespeare's 'official' style – dignified, regular, as in the King's long speeches in Act III Sc. 2

> 'By being seldom seen, I could not stir
> But, like a comet, I was wondered at;
> That men would tell their children, 'This is he!'
> Others would say, 'Where? Which is Bolingbroke?'
> And then I stole all courtesy from heaven,
> And dressed myself in such humility
> That I did pluck allegiance from men's hearts,
> Loud shouts and salutations from their mouths
> Even in the presence of the crowned King.
> Thus did I keep my person fresh and new,
> My presence, like a robe pontifical,
> Ne'er seen but wondered at; and so my state,
> Seldom but sumptuous, showed like a feast
> And won by rareness such solemnity.
> The skipping King, he ambled up and down
> With shallow jesters and rash bavin wits,
> Soon kindled and soon burnt; carded his state;
> Mingled his royalty with cap'ring fools;
> Had his great name profanèd with their scorns
> And gave his countenance against his name,
> To laugh at gibing boys, and stand the push
> Of every beardless vain comparative;
> Grew a companion to the common streets,
> Enfeoffed himself to popularity;
> That, being daily swallowed by men's eyes,
> They surfeited with honey and began
> To loathe the taste of sweetness, whereof a little
> More than a little is by much too much.
> So, when he had occasion to be seen,
> He was but as the cuckoo is in June,
> Heard, not regarded; seen, but with such eyes

As, sick and blunted with community,
Afford no extraordinary gaze,
Such as is bent on sunlike majesty
When it shines seldom in admiring eyes;
But rather drowsed and hung their eyelids down,
Slept in his face, and rendered such aspect
As cloudy men use to their adversaries,
Being with his presence glutted, gorged, and full.
And in that very line, Harry, standest thou;
For thou has lost thy princely privilege
With vile participation. Not an eye
But is aweary of thy common sight,
Save mine, which hath desired to see thee more;
Which now doth that I would not have it do –
Make blind itself with foolish tenderness.'

(*ii*) The freer, more 'racy' style, especially in Hotspur's lines, e.g. the 'popinjay' speech in Act I
Sc. 3.

'My liege, I did deny no prisoners.
But I remember, when the fight was done,
When I was dry with rage and extreme toil,
Breathless and faint, leaning upon my sword,
Came there a certain lord, neat and trimly dressed,
Fresh as a bridegroom, and his chin new reaped
Showed like a stubble land at harvest home.
He was perfumed like a milliner,
And 'twixt his finger and his thumb he held
A pouncet-box, which ever and anon
He gave his nose, and took't away again –
Who therewith angry, when it next came there,
Took it in snuff – and still he smiled and talked;
And as the soldiers bore dead bodies by,
He called them untaught knaves, unmannerly,
To bring a slovenly unhandsome corse
Betwixt the wind and his nobility.
With many holiday and lady terms
He questioned me, amongst the rest demanded
My prisoners in your Majesty's behalf.
I then, all smarting with my wounds being cold,
To be so pestered with a popinjay
Out of my grief and my impatience
Answered neglectingly, I know not what –
He should, or he should not; for he made me mad
To see him shine so brisk, and smell so sweet,
And talk so like a waiting-gentlewoman
Of guns and drums and wounds – God save the mark! –
And telling me the sovereignest thing on earth
Was parmacity for an inward bruise,
And that it was great pity, so it was,
This villainous saltpetre should be digged
Out of the bowels of the harmless earth,
Which many a good tall fellow had destroyed
So cowardly and but for these vile guns,
He would himself have been a soldier.
This bald unjointed chat of his, my lord,
I answered indirectly, as I said,
And I beseech you, let not his report
Come current for an accusation
Betwixt my love and your high Majesty.'

(*iii*) A lyrical, romantic exuberance, as in the speeches of Glendower and Mortimer in Act III
Sc. 1 or Vernon's description of the Prince in Act IV Sc. 1.

Prose

 (*i*) The splendid everyday conversation of the carters in Act II Sc. I.

(*ii*) The inventive rhetoric of abuse in the slanging match between the Prince and Falstaff in
       Act II Sc. 4.

Prince What's the matter?

Falstaff What's the matter? There be four of us here have ta'en a thousand pound this day morning.

Prince Where is it, Jack, where is it?

Falstaff Where is it? Taken from us it is. A hundred upon poor four of us!

Prince What, a hundred, man?

Falstaff I am a rogue if I were not at half-sword with a dozen of them two hours together. I have scaped by miracle. I am eight times thrust through the doublet, four through the hose; my buckler cut through and through; my sword hacked like a handsaw – ecce signum! I never dealt better since I was a man. All would not do. A plague of all cowards! Let them speak. If they speak more or less than truth, they are villains and the sons of darkness.

Prince Speak, sirs. How was it?

Gadshill We four set upon some dozen –

Falstaff Sixteen at least, my lord.

Gadshill And bound them.

Peto No, no, they were not bound.

Falstaff You rogue, they were bound, every man of them, or I am a Jew else – an Ebrew Jew.

Gadshill As we were sharing, some six or seven fresh men set upon us.

Falstaff And unbound the rest, and then come in the other.

Prince What, fought you with them all?

Falstaff All? I know not what you call all, but if I fought not with fifty of them I am a bunch of radish! If there were not two or three and fifty upon poor old Jack, then am I no two-legged creature.

(*iii*) The parody of euphuism by Falstaff in Act II Sc. 4.

(*iv*) The witty repartee (it must be allowed that this has dated).

(*v*) The sustained rhythmical flight of Falstaff's major speeches.

Falstaff and Doll Tear-Shelt in the Boar's Head Tavern (Henry IV Part II, Act II sc. 4)

Flora Robson as Isabella, *Measure for Measure*
(Old Vic 3rd Dec. 1933)

Measure for Measure

Since more than one play by Shakespeare is usually prescribed for A-level study, it is often useful to be able to make comparisons between them.

(*a*) *General points* No historical background of the kind needed for *Henry IV pt I* is involved here and the sources of the story are of rather vestigial interest. It is perhaps a play of which more can be taken in at a first reading, though it is hardly necessary to say that it cannot be fully understood without an awareness from the outset of its moral and religious assumptions. Further study as the exam approaches should be directed to deepening this awareness and noting how these assumptions are illustrated in the play.

(*b*) *Position in the canon of Shakespeare's works* It was written in 1604 (later than the histories) not long after *Hamlet,* with whose moral and religious background it has affinities. Therefore, in the middle of the tragic period, it belongs with the other so-called 'problem' plays. Why so called? Not just because they pose ethical problems, though they certainly do, but also because it is difficult to fit them into any neat category. *Measure for Measure* may be considered a 'comedy' in the sense that, after intrigue and confusion all is cleared up and ends with wedding bells (like *All's Well That Ends Well),* though not *Troilus and Cressida.* But the road to the happy ending is not, as in, say *Twelfth Night,* in itself a particularly merry one. The play is pervaded by satire and cynicism. Its view of life, while allowing that there is good in human nature, is often pessimistic, approaching tragic, but without the elevation of feeling and tone that redeems the tragedies from the sourness.

(*c*) *Structure* The play is simpler than *Henry IV pt I.* The low-life scenes have hardly any bearing on the main action and exist chiefly to illustrate the depravity of 'Vienna' and the disregard of law, as well as providing something for the groundlings to guffaw at. Lucio serves as a 'link' character with the weightier matter, but does not measure up to Falstaff in any sense. Once the sequence of events is firmly grasped, it will be seen that the action develops in a straightforward 'linear' fashion with successive crises clearly identified. Note how tension is maintained by the unexpected twist given to events by Angelo ordering Claudio's immediate execution. Also in Act V we know Angelo is going to be unmasked. He repeatedly avoids exposure; we wonder just how and when it will come.

(*d*) *Atmosphere and ideology* The play's institutions and morality are nominally Catholic – may be largely for dramatic convenience – nunneries and friar's hoods are useful for practical purposes. Claudio's apparent belief in the doctrine of Purgatory (as in *Hamlet*) adds force to his fear of death. On the other hand, the acceptability of the bed-trick (as in *All's Well That Ends Well*) to a supposedly severe moralist and near nun-like Isabella has been questioned. Death for fornication smacks more of Calvin's Geneva than any Catholic state and the Duke's impersonation of a friar, purporting to confess and give absolution is surely a mortal sin. In all this, Shakespeare probably reflects the state of mind of many contemporaries who had a considerable hangover of ideas from pre-Reformation times.

The play, of course, is constructed around sexual behaviour and motives, which make it very different from *Henry IV pt I* and links it with *Hamlet, Othello* and very much to *Lear*, especially in its concentration on the sleazier physical aspects. There is an obsession with female virginity which may seem strange to many young people today. The brothel-life of *Measure for Measure*, the jokes about venereal diseases are more brutal than anything in the *Henry IV* plays. The prison scenes are also very typical of Shakespeare's age in the mixture of brutality with easy-going informality.

(*e*) *Characterization* presents difficulties, especially with the Duke and Isabella. The Duke, despite individual touches such as a dislike of popularity which he shared with James I, is more of a symbol than an individual. What looks like his personal busy-bodying must be related to that preoccupation with the position and duties of a ruler already noted in relation to Prince Hal. In a hierarchical society, thought of as reflecting universal order, the ruler is the counterpart of God; his highest duty to incarnate and dispense justice. The Duke puts himself into disguise so that, like God, he may see into men's hearts and so do perfect justice, tempered with mercy, at the end. It looks like an almost malicious cat-and-mouse game; spinning out Claudio's and Isabella's distress and letting Angelo think he is going to get away with his misdeeds, may be compared with the mysterious ways of God to man. Heaven punishes the bad and proves the best. But the suggestion that the Duke is almost a representation of God must not be pressed too far; after all, if he didn't behave as he does there would be no play.

Isabella is an ambiguous character. Apart from her connivance in the bed-trick already mentioned, 'the lady doth protest her chastity too much'. Note how readily she hurries off to virtuous sheets at the end; we hear no more of her vocation to a nunnery.

Angelo is in many ways more credible, as a picture of the man who has but slenderly known himself, having never before been tempted. He incarnates the old theme of the punishment of 'hubris' without becoming in any way a lay figure and enables Shakespeare to satirize the abuse of power.

The other main characters – Lucio, Claudio, Pompey – are more 'natural' though Lucio is a mass of contradictions. He is cynical and debauched, a liar and a slanderer who shops his associates for no apparent reason, seems genuinely fond of Claudio and does what he can to help him.

(*f*) *The play as Art rather than Nature* Even this brief run-through of the characters shows that they are much less easy to grasp than those in a play like *Henry IV pt I*. To a large extent 'natural' behaviour is subordinated to the demand of the fable. The same point can be made about many of the situations and events. Isabella is just about to take the veil when she is recalled to contend with the Flesh and the Devil. Her calling as a nun seems rather a patent device to heighten the interest of her situation. The parallels between the Claudio/Juliet and Angelo/Mariana relationships seem a remarkably happy coincidence (though the impediment to each marriage is one typical of the age – a matter of dowry). Angelo heaps damnation on himself in a very obvious way from the beginning – as soon as he utters

> 'When I, that censure him, do so offend
> Let mine own judgement pattern out my death
> and nothing come in partial'

Act II Sc. 1 – we can hear the Infernal Machine creaking into action, the bed-trick substitution seems improbable even if all cats are grey in the dark; the convenient death of Ragozine and his resemblance to Claudio are almost perfunctory solutions to the problem of avoiding violent death in a comedy. *But* we are not meant to apply the test of 'could it all really have happened?' Take account of these improbabilities, by all means, but recognize that the play is a kind of fable in which they are to be accepted to heighten dramatic impact and underline moral issues.

(*g*) *Language* As always, the power of Shakespeare's language carries us along and suspends our disbelief. In *Measure for Measure* his verse has developed a range beyond that of *Henry IV pt I*. We still have, of course, his 'official' style which the Duke employs to explain his actions or to preach resignation; but Claudio's 'Ay, but to die and go we know not where', is very reminiscent of *Hamlet*. The flexible and superbly articulated style of the two great debates between Angelo and Isabella, touching matters far deeper than anything in *Henry IV pt I* and Angelo's self-probing soliloquies, with their blend of passion and reasoning, take us into the world of the great tragedies. On the other hand, apart from Lucio's witty sallies in the 'smart young man' vein, the prose is rather undistinguished. The comic malapropisms of Elbow (like the other character, Dogberry) and the vulgar loquacity of Pompey (who is given his name so that jokes may be made about it) are unambitious popular stuff. Much of the prose is devoted to giving practical information e.g. for the bed-trick and the description of Angelo.

ANALYSIS AND COMMENTARY

The following passage should help you analyse the difficult language of Shakespeare's plays. Although there is probably far more detail here than you would need in an examination answer, if you absorb most of the information you will give yourself a good chance of giving the examiner what he is looking for.

Hamlet, Act I, Sc. IV, lines 23-38

(Hamlet's father, the King of Denmark, has recently died and been succeeded by his brother Claudius, who has married the widowed Queen, Hamlet's mother. Much grieved by these events, Hamlet has been further distressed by learning that his father's ghost has appeared to the sentries on the ramparts of the castle of Elsinore.)

> 1 So, oft it chances in particular men,
> That, for some vicious mole of nature in them,
> As, in their birth, – wherein they are not guilty,
> Since nature cannot choose his origin, –
> 5 By the o'ergrowth of some complexion,
> Oft breaking down the pales and forts of reason,
> Or by some habit that too much o'er-leavens
> The form of plausive manners; that these men,
> Carrying, I say, the stamp of one defect,
> 10 Being nature's livery, or fortune's star,
> Their virtues else, be they as pure as grace,
> As infinite as man may undergo,
> Shall in the general censure take corruption
> From that particular fault: the dram of evil
> 15 Doth all the noble substance of a doubt,
> To his own scandal.

(*a*) *Context* It is night. Hamlet is keeping watch with the soldiers to see if the ghost will appear again. There has just been a burst of noisy revelry from the castle hall where the King 'drains his draughts of Rhenish down'. Hamlet remarks to his friend Horatio that this Danish delight in drinking is a fault which tarnishes the country's reputation, and goes on to speak the lines above. Immediately afterwards the ghost appears.

(*b*) *Meaning and expression* The whole passage is an extended comparison in which the speaker draws a parallel between the consequences of a defect in national character and of one in individuals ('particular men'). The language makes considerable use of metaphor. The weakness, of whatever kind, is compared with a physical blemish (a 'mole'), and the first example we are given is illegitimacy, for which, as Hamlet charitably observes, the bastard child is not responsible – he 'cannot choose his origin'. (Note here our ancestors' view of bastardy as an indelible taint, very possibly fitting one to play a villain's part – think of Edmund in *King Lear*, or Don John in *Much Ado About Nothing*.) Next comes disturbance of the mind. Here the individual's sanity is compared with a beseiged garrison protected by palisades ('pales') and fortifications set up by reason, but battered down by a combination of physical and temperamental factors ('complexion') grown too strong to resist. Lastly comes outward eccentricity, working too powerfully ('o'er-leavens' – like too much yeast producing excessive fermentation) on a normally pleasing ('plausive') manner and behaviour. Here we can see reflected the preoccupation of Shakespeare's age, especially in the drama, with 'humour', i.e., extreme oddity of

David Warner as Hamlet, Prince of Denmark

dress, behaviour, and ideas arising from an obsessive ruling passion. Any of these defects is stamped on a man as an impression is stamped on a coin; it is like a badge ('livery') bestowed on him by nature as noblemen gave badges to be worn by their servants, or like a star which, according to astrology, controls his life as fate ('fortune') decrees.

We find in these lines a number of words still used in modern English, but with a change of meaning, e.g. 'complexion'. Another example not yet mentioned is 'censure', in line 13, which means, not 'blame', as it always does today, but simply 'judgment' or 'opinion'.

If you have paid some attention – as you should – to what is called 'textual criticism', you will know that lines 14-15 present editors with a considerable difficulty. Some have chosen to follow the version of

'the dram of eale
Doth all the noble substance of a doubt,'

which seems meaningless. 'Eale' is probably a misprint. The version we have printed makes better sense: 'the small drop of evil often quenches ('douts') a man's noble qualities.'
(*Note* Examining Boards generally announce which edition of Shakespeare, and sometimes of other older writers, they will use for setting passage-based questions. You should check that your edition is the same as your Board's, or that you can refer to the nominated edition when textual problems arise.)

The whole of this passage down to 'particular fault' (line 13) is one long sentence. It is not incoherent, but Hamlet does seem to feel the need to remind himself of what he is talking about in

'. . . . that these men,
Carrying, I say, the stamp. . . .'
(lines 8-9)

This slight tendency to ramble and lose one's thread contrasts with, and is possibly restrained by the comparative strictness of the verse. Differing in this respect from Shakespeare's later plays, the lines are fairly regular, although many have an extra syllable which gives variety to the metre, and most of them are end-stopped.

(*c*) *Character* Though Hamlet begins the speech from which these lines are taken by addressing Horatio, it could be argued that in the part of it quoted he is really talking to himself, meditating on an aspect of human life. As we learn elsewhere, though some thirty years old, he has until very lately been a student at the University of Wittenberg, and he exhibits here some of the features of a certain kind of scholarly mind – systematic up to a point, inclined to digression and elaboration, but never quite losing his thread. If we think of him as continuing to speak to Horatio throughout, then indeed his words have a good deal of the tone we might expect in a teacher or a lecturer.

(*d*) *Importance to the plot* The passage does not contribute to the development of the action. Events stand still while, as so often in this play, we are offered comment and reflection.

(*e*) *Stage effect, atmosphere* The suspension of action certainly does not mean that interest is lost. On the contrary, if the full context of the speech is called to mind, or if, better still, we are seeing the play in performance, we experience a feeling of uneasy suspense. There is a contrast between the King's noisy revelry in the lighted hall and the silence, cold, and darkness of the ramparts of Elsinore. Among the little group of soldiers, Hamlet is already an isolated, preoccupied figure. We are instinctively prepared for something strange to happen at any moment – as indeed it does ('Look, my lord, it comes') – to interrupt his musings.

In a modern production in an indoor theatre we would expect much use to be made of lighting to help create the eerie midnight atmosphere. In Shakespeare's theatre, of course, the performance would take place in daylight, but there would be plenty of sound effects – kettle-drums and trumpets are specifically called for a little earlier – and the actors in this scene would be in the gallery or upper stage.

(*f*) *Themes* In this respect the importance of the passage is considerable. It is often cited to support the view that a tragic hero is a man with great qualities destroyed by a fatal flaw. Hamlet, it is argued, is really thinking of himself, and already conscious of that weakness he repeatedly accuses himself of throughout the play – excessive introspection, reluctance to act, 'thinking too precisely on the event', all of which seems to him to carry with it the taint of cowardice. Whether his self-accusation is justified, whether the 'fatal flaw' theory of tragic character is sound, are matters for discussion.

The lines also show beyond question an acceptance of the influence of factors they cannot control upon men's lives, an awareness of the way character and fate work hand in hand, which is felt in Hamlet as in all great tragedy.

Finally, in lines 5-8 we can see foreshadowed two important elements in the later course of the play: Hamlet's fears for his own sanity, and his assumption of an 'antic disposition' which disguises his normally 'plausive manners'.

COMMON ERRORS TO BE AVOIDED IN ANSWERING SHAKESPEARE QUESTIONS

Weaknesses noted in candidates' work do not change much over the years, as we find by looking through old reports.

1 On context-type questions

(a) Candidates spend much too long placing passages in context often virtually telling the whole story of what has gone before, while still omitting points relevant to the passage.

(b) Asked to comment on language and style, too many take refuge in paraphrase. Others seem to believe that identification is enough and reel off lists of metaphors without explanation of meaning or suggestions about effect.

(c) There is too much use of technical terms – caesura, onomatopoeia and so on – usually without understanding.

(d) Many believe that punctuation in itself has some kind of magical power – to quote from a recent report 'Punctuation is a mere indicator of *syntax*. Lots of commas do not show emotion, but disturbed syntax and short phrases marked off by commas *can* do in certain cases.'

2 Essay questions

(a) Here the major fault is the belief that every question can be answered by lengthy narrative. Candidates do not address themselves closely enough to the requirements of the question and are weak in constructing logically-argued answers.

(b) Prepared answers rarely fit the questions. Genuine personal response is what the examiner is looking for.

(c) In general, candidates lack understanding of critical terms. 'Plot' is generally taken to mean no more than 'story', 'action' and 'drama' are too often equated with sensational events.

(d) Introductions to answers are often excessively long, and conclusions are pointlessly repetitive.

(e) On the vexed issue of the use of quotations, I can do no better than quote from a recent JMB report. 'Candidates waste their energies when the page becomes a series of verse passage punctuated by the odd line of literally pointless prose. A line or two, or a phrase, often from the second soldier rather than from the set speech of a major character, can be (and in the best scripts is) far more valuable. Quotations easily become clichés, and candidates should be advised firmly and clearly that the examination is *not* a test of mechanical memorization. Clear allusion is often as effective as quotation in providing argued proof, unless linguistic or poetic matters are involved. Then, indeed, quotation is obligatory, and must be accurate if it is to have any value.'

EXAMPLES OF ANSWERS TO ESSAY QUESTIONS

We have taken several actual scripts from recent examinations of the Scottish Examination Board. These are facsimiles, and are thus able to recapture those features of handwriting and layout which contribute to our impression of a candidate's work. The questions are reproduced below, together with the detailed Marking Instruction, and a brief statement of the examiner's attitude to the candidate's response. The facsimile answers are reproduced on pp. 83-6.

1 1973, Question 3

In any play that you know well discuss the importance of conflict – for example, an internal conflict in one character, or a conflict between two characters, or a conflict between one character and the circumstances in which he finds himself. (For answer see facsimile 1 on p. 83).

Marking instructions

Most candidates may be expected to choose a conflict of one kind only, but many will discuss conflicts of different kinds. Either treatment is acceptable, though those who choose the former will presumably treat the subject in more detail than those who choose to cover a wider field. The kinds of conflict listed are not intended to be exclusive. If any other kind is discussed it should be accepted if at all possible. Shakespeare is acceptable here (and throughout Section 1).

Examiner's comments

This is clearly an answer of very high quality. The candidate treats the topic of conflict on several levels and over the whole range of characters in the play, but manages to cover this very wide range of material without any sacrifice of depth. He clearly has a very thorough knowledge of the play, both in its detailed incidents and in its overall significance, and this knowledge he demonstrates not by a mere re-telling of incidents but by copious and apt allusions and quotations. There are some minor inaccuracies in some of these quotations, admittedly, but they never depart significantly from the original. The answer reveals great competence in vocabulary, sentence structure, punctuation and overall structure. It would no doubt be possible to pick out a few places where the quality of expression could be slightly improved, but to do so would be hypercritical. Considering the stresses to which examination candidates are subjected, this answer reveals a mature, thoughtful and skilful candidate who deserves to be highly rewarded. Answers even better than this do turn up occasionally, but this is surely as good as we have any right to expect.

2 1975, Question 1

From any Shakespearian tragedy choose one soliloquy, episode, or scene that seems to you to reveal clearly the main theme of the play. Make clear what you consider this theme to be, and show in detail how the extract of your choice brings it out.

Shakespeare's 'Lear' makes most of its impact through the overwhelming universality of its theme, and consequently the main conflict of the play is that very basic and fundamental one for which our existence provides an arena — the conflict of good with evil.

To this end most of the characters are protagonists in the conflict, agents of either force. The size and nature of this elemental theme is so large and urgent that it dominates much of the treatment of characters and events in the play and one would not expect Shakespeare to leave room for other conflicts. Nevertheless they are there.

Most of the characters are as I have said involved with the forces of good or evil. Extreme characters such as Edmund or Cordelia have no 'internal' conflict — they perform their roles quite naturally. 'Legitimate Edgar, I'll have your land!' says Edmund, without scruple or conscience of any sort. He is essentially an amoral creature dedicated to self-advancement (rather cheerfully so) and only at the end when he is dying do we see another element intrude upon his character in the realization of death — 'some good I mean to do ere I die...'

Other characters do undergo some form of moral conflict; most notably Albany, who finds himself in the evil camp through his marriage to Goneril, but all his sympathies and instincts lie on the side of good. However he is a patient, courageous character and oblivious to the seductions and taunts of his wife ('Marry, your manhood — Mew! — Milk-liver'd man, thou bearest a cheek for blows, a head for wrongs'...) unlike Macbeth in another play, he plays his part in asserting good at the end, challenging Edmund.

Some characters, notably Gloucester and 'legitimate Edgar' undergo deeper spiritual conflicts relating to their conception of the universe, as a result of their suffering — they are victims (but eventually victors) of the greater good – versus – evil conflict. Edgar, satirised and outcast, comes to the lowest depth of human existence as Poor Tom and is frequently tempted to despair — upon seeing the king mad, and upon finding his blinded father, for example. However, in each case his natural buoyancy triumphs — ' 'When we our betters see ' bearing even worse catastrophes, Edgar knows 'this is not the worst' in the first instance. In the second he is also tempted — 'I am worse than e'er I was' — but triumphs again. Similarly his father Gloucester is led to some given conclusion: 'It is the time's plague, when madmen lead the blind ... As flies to wanton boys, are we to the Gods; they kill us for their sport.' He even attempts suicide. But he lives long enough to be reconciled with his son.

These can be seen as manifestations of this great conflict of good with evil. Lear's struggle with the more unsavoury aspects of his nature, and finally with insanity ('Hysterica passio.....down, thou climbing sorrow!...) are similarly so. Lear capitulates to insanity but gains a new and truer insight into things, as some of his mad speeches reveal.

But the primary conflict which infests the play, that of good with evil, is employed on a vaster scale. The physical opposition of 'good' characters — Lear, Cordelia, Gloucester, Edgar, Kent, Albany — with evil ones — Edmund, Cornwall, Goneril, Regan, Oswald — is evidence of this. At the beginning, this conflict is manifest in rivalries and intrigue. By the end of the play it resolved in open physical combat — the battle and its results and, in some ways the dramatization in miniature of this conflict, the duel between Edgar and Edmund. Shakespeare uses

language and imagery and atmosphere to help this division of good from evil. The latter is associated with darkness, bestial imagery (Goneril is described by Albany as 'this gilded serpent', Gloucester speaks of the visitors 'boarish tusks', they are compared with tigers and pelicans and monsters) and especially, 'unnatural' references. The rebellion against parental law as performed by Edmund, Goneril and Regan was seen by the Elizabethans as a serious disruption of the forms of natural order as well as a personal cruelty. This is hinted at in Gloucester's observance of heavenly upsets — 'these late eclipses in the sun portend no good to us.' Nature reflects the unnatural situation — the great storm of course symbolizing the upset and strife and conflict of the characters. When such a situation arises, we are told, 'humanity perforce must prey upon itself, like monsters of the deep.'

Contrasted with this are the forces of good, particularly as embodied in Cordelia. The Gentleman's description of Cordelia to Kent in Act IV scene 3 is full of imagery connected with light, healing and balm and things celestial. Dover is seen as a sort of counter to the evil atmosphere around, for there lies hope — Cordelia and the French forces. Edgar, Gloucester, Lear, Kent all make their various ways to Dover.

So how does this titanic conflict resolve? Shakespeare's answer I think is intentionally ambiguous — life is both good and evil. Good reasserts itself, but at a tremendous cost — Cordelia unexpectedly murdered in the final example of one of those sudden catastrophic reversals of situation current throughout the play..... Gloucester and Lear himself are dead. The survivors are shattered, worn out, and Kent must die soon too — 'My master calls me, I must not say no.' There is a mood of fatalistic acceptance, wearied by the conflict. Old Lear's death itself is equivocal, dying in the delusion that Cordelia still lives — 'Look, look on her lips!'

It is Albany who bids Edgar let the old man be: 'He hates him that would on the rack of this tough world stretch him out longer.' The forces of evil are crushed, but it is no glib triumph.

1. 1973, Question 3

1

Arguably, the witches' scene in Shakespeare's Macbeth reveals the main theme of the play, but to my mind the scene which best introduces the theme of Macbeth's torment and downfall is the murder scene. Set in a shady court of Inverness castle, the audience is informed of the murder by the simple but effective words 'He is about it' from the lips of Lady Macbeth. Here the setting and complete simplicity of the message convey to a very high degree the distaste and evil in Duncan's murder.

What is more terrifying, however, is the consequence of the murder which the scene attempts to adumbrate. Already in Macbeth's tortured thoughts the theme emerges. 'Glamis hath murdered sleep', and therefore will sleep no more. What greater torment could there be than to kill '...the innocent sleep, that knits up the ravell'd sleave of care'?

This theme emerges more strongly throughout the play, particularly in the contrast between Macbeth and Lady Macbeth. Lady Macbeth in the murder scene had appeared callous, urging Macbeth to a foul deed which he himself was terrified! Yet we must remember that Lady Macbeth at least had required some wine to fortify her thought against Duncan's murder, whereas Macbeth himself, later on (indeed the next morning) executes some casual slaughter without even a second thought.

2

As the play progresses, Lady Macbeth's mind is unbalanced by the horror of 'it all', and she eventually dies in madness. Macbeth, on the other hand, also becomes mentally unbalanced, to the point where even his wife's death leaves him untouched –
'She should have died hereafter
There would have been time for such a word.'
His form of 'insanity' is that of insane evil He can slaughter Duncan's guards, Banquo, even Fleance and Macduff, without remorse. Once he had murdered Duncan, once he had surmounted his initial mental bloc to such a deed, then murder came easily to him.

Another aspect of the downfall theme which emerges later on is the fact that Macbeth is tortured by ghosts and evil spirits, who haunt and terrify him, even when he is in the middle of a jovial, feasting company. This aspect was successfully foreshadowed again in the murder scene with the theme of Duncan's blood forever on Macbeth's hands.

So from this scene the overall theme of his downfall becomes apparent. Yet at the end of the play the audience does not despise Macbeth for an evil individual rather we pity him, indeed sympathise with him. This is why the play is a tragedy, and it seems there must be yet another element present in the theme.

3

That element is Macbeth's helplessness (for lack of a better word). As soon as Macbeth commits the murder and becomes king, the audience is aware that by his one deed he had set a ball rolling which would inexorably crush him spiritually, and then physically. To the audience Macbeth could not help his downfall; it was inevitable.

In conclusion, the scene establishes the theme of his downfall: the mental decline, the murder, the alienation, and the inevitability.

The first scene of Hamlet begins on the very first line, with mystery, and fear, when the sentry on guard is challenged instead of the other way round. The sentry is relieved and in the comments the idea of something frightening and mysterious. Later it is explained that a Ghost has been seen. The Ghost appears twice and dissappears when the cock crows. Mean while Horatio explains that preparations for war are being made by the son of one of the elder Hamlets ennemies, who is trying to regain his fathers lands. Later in the play Hamlet compares himself to him and this helps to establish the custom of the time which Hamlet refuses to follow.

The appearance of the Ghost has taken the collection of Elisabethan people off the street and turned them into an audience. The Ghost also appears to Hamlet and during their talk the cock crows. Thus in the first act Shakespeare lays the foundations for later tensions.

The rest of Act One reveals that Claudius has murdered the elder Hamlet and married his wife, and that Hamlet is sworn to find his revenge.

It is also established that Laertes is to

act as a foil for Hamlet. When Laertes asks permission to go to Paris, Hamlet asks to go to Wittenberg to study. Also, Laertes returned for the wedding and not the funeral. Hamlet mourned during the wedding. Later in the play Hamlet is killed by Laertes, taking revenge for his father; the very deed Hamlet could not bring himself to do.

Also Hamlet's procrastination and religious fervour are both expressed in Act One. These eventually bring about his death in the classical manner of the 'Tragic flaw'.

In Shakespeare's play Othello there two characters who aptly fit the roles of 'tragic' and 'pathetic'. The central character Othello is of course the tragic character while Roderigo fill the place of the pathetic one.

Othello is tragically reduced from the 'valiant Moor' to the 'credulous fool' during the process of the play and we cannot help but sympathise with him. The weaknesses which Iago exploits are shown early — Othello is too proud and sure of himself.

'My parts my title and my perfect soul shall manifest me rightly'

'I'll see before I doubt and when I doubt profe' This in fact he does not do, instead he allows emotion to take control

'My blood begins my better guids to rule'.

Perhaps the greatest tragedy is we see a man • losing love and losing love himself 'Perdition catch my soul but I do love thee And when I love thee not, chaos is come again.' Farewell tranquil mind, farewell content.' Othello is destroyed in the end, ruined by Iago and his own great weakness — jealousy. He is a tragic character unable to cope with the truth .

'An honourable murder I say'

'Of one who loved not wisely but too well.' It is not the case Othello loved too well, but he was 'perplexed in the extreme' and we can sympathise with him—and do.

Roderigo on the hand is a dupe. He changes from a man desiring someone elses wife, to an attempted murderer. Iago uses him throughout

'Thus do I ever make my fool my purse.' He never see through Iago and allows himself to be badly misused. He feels emotion Iago does not.

'A lust of the blood, a permission of the will.' Iagoes word on sex when Roderigo is contemplating suicide. Bankrupt and ruined he believes Iago again, though he is the very person whom Iago told

'I am not what I am' It is only when dying Roderigo comes to himself and calls Iago

'Inhuman dog.

He is of course right, but to late to deserve real sympathy — pity yes.

Othello is used because he is blinded and never acts against his conscience, he is a tragic character. Roerigo is used because he allows it hoping for gain, for him we have on the pity we would give to a fool.

Marking instructions

You may disagree with the candidate's choice of 'main theme', but you should accept it if at all possible and judge the answer on the way this theme emerges from the candidate's handling of the chosen stretch of text.

Examiner's comments

This candidate writes in a good, clear style, apparently simple but in fact (apart from some minor slips) revealing good vocabulary and mastery of all the technicalities of writing. Even the very first word gives some indication of the quality to come. The theme of the play is at once stated as being 'Macbeth's torment and downfall'. This is very much open to question but it must be accepted in view of the Marking Instructions. Once the theme is stated, the candidate consistently relates everything to the ways in which it is 'adumbrated' in the scene of his choice. Paragraph three is perhaps not too well related to the theme, although it manages to show that the seeds of the estrangement between Macbeth and his wife are present even as early as the murder scene. Throughout his answer, the candidate reveals a thorough knowledge of the play, amply illustrated by apt reference and quotation. He shows, moreover, not mere knowledge of people and events but a very good understanding of the overall nature of the play, particularly towards the end when he discusses the additional element of Macbeth's 'helplessness' in an attempt to justify our sympathy for him. Questions on Macbeth very often produce responses which are drab and predictable, with nothing of the candidate himself present. In this case, however, there is no doubt that the candidate is presenting his own response to the play and to the teaching he has had. It is clearly an answer of high quality, but probably not in the highest range. The rather weak choice of theme must be accepted, but it results in an answer which, for all its merits, lacks that fullness of treatment which marks the very best.

Peter Egan and Kirka Markham in the Mark Cullingham production of *Macbeth* (Thorndike Theatre)

3 1973, Question 1

Examine Act One of any play by Shakespeare, showing the skill with which the author establishes 'atmosphere', suggests a theme, and lays before the audience the situation from which the ensuing drama will spring. What expectations are aroused in us at the end of Act One, and how are these expectations later fulfilled?

Marking instructions

'Act One' need not be too literally interpreted, as long as only the early part of the play is considered. An answer which deals with only part of Act One will penalize itself; an answer which goes significantly beyond Act One should be marked out of 15. Answers should deal with both sentences in the rubric, but candidates are free either to give them equal weight or to concentrate on one more fully than the other. Assessment of the answer should be based chiefly on the candidate's awareness of the author's skill as a dramatist. Mere storytelling must fail.

Examiner's comments

Obviously there are many weaknesses in this answer. It would be a mistake, however, to allow these weaknesses to obscure the merits that are also present. The most obvious linguistic weakness is merely one of spelling, yet this amounts in fact to only about five errors. There is no question of communication breaking down through bad spelling, and therefore if it is to be penalized the penalty should take the form of an overall deduction on the paper (a maximum of 2 marks) rather than a deduction on each individual question. The apostrophe is omitted on almost all occasions when it would normally be expected, but again no breakdown of communication occurs thereby. Something has gone far astray in the second sentence, but apart from that the sentence structure and use of full stops are perfectly sound. The candidate's expression, then, is faulty but not seriously so. In his favour it can be said that he knows the play and that he tries hard, in a complex question, to deal with everything asked for. He does examine Act One, and throughout he points to significances, as in his references to Fortinbras (unnamed) and Laertes, for example. He is quite good on 'atmosphere', less on 'the situation from which the ensuing drama will spring', and not at all good on 'theme'. The second sentence of the rubric is complied with by implication at least. Unlike many weak candidates, he makes no attempt to seek refuge in story-telling, but keeps trying hard to stick to the question. On balance, he has done enough to merit the bare or marginal pass.

4 1974, Question 1

We admire and sympathize with a tragic character; we feel merely pity for a pathetic character.

From your knowledge of Shakespearean tragedy, choose two characters, one of whom you would describe as 'tragic' and the other as 'pathetic', and discuss the means by which the appropriate feelings for the characters are aroused.

(You may choose characters from different plays.)

Marking instructions

Candidates are not invited to dispute the statement but to discuss the means by which the three feelings are aroused. Obviously it would be unreasonable to expect an equal balance between the two characters chosen, but answers should treat all three areas (admiration, sympathy, and pity).

Examiner's comments

The choice of characters is not an unreasonable one. On the positive side, the candidate demonstrates some knowledge of the play and makes an honest effort to answer the question, avoiding the pitfalls of so many answers – mere narrative. It is, however, a very thin answer and would not satisfy the requirements of marking criterion (a) 'degree of textual knowledge displayed'. There is no treatment of the element of 'admiration', nothing at all, as we might reasonably expect, about Othello's positive qualities, and the 'sympathy' which is aroused is largely for his 'weaknesses' and his downfall. In arguing for 'pity' for Roderigo he comes nearer to proving the case for contempt. The answer is badly organized. The candidate, having learned his quotations by the yard, is determined to use them, and his text is a thin way of stringing them together. Remove the quotations and there is little left.

Olivier's Othello

The quality of the expression is unsatisfactory and indicates a considerable degree of carelessness.

Such an answer will not pass, but some account should be taken of the fact that there has been an honest attempt to do what was asked. One can extend more charity to an answer of this kind than to one which ignores the rubric and wallows in simple narrative.

CHOOSING AND READING EXAMINATION QUESTIONS ON SHAKESPEARE

It will be useful to share a few thoughts on the subject of the ways in which candidates in English examinations choose examination questions and how they read them when they have chosen them.

We will begin with the choice. The results of a survey over a number of years have demonstrated that, given the choice of two questions on a text, most candidates, in the approximate proportion of 60-40 will choose the first, and, given the choice between a long question and a short question, most candidates, in the approximate proportion of 70-30, will choose the short question. If, therefore, there is a short first question, and a long alternative, it does not take a computer to work out the odds. The reason for this would seem to be that, for many candidates, if the first question seems not impossible (or even, at first sight, easy) then many candidates do not go on to read the alternative at all, even though, when the heat of battle has died down, they may come to see that it was even more to their liking. Long questions seem to put some students off by their mere appearance on the page, although, by their very nature, they often give the candidate important and useful information and are therefore, in that sense, 'easier' than shorter, more open-ended questions of the 'is *King Lear* a tragedy?' variety.

Choice is given by examiners in order to try to give opportunities of as wide a range of interest and ability as possible. Examiners are trying to create opportunities to reward the hard-working, possibly rather limited candidate as well as the perceptive, talented individual who might even make something of the daunting *King Lear* question. Many of the more limited candidates ignore questions that would be very suitable for them, possibly for the reasons already given, and embark on more perilous seas. All A-level Shakespeare questions demand some discussion and analysis and not merely 're-telling the story' but some questions, by their very nature, demand a more discursive approach than others. It will repay students, therefore, to decide what kind of questions they are more competent to deal with and then to spend a little time in making their choice.

Once the choice has been made, of course, the great problem, familiar to all teachers of English, is irrelevance. The reasons are, no doubt, complex, but we are convinced that one major reason is that the questions are read as *words* and not as *sentences*. If we may explain this a little further: in the very understandable moment of nervous panic when a candidate first sees the examination paper, he or she is likely to be immensely reassured by two things – firstly, that the books studied are those appearing on the paper and the head of English has not misread the syllabus (an emotion shared by the head of English!) and, secondly, that the characters' names are familiar. It is at this stage that mistakes occur. Seeing the name 'Ophelia' in the question the candidate jumps to the conclusion that a character-sketch of Ophelia is required and promptly supplies one whereas the question might have read 'Discuss the view that not Ophelia but Gertrude is the real victim in *Hamlet*'. This is an extreme example (and an appalling question) but it will serve as an illustration. If the candidate reads the question as a sentence and notes its sense and progression, there is a fair chance that he or she will answer it. It is also useful to remind the examiner from time to time that the question is being dealt with – e.g. 'having considered X we now turn to Y' – providing that this technique is not carried to absurd lengths.

The most depressing thing in examining Shakespeare is seeing young people misapplying knowledge that they have acquired by conscientious application and hard work over two years. No examiner should ever set out to 'fail' anyone; the effort should always be to mark positively and to reward knowledge, perception and understanding wherever it appears. Unfortunately, many candidates make it very difficult for themselves and for the examiners by being so completely off-target and a few extra minutes spent over the choice of question and then a careful reading of exactly what is being asked, can help to ensure that the student's hard work and that of the English staff over the two years of the course is not thrown away at the first fence.

3 Practical criticism of drama

Introduction

In Drama writers have only the actual words spoken by their characters through which to tell their story and make their effects. Of course, when the play is seen on the stage, it receives a great deal of help from the skill of the actors, the interpretation of the producer and the lighting, set, costumes and music.

In Practical Criticism of Drama, you are faced with the words alone. The basis for whatever you say in your analysis of the passage must come from the text.

In any passage of drama, the dramatist tries to include the following:

1 General atmosphere of the scene, e.g. the three witches on the heath at the beginning of *Macbeth*.

2 Indications of actions, past, present and future.

3 Indications of character by what the characters say themselves, what is said about them and their actions.

4 Indications of the moral attitude of the dramatist through the speeches and actions of the characters and the implied beliefs of the dramatist him- or herself. Most writers – and this applies to dramatists as well as to novelists – are not just telling stories or creating characters; they are also indicating attitudes to life which they feel are right and which they want us to share.

It is very difficult, if not impossible, to comment on a passage from a play in isolation from the rest of the work. Where the passage to be discussed is from a play prescribed for an examination, no difficulty should be experienced by a candidate who has prepared it thoroughly. Passages of drama are not often set 'unseen' in Appreciation papers; where they are, examiners will supply the appropriate background information. In presenting the passages in this book, some account of the plays from which they are taken is given. In the detailed comments, incidental reference to events elsewhere in the play should suggest how this could be done most effectively in an examination answer. We hope that the passages are sufficiently interesting in themselves to inspire you to go on and read the complete plays. Your background knowledge will benefit from this, even if none of them is in your examination syllabus.

In the following passages from well-known plays, which have frequently been set for A level, an A-level examiner has given a commentary for each passage, bringing out the main areas a candidate should examine when preparing an A-level answer. They are *not* 'model answers'. As in most exercises on Practical Criticism, practice is the key word. Too often candidates feel they will achieve a good grade by natural flair and ability without any previous experience of writing commentaries in examination conditions. Try to read the passage aloud to yourself as though you are acting it. It will help to supply the right dramatic intonations. Check up on your ideas of what the playwright is trying to do and make your own notes with the text to help you.

Passages in chronological order with commentaries

Christopher Marlowe	*Edward II*	George Farquhar	*The Beaux-Stratage*
John Webster	*The Duchess of Malfi*	George Bernard Shaw	*Man and Superma*
Ben Jonson	*Volpone*	Arthur Miller	*Death of a Salesma*
William Congreve	*The Way of the World*		

Edward II and *The Duchess of Malfi*

Violent death on-stage was an obligatory feature of the Elizabethan or Jacobean tragedy. We give here two death-scenes from plays often prescribed for A level: Marlowe's *Edward II* (c. 1593), and Webster's *The Duchess of Malfi* (c. 1623). A comparison of these extracts will help to indicate some of the ways in which English drama developed during a period of about thirty years.

Note We will sometimes refer to aspects of the plays outside the passages quoted. If you have prepared a play for A Level, you ought to be able to do this, and will probably be expected to do so.

Edward II

(*Synopsis of previous events. Edward,* unable to control his turbulent barons, humiliated by his defeat at Bannockburn, and accused of taking advice only from his homosexual lovers, has been imprisoned in Berkeley Castle by the ambitious *Mortimer* and the Queen, now Mortimer's mistress. Attempts to bring about his death by subjecting him to humiliating maltreatment – shaving off his beard with ditch-water, keeping him in the castle sewers – having failed, Mortimer has engaged an assassin, *Lightborn,* to murder him. *Matrevis* and *Gurney* are two gentlemen acting as the King's keepers. Just before this passage, Lightborn has hypocritically pretended to pity him.)

> *King Edward* Weep'st thou already? list a while to me,
> And then thy heart, were it as Gurney's is,
> Or as Matrevis', hewn from the Caucasus,
> Yet will it melt ere I have done my tale.
> This dungeon where they keep me is the sink
> Wherein the filth of all the castle falls.
> *Lightborn* O villains!
> *King Edward* And there, in mire and puddle, have I stood
> This ten days' space; and, lest that I should sleep,
> One plays continually upon a drum;
> They give me bread and water, being a king;
> So that, for want of sleep and sustenance,
> My mind's distemper'd, and my body's numb'd,
> And whether I have limbs or no I know not.
> O, would my blood dropp'd out from every vein,
> As doth this water from my tatter'd robes!
> Tell Isabel the queen, I look'd not thus,
> When for her sake I ran at tilt in France,
> And there unhors'd the Duke of Cleremont.
> *Lightborn* O, speak no more, my lord! this breaks my heart.
> Lie on this bed, and rest yourself a while.
> *King Edward* These looks of thine can harbour naught but death;
> I see my tragedy written in thy brows.
> Yet stay a while; forbear thy bloody hand,
> And let me see the stroke before it comes,
> That even then when I shall lose my life,
> My mind may be more steadfast on my God.
> *Lightborn* What means your highness to mistrust me thus?
> *King Edward* What mean'st thou to dissemble with me thus?
> *Lightborn* These hands were never stain'd with innocent blood,
> Nor shall they now be tainted with a king's.
> *King Edward* Forgive my thought for having such a thought.
> One jewel have I left; receive thou this: [*Giving jewel.*

> Still fear I, and I know not what's the cause,
> But every joint shakes as I give it thee.
> O, if thou harbour'st murder in thy heart,
> Let this gift change thy mind, and save thy soul!
> Know that I am a king: O, at that name
> I feel a hell of grief! where is my crown?
> Gone, gone! and do I [still] remain alive?
> *Lightborn* You're overwatch'd, my lord: lie down and rest.
> *King Edward* But that grief keeps me waking, I should sleep;
> For not these ten days have these eye-lids clos'd.
> Now, as I speak, they fall; and yet with fear
> Open again. O, wherefore sitt'st thou here?
> *Lightborn* If you mistrust me, I'll be gone, my lord.
> *King Edward* No, no; for, if thou mean'st to murder me,
> Thou wilt return again; and therefore stay.   [*Sleeps.*
> *Lightborn* He sleeps.
> *King Edward* [*waking*] O, let me not die yet! O, stay a while!
> *Lightborn* How now, my lord!
> *King Edward* Something still buzzeth in mine ears,
> And tells me, if I sleep, I never wake:
> This fear is that which makes me tremble thus;
> And therefore tell me, wherefore art thou come?
> *Lightborn* To rid thee of life. – Matrevis, come!
>
> *Enter* MATREVIS *and* GURNEY.
>
> *King Edward* I am too weak and feeble to resist. –
> Assist me, sweet God, and receive my soul!
> *Lightborn* Run for the table.
> *King Edward* O, spare me, or despatch me in a trice!
>   [*Matrevis brings in a table. King Edward is murdered
>   by holding him down on the bed with the table, and
>   stamping on it.*
> *Lightborn* So, lay the table down, and stamp on it,
> But not too hard, lest that you bruise his body.
> *Matrevis* I fear me that this cry will raise the town,
> And therefore let us take horse and away.
> *Lightborn* Tell me, sirs, was it not bravely done?
> *Gurney* Excellent well: take this for thy reward.
>   [*Stabs Lightborn, who dies.*
> Come, let us cast the body in the moat,
> And bear the king's to Mortimer our lord:
> Away!   [*Exeunt with the bodies.*

Marlowe could count on two built-in advantages in choosing the reign of Edward II for his subject. Firstly, the 'fall of princes' was universally recognized as the great tragic theme, its awesomeness increased by the reverence for kings carefully inculcated in the subjects of our Tudor monarchs; secondly, Edward II was, like Shakespeare's Richard II, well known as one of the most unhappy of English kings, and the story of his troubled life and miserable end a familar one.

It is easy to see how these advantages are exploited in the passage. Edward is made to dwell with much feeling on the contrast between his present wretchedness and the days when he cut a brave figure in the lists ('ran at tilt in France'). A more extreme change of fortune would be hard to imagine. Natural pathos is introduced by his implied hope that the Queen's heart may be softened towards him if she is reminded of other times. He laments the loss of his crown as if it were not just his most treasured personal possession, but rather the very principle of his life. One sometimes thinks that, in the popular mind of the age of Shakespeare, kings were supposed to wear their crowns wherever they went or whatever they did, and indeed they seem to have done so on the Elizabethan stage. To see a stage king without his property crown on his head must have been enough to signify that he had fallen from his high estate.

The human aspect of Edward's sufferings is, of course, greatly heightened by his fear that he will be murdered in his sleep, his wish to meet his end awake, so that his thoughts may be consciously directed towards God (a matter of importance in a religious age), and his parting with his last remaining jewel in the faint hope of bribing Lightborn, whose intentions he divines all too clearly, to spare him. Lightborn's own behaviour may not be altogether as easy to explain as at first appears. Certainly his professed sympathy and assurances that he means Edward no harm can be interpreted adequately enough as sadistic trifling with his victim for his own amusement, and as such is dramatically effective in prolonging the tension of the episode and intensifying the atmosphere of cold horror that envelops it. His assertion that his hands 'were never stain'd with innocent blood' fits well with this view of his motives, as an example of devilish equivocation; as we have been told a little earlier, he specializes in murder by subtle means, not by crude blood-letting. Indeed, one reason for his wishing to lull Edward to sleep before he sets to work on him is, presumably, to avoid a struggle, with consequent marks of violence on the body. But are there perhaps other, almost instinctive reasons? If he kills Edward awake and calling on God, the murder becomes doubly heinous; there is the old belief that the image of the murderer is imprinted on his victim's open eyes; and finally, after all, Edward had been an anointed king, and to look such a person in the eyes and kill him was a fearful deed – one that Macbeth shrinks from. We can be pretty sure that thoughts of this nature were in the minds of Marlowe's audience as they watched the representation of the killing of a king with fascinated horror.

In any case, to treat a monarch disrespectfully on the stage (unless he were one of the officially-labelled bad kings like Richard III) was a somewhat ticklish business, as Shakespeare's company found when the authority required the deposition of Richard II to be cut out of the printed version of the play, and there were limits to what could decently be shown on the stage. Marlowe has skirted round the peculiarly revolting way in which the chroniclers report that Edward was killed, though he drops hints that would have been readily taken in his day. Earlier, Lightborn has boasted to Mortimer that he knows 'a braver way' to kill a man, one that he intends to keep to himself as a professional secret, and has ordered Matrevis and Gurney to heat a spit red-hot. We are not shown it in use, but it is hard to imagine how Edward, in the process of being smothered, could emit the awful shriek which traditionally awoke the whole sleeping countryside, and to which Matrevis refers in
'I fear me that this cry will raise the town.'

Background knowledge will help us to appreciate more fully the impact of this episode on Marlowe's contemporaries, but its dramatic power can still be felt by audiences today. The increase of tension and the drawing out of Edward's agony during his conversation with Lightborn has already been mentioned; the end, when it actually comes, is appalling in its sudden violence, following the dreadful words, 'To rid thee of thy life'. Note here the irony, whether conscious or otherwise: life has indeed become a burden to Edward, of which he has wished to be rid
'O, would my blood dropp'd out from every vein'
though not by such means, and therefore, in a certain sense, Lightborn is doing him a service.. The immediate killing of Lightborn in his turn, when he is expecting congratulation, does not indeed come as a complete surprise to the spectator, because we already know that this was part of Mortimer's plan; still, it remains a dramatically effective, if perhaps rather obviously contrived *peripeteia* (i.e. sudden change of fortune), and satisfies the moral sense by visiting immediate retribution on the murderer, even if at the hands of his accomplices.

No comment on the passage would be complete without reference to the language and versification. Despite the command shown elsewhere in Marlowe's work of high-flown imagery and exuberant diction, the style here, despite the emotionally-charged content, is restrained, almost austere. Certainly this is not 'tragical rant'. There is hardly an image from beginning to end. Further, and most notably, the strict iambic measure is rigorously observed throughout, with a high proportion of end-stopped lines. Even in death, Edward keeps regular metre
'O, spare me, or despatch me in a trice!'
– one almost feels that he might have added 'And in one line of five iambic feet'. The effect is very unlike natural speech, and indeed naturalism was not Marlowe's objective. Instead he depicts the atrocious action in language and verse which give it a kind of formal dignity; to adapt Hamlet's words about the kind of acting he approves, in the very torrent, tempest and whirlwind of passion, it begets a temperance.

The Duchess of Malfi

(*Synopsis of previous events* The young and beautiful *Duchess,* having recently lost her husband, has disregarded the wishes of her two brothers that she should remain a widow, and has secretly married her steward, *Antonio,* a gentleman of high personal accomplishments but of undistinguished family. Her remarriage and subsequent bearing of a son, are revealed to the brothers by another gentleman of her household, the discontented and ambitious *Bosola.*

Incited by resentment of the misalliance, and in the case of one of them, *Ferdinand, Duke of Calabria,* by incestuous jealousy, the brothers, after some time has passed, seize their sister and imprison her together with her gentlewoman, *Cariola.* They then employ Bosola, first to torment her, and finally, in the scene that follows, to supervise her murder. Prior to this, Ferdinand has visited her in the dark and given her a dead man's hand, following which Bosola exhibits to her the waxwork figures of Antonio and her children as if they are dead. Subsequently, her apartments are invaded by a crew of madmen sent by her 'tyrant brother'. At last Bosola appears, 'disguised as an old man', followed by 'executioners with a coffin, cords, and a bell'.)

Bosola This is your last presence-chamber.
Cariola Oh, my sweet lady!
Duchess Peace; it affrights not me.
Bosola I am the common bellman,
    That usually is sent to condemn'd persons
    The night before they suffer.
Duchess Even now thou said'st
    Thou wast a tomb-maker.
Bosola 'Twas to bring you
    By degrees to mortification.   Listen:

        Hark, now everything is still,
        The screech-owl and the whistler shrill
        Call upon our dame aloud,
        And bid her quickly don her shroud!
        Much you had of land and rent;
        Your length in clay's now competent:
        A long war disturb'd your mind;
        Here your perfect peace is sign'd.
        Of what is 't fools make such vain keeping?
        Sin their conception, their birth weeping,
        Their life a general mist of error,
        Their death a hideous storm of terror.
        Strew your hair with powders sweet,
        Don clean linen, bathe your feet,
        And (the foul fiend more to check)
        A crucifix let bless your neck:
        'Tis now full tide 'tween night and day;
        End your groan, and come away.

Cariola Hence, villains, tyrants, murderers! alas!
    What will you do with my lady? – Call for help.
Duchess To whom? to our next neighbours? they are mad folks.
Bosola Remove that noise.
Duchess Farewell, Cariola.
    In my last will I have not much to give:
    A many hungry guests have fed upon me;
    Thine will be a poor reversion.
Cariola I will die with her.
Duchess I pray thee, look thou giv'st my little boy
    Some syrup for his cold, and let the girl
    Say her prayers ere she sleep.
             [*Cariola is forced out by the Executioners.*
    Now what you please:
    What death?
Bosola Strangling; here are your executioners.
Duchess I forgive them:
    The apoplexy, catarrh, or cough o' the lungs,
    Would do as much as they do.
Bosola Doth not death fright you?
Duchess Who would be afraid on 't,
    Knowing to meet such excellent company
    In the other world?
Bosola Yet, methinks,
    The manner of your death should much afflict you:
    This cord should terrify you.

Duchess Not a whit:
    What would it pleasure me to have my throat cut
    With diamonds? or to be smothered
    With cassia? or to be shot to death with pearls?
    I know death hath ten thousand several doors
    For men to take their exits; and 'tis found
    They go on such strange geometrical hinges,
    You may open them both ways: any way, for heaven sake,
    So I were out of your whispering. Tell my brothers
    That I perceive death, now I am well awake,
    Best gift is they can give or I can take.
    I would fain put off my last woman's fault,
    I'd not be tedious to you.
First Executioner We are ready.
Duchess Dispose my breath how please you; but my body
    Bestow upon my women, will you?
First Executioner Yes.
Duchess Pull, and pull strongly, for your able strength
    Must pull down heaven upon me:
    Yet stay; heaven gates are not so highly arch'd
    As princes' palaces; they that enter there
    Must go upon their knees.   [*Kneels.*] – Come, violent death,
    Serve for mandragora to make me sleep! –
    Go tell my brothers, when I am laid out,
    They then may feed in quiet.
                [*The Executioners strangle the Duchess.*]
Bosola Where's the waiting-woman?
    Fetch her: some other strangle the children.
             [*Cariola and Children are brought in by the Executioners;*
                who presently strangle the Children.
    Look you, there sleeps your mistress.
Cariola Oh, you are damn'd
    Perpetually for this! My turn is next;
    Is't not so order'd?
Bosola Yes, and I am glad
    You are so well prepar'd for 't.
Cariola You are deceiv'd, sir,
    I am not prepar'd for't, I will not die;
    I will first come to my answer, and know
    How I have offended.
Bosola Come, dispatch her. –
    You kept her counsel; now you shall keep ours.
Cariola I will not die, I must not; I am contracted
    To a young gentleman.
First Executioner Here's your wedding-ring.
Cariola Let me but speak with the duke; I'll discover
    Treason to his person.
Bosola Delays: – throttle her.
First Executioner She bites and scratches.
Cariola If you kill me now,
    I am damn'd; I have not been at confession
    This two years.
Bosola [*To Executioners.*] When?
Cariola I am quick with child.
Bosola Why, then,
    Your credit's sav'd.   [*The Executioners strangle Cariola.*]
    Bear her into the next room;
    Let these lie still.
          [*Exeunt the Executioners with the body of Cariola.*]

In this play the dramatist is using matter not from familiar English history, but from a mainly fictitious story. The action is, however, located in a 'country of the mind' familiar enough to English audiences – Renaissance Italy, where high civilization and base treachery and murder went hand in hand, and where Marlowe's Lightborn boasts of having learnt his trade – and at a not too remote time: the year 1504 is specifically mentioned in the text.

Our critical awareness of the ingenuity, psychological depth and the variety of language of Jacobean tragedy should not be blunted by the horror it displays.

Consider first the characterization in this extract. The Duchess is not of royal rank, but she displays such regal dignity and composure in her last dreadful moments that even Bosola is impressed. He tries, and fails, to shake her calm by dwelling on the means to be used with her, to which she replies, like a stoic philosopher, that death is death, however it comes. She even manages two jesting remarks – once to Cariola, when she regrets that she will not have much to leave her for a legacy (note the dramatic irony here: she supposes that Cariola will survive her), and once to Bosola, when she apologizes with mock humility for holding up the business with her 'last woman's fault', i.e., talking too much. But underneath her disdainful manner may be glimpsed a great weariness with the persecution she has endured, and a willing acceptance of escape to a better world. Her last words breathe ironical contempt for her brothers. At the same time, she humbles herself before Heaven: unlike princes' palaces, one may only enter there upon one's knees; yet, for all this religious humility, she seems to need no priest to hear her last confession or strengthen her for her ordeal. Such superb self-possession might have made her seem almost inhuman, were it not that Webster has taken care to add the natural touch. She shows a touchingly homely concern for her children: the little boy is to take his cough-mixture, and the girl is to say her prayers. (Here again, dramatic irony is strongly felt: she does not know and, by probably unintentional mercy, she is spared the knowledge that the little boy's cold will soon be the cold of death, and the little girl's sleep eternal.) Her gentle modesty, in her request that her body shall be given to her women for laying out.

Unlike Marlowe, Webster heightens the dramatic impact of the scene by introducing another person facing the same death at almost the same moment. The nobility of the Duchess is thrown into relief by the very different behaviour of Cariola. As is foreshadowed by her vain and noisy clamour for help (which the Duchess disdains to join in), and despite her assertion that she will die with her mistress, when it comes to the point the poor girl screams and struggles in a way which is, God knows, natural enough, but shows that she is made of different stuff. Her desperate outcry, in which she makes, one after another, all the customary pleas for a stay of execution (including, unlike the Duchess, a demand for the comforts of religion) is pathetic and moving, but falls below the level of the tragic. This does not necessarily indicate that she is of low birth and breeding. The women attendants of great ladies in the age when Webster wrote were themselves gentlewomen, and Cariola is as much a 'lady' as Antonio, the sometime steward, is a 'gentleman' – or, for that matter, Malvolio (*Twelfth Night*). It is worth remembering that, in *Antony and Cleopatra,* Shakespeare has shown Cleopatra's maid's, Charmain and Iras, facing the moment of death with courage that matches that of their mistress. No, the difference between the Duchess and Cariola is not so much one of rank as of character.

A great advance beyond Marlowe's simple characterization is to be observed in Bosola, an enigmatic figure far more complex than Lightborn, and one whose role changes sharply in the play. Presented to us at first as a typical 'malcontent', willing to do anything to advance his fortunes, he appears to be no more than a 'serviceable villain'. In this episode, however, he seems to have found his true vocation as a specialist in human agony. He begins this extract with a grimly ironical reference back to the great position the Duchess once held, when she would receive courtiers and petitioners in her 'presence chamber'. Just before this he has been impersonating a grave-digger, and it is now in the guise of the 'common bellman', one of whose duties in Webster's day is explained in the text, that he recites the verses beginning 'Hark, now everything is still'. A little later he is coldly probing the Duchess's reaction to the fatal cord. His manner to Cariola is throughout contemptuous and callous, from 'Remove that noise' to the unfeeling sneer, 'Why then, your credit's sav'd' as she is strangled. His detached indifference to the horror of what he is doing is worthy of one of Hitler's death-camp doctors; yet, after it is done, he experiences revulsion, and when Ferdinand, unable in his turn to face up to his crime, sends him packing without the expected reward, Bosola becomes the Duchess's avenger and attracts much of our sympathy.

If we consider the poetic style of the passage, perhaps the first thing that strikes us is the introduction of the rhyming dirge spoken – or rather chanted – by Bosola. Though at times it has something of a popular or proverbial flavour, it is in fact a highly polished little piece, making skilful use of the octosyllabic couplet, varied by the introduction of seven-syllable lines, and moralizing on the misery of life and the vanity of worldly greatness in words that are perhaps better suited to console than to terrify. The blank verse has completely abandoned the rigidly iambic beat and end-stopped lines we find in Marlowe, and the speakers no longer address each other in complete lines of verse. The Duchess's last line has only three feet. Some of the shorter speeches cannot be fitted into any regular blank-verse pattern at all, especially in the last abrupt and broken exchanges between Bosola and Cariola. The metre, in fact, responds to the mood of the moment, and the rhythms are much closer to those of natural speech than are Marlowe's. Nevertheless, we are always aware that, despite the freedom of the verse, its basic structure is still the good old five-foot iambic line.

In diction and imagery, Webster often strikes the true metaphysical vein, both in his vivid and arresting turns of phrase, e.g.

> 'What would it pleasure me to have my throat cut
> With diamonds?'

or

> 'any way, for heaven sake,
> So I were out of your whispering.'

and in his original imagery, e.g. the ten thousand doors of death and their 'strange geometrical hinges', or the gates of heaven which are 'not so highly arch'd as princes' palaces'.

Many features of *The Duchess of Malfi* suggest that it was written not for the public play-house that Marlowe catered for so well with his clear and simple actions and vigorous declamatory verse, but for the indoor private or 'chamber' theatre, where a more discriminating and aristocratic audience would appreciate subtler dramatic effects. Much of the play – including the episode we have been discussing – is supposed to take place in at least semi-darkness, to which a candle-lit interior would be more adaptable.

Volpone (1605): Ben Jonson

In *Volpone* there is not a great range of humours (see Glossary and pp. 54-5), nearly all the personages being dominated by greed in a variety of forms. The scene is Venice, and they bear the Italian names of birds and beasts: *Volpone* (the Fox, celebrated for his cunning), *Mosca* (the Fly), *Voltore* (the Vulture), *Corbaccio* (the Crow), *Corvino* (the Raven) – all the last four having in common a propensity to feed on carrion. In the play, Volpone is a wealthy nobleman in the prime of life, with a highly developed appetite for sensual pleasure, but above all else a worshipper of gold, to which he prays as to a god every morning. Assisted by his parasite or hanger-on, Mosca, he pretends to be at death's door in order to attract a crew of legacy-hunters, each of whom believes that he is to be Volpone's sole heir.

In the following passage Corvino, a merchant, has just entered with rich gifts for Volpone, who lies motionless in bed, his face plastered with ointments, while Mosca plays the intermediary.

Corvino Say,
    I have a diamond for him, too.
Mosca Best shew it, sir;
    Put it into his hand; 'tis only there
    He apprehends: he has his feeling, yet.
    See how he grasps it!
Corvino 'Las, good gentleman!
    How pitiful the sight is!
Mosca Tut! forget, sir.
    The weeping of an heir should still be laughter
    Under a visor.

Corvino O, my dear Mosca! [*They embrace.*] Does he not perceive
    us?
Mosca No more than a blind harper. He knows no man,
    No face of friend, nor name of any servant,
    Who 'twas that fed him last, or gave him drink:
    Not those he hath begotten, or brought up,
    Can he remember.
Corvino Has he children?
Mosca Bastards,
    Some dozen, or more, that he begot on beggars,
    Gypsies, and Jews, and black-moors, when he was drunk.
    Knew you not that, sir? 'tis the common fable.
    The dwarf, the fool, the eunuch, are all his;

He's the true father of his family,
In all, save me: – but he has given them nothing.
Corvino That's well, that's well! Art sure he does not hear us?
Mosca Sure sir! why, look you, credit your own sense.
                                        [*Shouts in Volpone's ear.*
The pox approach, and add to your diseases,
If it would send you hence the sooner, sir,
For your incontinence, it hath deserv'd it
Thoroughly, and thoroughly, and the plague to boot! –
You may come near, sir. – Would you would once close
Those filthy eyes of yours, that flow with slime,
Like two frog-pits; and those same hanging cheeks,
Cover'd with hide instead of skin – Nay, help, sir –
That look like frozen dish-clouts set on end!
Corvino [*aloud.*] Or like an old smoked wall, on which the rain
Ran down in streaks!
Mosca Excellent, sir! speak out:
You may be louder yet; a culverin
Discharged in his ear would hardly bore it.
Corvino His nose is like a common sewer, still running.
Mosca 'Tis good! And what his mouth?
Corvino A very draught.
Mosca O, stop it up –
Corvino By no means.
Mosca 'Pray you, let me:
Faith I could stifle him rarely with a pillow,
As well as any woman that should keep him.
Corvino Do as you will; but I'll begone.
Mosca Be so:
It is your presence makes him last so long.
Corvino I pray you, use no violence.
Mosca No, sir! why?
Why should you be thus scrupulous, pray you, sir?
Corvino Nay, at your discretion.
Mosca Well, good sir, begone.
Corvino I will not trouble him now, to take my pearl.
Mosca Puh! nor your diamond.   What a needless care
Is this afflicts you?   Is not all here yours?
Am not I here, whom you have made your creature?
That owe my being to you?
Corvino Grateful Mosca!
Thou art my friend, my fellow, my companion,
My partner, and shalt share in all my fortunes.
Mosca Excepting one.
Corvino What's that?
Mosca Your gallant wife, sir, –   [*Exit Corvino*
Now is he gone: we had no other means
To shoot him hence, thus this.
Volpone My divine Mosca!
Thou hast to-day outgone thyself. [*Knocking within.*] – Who's there?
I will be troubled with no more.   Prepare
Me music, dances, banquets, all delights;
The Turk is not more sensual in his pleasures,
Than will Volpone.   [*Exit Mosca*]   let me see; a pearl!
A diamond! plate! chequines! Good morning's purchase.
Why, this is better than rob churches, yet;
Or fat, by eating, once a month, a man –

The most immediately striking aspect of this scene is the skill and malicious glee with which Mosca manipulates the dupe, Corvino. First, he assures him that he is to be the sole heir, and that they can speak and act with perfect freedom since Volpone sees nothing and knows nobody – not even 'those he hath begotten'. This seemingly artless mention of possible rivals for the inheritance alarms Corvino, as it is intended to do ('Has he children?'), but he is reassured by 'he has given them nothing.' The sneering references to Volpone's supposed offspring ('The dwarf, the fool, the eunuch' are members of a private circus of 'freaks' kept by Volpone for his entertainment) serve to confirm that the supposedly dying man is deaf as well as blind, which Mosca proceeds to demonstrate by bawling foul abuse into his ear, inciting Corvino to join in. He follows this up with the suggestion that he could very easily give Volpone the last little push to launch him into Eternity, and that, in the circumstances, Corvino being so close to realising his hopes, it is not worth troubling to prise the jewels out of Volpone's tenacious grasp. The precious pair then exchange vows of eternal gratitude, which Mosca cuts short by bringing in an allusion to Corvino's 'gallant (i.e. handsome and high-spirited) wife'. This sends the jealous husband packing.

Corvino, naturally, has the passive part of this conversation, but his thoroughly unpleasant character is strongly brought out. He is at first hypocritically conventional: .

> "Las, good gentleman!
> How pitiful the sight is!'

but shows himself indecently ready to drop the pretence when convinced that Volpone cannot hear him; the meanness of his nature is thus demonstrated. He objects, for form's sake, to Mosca's suggestion of a little timely homicide ('By no means'), then immediately makes it plain that he has no real scruples, provided the deed is done discreetly, and not in his presence. His jealousy of his wife, played on at the end, introduces a new element in the plot, which is to assume major importance later.

The dramatic impact of the passage is undeniable. Note, first, that the whole comedy is enacted for the enjoyment of Volpone, and that we inevitably associate ourselves with him, however much we may dislike him, seeing it through his eyes, watching Corvino reveal his true self, and hugely relishing the way in which he is being gulled. After his departure, when Volpone throws off the disguise of sickness and exultantly devotes the rest of the day to pleasures more exquisite than those of the Grand Turk (i.e., the Sultan of Turkey), the atmosphere is swiftly and powerfully transformed. It is hard not to admire someone who is so uninhibited in his triumph over crawling baseness and his enjoyment of the accrued profits. The scene demonstrates rather strikingly at the end that we do not always have to find a character attractive in order to feel a degree of sympathy with him.

Apart from the major ironies, there are other subtler details which add depth and texture to the effect of the episode. Does it not seem, for example, that Mosca's reviling of Volpone goes rather beyond what the situation requires, and breathes a real hatred? Does Mosca in fact loathe his patron and the part he is obliged to play? Certainly he attempts to perpetrate an enormous double-cross at the end of the play. The allusion to Volpone's grasp of whatever is put into his hand ironically points to a real feature of his character, as well as to a kind of assumed 'rigor mortis'. Other seemingly incidental references suggest a background of a corrupt society in which cheating, and graver crimes, are commonplace. If Volpone (who can see perfectly well) can perceive 'no more than a blind harper', then it seems to follow that blind harpers, and similar itinerant musicians, were no more blind than Volpone really is. When Mosca says that he could stifle him

> 'with a pillow
> As well as any woman that should keep him'

the casual tone of the comparison implies that it was quite usual for nurses to get rid of their patients this way.

I have referred to *Volpone* as a comedy, but – as the extract makes plain – it is a very black kind of comedy. All the main characters are morally vile (though there is a kind of depraved splendour about Volpone himself), and all, in the end, are exposed and sentenced by judges as corrupt as themselves to punishments which have little of the comic about them – whipping and the galleys, imprisonment in chains, disbarring and banishment, confinement to a monastery, and the pillory.

The play is unlike Jonson's other major comedies in two ways. Firstly, it takes place, not in contemporary London, but in Venice. Why Jonson should have chosen this exotic location is not altogether clear. Venice certainly meant much to the English writers of his day – Shakespeare among them. To Jonson, the great merchant city may well have seemed to symbolize wealth, luxury, and depravity of morals, and by giving his work a foreign setting he may have intended to emphasize the international, indeed the universal nature of the human vices he satirizes.

Secondly, *Volpone,* unlike the others again, is almost entirely composed in blank verse. It must be allowed that, in this passage, there is great energy and inventiveness in the language, especially in that of Mosca's longest speech. Whether it is the language of poetry may be disputed by those who think that poetry must be 'beautiful'. (Elsewhere in the play the style attains an undeniable splendour.) What must be allowed is Jonson's skill in the writing of lively dialogue in verse. The short exchanges between Mosca and Corvino look like prose, but a more careful examination shows that in fact they form perfect pentameters:

> ''Tis good! And what his mouth?/ A very draught.
> O, stop it up –/ By no means./ Pray you, let me.'

(the unstressed extra syllable at the end of the second line being always permissible in dramatic blank verse). To combine such strict observance of metre with such racy freedom of speech may not be the most that poetry is capable of, but it is certainly craftsmanship of a very high order.

Two Restoration comedies: *The Way of the World,* **William Congreve (1700)**
The Beaux-Stratagem, **George Farquhar (1707)**

'Restoration comedy' may seem something of a misnomer for two plays belonging to the first years of the eighteenth century, long after 'Good King Charles's golden days.' Nevertheless, the kind of comedy written during the fifty years or so after the restoration of the monarchy in 1660, though it certainly developed, did not change fundamentally during that period. For a full account of the new theatre which emerged in the 1660's you must consult a history of English drama. A few important background points are given on pp. 55-6 of this book.

The Way of the World

By common consent the finest example of its kind, this play has a very involved plot. There are many characters, and they are all engaged in elaborate schemes involving a great deal of double-crossing – such, as Congreve suggests by the title, is 'the way of the world'. At the centre of the action is *Mirabell's* plan to marry the far-from-unwilling *Millament* despite the hostility of her aunt and guardian, *Lady Wishfort,* without whose consent Millament loses her fortune. On p. 58 of this book you will find a diagramatic representation, showing its complexity. In the passage that follows, Mirabell proposes, and is accepted – on certain conditions.

> *Millament* Ah! I'll never marry, unless I am first made sure of my will and pleasure.
>
> *Mirabell* Would you have 'em both before marriage? Or will you be contented with the first now, and stay for the other 'till after grace?
>
> *Millament* Ah, don't be impertinent – My dear liberty, shall I leave thee? My faithful solitude, my darling contemplation, must I bid you then adieu? Ay-h, adieu – my morning thoughts, agreeable wakings, indolent slumbers, all ye *douceurs,* ye *someils du matin,* adieu – I can't do't, 'tis more than impossible – Positively, Mirabell, I'll lye abed in a morning as long as I please.
>
> *Mirabell* Then I'll get up in a morning as early as I please.
>
> *Millament* Ah! Idle creature, get up when you will – And d'ye hear, I won't be called names after I'm married; positively I won't be called names.
>
> *Mirabell* Names!
>
> *Millament* Ay, as wife, spouse, my dear, joy, jewel, love, sweetheart, and the rest of that nauseous cant, in which men and their wives are so fulsomly familiar – I shall never bear that – Good Mirabell, don't let us be familiar or fond, nor kiss before folks, like my Lady Fadler and Sir Francis: nor to go Hide Park together the first Sunday in a new chariot, to provoke eyes and whispers; and then never be seen there together again; as if we were proud of one another the first week, and ashamed of one another ever after. Let us never visit together, nor go to a play together, but let us be very strange and well bred: let us be as strange as if we had been married a great while; and as well bred as if we were not married at all.
>
> *Mirabell* Have you any more conditions to offer? Hitherto your demands are pretty reasonable.
>
> *Millament* Trifles, – as liberty to pay and receive visits to and from whom I please; to write and receive letters, without interrogatories or wry faces on your part; to wear what I please; and chuse conversation with regard only to my own taste; to have no obligation upon me to converse with wits that I don't like, because they are your acquaintance; or to be intimate with fools because they may be your relations. Come to dinner when I please, dine in my dressing-room when I'm out of humour, without giving a reason. To have my closet inviolate; to be sole empress of my tea-table, which you must never presume to approach without first asking leave. And lastly, wherever I am, you shall always knock at the door before you come in. These articles subscribed, if I continue to endure you a little longer, I may by degrees dwindle into a wife.
>
> *Mirabell* Your bill of fare is something advanced in this latter account. Well, have I liberty

> to offer conditions – that when you are dwindled into a wife, I may not be beyond
> measure enlarged into a husband?
>
> *Millament* You have free leave, propose your utmost, speak and spare not.
>
> *Mirabell* I thank you. *Imprimis* then, I covenant that your acquaintance be general; that
> you admit no sworn confident or intimate of your own sex. . . . *Item,* when you shall be
> breeding –
>
> *Millament* Ah! name it not.
>
> *Mirabell* Which may be presumed, with a blessing on our endeavours –
>
> *Millament* Odious endeavours!
>
> *Mirabell* I denounce against all strait lacing, squeezing for a shape, 'till you mould my
> boy's head like a sugar-loaf; and instead of a man-child, make me father to a
> crooked-billet.

Here we can enjoy a lively example of that 'duel of the sexes' which is, and always has been, one of the mainstays of comedy. (Cf. Beatrice and Benedick in Shakespeare's *Much Ado About Nothing*.) The duellists are well-matched: Mirabell, i.e. 'the admirable' and Millament, i.e., 'she who has a thousand lovers'. Millament is presented as full of caprice and affectation, exceedingly self-centred, and determined to be as different as possible from conventional people. We see her first delighting in her indolent mornings abed – not forgetting to smatter a little fashionable French – and pretending that, if she is expected to give them up, that would be an insuperable objection to marriage

'I can't do't, 'tis more than impossible'

though immediately afterwards she implies her consent with

'Positively, Mirabell, I'll lye abed in a morning as long as I please.'

She expresses a comprehensive contempt for homely endearments ('that nauseous cant'), her list of 'trifles', taken as a whole, adds up to a declaration of domestic independence, and her reaction to the prospect of child-bearing, generally taken to be the whole point of marriage, is comically squeamish. Her professed ideal of the married state is given in 'Let us be as strange (i.e. distant) as if we had been married a great while; and as well bred as if we were not married at all': an ideal which, translated into practice, is summed up by 'Wherever I am, you should always knock at the door before you come in'.

Mirabell, being an accomplished gentleman, takes all these airs and graces with imperturbable good humour, though he goes on to make a string of stipulations on his side, too long to be quoted here. Notice how the humour of the situation is enhanced by the legalistic turns of phrase – 'these articles subscribed', *'imprimis' 'item'*. From this point of view, the episode is almost a parody of the drawing up of a contract between two prospective business partners.

We, however, do not share Mirabell's attitudes and conventions; yet we too find Millament enormously appealing. Why is this? It is not just because a beautiful young woman is traditionally allowed to be whimsical and capricious. The real reason is surely that, as so often in great comedy, there is seriousness – perhaps, indeed, pathos – underlying the wit and the high spirits. We reflect that Millament's freedom to tease and play hard to get depends entirely on youth, beauty, and her single state. The first two are proverbially transient, while the independence she enjoys and prizes while single was, in fact, incompatible in her day with marriage. However politely a wife might be treated, her property (apart from what might be reserved for her in the marriage settlement) became her husband's, and her personal freedom was restricted in many ways sanctioned both by law and by custom. Congreve, we may be pretty certain, was perfectly aware of all this reality underlying the parade of courtship and fine manners. He makes fun of Millament, true, but in a wholly unmalicious way. Despite the easy assumptions made today about the male-dominated society of other times, it is fair to say that his view of women – or, at least, of women in Millament's situation – is basically sympathetic.

As in so many Restoration comedies, we are here given some rather satirical glimpses of the social life of London and the current practices of the 'beau monde': driving round Hyde Park in one's 'chariot' (not of the Boadicea type, of course!) to see and be seen, paying formal calls on acquaintances, going to the play, taking tea with much ceremony, and submitting to ferocious tight-lacing even during pregnancy.

When we compare the prose style of *The Way of the World* with that of the comedies of some sixty years earlier, we realize that a great watershed has been passed, and that what we have here, for all its elegance and its outmoded expressions, is essentially modern English. The sentence structure is neat and compact. The language combines colloquial ease with carefully studied effects, e.g., the paradox and antithesis in the sentence already quoted ('Let us be as strange . . .' etc.) or the delicate hesitations and qualifications of

'These articles subscribed,/ *if* I continue to endure you a little longer,/ I *may*/ by degrees/ *dwindle* into a wife.'

Enough has been said to show why Millament should see marriage as a 'dwindling', a diminution. Note also how these two examples of Congreve's fine sense of style serve to bring important speeches to a decisive conclusion.

The Beaux-Stratagem

This play is in many ways a transitional one, anticipating, for example, Goldsmith's *She Stoops to Conquer* (see p. 59) in its provincial setting (Lichfield) and its good-humoured – at times, positively sentimental – tone. It also contains a rich array of picturesque and original minor characters: an innkeeper in league with the local highwaymen, his daughter with ideas above her station, three comically inept robbers, an Irish priest pretending to be a Frenchman, a captive French officer. The dominant point of view throughout is, however, the same as in other plays of this genre, i.e. that of fashionable London, represented by the 'beaux' of the title, *Archer* and *Aimwell,* 'two gentlemen of broken fortunes' who have left town, travelling as master and servant turn and turn about, to make good their losses by the 'stratagem' of marrying an innocent country girl with a fortune and splitting the profits between them. The family which becomes the object of their attentions is that of *Squire Sullen* (the name immediately typecasts the character), who has recently married a fine London lady. The Squire also has an extremely eligible half-sister, *Dorinda.* The extract that follows is from the scene in which we first meet *Mrs Sullen.*

Dorinda But supposing, madam, that you brought it to a case of separation, what can you urge against your husband? My brother is, first, the most constant man alive.

Mrs Sullen The most constant husband, I grant ye.

Dorinda He never sleeps from you.

Mrs Sullen No, he always sleeps with me.

Dorinda He allows you a maintenance suitable to your quality.

Mrs Sullen A maintenance! do you take me, madam for an hospital child, that I must sit down, and bless my benefactors for meat, drink, and clothes? As I take it, madam, I brought your brother ten thousand pounds, out of which I might expect some pretty things, called pleasures.

Dorinda You share in all the pleasures that the country affords.

Mrs Sullen Country pleasures! racks and torments! Dost think, child, that my limbs were made for leaping of ditches, and clambering over stiles? or that my parents, wisely foreseeing my future happiness in country pleasures, had early instructed me in rural accomplishments of drinking fat ale, playing at whisk, and smoking tobacco with my husband? or of spreading of plasters, brewing of diet-drinks, and stilling rosemary-water, with the good old gentlewoman my mother-in-law?

Dorinda I'm sorry, madam, that it is not more in our power to divert you; I could wish, indeed, that our entertainments were a little more polite, or your taste a little less refined. But, pray, madam, how came the poets and philosophers, that laboured so much in hunting after pleasure, to place it at last in a country life?

Mrs Sullen Because they wanted money, child, to find out the pleasures of the town. Did you ever see a poet or philosopher worth ten thousand pounds? if you can show me such a man, I'll lay you fifty pounds you'll find him somewhere within the weekly bills. Not that I disapprove rural pleasures, as the poets have painted them; in their landscape, every Phillis has her Corydon, every murmuring stream, and every flowery mead, gives fresh alarms to love. Besides, you'll find, that their couples were never married: – but yonder I see my Corydon, and a sweet swain it is, Heaven knows! Come, Dorinda, don't be angry, he's my husband, and your brother; and, between both, is he not a sad brute?

Dorinda I have nothing to say to your part of him, you're the best judge.

Mrs Sullen O sister, sister! if ever you marry, beware of a sullen, silent sot, one that's always musing, but never thinks. There's some diversion in a talking blockhead; and since a woman must wear chains, I would have the pleasure of hearing 'em rattle a little. Now you shall see, but take this by the way. He came home this morning at his usual hour of four, wakened me out of a sweet dream of something else, by tumbling over the tea-table, which he broke all to pieces; after his man and he had rolled about the room, like sick passengers in a storm, he comes flounce into bed, dead as a salmon into a fishmonger's basket; his feet cold as ice, his breath hot as a furnace, and his hands and his face as greasy as his flannel night-cap. O matrimony! He tosses up the clothes with a barbarous swing over his shoulders, disorders the whole economy of my bed, leaves me half naked, and my whole night's comfort is the tuneable serenade of that wakeful nightingale, his nose! Oh, the pleasure of counting the melancholy clock by a snoring husband! But now, sister, you shall see how handsomely, being a well-bred man, he will beg my pardon.

And, of course, the Squire fully lives up to his wife's expectations:

Enter Squire SULLEN

Squire Sullen My head aches consumedly.
Mrs Sullen Will you be pleased, my dear, to drink tea with us this morning? it may do your head good.
Squire Sullen No.
Dorinda Coffee, brother?
Squire Sullen Psha!
Mrs Sullen Will you please to dress, and to go church with me? the air may help you.
Squire Sullen Scrub!   [*Calls.*

Enter SCRUB.

Scrub Sir!

Squire Sullen What day o' th' week is this?
Scrub Sunday, an't please your worship.
Squire Sullen Sunday! bring me a dram; and d'ye hear, set out the venison-pasty and a tankard of strong beer upon the hall-table, I'll go to breakfast.   [*Going.*

Unlike the passage from *The Way of the World,* this is not a conversation, still less an intellectual contest between two equally-matched antagonists. Dorinda's role in it, as indeed throughout the play, is essentially a passive one, though she is allowed a little gentle irony of her own in 'I could wish, indeed, that our entertainments were a little more polite, or your taste a little less refined'. But, in the main, her function is simply to prompt Mrs Sullen to inveigh against marriage and country life – not that she needs much prompting! Dorinda's interventions also serve to break up what might otherwise come close to being a monologue into sections, each of which attacks the central topics from a new angle.

The first point to note in Mrs Sullen's tirade is the way she bridles at the word 'maintenance'. She has brought her husband a fortune (what ten thousand pounds in 1707 represents in today's money is almost beyond calculation) and in return she is expected to be as grateful for what he allows her as an 'hospital child' (i.e., one who is being brought up in a charitable institution) to her benefactors. A standard grievance, this: the loss of independence by marriage which is so much in Millament's mind. Her satirical account of the 'accomplishments' of the country gentry again strikes a familiar note, enlivened though it is by the detailed examples; playing cards ('whisk' is whist), smoking, and drinking strong ale (pleasures shared in common with their tenants and labourers) for the men; for the women, administering home-made remedies to the local poor. (The 'good old gentlewoman' is Mrs Sullen's mother-in-law, Lady Bountiful.)

The next stage in the indictment is to pour scorn on the idealization of country life by poets and philosophers, all of whom, in the lady's view, would have much preferred to live in town could they have afforded it. ('Within the weekly bills' means 'in London', where the parishes published weekly lists of burials.) We are still, at this point, being offered ideas which are part of the common stock-in-trade of Restoration comedy, though in a particularly lively fashion, but the approach of Squire Sullen prompts as ludicrous and homely a picture of domestic discomfort as we can find anywhere in the repertoire of English comedy. Note that not the least of the Squire's offences is to have broken his wife's tea-table.

Mrs Sullen, of course, has nothing of sullenness about her except the name she is obliged to bear by her unfortunate marriage. She is, indeed, an extremely vivacious character, endowed by Farquhar with a happy turn of phrase, especially in satirical exaggeration and ironical mockery. It would be hard to better the concision with which she sums up the alleged pleasures of a walk in the country – 'leaping of ditches and clambering over stiles'. One has to be of a special breed, she suggests, to cope with such an obstacle course. She finds much amusement in echoing the language of artificial pastoral poetry, wherein shepherd and shepherdesses with traditional Greek names like Phillis and Corydon make delicate love amid murmuring streams and flowery meads, and then dismissing the whole pretty picture with the tart remark that these couples were never married. The sight of her own 'sweet swain' prompts her to expressions which stress the contrast between poetic illusion and reality – 'A sad brute' (i.e., a contemptible boor), 'a sullen, silent sot, one that's always musing, but never thinks'. Her description of the Squire's return to the matrimonial bedchamber, funny in itself, is made even more so by the comparisons she employs: – he and his manservant (Scrub) roll about the room 'like sick passengers in a storm' before he 'comes flounce into bed, dead as a salmon into a fishmonger's basket', 'his hands and his face as greasy as his flannel nightcap'. Notice how, throughout the passage, her manner of addressing Dorinda very naturally changes as she warms to her theme; she begins with the formal 'madam', but soon switches to the more familiar 'child' and 'sister'. Note too, in the second short extract, how she ironically assumes a polite and concerned manner of speaking – 'Will you be pleased, my dear, to drink tea with us this morning?' – in order to underline the Squire's oafishness and so provide proof of what she has been saying about him to Dorinda.

We must, however, admire Squire Sullen when we hear of the kind of breakfast he is prepared to tackle despite his shocking hangover.

This introduction of Mrs Sullen makes it clear that she finds her present state so intolerable that she will be only too ready to fall into the arms of any young spark with a whiff of London elegance about him. So, indeed, it proves, and at the end of the play she separates from her husband (to his infinite relief) and goes off with Archer and – marvellous indeed! – with her fortune as well. Aimwell of course, marries Dorinda. The last lines spoken on stage are a couplet recommending divorce of incompatible couples by mutual consent – a liberal enough idea even today.

> 'Consent, if mutual, saves the lawyer's fee.
> Consent is law enough to set you free.'

Man and Superman (1903): George Bernard Shaw

(If you have not already read the section on Shaw on p. 6 of this book, it will be helpful to do so before reading this commentary.)

The passages that follow are from the beginning of Act II of *Man and Superman,* an extremely long play mainly concerned with the relationship between men and women and the possible evolution of the human race. *Jack Tanner* is a wealthy young man who enjoys playing with radical ideas regarded by his stuffier acquaintances as shocking. He has just been driven down from London in his new toy, a motor car.

> On the carriage drive in the park of a country house near Richmond an open touring car has broken down. It stands in front of a clump of trees round which the drive sweeps to the house, which is partly visible through them: indeed Tanner, standing in the drive with his back to us, could get an unobstructed view of the west corner of the house on his left were. he not far too much interested in a pair of supine legs in dungaree overalls which protrude from beneath the machine. He is watching them intently with bent back and hands supported on his knees. His leathern overcoat and peaked cap proclaim him one of the dismounted passengers.

The Legs Aha! I got him.
Tanner All right now?
The Legs Aw rawt nah.

> *Tanner stoops and takes the legs by the ankles, drawing their owner forth like a wheelbarrow, walking on his hands, with a hammer in his mouth. He is a young man in a neat suit of blue serge, clean shaven, dark eyed, square fingered, with short well brushed black hair and rather irregular sceptically turned eye-brows. When he is manipulating the car his movements are swift and sudden, yet attentive and deliberate. With Tanner and Tanner's friends his manner is not in the least deferential, but cool and reticent, keeping them quite effectually at a distance whilst giving them no excuse for complaining of him. Nevertheless he has a vigilant eye on them always, and that, too, rather cynically, like a man who knows the world well from its seamy side. He speaks slowly and with a touch of sarcasm; and as he does not at all affect the gentleman in his speech, it may be inferred that his smart appearance is a mark of respect to himself and his own class, not to that which employs him.*

After some conversation between Tanner and his chauffeur, Straker by name, the two motorists are joined by Tanner's friend, Octavius Robinson, a sensitive youth romantically in love with the girl who is determined to marry Tanner.

Tanner By the way, let me introduce you. Mr Octavius Robinson: Mr Enry Straker.

Straker Pleased to meet you, sir. Mr Tanner is gittin at you with is Enry Straker, you know. You call it Henery. But I dont mind, bless you!

Tanner You think it's simply bad taste in me to chaff him, Tavy. But youre wrong. This man takes more trouble to drop his aitches than ever his father did to pick them up. It's a mark of caste to him. I have never met anybody more swollen with the pride of class that Enery is.

Straker Easy, easy! A little moderation, Mr Tanner.

Tanner A little moderation, Tavy, you observe. You would tell me to draw it mild. But this chap has been educated. Whats more, he knows that we havn't. What was that Board School of yours, Straker?

Straker Sherbrooke Road.

Tanner Sherbrooke Road! Would any of us say Rugby! Harrow! Eton! in that tone of intellectual snobbery? Sherbrooke Road is a place where boys learn something: Eton is a boy farm where we are sent because we are nuisances at home, and because in after life, whenever a Duke is mentioned, we can claim him as an old school-fellow.

Straker You dont know nothing about it, Mr Tanner. It's not the Board School that does it: it's the Polytechnic.

Tanner His university, Octavius. Not Oxford, Cambridge, Durham, Dublin, or Glasgow. Not even those Nonconformist holes in Wales. No, Tavy. Regent Street! Chelsea! the Borough! – I dont know half their confounded names: these are his universities, not mere shops for selling class limitations like ours. You despise Oxford, Enry, dont you?

Straker No, I dont. Very nice sort of place, Oxford, I should think, for people that like that sort of place. They teach you to be a gentleman there. In the Polytechnic they teach you to be an engineer or such like. See?

Tanner Sarcasm, Tavy, sarcasm! Oh, if you could only see into Enry's soul, the depth of his contempt for a gentleman, the arrogance of his pride in being an engineer, would appal you. He positively likes the car to break down because it brings out my gentlemanly helplessness and his workmanlike skill and resource.

Straker Never you mind him, Mr Robinson. He likes to talk. We know him, dont we?

Octavius [*earnestly*] But theres a great truth at the bottom of what he says. I believe most intensely in the dignity of labor.

Straker [*unimpressed*] Thats because you never done any, Mr Robinson. My business is to do away with labor. Youll get more out of me and a machine than you will out of twenty laborers, and not so much to drink either.

Tanner For Heaven's sake, Tavy, dont start him on political economy. He knows all about it; and we dont. Youre only a poetic Socialist, Tavy: he's a scientific one.

Straker [*unperturbed*] Yes. Well, this conversation is very improvin; but Ive got to look after the car; and you two want to talk about your ladies. *I* know. [*He pretends to busy himself about the car, but presently saunters off to indulge in a cigaret*].

Tanner Thats a very momentous social phenomenon.

Octavius What is?

Tanner Straker is. Here have we literary and cultured persons been for years setting up a cry of the New Woman whenever some unusually old fashioned female came along, and never noticing the advent of the New Man. Straker's the New Man.

It is, of course, impossible to do justice to the abundant variety of Shaw's work in a short extract from one play. For the higher flights of Shavian eloquence in *Man and Superman* you must turn to the 'Don Juan in Hell' episode in Act III, where Tanner, in a dream sequence, becomes Don Giovanni, the hero of Mozart's opera, and discusses the future of mankind, at enormous length, with other characters similarly transformed. Nor could it be claimed that our extract is directly related to the main themes of the play. Nevertheless, it illustrates quite a number of the features of Shavian drama outlined on pp. 60-61.

One of these is obviously the introductory stage direction. It begins with a rather panoramic view of the setting – a country house, a clump of trees, a drive – not easy to represent in an early twentieth-century theatre still largely wedded to the tradition of pictorial realism in décor. Notice how the general scene description is artfully merged with the particular situation: we are told what Tanner *could* see, were he not preoccupied with something else – 'the legs' which serve at first, comically enough, for the name of their owner; comical, too, is the posture he is compelled to adopt as he emerges from beneath the car. There is, however, nothing inherently ridiculous about the chauffeur himself – rather the reverse. See how systematically Shaw describes him: dress, physical appearance, movements, manner, style of speech – all building up a strong impression of a young man who is nobody's fool, least of all his employer's.

Anyone familiar with the sparse stage directions of most earlier drama will realize at once that all this goes well beyond the conveying of essential information, and is in fact a piece of studied prose to be *read* with enjoyment, but containing much that cannot possibly be conveyed by the actor playing Straker before he has done more than get to his feet. In his use of stage directions Shaw often adopts the novelist's approach in introducing new characters.

The conversation that follows is very much one between equals, though Octavius has only a small share in it. In 1903, when traditional class distinctions were still widely accepted, this must have seemed a piquant departure from the normal master-servant relationship. Slyly impudent and deceitful servants are, of course, stock figures of comedy, but not servants who treat their masters with Straker's easy familiarity. As Tanner says of him, he is a New Man. It is true that Tanner, to whom Shaw has given much of his own love of exaggeration, is not always to be taken literally, and in his 'chaffing' of Straker and glorification of his education (as well as in making fun of his pronunciation of 'Enry') we can detect obvious irony and an undertone of patronizing superiority. Nevertheless, there is, setting aside the matter of Tanner's sincerity, a fine comic contrast between the way that he, with a public school and Oxbridge background, denounces Eton and Oxford, and the benign indifference of Straker to these venerable institutions –
'Very nice sort of place, Oxford, I should think, for people that like that sort of place.'
Highly entertaining, too, are his deprecation of his employer's exuberant assertions – Easy, easy! A little moderation, Mr Tanner,' and his appeal to Octavius as one sensible man to another.
'Never you mind him, Mr Robinson. He likes to talk. We know him, dont we?'
(Notice, though, that he does not deny Tanner's claim that he 'positively likes the car to break down'.) But when Octavius comes out with his little cliché about 'the dignity of labor' – one that Shaw must have heard countless times on the Socialist platforms where he himself was given to holding forth – Straker squashes him with the devastatingly down-to-earth rejoinder, 'That's because you never done any.' At the end of the episode, far from asking Tanner's permission to attend to the car, Straker simply turns his back on the gentlemen, saying, in effect, that he has better things to do than to stand there talking nonsense.

There are doubtless more brilliant passages of repartee in Shaw's plays, but this may be taken as a very representative sample of his stage dialogue. It abounds in neatly-turned and provocative sallies: 'This man takes more trouble to drop his aitches than ever his father did to pick them up'; 'Eton is a boy farm where we are sent because we are nuisances at home'; the universities are 'mere shops for selling class limitations'. We can also enjoy the accurate reproduction of Cockney pronunciation ('Aw rawt nah'), faulty grammar ('You dont know nothing about it'), and typical idiom ('they teach you to be an engineer or such like. See?') As an Irishman living in London, Shaw had a keen ear for such speech habits.

Running through the whole passage, and effectively summed up by Tanner at the end, is an awareness of social change. It is not altogether hyperbolical to make him call Straker 'a very momentous social phenomenon'. We may be tempted to a superior smile at some of the aspects of motoring in the days when Old Crocks were new models – the heavy protective clothing, the unreliability of the machines. Evidently Shaw himself was not unaware that motoring had its funny side; but, more important, he was acute enough to see in what many still regarded as a toy or a nuisance, and in the advent of people like Straker who could make it work, a portent for the future. European civilization was about to enter a new phase of technological development which would greatly affect the structure of society. Nor have we ceased today to hear traditional education disparaged – rightly or wrongly – as irrelevant to the needs of modern life.

Death of a Salesman (1949): Arthur Miller

Apart from a few exceptions like TS Eliot's *Murder in the Cathedral* and *The Cocktail Party* (see pp. 62-3), poetic drama – if by that we mean plays written in verse – has failed to establish itself in the twentieth-century theatre. The medium of drama remains overwhelmingly prose. Nevertheless, there are many works by contemporary dramatists which are essentially poetic in their appeal to feeling and imagination and in their use of language, even when it is, in general, what Wordsworth called, in another connection, 'the language of conversation in the middle and lower classes of society'.

Among plays falling into this category are those of Arthur Miller, which, despite their distinctively American qualities, have quickly become recognized as modern 'classics' in the theatre of the English-speaking world.

Death of a Salesman presents the last days in the life of a 63-year-old commercial traveller, *Willy Loman*. Willy has 'worked' New England for 34 years as the representative of the New York firm of Wagner's. At one time he was – or so he says – so successful that the firm's founder, 'old man Wagner', virtually promised him a partnership. Now he is old and exhausted. His whole life has been founded on self-deception and illusion, and the pursuit of worthless and unrealizable aims. Moreover, his relationship with his two sons, still known by their family nick-names as *Biff* and *Happy,* for whom he also cherished high hopes, has gone sour – especially with Biff, the elder.

The play is a notable example of imaginative stagecraft. As the author himself has explained, it began from the presumption that the distinction we make between our past and our present is unreal: everything in our lives exists simultaneously in our minds. Indeed, Miller's first tentative name for the play was *The Inside of His Head,* and he pictured a set in the form of 'an enormous face the height of the proscenium arch which would appear and then open up, and we would see the inside of a man's head'. This was subsequently modified to a kind of vertical section through Willy's house in Brooklyn, overshadowed by a suggestion of more recently built apartment blocks, and with a front-stage acting area on which is performed everything that happens outside the house. Just as the location of events is supposed to alter as the play requires, without change of scene, so events from Willy's past and, in at least one case, events that never happened, fuse with the action in the present, showing how past and present co-exist in Willy's mind.

A significant figure always in Willy's thoughts, particularly when he is most depressed, is his much older brother, *Ben,* who has recently died in Africa – where, we are told, he made a great fortune. Apparently he once visited Willy in Brooklyn on his way to complete a big deal in Alaska and – so at least Willy has convinced himself – offered him a job in that distant land of opportunity. Willy earnestly believes that Ben had the secret of success, and regularly wonders what it was, but Ben never gives him any real advice. All he will do is to pronounce a kind of magic formula: 'When I was seventeen I walked into the jungle, and when I was twenty-one I walked out. And by God I was rich.'

Just before the extract which follows, Willy has gone to his firm's head office to ask if, in view of his long service, he can be taken off the road and given a permanent job in New York. Young *Howard Wagner,* who now runs the business, is much more interested in his latest gadget, a tape-recorder, than in Willy's problems. As Willy tries to press his point, Howard makes it increasingly clear that it is time for Willy to go for good. In the end, Willy is reduced to pleading to be allowed to make the trip to Boston he originally hoped to avoid.

> *Willy* [*grasping Howard's arm*] Howard, you've got to let me go to Boston!
> *Howard* [*hard, keeping himself under control*] I've got a line of people to see this morning. Sit down, take five minutes, and pull yourself together, and then go home, will ya? I need the office, Willy. [*He starts to go, turns, remembering the recorder, starts to push off the table holding the recorder.* Oh, yeah. Whenever you can this week, stop by and drop off the samples, You'll feel better, Willy, and then come back and we'll talk. Pull yourself together, kid, there's people outside.
> *Howard exits, pushing the table off left. Willy stares into space, exhausted. Now the music is heard – Ben's music – first distantly, then closer, closer. As Willy speaks, Ben enters from the right. He carries valise and umbrella.*
> *Willy* Oh, Ben, how did you do it? What is the answer? Did you wind up the Alaska deal already?
> *Ben* Doesn't take much time if you know what you're doing. Just a short business trip. Boarding ship in an hour. Wanted to say good-by.
> *Willy* Ben, I've got to talk to you.
> *Ben* [*glancing at his watch*] Haven't the time, William.
> *Willy* [*crossing the apron to Ben*] Ben, nothing's working out. I don't know what to do.
> *Ben* Now, look here, William. I've bought timberland in Alaska and I need a man to look after things for me.
> *Willy* God, timberland! Me and my boys in those grand outdoors!
> *Ben* You've a new continent at your doorstep, William. Get out of these cities, they're full of talk and time payments and courts of law. Screw on your fists and you can fight for a fortune up there.
> *Willy* Yes, yes! Linda, Linda!
> *Linda enters as of old, with the wash.*
> *Linda* Oh, you're back?
> *Ben* I haven't much time.
> *Willy* No, wait! Linda, he's got a proposition for me in Alaska.
> *Linda* But you've got – [*To Ben*] He's got a beautiful job here.
> *Willy* But in Alaska, kid, I could –
> *Linda* You're doing well enough, Willy!

Ben [*to Linda*] Enough for what, my dear?

Linda [*frightened of Ben and angry at him*] Don't say those things to him! Enough to be happy right here, right now. [*To Willy, while Ben laughs*] Why must everybody conquer the world? You're well liked, and the boys love you, and someday – [*to Ben*] why, old man Wagner told him just the other day that if he keeps it up he'll be a member of the firm, didn't he, Willy?

Willy Sure, sure. I am building something with this firm, Ben, and if a man is building something he must be on the right track, mustn't he?

Ben What are you building? Lay your hand on it. Where is it?

Willy [*hesitantly*] That's true, Linda, there's nothing.

Linda Why? [*To Ben*] There's a man eighty-four years old –

Willy That's right, Ben, that's right. When I look at that man I say, what is there to worry about?

Ben Bah!

Willy It's true, Ben. All he has to do is go into any city, pick up the phone, and he's making his living and you know why?

Ben [*picking up his valise*] I've got to go.

Willy [*holding Ben back*] Look at this boy!

Biff, in his high school sweater, enters carrying suitcase. Happy carries Biff's shoulder guards, gold helmet, and football pants.

Willy Without a penny to his name, three great universities are begging for him, and from there the sky's the limit, because it's not what you do, Ben. It's who you know and the smile on your face! It's contacts, Ben, contacts! The whole wealth of Alaska passes over the lunch table at the Commodore Hotel, and that's the wonder, the wonder of this country, that a man can end with diamonds here on the basis of being liked! [*He turns to Biff*] And that's why when you get out on that field today it's important. Because thousands of people will be rooting for you and loving you. [*To Ben, who has again begun to leave*] And Ben! when he walks into a business office his name will sound out like a bell and all the doors will open to him! I've seen it, Ben, I've seen it a thousand times! You can't feel it with your hand like timber, but it's there!

Ben Good-by, William.

Willy Ben, am I right? Don't you think I'm right? I value your advice.

Ben There's a new continent at your doorstep, William. You could walk out rich. Rich! [*He is gone*]

Willy We'll do it here, Ben! You hear me? We're gonna do it here!

Let us first consider the fluid treatment of time and place, and the significance of the stage properties and sound effects. The tape-recorder on its trolley locates the action in Howard's office. After he has wheeled it off, though Willy does not physically move, the scene changes to the Loman house in Brooklyn, and the time is now that of Ben's visit long ago. Ben's entrance is heralded by a musical theme (as in a Wagner opera, he has his *leitmotiv*); his case and umbrella indicate that he is just passing through, travelling from one end of the world to the other on his mysterious but profitable business. Ben can never stay long. When Linda, Willy's wife, enters 'as of old', i.e., as in former days, she is, of course, younger in appearance and carries a basket full of washing, symbolizing her devotion to her household tasks. Finally appears Biff as he was in his High School days, attended by his admiring and envious younger brother carrying his football kit – for there is to be an important game this afternoon, and Willy has already decided that Biff will be the hero of the match.

Notice next how the attitudes of the characters are conveyed. Howard is both embarrassed and irritated by Willy's desperate appeal to be allowed to go to Boston. As people in his position often do, he tries to put an end to the interview by claiming that he is a busy man. He appears to be worried about Willy – 'Pull yourself together, kid' – and hints that he *may* be able to do something for him when he feels better – 'Come back and we'll talk' – but we know that his real object is to get rid of Willy with as little fuss as possible. 'Stop by and drop off the samples' makes it very clear, despite the show of concern, that Willy is really being sacked.

In the conversation with Ben, who is throughout fidgeting to be off, Willy's inconsistency and his ability to swing round on a completely different tack are sharply revealed. At one moment 'nothing's working out' and he hears the call of the wide open spaces – 'God, timberland! Me and my boys in those grand outdoors!'; the next, he asserts that he is 'building something with this firm' and that he's 'gonna do it here'. All his aspirations are romantic dreams. The business success he yearns for is as far beyond his grasp as the new life on the Last Frontier. Ben jolts him by asking what solid achievement he can point to, but Linda – who, at this stage is wholly converted to Willy's view of life – comes to his aid. She reminds him of a veteran salesman (his name is Dave Singleman) who can still make an easy living because of his contacts and popularity, which in turn prompts Willy to a rhetorical outburst celebrating 'the wonder of this country' where deals involving as much wealth as can be found in the whole of Alaska are settled over lunch in a New York hotel.

Running through most of the episode is the spurious claim that all things will be added to you if you are 'well liked'. Linda, no doubt echoing what she has so often heard from Willy himself, reminds him that he is well liked; evidently Dave Singleman at 84 is well liked; 'a man can end with diamonds here on the basis of being well liked' – he doesn't have to go to Africa, like Ben, to find them. (It is almost predictable, after all this, that not one of Willy's business acquaintances will turn up at his funeral.) Most of all is it important that Biff, Willy's golden boy – as he is, literally, in one way, his football helmet being lacquered gold – should be well liked. The game of football, as Willy sees it, is not just an important sporting event: it marks the beginning for Biff of a spectacularly successful career in which all doors will fly open before the popular young sportsman with the big smile and the wide circle of useful friends. Already, boasts the proud father, 'three great universities' are competing for the privilege of admitting Biff as a student. It is, of course, only natural that Willy's ambitions for Biff should lead him to preach the false gospel of success incessantly, and that a relationship in which success is so harped on will be greatly strained when success is not in fact achieved.

The conversation is carried on for the most part, in the everyday speech of contemporary New Yorkers. There are moments when it achieves great pathos by its simplicity: 'Oh, Ben, how did you do it? What is the answer?' . . . . 'Ben, nothing's working out. I don't know what to do.' At other times, however, when Willy is carried away by his triumphal visions, his language is inspired rather as Volpone's is by the contemplation of his gold – 'And Ben! when he walks into a business office his name will sound out like a bell and all the doors will open to him!' One almost expects him to add that all the trumpets will sound for him on the other side – of the President's teak portals.

Miller has denied that the play is either an indictment of American capitalism or an analysis of family relationships gone wrong, though any reader or spectator is bound to feel that these are elements in it. His explanation of what he intended it to be about is a good deal more complex than the play itself. It is perhaps sensible to see it as primarily an attempt – a very powerful and moving one – to demonstrate what goes on in the mind of a man defeated by life and betrayed by the fantasies and illusions which have become necessary to him. Such people are to be found by the tens of thousands in all societies. Miller seems to think that Willy gains a kind of victory at the end by suicide, and that, while he is not a tragic figure in the Aristotelian sense, i.e., one who, before his downfall, is 'highly renowned and prosperous', he has the kind of tragic stature which our civilization allows. However that may be, we can agree, in the 'century of the common man', that he is something of an Everyman figure ('Loman = 'Low man'?), and the play a modern Morality.

Part IV The novel and other prose works

1 General
2 Practical criticism

INTRODUCTION

Questions on prose works, which in most cases mean novels, but also include collections of short stories, essays and good examples of other genres, such as letters or biography, take up about a third of those asked by all the Examining Boards; the other questions consist of those on poetry and drama.

The Oxford Board illustrates this proportion well enough in its two papers, of which the first, besides Shakespeare and Chaucer or Milton, offers a major (usually Victorian) novel as an option instead of either Chaucer or Milton. The second paper may be chosen from five periods of literary history, in which approximately a third are prose works, though the proportion varies according to the period. Some periods are more productive of good prose than others, which may be strongest in poetry or drama. The modern period is well represented by all three main categories of literature.

It is not usually possible, and in any case inadvisable, to miss entirely preparation for texts in any one of these categories. You should read carefully the rubric of your Board to ascertain what the exact requirements are. For example, you should find out how far candidates are encouraged to read parallel literature, what proportion and what types of questions are asked on such, and what choice is allowed on the prescribed texts.

The majority of examination boards set two types of question on prose works. The first is the general essay question and the second the practical criticism or critical appreciation question on an unseen passage or passages.

Oxford and JMB also set questions which ask for comment on a printed passage or passages from a prescribed work. (The relevant syllabuses give details.) In tackling this type of question you should follow the general guidelines in the section on practical criticism (p. 90). You will *also* be expected to show evidence of your knowledge of the work as a whole. For example, if characters are involved in the passage chosen, you should be able to analyze them more effectively because of your study of their development throughout the work. You should be very careful to confine yourself to remarks that are relevant to the printed passage.

1 General

NOTE ON NON-FICTION TEXTS

Although the novel from Defoe to William Golding holds, rightly, the pride of place in sections devoted to prose on the syllabuses, works from other genres may conveniently be noted here as they appear among the prose texts set:
Essays (Bacon, Milton, Addison, Johnson, Lamb, Hazlitt);
Biographies and autobiographies (De Quincey, Boswell, Gibbon, Johnson, Charles Darwin, Gosse);
Diaries (Pepys and John Evelyn);
Letters (of many good collections of these the one normally found is a selection of Keats' and even this usually in conjunction with the poetry);

Criticism Prescribed for its own excellence of style and the light thrown upon the thought of the critics themselves, since those chosen for A-level study are usually great writers in other genres too: Dryden's Prefaces and 'Essay on Dramatic Poetry', Addison on Milton, Johnson, Wordsworth, Coleridge, Matthew Arnold, Shaw, Lawrence, Eliot and Auden.

Occasional works in other genres specially chosen for their intrinsic merit or special interest with regard to English language or literature: philosophy (Browne, Bacon, Hobbes); natural history or sociology (Gilbert White, Richard Jefferies, Flora Thompson's *Lark Rise to Candleford;* linguistics (Sir Ernest Gowers' *Complete Plain Words*).

This list is not exhaustive but will give an indication of the range of works set.

INTRODUCTION

Depending on the sort of novel prescribed (and for convenience I will include other kinds of prose work under this head in future) there are likely to be certain common features in the questions. The candidate must know the principal features of the book he or she has chosen, for it is usually these features that are singled out for the questions, not more peripheral concerns. You must therefore grasp firmly and thoroughly whichever of the following (points 1-9) forms one or more of the main features of the novel you are studying.

1 SATIRICAL, POLEMICAL OR DIDACTIC ELEMENTS

Nearly every great novel, to a greater or lesser degree, or more or less profoundly, bears examination on the following points:

(a) Is the author trying to change, reform or attack anything?

(b) Is the author holding anything up for ridicule, or even harmless amusement?

(c) Is the author bitter about any social abuses or other forms of folly or wickedness?

If you decide the novel you are studying does have satirical, polemical or didactic elements, you should analyse how such elements can be identified and the manner of their expression.

If the novel you are studying is not contemporary and satirizes a political or social situation of its own time, you should ask yourself:

(a) How effective was the satire? Did it change anything?

(b) What proportion of the novel is devoted to such elements? Is the novel still valuable if the cause or motive for the satire is now past?

(c) If the cause is not yet dead, is the satire still relevant?

(d) Does the satire take on new significance in the light of events that have occurred since the work was written?

With regard to the continuing 'relevance' of satirical works, you should note that political satire may be regenerated if history repeats itself. Much 'moral' satire is of course perennial. For instance, vanity may present itself in different guises, but underlying vice is the same.

It should be remembered that even in the case of a primarily satirical novel or essay, other elements may play a very important part. You should decide whether the characters survive the burden of their satiric intent, as do many of Dickens' characters, for example. Are they credible and 'solid' or are they mere 'types'? Are they intended as 'types' (for this, their names may give a clue, for example, 'Hypocrisy' in *The Pilgrim's Progress*).

2 CHARACTER

It is important to remember that characters are not 'persons' who can be detached from their books as people can be taken from their normal lives; they are a part of their story and very often closely interrelated with several other characters of the book. Even Hemingway's lonely old man (*The Old Man and the Sea*) owes much of his character to the people of his memories and daydreams, as well as to the boy through whose eyes we see him. He is the centre of a parable created by the author to make a certain point about human endeavour, and man's place and state in life.

You may find it useful to prepare 'character studies' of all the main characters in the novels you are studying as an exercise in preliminary memorizing or foundation work. However, while at GCSE such preparation can form a basis for examination answers, A-level questions require more subtle treatment. The isolated character study is likely to prove too mechanical for the questions that are asked. They will require a more selective treatment, with more assessment and comparison of aspects of character based upon an overall close understanding of the whole work. One cannot dispense with close reference, examples and supporting details to illustrate generalizations and therefore you cannot afford to despise the sort of information gathered in 'character studies'. You should however be able to transcend the method, and without knowing substantially less, know how to arrange the material more sensitively, because it is better digested and related to other characters, themes and subject matter.

A more useful preparation on character would almost certainly be intelligent and well-informed discussion with other students, perhaps led by an instructor with special knowledge of the book. (Sixth form conferences can be very helpful in this.) Such discussions should include considerations such as the comparison of one character with another, the motives of their actions, their characteristic outlook and thinking, their values and their special foibles or traits.

You should examine not only how the characters operate but also in what manner they are operated upon and with what result. ('Tess' of Hardy's novel *Tess of the D'Urbervilles* is a good example of the fruitfulness of this line of thinking.) A good light upon character is thrown by examining a character's reactions to events. For example, in Hardy's *Far From the Madding Crowd,* Bathsheba's vanity and frivolity cause her to write Mr Boldwood a valentine; his stern, humourless and intense nature causes him to take it seriously. These small beginnings, mixed with the extraordinary personality of Sergeant Troy, lead to murder and suicide. Again, in Jane Austen's *Northanger Abbey,* Catherine's earlier predilection for the ridiculous 'Gothic horror' novels – an affected fashion of the time – leads directly to her unfortunate misunderstandings in the country mansion, her head being full of romantic nonsense. This aberration of course can be and is dispelled, making her a maturer, wiser woman. Similar romantic delusions derived from reading, pervert the behaviour and thought of characters as diverse as DH Lawrence's Miriam Leivers (*Sons and Lovers*), and Joseph Conrad's *Lord Jim.*

You should consider a character's role in the novel: Mrs Ramsay's centrality in Virginia Woolf's *To the Lighthouse* for example, or Nostromo's in Conrad's novel of that name. A-level questions often ask for comment on a character's achievement or failure in some endeavour, or on how far a character or a set of characters express their nature in a certain key chapter or scene.

Characters may also be assessed as to how far they are realistic, credible, natural, or heightened for special purpose such as satire, humour or tragic grandeur. They may range from cardboard stereotypes, or mere personifications of qualities as in an allegory; through grotesqueness or exaggeration of traits to heroically idealized or deliberately demeaned persons such as are often found in moralities like some Victorian novels and twentieth-century books such as *The Lord of the Flies* by William Golding. There is, for example, the interesting trio of Angel Clare, Tess and Alec d'Urberville in Hardy's *Tess of the D'Urbervilles.*

It is worth remembering that a first-person narrator in a novel is not the novelist but a character who sees things only in the light of his or her own point of view, and coloured by his or her personality. Thus in Conrad's *Lord Jim,* after some pages of authorial third-person narration, we begin to view things as Marlow saw them, and later as did the girl Jewel in Patusan, and even (since Marlow was not present at the later scenes) as did Gentleman Brown, a biased villain. Conrad gains variety and depth by the use of these different viewpoints. Conrad's *Nostromo* is far more complex in the use of the same technique, and Henry James' *What Maisie Knew* and *The Ambassadors* are remarkable in their application of this principle. You should resist the temptation to assume that the author's main character is synonymous with the author. For example, Stephen Dedalus in Joyce's *A Portrait of the Artist as a Young Man* and *Ulysses* is not necessarily representing Joyce himself. Autobiographical knowledge of an author can be enlightening but should be handled with caution. Identification of any fictional character with a prototype in real life is a bad practice; many characters are combinations of different people, not to mention the author's creative additions. An autobiographical persona such as Daedalus in Joyce's *A Portrait of the Artist as a Young Man* or *Ulysses,* Birkin in Lawrence's *Women in Love,* or David Copperfield or Pip in Dickens, are not to be taken as complete or even accurate portraits of their authors – they are often no more than studies in self criticism. In the same way, the innumerable portraits by artists of their friends, enemies or acquaintances are notoriously one-sided, exaggerated and even on occasion libellous. Hence the familiar disclaimer on many novels' title pages.

To summarize on 'Character' in novels students should ask themselves these elementary questions.

(1) Is what other characters say or think about this character true?

(2) Is what the character says or thinks about him- or herself true?

(3) Is his or her character revealed in action or in suffering of events?

Rosemary Harris and Christopher Lahr in *To The Lighthouse* (BBC Copyright Photograph)

Peter Lorre in *The Secret Agent*

(4) How is his or her character revealed by what he or she says and thinks, and in what terms does he or she express his or her thoughts?

(5) Does the author use 'all knowing' privilege to throw any light upon the character?

(6) Does the character undergo any significant change in the story?

You should also ask yourself more subtle questions:

(1) Does the character carry conviction?

(2) Is the character consistent? Is he or she played off against another/other character(s)?

(3) Does the character come to life or remain as a stereotype – if the latter, is this for a special purpose?

(4) Do we ever care what is happening to the character?

(5) Do we wonder how the character will behave – are we ever suprised by his or her behaviour?

(6) Does the character play a brief or minor role, if so how necessary is he or she to the action?

(7) What is his or her role if a major character – do his or her words or actions carry themes?

(8) Does he or she influence events and lives – if so how far?

(9) Is he or she used as a mouthpiece for authorial ideas or opinion?

It is by these and similar investigations that questions on character may be prepared for.

3 THEME

Care must be taken not to confuse the theme and plot as sometimes happens in the case of strongly plotted novels such as George Eliot's *Silas Marner* and Dickens' *A Christmas Carol*.

A *combination* of plot, characters and language may form the vehicle for whatever themes the novel has. A simple (and simplified) definition would be that the novel's theme is what it is about and its plot is what happens in it.

It is very common, of course, for novels to have no themes at all and yet still display wonderful plots (e.g. *Tarzan of the Apes*, E Rice Burroughs; *Enter the Saint*, Leslie Charteris). A vast flood of such works is released on to the market in every generation to enable people to pass otherwise unoccupied time agreeably and to make money for their authors.

Important themes, that is, those that advance or restate in satisfying new ways our understanding of ourselves and our world, are 'hallmarks' of good literature. The book of trivial or no theme, unfortunately, is the one often acclaimed and widely read, although it will not be found on A-level syllabuses.

Many fine, even great, novels, though they cannot be such without themes, can and do dispense with any recognizable plot. Short stories exemplify this; many are little more than 'studies' or situations. Where there is no real plot the theme must necessarily be carried by character and/or language; but if such are the heart, the theme is the soul of the work.

Novels that are thematic rather than plotted, such as Virginia Woolf's *The Waves* are often considered 'difficult'. The attitude reflected in EM Forster's resigned dictum 'yes–oh dear–yes– the novel tells a story' is still common. Chapter 2 of EM Forster's *Aspects of the Novel* (see p. 160) is stimulating reading on this subject and has been used as a basis for A-level questions.

The importance placed on themes in A-level questions may be illustrated by a paper where only one alternative was set on Lawrence's *The Rainbow*. The first option was 'What do you think Lawrence is trying to tell us about marriage and parenthood in *The Rainbow*?'; the second 'Why do you think Lawrence called his novel *The Rainbow*'?

It is not uncommon for a novel's major theme to be suggested by its title. Other examples of this include *To the Lighthouse* (Virginia Woolf), *The Way of All Flesh* (Samuel Butler), *The Lord of the Flies* and *The Inheritors* (William Golding); *Heart of Darkness* (Joseph Conrad). The titles of a novel's parts may also be used in this way, as: 'The Mosque', 'The Caves', 'The Temple' (*A Passage to India*, EM Forster). 'The Silver of the Mine', 'The Isabels', 'The Lighthouse' (*Nostromo*, Joseph Conrad). (See also pp. 131-2 where we discuss symbolism, imagery and 'motifs'.)

It is necessary to identify themes from whatever element in the novel is enlisted to express them whether the story, character or language. For example *A Portrait of the Artist as a Young Man* by James Joyce, may at first reading and at a first level, seem not much more than just that – a neutral if faithful exercise in autobiography with the character Stephen Daedalus representing Joyce himself. However, as the book develops, if you like at a second level, there is growing evidence that what it is really about at least includes the imperative need to escape from all that Dublin contains: family, religion, friends and academicism, to be free to be his creative self. One of the characteristic motifs of the novel is 'I will not serve'. It is about the growing awareness of Stephen of his genius and what threatens to destroy it. It is therefore, at a third level, also about how the human spirit may be enslaved by the dead, corrupt and sham elements of its environment and in that sense the novel is of universal application and embodies a theme as old as Exodus. Thus in order to get to the heart of a novel's theme you should learn to look and then look again.

An interesting example of the use of images or 'motifs' to help convey the essential themes of a novel, is to be found in *The Inheritors* by William Golding. As the title indicates and as is expanded in the book, the overall theme is the supercession of the old – comfortable as it may be – by the new, because more technically advanced and intellectually vigorous. In the clash and interplay of these two worlds lies all the tension and interest of the book. For example, the Old People hate water, but the New Ones have mastered it, and the presence and sound of the roaring waterfall is intermittently referred to throughout the book: the New People cross the river on canoes never seen before by the Old, who can scarcely cross a creek as their log bridge has been removed.

When deciding on a novel's major themes, it is a useful procedure to begin with the most obvious and work down to the smallest details and incidents, noting how these fit in and build up the picture. If details are taken irrespective of any overall theme, it is easier to be irrelevant and waste time over less important aspects.

By dovetailing the small pieces into the larger ones, the selection or pursuit of irrelevancies may be avoided. The thematic reasons for placing Gulliver (*Gulliver's Travels*, Jonathan Swift) first in Lilliput, then in Brobdingnag, then Laputa and other places and lastly the country of the Houyhnhnms and Yahoos, should be well grasped before any of the lesser activities in any place may be well understood. The broader gradations and differing emphases of satire should be noted in the *whole* work, the better to understand local episodes. In the first two, betrayals by royalty ('of so little weight are the greatest Services to Princes, when put into the balance with a Refusal to gratify their Passions') are set against services and kindnesses, while in 'Laputa' Swift gives freer reign to his attacks on pedantic folly, and in the last part he achieves the greatest power of the famous 'saeva indignatio' in the contrast between the two kinds of creature. Gulliver, as the 'normal' man moves through these scenes as a foil for the ways of life of the creatures in them, expressing the likely reaction of the reader rather like a Greek chorus. Our moral or political positions are shown up in various lights, although of course the eighteenth century context makes a good deal of this special to that time and in some cases peculiar to Swift. Presumably the Royal Society would not agree with all of his attitudes to scientific research, nor would modern scientists who have descended from them. (It should be observed here that very often, perhaps due to the length of the novel, Parts I and II only of this novel are set for A Level.)

Similarly the content and thematic contributions of each of the three sections of *Nostromo* and *A Passage to India* must be balanced and assessed for their place in the whole work; indeed, in the case of the latter, to appreciate why the third part was added to it at all. This is a good example of a book which if read for the story only seems to be all over by the end of the 'Caves'. Unless the transcending yet also immanent theme of communication or its failure between men, between races and between men and their land, or men and God, is deduced from the characters, incidents and language of all three parts, there is little value in criticizing any one part or paragraph of *A Passage to India*.

Finally it must be said that for much the same reason, other novels, poems or essays by, and good biographies about, these and other great novelists whose work is prescribed, most emphatically repay attention. You can then trace themes and give weight to your opinions.

4 PLOT

Although A-level questions seldom, if ever, require straightforward plot narration, the student should know thoroughly every stage of development of the plot, especially every stage of the development of the relationships of the leading characters with their attendant circumstances. It is helpful to draw diagrammatic plot plans to bring out more clearly circumstances on a time line. These emphasize the significant 'turns' and advances, the main crises and clarify complications such as time-shifts or changes of scene. Time-shifts include gaps or leaps of time forward as well as backward, and simultaneous action in other scenes.

An obvious warning should be recorded here: candidates should be particularly on their guard against being drawn into an irrelevant parade of such knowledge; questions always require you to judge, select and make new rearrangements of the prepared material, rarely to trot it straight out, unless by a happy coincidence a particular question has been fully prepared in advance. This warning holds good for lengthy quotations; these should not be uncritically or unselectively quoted simply because known. You should only quote the relevant lines, and not too many of them. For example, no question is likely to ask a candidate to reproduce in full any particular episode of, say, *Middlemarch* by George Eliot, but in answer to a question on how far Dorothea, its heroine, gains in self-knowledge, the candidate is called upon to refer to such episodes and incidents of the novel as properly illustrate circumstances in which she becomes aware of her strengths, her limitations, in short, aware of herself. Here, the art is to be as comprehensive as possible: the examiner is likely to have as a guide a list of the possible areas of reference relevant to this question, and it behoves candidates aspiring to full marks to be as complete as possible, and not to dwell too long on one or two episodes they perhaps know better than others. This requires a period of steady and concentrated thinking in advance, with possibly a few notes jotted down as aides-memoire.

If the question is actually based on the plot, as for example, 'Show how the separate strands of *Middlemarch* are blended into a unified whole' then the same principle applies: large sketches of each 'strand' including the leading story should be left in favour of consideration of the actual manner in which such 'strands' are linked one with the other – by character, cross-over of thematic or narrative material, or symmetry of structure. Notice how closely the need for actual knowledge of the material goes hand in hand with the successful answering of such questions. It cannot be denied that a judicious and discriminating intelligence is necessary for tackling A-level questions; fortunately these days the pomposity and jargon of the old phrasing of questions in which simple and straightforward ideas were wrapped up in obscurity, are no longer inflicted on the candidate.

A further illustration of comprehensiveness in the selection of relevant plot material can be given by a question which requires an examination of Walter Morel's status in and popularity with his family in DH Lawrence's *Son and Lovers*. The times when he is accepted by the children should be cited as well as the more immediately obvious drunken bullying and loss of sympathy; the special relationship with Mrs Morel should be noted and distinguished from the implacable hatred of the sick Paul, and the latter's uncompromising rejection of Walter's clumsy attempts at sympathy and communication. In a consideration of the attitudes of the parents to their children, Walter's reception of the news of William's death may be usefully compared or contrasted with Gertrude's where the only thing that brings her back to life is the near death of her youngest son and next object of possessive love, Paul.

The following examination question on Joyce's *A Portrait of the Artist as a Young Man* is a thematic question but required selection from the plot may demonstrate the reverse process: thus, 'What chiefly motivates Stephen is an increasing desire for freedom. Discuss', necessitates the survey of the novel with a view to writing on this subject. The candidate might turn over in his or her mind all the respects in which Stephen is restricted or cramped or frustrated; as he grows up, he is hampered by conditions in his home, by the schools he attends, by his ignorant and insensitive companions, by hidebound teachers, by his mother's religion and Jesuitical indoctrination, by sexual frustration and the terror of damnation springing from sermons and by artistic narrowness and Philistinism, and by the 'dear dirty' city of Dublin itself. Growing impatience and restiveness under it all leads in the end to self-appointed exile – a complete break with his entire background. He gains freedom from all previous shackles as he applies his 'Non serviam' to each one. Relevant quotation may be made; in particular, remarks about Stephen's mother; his refusal of her dying entreaty that he should make his communion. But as the question invites one to 'discuss' this proposition, it should be noticed that it is quite relevant to consider, more briefly because less significantly, the other possible motivations for Stephen's actions in his early life – that is the period covered by this book (he appears again in *Ulysses*). We have examined what 'chiefly' motivates Stephen, but there are such drives as his desire for intellectual supereminence; his desire for others' recognition of this and his desire to be an artist. These things are more positive than his urgent need for freedom – he needs to be free for something, and gaining his freedom is the prerequisite for his larger ambitions. His 'epiphanies' especially the one of the girl on the beach, give him some of the evidence to justify these motives.

There are two main types of plot found in novels: the first is the highly structured, architectonic story, with artfully arranged parallels, contrasts, discoveries, shifts of scene and time, character groupings or major character establishment (e.g. the parallel or contrasting pairs in Conrad's *Victory*, the police and anarchist groups in *The Secret Agent*, and Nostromo and

Decoud in *Nostromo*), the engineering of coincidences, concealed with varying success so as to appear natural or inevitable. It may be that the structure of this type may be loose, or full of unresolved beginnings or dead ends, but the principal test of such plots is that they may be easily paraphrased or told as stories. Time shifts may be rearranged to be chronological as the film of *Lord Jim* did for that novel and generally speaking there is a strong air of 'what happens next' in such plots.

The second type may be called 'episodic' or 'organic': there is less concern with 'a story' and more with the growth and development of affairs, or the progress of events, as in life. The progress through time of a character or set of characters, merely to see where they will arrive, is one of the examples of this type such as in *War and Peace, The Rainbow, Mrs Dalloway, The Forsyte Saga, Tristram Shandy:* usually only parts, if anything, of such novels can be related as 'stories'. Events grow naturally from prior events, with no obvious plan (though of course with unifying themes).

A third type of novel may be considered to have scarcely any plot, but since the content of such novels may be described, and as this type includes very good novels, I mention them here: they are the 'poetical' novels, almost prose poems; the action subsists in character and language, in some extreme cases in language alone. This is a type which not so long ago would not have been regarded as a novel at all, but with the work of Woolf (*The Waves*), Joyce (*Finnegans Wake*) and Beckett (*Watt, The Unnameable, How It is*), the definition or boundaries of the novel have to be redrawn to accommodate them: there is a decided and firm, even formal, structure to such novels, but it is a structure of their material and language rather than a plot structure.

5 SETTING AND BACKGROUND OF NOVELS

The geographical and social background of most novels is significant and should be studied for itself, whether it be the Victorian London of Dickens' *Our Mutual Friend,* the Mexico of Graham Green's *The Power and Glory,* or, should it ever be set, Lawrence's *The Plumed Serpent* or the lovely Wessex of nearly all of Hardy. Most authors of such novels, of course, know their country very well at first hand. However, it is not necessarily the authenticity that makes the setting so important, but its use in many novels not only as a background but actually as a force in the novel, for thematic or other purposes. Whether it was poets or novelists who first consciously conceived the idea of turning backgrounds into active partners is hard to say: the honour may even be Shakespeare's; it is sufficient to be aware of their employment as such.

The Lord of The Flies (Directed by Peter Brooke)

Wuthering Heights

Hardy's settings for example, often of several distinct kinds in one novel, are as vital to the understanding of his themes as the deliberately exploited landscape features of the poet WH Auden's *Bucolics*. Certainly an imaginative power akin to that of fine nature poetry is achieved by such novels as Hardy's *The Return of the Native*. Here, the famous first chapter which develops the atmosphere of Egdon Heath establishes a mood that prevails over the book, and which the characters seem to share. This conscious handling of scenery is a kind of Wordsworthian alchemy, in which moral, sensuous, spiritual or even intellectual concepts may be established. At its plainest we find this in open allegory such as Spenser's epic *The Faerie Queene* which is a set of narrations in verse, and Bunyan's *The Pilgrim's Progress,* or in concealed allegory such as *The Spire* or *The Lord of the Flies,* both by William Golding. The allegory may become very subtle in works such as *The Rainbow* or *Women in Love* by DH Lawrence, in Hardy's *Far from the Madding Crowd* and *Tess of the D'Urbervilles*, in Emily Bronte's *Wuthering Heights* or Conrad's *The Heart of Darkness*.

A fine example of the suggestive painting of a setting is the first chapter of *The Rainbow* with its delicate allusions to the pressures and impulses in the lives of the inhabitants of the environs of Cossethay, from which the characters of the ensuing novel are to be drawn from one generation to another. See also the treatment of *The Man Who Loved Islands* by Lawrence, where the theme is paralleled by the successive series of diminishing islands in which the man hopes, self-deludingly, to be happy. In Conrad's *Victory* there is a supposedly paradisal island, but its derelict coal mine, black jetty and abandoned rails, offices and bungalows unmistakably suggest the vanity of trying to escape, and the violent storm, as so often in Conrad, heralds the catastrophe. Axel Heyst is forcibly returned to the evil realities of existence, as the setting so ominously suggests he will be.

On pp. 133-4 there are extracts from two novels which show how skilfully settings can be used.

To summarize: the ordinary function of the setting is to provide realism of context to plot and character; it gives them a historical, social and geographical background which enhances their authenticity; it adds atmosphere, colour and interest; as a side effect it can provide documentary knowledge of place rather in the manner of a travel guide and this can also add interest, verisimilitude and satisfaction to our normal curiosity about our world and its affairs. Many novelists have first-hand experience or do careful research on their settings (e.g. Conrad for *Nostromo* as he had never experienced life on a Caribbean island). Novels, even bad ones, may therefore be mines of information but the main and organic function of setting remains the provision of a living and cooperative medium for the better understanding of character, plot and, above all, themes.

A still from the first film version of Tess of the D'Urbervilles

6 COMPARISON OF THE NOVEL WITH OTHER GENRES

Occasionally questions are set at A Level which touch on the similarity of a novel to a work or works of another genre, either in its structure or its method. Such questions presuppose a good knowledge of, and ability to define at least competently, the genre for comparison. For example, medieval morality and allegory lie behind Bunyan's *The Pilgrim's Progress* and social history behind Dickens' *A Tale of Two Cities* and Elizabeth Gaskell's *North and South*.

Tragedy

It is particularly necessary to be able to define, and know some good examples of, tragedy, as this has a large body of theory and practice built up over the centuries. Some ages in history tend to produce tragic novels rather than tragedies: *Tess of the D'Urbervilles, Jude the Obscure* and *The Mayor of Casterbridge* are examples from the nineteenth century. For generally dramatic treatment in the eighteenth century there are Henry Fielding's *Joseph Andrews* and Oliver Goldsmith's *The Vicar of Wakefield*.

Journalism diaries and letters

Documentary journalism may be referred to in connection with novels such as Daniel Defoe's *Moll Flanders* and the journal or diary in connection with, for example, the same author's *Journal of the Plague Year*.

Biography and autobiography

Biography and autobiography are very closely linked to the novel, so that different kinds of prose work as set may be required to be compared with kinds not set. As for novels, the features and elements of the genre not prescribed have to be recognized in the work that is: if the work is any way similar to another genre such features need to be analysed in advance of probable questions. Although it is not normally expected for autobiographical novels, that the candidate should necessarily be conversant with the life of the author and where the parallels lie, it is useful and certainly often very interesting to read a good biography of those novelists who are particularly strong in autobiographical material in their work, or some of it. A short list here should include:

Compton Mackenzie (*Sinister Street*)
Somerset Maugham (*The Razor's Edge*)
Orwell (*Burmese Days, A Clergyman's Daughter* – others of his books are frankly autobiographical such as *Down and Out in Paris and London, Homage to Catalonia*)
Lawrence (*Sons and Lovers*)   Scott Fitzgerald (*Tender is the Night*)
Hemingway (*A Farewell to Arms*)   Conrad (*Youth, The Heart of Darkness*)

In the nineteenth century

Dickens (*David Copperfield*)
Hardy (*A Pair of Blue Eyes*)
George Eliot (*Scenes from Clerical Life, The Mill on the Floss*)
Melville (*Bartleby*)
Samuel Butler (*The Way of All Flesh*)
Kipling (*Kim, Stalky and Co.*)

Autobiographies occasionally seen on the syllabuses may be noted here: Johnson's *Journey to the Western Islands of Scotland* which should be read in conjunction with Boswell's *Journal of a Tour to the Hebrides;* Edmund Goss's *Father and Son,* Darwin's *The Voyage of the Beagle;* Conrad's *A Personal Record,* and *The Mirror of the Sea;* Sassoon's *Memoirs of an Infantry Officer;* Graves' *Goodbye to All That;* Cyril Connolly's *Enemies of Promise;* TE Lawrence's *The Mint;* Koestler's *Darkness at Noon;* Ford Madox Ford's *Memories and Impressions* read in conjunction with *The Good Soldier.* In the same way Graves, Lawrence, Hardy and Sassoon should be read with their related poetry, and Keith Douglas's *Alamein to Zem Zem* with his Second World War poems. Many poets have written at least one novel, and beside Hardy's double achievement should be read his autobiography published under the name of a biography by his second wife and secretary, Florence Emily Hardy.

Political theory

Behind George Orwell's *1984,* stemming from the political allegory of *Animal Farm,* for example, may be noted the political theory directly embodied in *Goldstein's Book* and elsewhere implicit in the ideas and action of the novel.

Useful reading

A useful book which relates the theory of tragedy to its foundation in Aristotle's Poetics is FL Lucas's *Tragedy.* Other studies of the different genres include an interesting series of essays published by Martin Secker titled *The Art and Craft of Letters:* Comedy, Parody, Satire, Ballad, Epic, Short Story and History are described. However, the best examples of the major practitioners remain the most useful frames of reference and comparison.

7 HUMOUR (*see also 'A humorous or serious tone' p. 138 and Comic style p. 142*)

If the novel or a large part of it is meant to be humorous, it is to be hoped that we still find it so even if the novel is 'dated'. Or if the novel is of our own age, we hope we shall find funny that which the author intended to be so. By far the best initial response to comic material is genuine amusement. This is true for texts as old as Apuleius, as well as those as recent as Evelyn Waugh.

With this in mind, readers should do their part by trying to appreciate exactly what sort of humorous effects the author intended, and what special conditions pertained in his or her time which gave the humour its point. Much humour, for instance, depends on satire and therefore relies for its effect on an appreciation of this and an understanding of what is being satirized.

Some kinds of humour wear better than others. In general, if the humour is derived from universally applicable and perennially relevant sources, it should survive. If it derives from topicalities, special fashions or tastes, or concerns limited by the circumstances common to the author and his contemporary readers, but not to those of a later age, it will fail unless historical research revives it.

On the whole, if you have been unable to react appropriately and genuinely to the humour of a particular novel, you will find it difficult to write convincingly about it, whether it be on character, situation or dialogue. In some questions for example, the candidate is asked to comment on the humorous elements, and these will not be evident if he or she has not been amused by anything. As preparation, however, it would be worth noting as you read through the book where the humorous elements occur and how a humorous effect is gained.

Humorous effects may be achieved by a combination of the following: incongruity, absurdity, sudden surprise accompanied by relief of tension, anticlimax, abrupt contrast or disappointed expectation. Better humour also involves the development of a sympathetic (i.e. credible) humorous character, whose behaviour or speech specially provokes laughter. Wit, clever neatness of expression, the 'epigrammatic' or brilliantly incisive turn of phrase also heighten the humorous atmosphere or help develop a humorous character.

Cruel humour

Much humour regrettably works by cruelty, perhaps on the psychological sense 'Thank God I'm not the one to be made ridiculous' (or even hurt). 'Slapstick' and other forms of humorous cruelty are funny usually precisely because not intended as serious: the actions are grotesque and they involve 'opposite' behaviour to that which is normally accepted. This is also partly how people can contemplate any work representing suffering: it is known not to be real. The pleasure and appreciation of all art in this sense is a form of broad and calm humour, 'good humour' as distinct from the sudden intense effect. This is why humorous novels may be less realistic than others; those with subordinate humorous parts (like the peasant scenes in Hardy's novels), may be less realistic in these parts than in the 'straight' scenes because of their dependence on increased incongruity or caricature. In plays, such scenes are often used as 'comic relief' to scenes of intense tragedy or high tension. When human foibles or weaknesses are exaggerated, humour joins hands with satire to create even greater opportunities for comic effect, as for instance in *The Secret Lives of Walter Mitty* (James Thurber) or *The Village Cricket Match* (George Macdonald).

Sadistic or sexual humour, both being grotesque distortions of themes of unfailing interest, are also a good deal 'softened' by being presented in the form and framework of traditional conventions, such as stage farce, elements of which often appear in novels, such as *My Family and Other Animals* (Gerald Durrell) which passes itself off as autobiography and thus increases the surprise that humour thrives on. If meant to be funny, violence or sex is usually endowed with more than usual absurdity to escape offending or disturbing 'sacred cows'.

Incongruity

Another convention often employed by humorous writers but expecially dramatists, from whose domain they originate, is the use of the 'unmatched pair' normally a 'straight man' (serious, pompous, slow witted, earnest, trying to maintain standards of ordinary morality) and a 'fall guy' (zany, outrageous, unserious, sharp, playful, deflating, etc). The process is most obviously seen in stage comedy but it is found also in many books of humour: in Mark Twain's two great novels, *Tom Sawyer* and *Huckleberry Finn,* in *Barchester Towers* (Mrs Proudie and Slope or Signora Neroni) and in most of the 'anti hero' novels (e.g. Kingsley Amis' Lucky Jim and his professor, Billy Liar and the majority of the adults he encounters in the real world). There is something of the 'David and Goliath' satisfaction as depicted by these pairings, since the 'straight man' is usually proud and powerful in some respect. When pride and powers are affected by a personality defect and are confronted by humility and a lively mind, the ingredients for comedy are present. A comic scene worthy of close attention for the manner of Victorian fictional humour, is the Rainbow Inn chapter of George Eliot's *Silas Marner.* The individualization of the villagers, their controversies and tensions, and the motives of these, Macey's ghost story culminating in an apparently genuine apparition with the sudden irruption of Silas, repay analysis. Most of the ingredients of good comedy are to be found here.

8 MORALITY

Questions such as the following might be asked and discussed on the novel.

1 What is its moral tone?

2 What is the accepted norm of its morality? (Although in Western literature this is usually more or less Christian or humanist, one should be aware that this is not necessarily so.)

3 Are the standards of what is good or bad, right or wrong, those of our society now, or the society of the novel's author, or both?

4 Is the novel especially concerned with the moral problems (as are those of Henry James and Conrad)?

5 If the hero's or any leading character's morality is perverted, or deviant from the norm of the author's background, does the author, or do the other characters approve?

If the author appears to condone lines of action of whose morality the reader disapproves, then such morality becomes at once debatable, but such debates are rarely relevant in written answers; the book is to be treated *per se*. Only differences in morality between the characters themselves are admissible subjects for written debate.

In a picaresque novel, such as Fielding's *Tom Jones,* or its twentieth-century counterparts such as *The Loneliness of the Long Distance Runner* (Allan Sillitoe) or *Autobiography of a Super Tramp* (WH Davies), we should ask whether the deeper layers of morality underlying the roguery or delinquency of the hero are more moral than those of 'respectable' or establishment characters with whom he is at odds, and whose laws he breaks? In this connection the misfortunes of Moll Flanders are also relevant; her prostitution being an angry indictment of the factors that lead her to this. The same thing applies a century and half later to 'The Artful Dodger', and Oliver Twist. In novels of more subtle morality there is greater ambiguity (although to be sure Moll Flanders is nothing if not a recognizable character drawn from the life): in *The Secret Agent* for example, if Winnie the murderess is clearly as 'right' as Tess, and Comarade Ossipon and the Professor clearly vile, what are we to make of the well-meaning but disastrous Verloc, or the equally double game-playing Chief Inspector Heat?

Great passion and intensity of purpose may override ordinary mortality, or at least rise above it, as for Heathcliffe in Emily Brontë's *Wuthering Heights* or Captain Ahab in Melville's *Moby Dick* or Jocelyn in William Golding's *The Spire*. Sometimes morality is almost externalized or allegorized as in a medieval morality play; for example, Golding's *The Lord of the Flies* or Melville's *Billy Budd*. Very seldom in our accepted great novels do we feel that the morality is bad to the core, as we do sometimes in the case of weak books which, apart from their failure as artistic works, may embody immoral concepts in their very values, e.g. some science fiction in which battles are enjoyed merely as battles, Tarzan books which make monsters out of ordinary animals, books which extol black magic, the great number of 'pornographic' books which make a virtue of lust. Perhaps worse, because they are accepted and more widely regarded as harmless, are the mass of sentimentalized 'love' stories which dangerously pervert reality with no hint of authorial criticism or irony, if indeed the author be capable of such.

Most English novels have as their reference point Christian ethics. Works that do not spring from Christian morality at all include those that may be termed 'existentialist' such as a French example *L'Etranger* (*The Outsider,* Camus), nihilistic (Beckett's *No's Knife,* especially *Texts for Nothing*), amoral and agnostic (*The Great Gatsby,* Scott Fitzgerald), fatalistic or pessimistic (*Jude the Obscure,* Hardy), Satanistic or superstitious in other ways – a host of novels probably specially churned out for the ready market (e.g. *The Exorcist*). Some oddities include experiments in surrealism (short stories in Dylan Thomas's *The Map of Love*) and mere verbal game-playing. Some experiments have yet to be properly accepted as authentic, yet are surely worthy of suspended judgement e.g. Joyce's *Finnegans Wake*.

9 STYLE AND LANGUAGE

The style and language in each novel you study need separate and sustained analysis. Vocabulary, diction and modes of sentence structure often vary from one generation to another and can give clear clues to the period of their composition, like music. On pp. 144-7 we discuss practical criticism of individual passages. You should apply also these critical techniques in your own preparation of your set novels.

Different styles may be deliberately employed in one work, apart from the varieties of dialogue, which suit their speakers' characters. There may be 'quasi-dialogue' or prose that is not dialogue as such, but which is in the style of a character's speech, commentating upon his or her actions or thoughts. 'Stream of consciousness' writing as found in Virginia Woolf's *Mrs Dalloway* is an example of this.

Characters' typical style is likewise used in 'point of view' writing, or when they are employed as narrators. Such styles may subtly change when the characters come to write letters, as they do in Emily Brontë's *Wuthering Heights,* Hardy's *Tess of the D'Urbervilles,* Conrad's *Nostromo* and many others. Mrs Durbeyfield, for instance, writes in an appropriately garrulous and illiterate manner, worse than her speech. There is, in ordinary narration, an extraordinary change of style near the end of *The Inheritors* (William Golding) to mark the sudden transition from a Neanderthal to New People's outlook. In *Ulysses* James Joyce employs a selective variety of styles in one chapter to indicate the evolution of prose over the centuries, as an analogue to the development during gestation of Mrs Purefoy's baby as she comes to childbed. However, the *tour de force* remains partly a verbal game. Hemingway in *A Farewell to Arms* manipulates style to parallel meaning, as for example in the impressionistic passage when a shell nearly kills the Lieutenant, and its actual effect on him as he loses consciousness is conveyed by mimetic prose.

> 'I ate the end of my piece of cheese and took a swallow of wine. Through the other noise I heard a cough, then came the chuh-chuh-chuh-chuch- then there was a flash, as a blast-furnace door is swung open, and a roar that started white and went red and on and on in a

rushing wind. I tried to breathe but my breath would not come and I felt myself rush
bodily out of myself and out and out and out and all the time bodily in the wind.'

Conrad uses a rapturous tone in *Youth* and a sardonic, consistently ironic style in *The Secret
Agent,* in keeping with their themes: boyhood's glowing, optimistic expectation, idealism and
romantic sensibility in the first; the shady scheming and terrible betrayals in the second.

Seventeenth century

We have cited below examples from the seventeenth century. Many would maintain that
this is the age in which the literary prose of the modern English was founded and perfected.
Milton habitually employs the colours of high rhetoric: (On false leaders in the Church)

'O let them not bring about their damned designs that stand now at the entrance of the
bottomless pit expecting the Watchword to open and let out those dreadful Locusts and
Scorpions, to re-involve us in that pitchy Cloud of infernal darkness, where we shall never
more see the Sun of thy Truth again, never hope for the cheerful dawn, never more hear
the Bird of Morning sing.'

Dryden affects a similar style though not with such an exalted tone: (On the plots of Roman
comedy)

'These are plots built after the Italian mode of houses, you see through them all at once;
the characters are indeed the imitations of nature, but so narrow as if they had imitated
only an eye or a hand, and did not dare to venture on the lines of a face or the proportion of
a body'

There is a slightly looser structure, but an increase of wit such as the use of the 'see through' and
'narrow'. The same interest in extended metaphor is evident however.

Sir Thomas Browne favoured a balanced, antithetical style, highly polished and with a love of
exact Latinate words (On funeral customs):

'Though the Funeral pyre of Patroclus took up a hundred foot, a piece of an old boat burnt
Pompey, And if the burthen of Isaac were sufficient for an holocaust, a man may carry
his own pyre.'

Bacon's style is similar to this, though much pithier and more terse, his words carry a greater
load of the content and thought, without much embroidery:

'In the youth of a state arms do flourish; in the middle age of a state, learning; and then
both of them together for a time; in the declining age of a state, mechanical arts and
merchandise.'

Eighteenth century

In the eighteenth century we still find great influence of the Ciceronian style, shown with great
power and vigour by Dr Samuel Johnson. Note there is a suppleness and fluency that renders
it agreeable to the modern ear.

'As there are none more ambitious of fame, than those who are conversant in poetry it is
very natural for such as have not succeeded in it to depreciate the works of those who have.'

(Addison from the *Spectator*, Dec 1711)

'Among the various methods of consolation to which the miseries inseparable from our
present state have given occasion it has been, as I have already remarked, recommended
by some writers to put the sufferer in mind of heavier pressures and more excruciating
calamities than those of which he has himself reason to complain,'

(from *The Rambler*, September 1750)

This gives a fair example of Johnson's love of full phrasing well weighed and balanced, and
drawing to an unhurried finish. There is less employment of fanciful images here – the influence
represented by Sprat, and the Royal Society now having taken effect. Sprat declared to the
Society that it was necessary for their Fellows 'to separate the knowledge of nature from the
colours of Rhetorick, the devices of Fancy, or the delightful deceit of Fables.'.

Nineteenth century

Even more translucence is added to the precision and rhythm of the phrases, by Jane Austen.
This, from *Emma:*

'She felt all the honest pride and complacency which her alliance with the present and
future proprietor could fairly warrant, as she viewed the respectable size and style of the

building, its suitable, becoming, characteristic situation, low and sheltered – its ample
gardens stretching down to meadows washed by a stream, of which the Abbey, with all
the old neglect of prospect, had scarcely a sight – and its abundance of timber in rows and
avenues, which neither fashion nor extravagance had rooted up.'

This well carpentered sentence leads the proud and complacent eye of Emma all over the estate
to which she has so strong a link. The novel was published in 1816, the great Romantic poets had
already brought out much of their main work, Keats was soon to be adding almost the last word
with *Poems* of 1821; prose was soon to be allowed to recapture some of its old colours. With
Charles Lamb, born in 1775, the effects are still subdued, the tone easy, the content light:

'Do you remember the brown suit, which you made to hang upon you, till all your friends
cried in shame upon you, it grew so thread-bare – and all because of that folio Beaumont
and Fletcher, which you dragged home late at night from Barker's in Covent Garden?'

But before long style is to resume most of all its old finery, and yet retain the perfect lucidity
learned from Johnson and Austen: 'For we are all so busy' (writes Robert Louis Stevenson in
Virginibus Puerisque of 1884), 'and have so many far-off projects to realise, and castles in the fire
to turn into solid habitable mansions on a gravel soil, that we can find no time for pleasure
trips into the land of Thought and among the Hills of Vanity.'

We must turn to the novels of the middle to late nineteenth century to see the new
imagination working at its fullest, and only two brief examples must be made to serve the
purpose: they have a continuing progeny among the novels of this century and even this present
age. This then of 1874, Hardy's first widely acclaimed novel *Far From the Madding Crowd*.

'The sheep-washing pool was a perfectly circular basin of brickwork in the meadows, full
of the clearest water. To birds on the wing its glassy surface, reflecting the light sky, must
have been visible for miles around as a glistening Cyclops' eye in a green face.'

– The first master of the cinematographic technique, with the bonus of a beautiful simile (as well
as apposite, in its reference to sheep, a hero and a monster)! The aerial view is put to good
service later in Hardy, notably in *The Dynasts*.

Our other example, from Dickens' *Bleak House* published twenty years earlier, illustrates the
energy of Victorian novels allied to their mythopoeic (myth-making) quality:

'We looked at one another, half laughing at our being like the children in the wood, when a
curious little old woman in a squeezed bonnet, and carrying a reticule, came curtseying
and smiling up to us, with an air of great ceremony.
"O"! said she. "The wards in Jarndyce! Ve-ry happy, I am sure, to have the honour! It is
a good omen for youth and hope and beauty, when they find themselves in this place and
don't know what's to come of it."
"Mad!" whispered Richard, not thinking she could hear him.
"Right! Mad, young gentleman," she returned so quickly that he was quite abashed.'

The Brothers Grimm would have admired this, especially as it goes the logical step further and
uses the whole machinery of the folk tale for the purpose of adding colour to the real jungle of
Chancery, and the real innocence of two victims of it, meeting the mad decrepitude of one
long-snared in its coils.

Ironic style

Some notable features of style may be due to some special purpose of the novelist, such as satire.
Irony is one of the chief stylistic weapons of the satirist, and is used by nearly all great authors
though not necessarily as a prevailing mode. Both passages from Victorian novels quoted above
are ironical, the first through the implications of the chosen image, the second through the
words of the old woman, who is knowingly being ironical, and whose 'Right! Mad . . .' contains
the consequent irony of her present state as the result of what the innocent pair are about to
plunge into.

Much of the plainest irony is achieved by the author's initial establishment of a certain
situation or set of circumstances, against the background of which, since these are present in
the mind of the reader, he or she may 'play off' speeches of characters themselves ignorant of
such circumstances, and which nevertheless refer to them in various ways that contain
significance for us, but not the the speakers. The old woman from *Bleak House* quoted above,
herself uses the technique on Richard Carstone and Esther Summerson, though she soon begins
to indicate what she really means.

A good sustained example of dramatic irony (working in plot and action rather than in
character development or narrative comment), is to be found in Conrad's *Under Western Eyes*.

We are shown the revolutionary Russian student Haldin desperately applying to a friend for help and asylum, after assassinating a political enemy. Haldin believes the views of his friend, Razumov, to be identical to his own, and has good reason to think so. But Razumov, from fear and a sense of outrage – the futility of such violence – refuses to grant what he begs, so Haldin tries to get out by himself, is betrayed by Razumov, arrested, and breathing no word of his interview with his friend, he is executed. His devoted mother and sister having been placed in Geneva for safety, meet Razumov who has been set by the police to spy on them and other political troublemakers. The subsequent scenes between Razumov and these women, particularly Miss Haldin, are promising ground for irony of which Conrad does not fail to take advantage.

Irony pervades Conrad's previous book *The Secret Agent* and reaches one of its peaks in the famous remark of Mr Verloc to his wife Winnie, when she has just discovered that her husband has caused the death of the one person she loves above all others, her 'simple-minded' brother: 'Do be reasonable, Winnie. What would it have been if you had lost me?' Beyond doubt, if Verloc had been killed she not only would have had her brother but been saved from an egocentric, vastly lethargic and completely deceitful husband, whom she shortly murders, thereby damning herself to a miserable suicide.

There are many shades and facets of irony, and the reader simply has to be alert and responsive to all the strands of the web that is being unfolded before him. We will conclude with a typical but subtle example from the greatest exponent of delicate, usually humorously gentle, but always penetrating irony, Jane Austen. In *Mansfield Park* Lady Bertram has learned of her daughters' escape from their parents and home, one to elope, the other (unhappily married), with a lover. Lady Bertram is a person whose main characteristic is never to stir herself, or upset herself, unnecessarily – which for her practically means never at all. The irony of the following makes its effect by innuendo and quite valid understatement:

> 'Lady Bertram did not think deeply, but, guided by Sir Thomas, she thought justly on all important points, and she saw therefore in all its enormity, what had happened, and neither endeavoured herself, nor required Fanny to advise her, to think little of guilt and infamy.'

Lady Bertram just manages in these circumstances to stir on her sofa and unsettle her lap-dog.

Twentieth century

We approach now the enormous variety of style and stylistic devices to be encountered among novels of our century. There was plenty of variety before, but since Henry James ushered in the modern novel, for those who took notice of him, there can be found in English and American – not to mention Irish and lately Australian, South African and even West Indian novels – every conceivable style except the stiffly formal. There are also the experiments – not all of them likely to prove dead-ends, of Woolf, Joyce, James Merrill in *The (Diblos) Notebook,* Salinger, Beckett, Anthony Burgess and others. None of the old facilities and felicities of rhetoric has been dispensed with. An example from Updike's *A Month of Sundays* can be quoted (a book which may one day appear on an A-level syllabus):

> 'The silence of this room m'effraie. It is not one silence but many; The lampshade is silent, the bulb silently burns, the bed in silence waits for my next oblivion, the bathroom mirror silently plays catch with a corner of my bathrobe, the carpeting is a hungry populace of individual acrylic silences, even the air-conditioning, today, is silent. Has the power failed? Has the desert cooled? Has the beautiful last beseeching of the Bible ('Even so, come, Lord Jesus' – *Rev.* 22.20) been at last answered, and Man's two millennia of Inbetweentimes ended? No, my clock says an hour to noon remains.'

There are more than enough rhetorical devices applied to this passage, and yet the whole is unquestionably of our era. The desert and Biblical reference may be explained by the situation in which a priest has been defrocked and banishd to a 'rest home' in the Arizona desert.

Some styles are flat 'reporting' to convey realism in scenes of horror or unusually violent action (Crane's *The Red Badge of Courage,* Hemingway's *A Farewell to Arms,* Greene's *The Power and the Glory*). Other novels favour a highly subjective, 'committed' style (Lawrence's *Kangaroo* and novellas); others may be emotive, suggestive or impressionistic rather than directly descriptive (*To the Lighthouse,* Virginia Woolf, *Dubliners,* James Joyce). Henry James' last four novels have taken the exploration of the possibilities of style far in the direction of refinement of sensibility, but all his splitting and resplitting of hairs are justified by the world such writing opens to us.

Conclusion

Faced with an essay question, the student must think: What are its implications? All relevant matter connected with the novel under question must be turned over, sifted, selected for use and arranged into a reasonable order for composition.

Broad, obvious ideas should occur at once: these, even after further thought, will probably form the backbone of the answer, but you should not take them straight into the essay without longer and deeper thought. Pursuit of the less obvious is just as necessary for completeness. Are all the possibilities exhausted? Minor points may well turn out to be quite vital to a satisfactory answer.

In any discussion, both sides of the case should be aired before judgement is made, even if the topic for discussion clearly seems a correct comment; e.g. 'Is *The Eustace Diamonds* a detective thriller?' – do not assume that it is not, nor assume that it is. Cast your mind over all the evidence that points to its being so, and welcome as equally useful any reservations that may lead eventually to the conclusion that the novel is not of the 'detective' or 'thriller' school. It is this 'pro' and 'con' discussion which gives the essay writers the meat of their answers.

Above all, the candidate needs to maintain a firm control of what is relevant to the answer and what is not. Many good students begin an essay well and proceed to forget or ignore the actual requirements of a particular question. Others go to the opposite (and worse) extreme, and in every paragraph reassert the terms of the question in their answer, as if the latter were revolving round the former like a moth round a candle. The first fault is often because good knowledge is not made to serve the limited requirement and specified field of thought; the second due to insufficient knowledge. The first is therefore that which may result in an injustice to the candidate.

---

2 Practical criticism of prose

By the practical criticism of prose, we mean the close and detailed analysis of relatively short pieces of writing, extracts from novels, short stories and essays, in order to determine how the writer obtains certain effects. These effects include the selection of language and the arrangement and structuring of ideas in order to achieve most effectively his or her purpose in writing.

It is very important to know how to evaluate prose writing as much writing today is carefully designed to manipulate our minds and condition us to the writer's way of thinking. A critical mind may help to develop a healthy critical awareness of the written word.

Practical criticism of prose, even literary prose, is in many ways more difficult than poetry. Novelists, through use of language in the creation of characters, description of events and so on, manipulate our responses just as effectively as poets, but, because their effects tend to be large-scale effects, we are not immediately aware of them. If a novel is successful, we are usually so absorbed in the action that we only notice techniques used by the author at the second or third reading. Do not worry if you are not consciously noting the author's technique in the first reading. Subsequent readings are for detailed study.

METHOD OF APPROACH

When you are faced with a prose passage for practical criticism, read the passage through carefully twice, aiming to comprehend fully the meaning of what is said.

Read thoroughly the part of this chapter beginning 'Aspects of character drawing' and see which of the criteria of style given apply to your passage. Although not all these aspects of style will be found, some will certainly be relevant and you must find illustrations of their use and discuss why the author has chosen them as I have done.

Examples from A-level set books are given for each of the aspects of style, which illustrate clearly what each is showing.

At the end of the chapter are two passages, one with a detailed model commentary and questions, the other just with questions for you to try. The answers you give will help to clarify your further reading of the passage. Then, to write your commentary, you must scrutinize the passage in great detail noting all the devices of writing the writer has employed and estimating why he or she has employed them and how succesfully. Before you write your commentary, read the passage slowly, trying to 'feel' the tone and the quality of the writing. You should then be in a position to write an informed critical appreciation of the passage.

ASPECTS OF CHARACTER DRAWING

Character can be revealed by the following methods:

1 **Action** (A character performing an action typical of him or her.)
In *Wuthering Heights* by Emily Brontë, there are many examples of characters revealing themselves through their actions. At the beginning of the novel, when Mr Lockwood meets Heathcliff, his coarse manner betrays his rough nature.

> I took a seat at the end of the hearthstone opposite that towards which my landlord advanced, and filled up an interval of silence by attempting to caress the canine mother, who had left her nursery, and was sneaking wolfishly to the back of my legs, her lip curled up, and her white teeth watering for a snatch. My caress provoked a long, guttural gnarl.
> 'You'd better let the dog alone,' growled Mr Heathcliff in unison, checking fiercer demonstrations with a punch of his foot. 'She's not accustomed to be spoiled – not kept for a pet.' Then, striding to a side door, he shouted again, 'Joseph!'

Another example of Heathcliff's frighteningly violent behaviour is when Mr Lockwood has a terrifying nightmare and Heathcliff's reaction is equally violent. Notice the phrases 'crushing his nails into his palms' and 'grinding his teeth'.

> 'Heathcliff stood near the entrance, in his shirt and trousers; with a candle dripping over his fingers, and his face as white as the wall behind him. The first creak of the oak startled him like an electric shock: the light leaped from his hold to a distance of some feet, and his agitation was so extreme, that he could hardly pick it up.
> 'It is only your guest, sir,' I called out desirous to spare him the humiliation of exposing his cowardice further. 'I had the misfortune to scream in my sleep, owing to a frightful nightmare. I'm sorry I disturbed you.'
> 'Oh, God confound you, Mr Lockwood! I wish you were at the . . .' commenced my host, setting the candle on a chair, because he found it impossible to hold it steady. 'And who showed you up to this room?' he continued, crushing his nails into his palms, and grinding his teeth to subdue the maxillary convulsions. 'Who was it? I've a good mind to turn them out of the house this moment!'

An example of the spoilt childhoods of Edgar and Isabella Linton at Thrushcross Grange is found in Chapter 5 of *Wuthering Heights* when Heathcliff and Catherine see the two children squabbling over a little dog.

> 'Both of us were able to look in by standing on the basement, and clinging to the ledge, and we saw – ah! it was beautiful – a splendid place carpeted with crimson, and crimson-covered chairs and tables, and a pure white ceiling bordered by gold, a shower of glass-drops hanging in silver chains from the centre, and shimmering with little soft tapers. Old Mr and Mrs Linton were not there; Edgar and his sister had it entirely to themselves. Shouldn't they have been happy? We should have thought ourselves in heaven! And now, guess what your good children were doing? Isabella – I believe she is eleven, a year younger than Cathy – lay screaming at the farther end of the room, shrieking as if witches were running red-hot needles into her. Edgar stood on the hearth weeping silently, and in the middle of the table sat a little dog, shaking its paw and yelping; which, from their mutual accusations, we understood they had nearly pulled in two between them. The idiots! That was their pleasure! to quarrel who should hold a heap of warm hair, and each begin to cry because both, after struggling to get it, refused to take it. We laughed outright at the petted things; we did despise them!'

2 **The way the characters reveal themselves in their speech**

In the first chapter of *Pride and Prejudice* by Jane Austen, Mr and Mrs Bennet are discussing the arrival of Mr Bingley, an eligible and wealthy bachelor. Mrs Bennet is desperate that he will marry one of their daughters, Mr Bennet feigns indifference. Note the length of Mrs Bennet's sentences compared with those of her husband.

Pride and Prejudice

It is a truth universally acknowledged, that a single man in possession of a good fortune must be in want of a wife. However little known the feeling or views of such a man may be on his first entering a neighborhood, this truth is so well fixed in the minds of the surrounding families, that he is considered as the rightful property of some one or other of their daughters.

'My dear Mr Bennet,' said his lady to him one day, 'have you heard that Netherfield Park is let at last?

Mr Bennet replied that he had not.

'But it is,' returned she; 'for Mrs Long has just been here and she told me all about it.'

Mr Bennet made no answer.

'Do not you want to know who has taken it?' cried his wife impatiently.

'You want to tell me and I have no objection to hearing it.'

This was invitation enough.

'Why, my dear, you must know, Mrs Long says Netherfield is taken by a young man of large fortune from the North of England; that he came down on Monday in a chaise and four to see the place, and was so much delighted with it, that he agreed with Mr Morris immediately; that he is to take possession before Michaelmas, and some of his servants are to be in the house by the end of next week.'

'What is his name?'

'Bingley.'

'Is he married or single?'

'Oh! single, my dear, to be sure! A single man of large fortune; four or five thousand a-year. What a fine thing for our girls!'

'How so! how can it affect them?'

'My dear Mr Bennet,' replied his wife, 'how can you be so tiresome! you must know that I am thinking of his marrying one of them.'

'Is that his design in settling here?'

'Design! nonsense, how can you talk so! But it is very likely that he may fall in love with one of them, and therefore you must visit him as soon as he comes.'

'I see no occasion for that. You and the girls may go, or you may send them by themselves, which perhaps will be still better, for as you are as handsome as any of them, Mr Bingley might like you the best of the party.'

'My dear, you flatter me. I certainly have had my share of beauty, but I do not pretend to be anything extraordinary now. When a woman has five grown-up daughters, she ought to give over thinking of her own beauty.'

'In such cases, a woman has not often much beauty to think of.'

'But, my dear, you must indeed go and see Mr Bingley when he comes into the neighborhood.

'It is more than I engage for, I assure you.'

'But consider your daughters. Only think what an establishment it would be for one of them. Sir William and Lady Lucas are determined to go, merely on that account, for in general, you know, they visit no newcomers. Indeed you must go, for it will be impossible for us to visit him if you do not.'

'You are over-scrupulous, surely. I dare say Mr Bingley will be very glad to see you; and I will send a few lines by you to assure him of my hearty consent to his marrying whichever he chooses of the girls; though I must throw in a good word for my little Lizzy.'

'I desire you will do no such thing. Lizzy is not a bit better than the others; and I am sure she is not half so handsome as Jane, nor half so good-humoured as Lydia. But you are always giving her the preference.'

'They have none of them much to recommend them,' replied he; 'they are all silly and ignorant, like other girls; but Lizzy has something more of quickness than her sisters.'

'Mr Bennet, how can you abuse your own children in such a way! You take delight in vexing me. You have no compassion on my poor nerves!'

'You mistake me, my dear. I have a high respect for your nerves. They are my old friends. I have heard you mention them with consideration these twenty years at least.'

'Ah! you do not know what I suffer.'

'But I hope you will get over it, and live to see many young men of four thousand a-year come into the neighborhood.'

'It will be no use to us, if twenty such should come, since you will not visit them.'

'Depend upon it, my dear, that when there are twenty, I will visit them all.'

Mr Bennet was so odd a mixture of quick parts, sarcastic humor, reserve, and caprice, that the experience of three-and twenty years had been insufficient to make his wife understand his character. Her mind was less difficult to develop. She was a woman of mean understanding, little information, and uncertain temper. When she was discontented, she fancied herself nervous. The business of her life was to get her daughters married; its solace was visiting and news.

3 By direct statement of the author on the character

Where the author tells you directly his or her opinion and what you ought to think of the character at this particular time in the novel.

In *Washington Square* by Henry James, the passage I have chosen appears at a crucial point where Morris Townsend knows he could marry Catherine, but has to weigh up whether he could do better. The following passage is an interesting example because of the double-edged nature of James' address to the reader.

He had slightly misrepresented the matter in saying that Catherine had consented to take the great step. We left her just now declaring that she would burn her ships behind her; but Morris, after having elicited this declaration, had become conscious of good reasons for not taking it up. He avoided, gracefully enough, fixing a day, though he left her under the impression that he had his eye on one. Catherine may have had her difficulties; but those of her circumspect suitor are also worthy of consideration. The prize was certainly great; but it was only to be won by striking the happy mean between precipitancy and caution. It would be all very well to take one's jump and trust to Providence; Providence was more especially on the side of clever people, and clever people were known by an indisposition to risk their bones.

The ultimate reward of a union with a young woman who was both unattractive and impoverished ought to be connected with immediate disadvantages by some very palpable chain. Between the fear of losing Catherine and her possible fortune altogether, and the fear of taking her too soon and finding this possible fortune as void of actuality as a collection of emptied bottles, it was not comfortable for Morris Townsend to choose – a fact that should be remembered by readers disposed to judge harshly of a young man who may have struck them as making but an indifferently successful use of fine natural parts. He had not forgotten that in any event Catherine had her own ten thousand a year; he had devoted an abundance of meditation to this circumstance. But with his fine parts he rated himself high, and he had a perfectly definite appreciation of his value, which seemed to him inadequately represented by the sum I have mentioned. At the same time he reminded himself that this sum was considerable, that everything is relative, and that if a modest income is less desirable than a large one, the complete absence of revenue is nowhere accounted an advantage.

These reflections gave him plenty of occupation, and made it necessary that he should trim his sail. Doctor Sloper's opposition was the unknown quantity in the problem he had to work out. The natural way to work it out was by marrying Catherine; but in mathematics there are many short cuts, and Morris was not without a hope that he should yet discover one. When Catherine took him at his word, and consented to renounce the attempt to mollify her father, he drew back skilfully enough, as I have said, and kept the wedding-day still an open question. Her faith in his sincerity was so complete that she was incapable of suspecting that he was playing with her; her trouble just now was of another kind. The poor girl had an admirable sense of honour, and from the moment she had brought herself to the point of violating her father's wish, it seemed to her that she had no right to enjoy his protection.

4 Description of characters in a novel by an omniscient narrator

In novels like Fitzgerald's *The Great Gatsby,* and Evelyn Waugh's *Brideshead Revisited,* the personalities of characters are revealed by the narrator, who is also one of the characters.

Charles, in *Brideshead Revisited,* gives us very clear and amusing character studies of two of his contemporaries at Oxford, Anthony Blanche and Sebastian Flyte.

He was tall, slim, rather swarthy, with large saucy eyes. The rest of us wore rough tweeds and brogues. He had on a smooth chocolate-brown suit with loud white stripes, suede shoes, a large bow-tie and he drew off yellow, wash-leather gloves as he came into the room; part Gallic, part Yankee, part, perhaps, Jew; wholly exotic.

This, I did not need telling, was Anthony Blanche, the 'aesthete' par excellence, a byword of iniquity from Cherwell Edge to Somerville. He had been pointed out to me often in the streets, as he pranced along with his high peacock tread; I had heard his voice in 'The George' challenging the conventions; and now meeting him, under the spell of Sebastian, I found myself enjoying him voraciously.

I knew Sebastian by sight long before I met him. That was unavoidable for, from his first week, he was the most conspicuous man of his year by reason of his beauty, which was arresting, and his eccentricities of behaviour, which seemed to know no bounds. My first sight of him was in the door of Germer's, and, on that occasion, I was struck less by his looks than by the fact that he was carrying a large teddy-bear.

'That,' said the barber, as I took his chair, 'was Lord Sebastian Flyte. A most amusing young gentleman.'

'Apparently,' I said coldly.

'The Marquis of Marchmain's second boy. His brother the Earl of Brideshead, went down last term. Now he was very different, a very quiet gentleman, quite like an old man. What do you suppose Lord Sebastian wanted? A hair brush for his teddy-bear; it had to have very stiff bristles, not, Lord Sebastian said, to brush him with, but to threaten him with a spanking when he was sulky. He bought a very nice one with an ivory back and he's having 'Aloysius' engraved on it – that's the bear's name.' The man, who, in his time, had had ample chance to tire of undergraduate fantasy, was plainly captivated. I, however, remained censorious, and subsequent glimpses of him, driving in a hansom cab and dining at the George in false whiskers, did not soften me, although Collins, who was reading Freud, had a number of technical terms to cover everything.

Jeremy Irons in *Brideshead Revisited* (Courtesy of Granada TV)

5 By association of one character with a recurrent image

In DH Lawrence's novel, *The Rainbow,* the Brangwen men have for generations farmed the land between Derbyshire and Nottinghamshire. Lawrence vividly suggests the closeness of the Brangwen men to the soil in the following passage.

> The Brangwens had lived for generations on the Marsh Farm, in the meadows where the Erewash twisted sluggishly through alder trees, separating Derbyshire from Nottinghamshire. Two miles away, a church-tower stood on a hill, the houses of the little country town climbing assiduously up to it. Whenever one of the Brangwens in the fields lifted his head from his work, he saw the church-tower at Ilkeston in the empty sky. So that as he turned again to the horizontal land, he was aware of something standing above him and beyond him in the distance.
>
> There was a look in the eyes of the Brangwens as if they were expecting something unknown, about which they were eager. They had that air of readiness for what would come to them, a kind of surety, an expectancy, the look of an inheritor.
>
> They were fresh, blond, slow-speaking people, revealing themselves plainly, but slowly, so that one could watch the change in their eyes from laughter to anger, blue, lit-up laughter, to a hard blue-staring anger; through all the irresolute stages of the sky when the weather is changing.
>
> Living on rich land, on their own land, near to a growing town, they had forgotten what it was to be in straitened circumstances. They had never become rich, because there were always children, and the patrimony was divided every time. But always, at the Marsh, there was ample.
>
> So the Brangwens came and went without fear of necessity, working hard because of the life that was in them, not for want of the money. Neither were they thriftless. They were aware of the last halfpenny, and instinct made them not waste the peeling of their apple, for it would help to feed the cattle. But heaven and earth was teeming around them, and how should this cease? They felt the rush of the sap in spring, they knew the wave which cannot halt, but every year throws forward the seed to begetting, and, falling back, leaves the young-born on the earth. They knew the intercourse between heaven and earth, sunshine drawn into the breast and bowels, the rain sucked up in the daytime, nakedness that comes under the wind in autumn, showing the birds' nests no longer worth hiding. Their life and inter-relations were such; feeling the pulse and body of the soil, that opened to their furrow for the grain, and became smooth and supple after their ploughing, and clung to their feet with a weight that pulled like desire, lying hard and unresponsive when the crops were to be shorn away. The young corn waved and was silken, and the lustre slid along the limbs of the men who saw it. They took the udder of the cows, the cows yielded milk and pulsed against the hands of the men, the pulse of the blood of the teats of the cows beat into the pulse of the hands of the men. They mounted their horses, and held life between the grip of their knees, they harnessed their horses at the wagon, and, with hand on the bridle-rings, drew the heaving of the horses after their will.

Another example of the use of recurrent imagery is found in *Dombey and Son* by Charles Dickens where the river, sea and ebbing tide imagery is linked with the child Paul Dombey.

> 'Another time, in the same place, he fell asleep and slept quietly for a long time. Awaking suddenly, he listened, started up and sat listening. Florence asked him what he thought he heard.
>
> "I want to know what it says," he answered, looking steadily in her face. "The sea, Floy, what is it that it keeps on saying?"
>
> She told him that it was only the noise of the rolling waves.
>
> "Yes, yes," he said, "But I know that they are always saying something. Always the same thing. What place is over there?" He rose up, looking eagerly at the horizon.
>
> She told him there was another country opposite, but he said he didn't mean that; he meant farther away – farther away!
>
> Very often afterwards, in the midst of their talk, he would break off, to try to understand what it was that the waves were always saying; and would rise up in his couch to look towards that invisible region, far away.'

George Eliot uses reptile imagery a good deal in *Middlemarch* and in Chapter 41 she compares Mr Rigg Featherstone with a frog, who may appeal to certain lowly people, but not to people of any intelligence.

> 'Having made this rather lofty comparison I am less uneasy in calling attention to the existence of low people by whose interference, however little we may like it, the course of the world is very much determined. It would be well, certainly, if we could help to reduce their number, and something might perhaps be done by not lightly giving occasion to their

existence. Socially speaking, Joshua Rigg would have been generally pronounced a super-fluity. But those who like Peter Featherstone never had a copy of themselves demanded, are the very last to wait for such a request either in prose or verse. The copy in this case bore more of outside resemblance to the mother, in whose sex frog-features, accompanied with fresh-coloured cheeks and well-rounded figure, are compatible with much charm for a certain order of admirers. The result is sometimes a frog-faced male, desirable, surely, to no order of intelligent beings. Especially when he is suddenly brought into evidence to frustrate other people's expectations – the very lowest aspect in which a social superfluity can present himself.'

6 By associating a character with one particular point of view or action with which he can be easily identified

In *The History Man,* a new A-level set book in which Malcolm Bradbury satirizes the intermesh-ings of human relationships between academics on the campus of a new university, Henry Beamish, a member of the Sociology Department, is lampooned by Bradbury for his complete clumsiness and ineptitude in every direction. In this passage, having damaged his wrist in an 'accident' at Howard Kirk's party, he tries to negotiate his tray through the queue at the university cafeteria. His public humiliation symbolizes his unlucky life.

> A very loud crash comes from the direction of the self-service line. The sociologists' heads all turn; in the line, someone, a bandaged person, has dropped an entire tray and its contents. 'Oh, God,' says Flora, 'it's Henry.' Henry Beamish stands transfixed in the line, with yoghurt all over his trousers;

7 By choice of words and picking out a particular feature or detail which calls a character vividly to mind

In Flaubert's novel, *Madame Bovary,* Emma Bovary, married to a country doctor, is totally bored and dissatisfied with her marriage. An incurable romantic, she longs for a lover who can satisfy her desires.

In the following passage Flaubert uses the imagery of the sea and the shipwrecked sailor to suggest her isolation.

> 'And all the time, deep within her, she was waiting for something to happen. Like a shipwrecked sailor she scanned her solitude with desperate eyes for the sight of a white sail far off on the misty horizon. She had no idea what that chance would be, what wind would waft it to her, where it would set her ashore, whether it was a launch or a three-decker, laden with anguish or filled to the portholes with happiness. But every morning when she woke she hoped to find it there. She listened to every sound, started out of bed, and was surprised when nothing came. Then at sunset, sadder every day, she longed for the morrow.'

Dickens uses the image of an engine to describe vividly Pancks in *Little Dorrit,* Chapter XIII.

> 'He had scarcely left the room, and allowed the ticking to become audible again, when a quick hand turned a latchkey in the house-door, opened it, and shut it. Immediately after-wards, a quick and eager short dark man came into the room with so much way upon him, that he was within a foot of Clennam before he could stop.
> "Halloa!" he said.
> Clennam saw no reason why he should not say "Halloa!" too.
> "What's the matter?" said the short dark man.
> "I have not heard that anything is the matter," returned Clennam.
> "Where's Mr Casby?" asked the short dark man, looking about.
> "He will be here directly, if you want him."
> "I want him?" said the short dark man. "Don't you?"
> This elicited a word or two of explanation from Clennam, during the delivery of which the short dark man held his breath and looked at him. He was dressed in black and rusty iron grey; had jet black beads of eyes; a scrubby little black chin; wiry black hair striking out from his head in prongs, like forks or hair-pins; and a complexion that was very dingy by nature, or very dirty by art, or a compound of nature and art. He had dirty hands and dirty broken nails, and looked as if he had been in the coals; he was in a perspiration, and snorted and sniffed and puffed and blew, like a little labouring steam-engine.
> "Oh!" said he, when Arthur had told him how he came to be there. "Very well. That's right. If he should ask for Pancks, will you be so good as to say that Pancks is come in?"
> And so, with a snort and a puff, he walked out by another door.'

Note how the 'layers' of images are built up with the idea of a steam engine developing from earlier metallic imagery: 'black and rusty', 'forks or hair-pins'.

Descriptive prose

The background against which the characters in a novel operate can either be merely a place in which they happen to live or can be inextricably linked with their characters. In most novels of any importance the author deliberately chooses the setting to illustrate or underline some aspect of his characters. For instance, in Hardy's novels, much use is made of the wild, inhospitable heathland to reflect the author's notion that man lives in an environment often hostile to him.

The following methods can be used to form a detailed description.

1 Selected detail to build up a complete picture

2 Concrete detail to make the reader feel the reality of the description

3 Comparisons to make the descriptions more vivid and easy to imagine

4 The use of words to appeal to our senses so that we see, feel and hear objects more precisely

5 The use of words as images to give us a good picture of what the author is trying to describe

Virginia Woolf

An excellent illustration of a building being used to highlight an integral part of a character is the description of the lighthouse in *To The Lighthouse* by Virginia Woolf. The lighthouse is used both as a setting and a symbol, highlighting fears and hopes within different characters.

> 'He was an awful prig – oh yes, an insufferable bore. For, though they had reached the town now and were in the main street, with carts grinding past on the cobbles, still he went on talking, about settlements, and teaching, and working-men, and helping our own class, and lectures, till she gathered that he had got back entire self-confidence, had recovered from the circus, and was about (and now again she liked him warmly) to tell her – but here, the houses falling away on both sides, they came out on the quay, and the whole bay spread before them and Mrs Ramsey could not help exclaiming, "Oh, how beautiful!" For the great plateful of blue water was before her; the hoary Lighthouse, distant, austere, in the midst; and on the right, as far as the eye could see, fading and falling, in soft low pleats, the green sand dunes with the wild flowing grasses on them, which always seemed to be running away into some moon country, uninhabited of men.
>
> That was the view, she said, stopping, growing greyer-eyed, that her husband loved.
>
> She paused a moment. But now, she said, artists had come here. There indeed, only a few paces off, stood one of them, in Panama hat and yellow boots, seriously, softly, absorbedly, for all that he was watched by ten little boys, with an air of profound content-ment on his round red face, gazing, and then, when he had gazed, dipping; imbuing the tip of his brush in some soft mound of green or pink.'

Another example of how settings are used as symbols for the emotions of the different characters is found in the descriptions of the Marabar Caves in EM Forster's novel *A Passage to India*.

> 'The caves are readily described. A tunnel eight feet long, five feet high, three feet wide, leads to a circular chamber about twenty feet in diameter. This arrangement occurs again and again throughout the group of hills, and this is all, this is a Marabar Cave. Having seen one such cave, having seen two, having seen three, four, fourteen, twenty-four, the visitor returns to Chandrapore uncertain whether he has had an interesting experience or a dull one or any experience at all. He finds it difficult to discuss the caves, or to keep them apart in his mind, for the pattern never varies, and no carving, not even a

bees' nest or a bat, distinguishes one from another. Nothing, nothing attaches to them and their reputation – for they have one – does not depend upon human speech. It is as if the surrounding plain or the passing birds have taken upon themselves to exclaim "extra-ordinary", and the word has taken root in the air, and been inhaled by mankind.

They are dark caves. Even when they open towards the sun, very little light penetrates down the entrance tunnel into the circular chamber. There is little to see, and no eye to see it, until the visitor arrives for his five minutes, and strikes a match.* Immediately another flame rises in the depths of the rock and moves towards the surface like an imprisoned spirit: the walls of the circular chamber have been most marvellously polished. The two flames approach and strive to unite, but cannot, because one of them breathes air, the other stone. A mirror inlaid with lovely colours divides the lovers, delicate stars of pink and grey interpose, exquisite nebulae, shading fainter than the tail of a comet or the midday moon, all the evanescent life of the granite, only here visible. Fists and fingers thrust above the advancing soil – here at last is their skin, finer than any covering acquired by the animals, smoother than windless water, more voluptuous than love. The radiance increases, the flames touch one another, kiss, expire. The cave is dark again, like all the caves.

Only the wall of the circular chamber has been polished thus. The sides of the tunnel are left rough, they impinge as an afterthought upon the internal perfection. An entrance was necessary, so mankind made one. But elsewhere, deeper in the granite, are there certain chambers that have no entrance? Chambers never unsealed since the arrival of the gods. Local report declares that these exceed in number those that can be visited, as the dead exceed the living – four hundred of them, four thousand or million. Nothing is inside them, they were sealed up before the creation of pestilence or treasure; if mankind grew curious and excavated, nothing, nothing would be added to the sum of good or evil. One of them is rumoured within the boulder that swings on the summit of the highest of the hills; a bubble-shaped cave that has neither ceiling nor floor, and mirrors its own darkness in every direction infinitely. If the boulder falls and smashes, the cave will smash too – empty as an Easter egg. The boulder because of its hollowness sways in the wind, and even moves when a crow perches upon it: hence its name and the name of its stupendous pedestal: the Kawa Dol.

* Note how the passage changes dramatically at this point. Boredom and confusion give way to delight when light is introduced into the cave.

THE WRITER'S OPINION

Often a novelist is strongly committed to a certain character or cause in the novel. The student should try to show how he reveals his opinions. Does he use rhetoric, emotional prose or calm reasoned argument? Does he make it clear that he sympathises with one character more than another? If so, how does he do this – by the character's speech and actions or by direct comment by the author in his role of omniscient narrator?

In *Animal Farm* George Orwell shows his contempt of both the Communist and autocratic methods of government. The pigs overthrow the cruel farmer, Mr Jones and replace his rule with a supposedly Utopian situation. They make Seven Commandments which are the moral rules for the guidance of all the animals. However, the corrupt pigs, led by Napoleon, with Squealer as his propaganda agent, soon turn the farm back to an almost exact replica of how it was under Mr Jones.

It was just after the sheep had returned, on a pleasant evening when the animals had finished work and were making their way back to the farm buildings, that the terrified neighing of a horse sounded from the yard. Startled, the animals stopped in their tracks. It was Clover's voice. She neighed again, and all the animals broke into a gallop and rushed into the yard. Then they saw what Clover had seen.

It was a pig walking on his hind legs.

Yes, it was Squealer. A little awkwardly, as though not quite used to supporting his considerable bulk in that position, but with perfect balance, he was strolling across the yard. And a moment later, out from the door of the farmhouse came a long file of pigs, all walking on their hind legs. Some did it better than others, one or two were even a trifle unsteady and looked as though they would have liked the support of a stick, but every one of them made his way right round the yard successfully. And finally there was a tremendous baying of dogs and a shrill crowing from the black cockerel, and out came Napoleon himself, majestically upright, casting haughty glances from side to side, and with his dogs gambolling round him.

He carried a whip in his trotter.

There was a deadly silence. Amazed, terrified, huddling together, the animals watched the long line of pigs march slowly round the yard. It was as though the world had turned upside-down. Then there came a moment when the first shock had worn off and when, in spite of everything – in spite of their terror of the dogs, and of the habit, developed through long years, of never complaining, never criticizing, no matter what happened – they might have uttered some word of protest. But just at that moment, as though at a signal, all the sheep burst out into a tremendous bleating of –

'Four legs good, two legs better! Four legs good, two legs better! Four legs good, two legs better!'

It went on for five minutes without stopping. And by the time the sheep had quieted down, the chance to utter any protest had passed, for the pigs had marched back into the farmhouse.

Benjamin felt a nose nuzzling at his shoulder. He looked round. It was Clover. Her old eyes looked dimmer than ever. Without saying anything, she tugged gently at his mane and led him round to the end of the big barn, where the Seven Commandments were written. For a minute or two they stood gazing at the tarred wall with its white lettering.

'My sight is failing,' she said finally. 'Even when I was young I could not have read what was written there. But it appears to me that that wall looks different. Are the Seven Commandments the same as they used to be Benjamin?'

For once Benjamin consented to break his rule, and he read out to her what was written on the wall. There was nothing there now except a single Commandment. It ran:

ALL ANIMALS ARE EQUAL
BUT SOME ANIMALS ARE MORE
EQUAL THAN OTHERS

TONE

The words an author actually uses gives us the most obvious indication of the tone of voice the writer is employing.

The tone may be

1 Formal or informal

2 Sympathetic or unsympathetic

3 Serious or comic

4 Emotional or restrained

5 Cynical or sentimental

6 Biased or impartial

You must imagine the author reading the passage and try to hear the intonation he would put into his words. This should let you know what tone the author intends to adopt.

Although examples of all different kinds of tone are too numerous to mention, I have tried to choose some of the main ones and give illustrations of them from passages of A-level set texts.

Pessimistic tone

Thomas Hardy in his novels reveals a fatalistic and pessimistic view of life. He feels that however his characters struggle against their fates, their movements and destinies are controlled by an arbitrary and sometimes malevolent being who seems often to conspire against them.

In *Tess of the D'Urbervilles* Tess is used and manipulated by Alec d'Urberville, whom she eventually kills. One might feel justice had been done but the courts find her guilty and she is hanged. Angel Clare, her true love, views her death from a distance.

Upon the cornice of the tower a tall staff was fixed. Their eyes were riveted on it. A few minutes after the hour had struck something moved slowly up the staff, and extended itself upon the breeze. It was a black flag.

'Justice' was done, and the President of the Immortals, in Aeschylean phrase, had ended his sport with Tess. And the D'Urberville knights and dames slept on in their tombs unknowing. The two speechless gazers bent themselves down to the earth, as if in prayer, and remained thus a long time, absolutely motionless; the flag continued to wave silently. As soon as they had strength they arose, joined hands again, and went on.

Hardy's exploration of the human condition of his society certainly had melancholy over-tones. This attitude of his met with severe critical comment when his novels were published. When *Jude the Obscure* was published as a complete novel in 1895, the *New York Bookman* said of it, 'It is simply one of the most objectionable books that we have ever read in any language whatsoever'; and a reviewer in *The World,* betraying the characteristic Victorian middle-class opinion that gloom is somehow socially undesirable, remarked that 'None but a writer of exceptional talent indeed could have produced so gruesome and gloomy a book'.

At the end of the fifth chapter of *The Return of the Native,* the returning native, Clym Yeobright, expresses his feelings that anything hopeful in his life has come too late for him.

> Yeobright's manner had been so quiet, he had uttered so few syllables since his re-appearance, that Venn imagined him resigned. It was only when they had left the room and stood upon the landing that the true state of his mind was apparent. Here he said, with a wild smile, inclining his head towards the chamber in which Eustacia lay, 'She is the second woman I have killed this year. I was a great cause of my mother's death; and I am the chief cause of hers.'
>
> 'I spoke cruel words to her, and she left my house. I did not invite her back till it was too late. It is I who ought to have drowned myself. It would have been a charity to the living had the river overwhelmed me and borne her up. But I cannot die. Those who ought to have lived lie dead; and here am I alive!'
>
> 'But you can't charge yourself with crimes in that way,' said Venn. 'You may as well say that the parents be the cause of a murder by the child, for without the parents the child would never have been begot.'
>
> 'Yes, Venn, that is very true; but you don't know all the circumstances. If it had pleased God to put an end to me it would have been a good thing for all. But I am getting used to the horror of my existence. They say that a time comes when men laugh at misery through long acquaintance with it. Surely that time will soon come to me!'
>
> 'Your aim has always been good,' said Venn. 'Why should you say such desperate things?'
>
> 'No, they are not desperate. They are only hopeless; and my great regret is that for what I have done no man or law can punish me!'

Cynical tone

The whole tone of *The History Man* expresses cynicism about human relationships. The main character, Howard Kirk, is a totally selfish individual who manipulates others both politically and sexually in the single minded pursuit of his goals. He becomes involved with one of his students, Felicity Phee, but tries to convince one of his other lady friends that he was acting totally unselfishly as she needed his help. Note how Miss Callendar treats Kirk briskly as if he were a tiresome child.

> 'The key question is now my relationship with Miss Phee. You remember Miss Phee' 'Do I?' says Miss Callendar. 'Yes,' says Howard, 'you saw me with her in my downstairs study, when you were leaving the party.' 'Then that was one of your episodes,' says Miss Callendar, 'I did rather think so.' 'It's a pity you don't know her better,' says Howard, 'then perhaps, instead of supporting Carmody's crazy story, you'd understand what repressed, evil nonsense it is.' 'I don't support his story,' says Miss Callendar, 'I don't know whether his interpretation of what he saw is right at all. I just have some reason, don't I, for thinking he saw what he saw.'
>
> 'But he saw nothing,' says Howard, 'he just looked in on me from outside and made corrupt deductions. Miss Phee's one of my advisees. She's a very sad creature. She's been through everything. Boy trouble, girl trouble, an abortion, the identity crisis, a break-down. . . .' 'The menopause,' says Miss Callendar. 'Not yet,' says Howard. 'Well, you've something to come,' says Miss Callendar, 'A scone? I made them myself.' 'Thanks,' says Howard. 'She had a crisis that night. A lesbian affair she was having was breaking up.' 'Isn't she rather hogging the problems?' asks Miss Callendar. 'She was in trouble,' says Howard, 'she went down there into my study, and started raking through my papers. She wanted to be caught, I think; anyway, I caught her.' 'The instinct of curiosity,' says Miss Callendar, 'Mr Carmody has that too.' 'Of course I was angry. But the meaning of the situation was obvious. She was crying out for attention.' 'So you laid her down and gave her some,' says Miss Callendar. 'No,' says Howard, 'it was very much the other way around.' 'Oh, God, how awful,' says Miss Callendar, 'did she attack you? Were you hurt?' 'I'm explaining to you that she has no attraction for me,' says Howard, 'I didn't want her at all. I wanted someone else. In fact, you. Out there beyond the window.' 'But in my absence you settled for her instead,' says Miss Callendar.

Sympathetic or unsympathetic tone

The author can either remain neutral or let you know which of his characters his sympathies are with. In *The Sandcastle,* Iris Murdoch seems to have mixed feelings about the matrimonial difficulties of the two main characters, Nan and Mor. Nan is a somewhat cold and unsympathetic character, but she wins in the end as she makes a speech putting forward her husband, Mor, as a political candidate. This makes it virtually impossible for him to continue his affair with Rain Carter as he now has to appear totally respectable.

'It has been for many years,' Nan went on, 'the dear wish and ambition of my husband, myself, and our children that he should serve his country in the highest role to which a democratic society can call its citizens – that of a Member of Parliament. After a long period of patient work, my husband has now the great happiness of being able to realize his lifelong ambition. The nearby borough of Marsington have decided to adopt him as their Labour candidate – and as we know, Marsington, with all respect to those present who are of the other party, is a safe Labour seat.'

Amazement, horror, and anger struggled within him; Mor could scarcely believe his ears. He turned his head to where Demoyte and Rain were sitting. Demoyte looked completely stunned; he was half turned towards Nan, his hand raised to his mouth. Then he turned sharply back towards Mor, a look of surprise, dismay, and accusation. But it was the face of Rain that made Mor almost cry out aloud. He had told her nothing of his political plans. She was hearing of them now for the first time. She looked towards him, her lips parting as if to question him, her eyes expressing astonishment and sheer horror, her whole face working in an agony of interrogation. Mor shook his head violently.

Nan was going on. 'As Shakespeare says, there is a tide in the affairs of men that taken at the flood leads on to fortune. This tide now runs for my husband, and for myself, and for our children. We have discussed the matter fully, and we are at last agreed that there is no other bond or tie which can prevent us from adventuring forward together. Courage is needed to make the great step. To delay would be fatal. Such a chance comes but once in a lifetime. Courage he has never lacked – nor is it likely that he will hesitate now when all his deepest and most cherished wishes are about to find so complete a fulfilment.'

Mor was breathing deeply. He was still almost deprived of breath by the shock. Who would have thought that Nan would be so ingenious – or so desperate? He knew that something vital, perhaps final, was happening to him, but he did not fully see what it was. He tried to keep Rain's eyes, but she turned away from him, grimacing with distress. Mor told himself that what he ought to do now, now this very minute, was to get up from his seat and lead Rain out of the room. Nan had attempted to corner him by a public gesture. She should be answered in the same way. To rise now and go out with Rain would set the seal on all his intentions. At last Nan had raised the storm. It was for him to ride it. But Rain had turned away her eyes – and although Mor struggled in his seat he could not bring himself to get up. A lifetime of conformity was too much for him. He stayed where he was.

Emotional and restrained tone

Often the author becomes very emotionally involved with the characters, especially when they are going through some crisis or traumatic event in their lives. In *The Millstone* by Margaret Drabble, Rosamund Stacey is the unmarried mother of a baby girl. Her baby becomes ill and is taken to hospital. Margaret Drabble, herself a mother, emotively narrates the scene where Rosamund confronts an irate Sister who is determined not to let her see her baby. This whole episode is told through the eyes of Rosamund. Mr Protheroe is the specialist paediatrician involved in the case.

'I told you this morning,' said Sister, 'that visiting is quite out of the question.'

'I don't care what you told me,' I said. 'I want to see my baby. If you don't take me straight there, I shall walk round until I find the way myself. She's not kept under lock and key, I assume?'

'Miss Stacy,' said Sister, 'you are behaving most foolishly, and I must ask you to leave at once.'

'I won't leave,' I said. 'You'd much better take me straight there, I don't want to be compelled to wander round upsetting the whole of your hospital until I find my baby.'

'Now then, now then,' said Sister, 'this is neither the time nor the place for hysterical talk like that. We must all be grateful that your child is . . .'

'Grateful,' I said. 'I am grateful. I admire your hospital, I admire your work, I am devoted to the National Health Service. Now I want to see my baby.'

She came over to me and took my arm and started to push me gently towards the door; I have spent so much of my life in intelligent, superior effort to understand ignorance that I recognized her look at once. She pitied me and she was amazed. I let her get me as far as the door, being unable at first to resist the physical sense of propulsion, but when we got to the door I stopped and said, 'No, I'm not going to leave. I'm going to stay here until you change your mind.'

'I have no intention of changing my mind,' she said, and once more took hold of my elbow and started to push. I resisted. We stood there for a moment; I could not believe that physical violence could possibly take place, but on the other hand I did not see what else I could do. So when she started to push, I started to scream. I screamed very loudly, shutting my eyes to do it, and listening in amazement to the deafening shindy that filled my head. Once I started, I could not stop; I stood there, motionless, screaming, whilst they shook me and yelled at me and told me that I was upsetting everybody in earshot. 'I don't care,' I yelled, finding words for my inarticulate passion, 'I don't care, I don't care, I don't care about anyone, I don't care, I don't care, I don't care.'

Eventually they got me to sit down, but I went on screaming and moaning and keeping my eyes shut; through the noise I could hear things happening, people coming and going, someone slapped my face, someone tried to put a wet flannel on my head, and all the time I was thinking I must go on doing this until they let me see her. Inside my head it was red and black and very hot, I remember, and I remember also the clearness of my consciousness and the ferocity of my emotion, and myself enduring them, myself neither one nor the other, but enduring them, and not breaking in two. After a while I heard someone shouting above the din, 'For God's sake tell her she can see the baby, someone try and tell her,' and I heard these words and instantly stopped and opened my eyes and beheld the stricken, confused silence around me.

'Did you say I could see the baby?' I said.

'Of course you can see the baby,' said Mr Protheroe. 'Of course you can see the baby. I cannot imagine why you should ever have been prevented from seeing the baby.'

A humorous or a serious tone

Different authors adopt or present different attitudes to an institution like marriage.

The attitude to marriage presented by Jane Austen is a paradoxical mixture of the romantic and the mercenary. Nowhere is this more apparent than in *Pride and Prejudice* where there is a spectrum of attitudes ranging from –

Wholly mercenary	*Partly mercenary*	*Romantic*
Mrs Bennet, Miss Bingley	Charlotte Lucas, Mr Wickham	Jane Bennet, Lydia Bennet, Mr Bingley

In this episode Charlotte is explaining how she can contemplate marriage to a man she does not love, namely Mr Collins, to her horrified friend, Elizabeth Bennet.

Miss Lucas called soon after breakfast, and in a private conference with Elizabeth related the event of the day before.

The possibility of Mr Collins' fancying himself in love with her friend had once occurred to Elizabeth within the last day or two; but that Charlotte could encourage him seemed almost as far from possibility as she could encourage him herself, and her astonishment was consequently so great as to overcome at first the bounds of decorum, and she could not help crying out –

'Engaged to Mr Collins! my dear Charlotte, – impossible!'

The steady countenance which Miss Lucas had commanded in telling her story, gave way to a momentary confusion here on receiving so direct a reproach; though, as it was no more than she expected, she soon regained her composure, and calmly replied –

'Why should you be surprised, my dear Eliza? – Do you think it incredible that Mr Collins should be able to procure any woman's good opinion, because he was not so happy as to succeed with you?'

But Elizabeth had now recollected herself, and making a strong effort for it, was able to assure her with tolerable firmness that the prospect of their relationship was highly grateful to her, and that she wished her all imaginable happiness.

'I see what you are feeling,' replied Charlotte, – 'you must be surprised, very much surprised – so lately as Mr Collins was wishing to marry you. But when you have had time to think it all over, I hope you will be satisfied with what I have done. I am not romantic, you know; I never was. I ask only a comfortable home; and considering Mr Collins' character, connections, and situation in life, I am convinced that my chance of happiness with him is as fair as most people can boast on entering the marriage state.'

Elizabeth quietly answered 'Undoubtedly'; – and after an awkward pause, they returned to the rest of the family. Charlotte did not stay much longer and Elizabeth was left to reflect on what she had heard. It was a long time before she became at all reconciled to the idea of so unsuitable a match. The strangeness of Mr Collins' making two offers of marriage within three days was nothing in comparison of his being now accepted. She had always felt that Charlotte's opinion of matrimony was not exactly like her own, but she could not have supposed it possible that, when called into action, she would have sacrificed every better feeling to worldly advantage. Charlotte the wife of Mr Collins, was a most humiliating picture! – And to the pang of a friend disgracing herself and sunk in her esteem, was added the distressing conviction that it was impossible for that friend to be tolerably happy in the lot she had chosen.

A much more cynical but vastly amusing view of marriage is presented in *Tristram Shandy* by Lawrence Sterne. This extract shows Widow Wadman's pursuit of Uncle Toby in Chapter XXIV.

> – I am half distracted, captain Shandy, said Mrs Wadman, holding up her cambrick handkerchief to her left eye, as she approach'd the door of my uncle Toby's sentry-box – a mote – or sand – or something – I know not what, has got into this eye of mine – do look into it – it is not in the white –
>
> In saying which, Mrs Wadman edged herself close in beside my uncle Toby, and squeezing herself down upon the corner of his bench, she gave him an opportunity of doing it without rising up – Do look into it – said she.
>
> Honest soul! thou didst look into it with as much innocency of heart, as ever child look'd into a raree-shew-box; and 'twere as much a sin to have hurt thee.
>
> – If a man will be peeping of his own accord into things of that nature – I've nothing to say to it –
>
> My uncle Toby never did; and I will answer for him, that he would have sat quietly upon a sofa from June to January (which, you know, takes in both the hot and cold months), with an eye as fine as the Thracian Rodope's beside him, without being able to tell, whether it was a black or blue one.
>
> The difficulty was to get my uncle Toby to look at one at all.
>
> 'Tis surmounted. And
>
> I see him yonder with his pipe pendulous in his hand, and the ashes falling out of it – looking and looking – then rubbing his eyes – and looking again, with twice the good-nature that ever Gallileo look'd for a spot in the sun.
>
> – In vain! for by all the powers which animate the organ – Widow Wadman's left eye shines this moment as lucid as her right – there is neither mote, or sand, or dust, or chaff, or speck, or particle of opake matter floating in it – There is nothing, my dear paternal uncle! but one lambent delicious fire, furtively shooting out from every part of it, in all directions, into thine –
>
> – If thou lookest, uncle Toby, in search of this mote one moment longer – thou art undone.

STYLE

You may be asked to comment on the style of a passage. These are the main areas that need to be examined.

Sentence structure and punctuation

You must decide what effect the sentence structure has and whether this effect is appropriate to the subject matter.

Language and imagery

Is the language and imagery suitable to the subject? Whether the subject be comic, serious or poetical the language and imagery should echo the subject.

Tone

Although this has been dealt with in greater detail in an earlier part of the chapter, an integral part of any discussion on style must contain a discussion of whether the tone is suitable to the passage; for instance is the tone ironical, comic or serious?

DIFFERENT TYPES OF STYLE AND EXAMPLES

Colloquial style

When the author deliberately uses dialect to suggest a working class, or regional atmosphere. Lawrence is a master of Nottingham dialect, as is Alan Sillitoe in *Saturday Night and Sunday Morning.*

In *Billy Liar,* Billy and his friend, Arthur, mockingly imitate the Yorkshire dialect of Councillor Duxbury. Billy mocks everything to do with his home background as he is trying

(a) and (b) Saturday Night, Sunday Morning

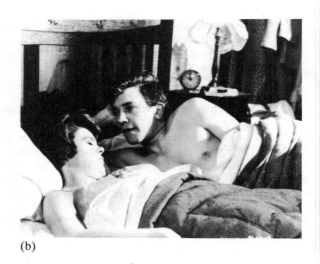

(b)

(c) Billy Liar

desperately to leave the North and become a script-writer in London. The author, Keith Waterhouse, uses this passage to show Billy's quick and intelligent mind and his ability to see the comic and grotesque side of any situation. It also shows his immaturity in fighting against his home background when he has neither the money or the talent to leave it.

> The door-bell tinkled and we put on our funeral faces but it was nobody, only Councillor Duxbury. He crossed the floor to his own office with an old man's shuffle, putting all his thought into the grip of his stick and the pattern of the faded, broken lino. A thick, good coat sat heavily on his bowed back, and there were enamelled medallions on his watch-chain. At the door of his room he half-turned, moving his whole body like an old robot, and muttered: 'Morning lads'.
>
> We chanted, half-dutifully, half-ironically: 'Good morning, Councillor Duxbury,' and directly the door was closed, began our imitation of him. 'It's Councillor Duxbury, lad, Councillor Duxbury. Tha wun't call Lord Harewood mister, would tha? Councillor, that's mah title. Now think on.'
>
> 'Ah'm just about thraiped,' said Arthur in broad dialect. The word was one we had made up to use in the Yorkshire dialect routine, where we took the Michael out of Councillor Duxbury and people like him. Duxbury prided himself on his dialect which was practically unintelligible even to seasoned Yorkshiremen.
>
> 'Tha's getten more bracken ivvery day, lad,' I said.
>
> 'Aye, an' fair scritten anall,' said Arthur.
>
> 'Tha mun wi't' gangling-iron.'
>
> 'Aye.'
>
> We swung into the other half of the routine, which was Councillor Duxbury remembering, as he did every birthday in an interview with the Stradhoughton Echo. Arthur screwed up his face into the lined old man's wrinkles and said:
>
> 'Course, all this were fields when I were a lad.'
>
> '– and course, ah'd nobbut one clog to mah feet when ah come to Stradhoughton,' I said in the wheezing voice.
>
> 'Tha could get a meat pie and change out o'fourpence –'
>
> 'Aye, an' a box at t'Empire and cab home at t' end on it.'
>
> 'Ah had to tak' a cab home because ah only had one clog.' said Arthur.

Didactic style

Didactic means 'fitted or intended to teach.' An author who writes didactically is intending to instruct his readers in the way they ought to think either about the ideas he is putting forward or his characters.

George Eliot is an ideal example of an author using didactic style. The passage represented here from *The Mill on the Floss,* where she criticises the narrowness of society, shows how George Eliot felt her own isolation from a narrow-minded society because of her relationship with GH Lewis. To understand much of George Eliot's writing we have to go back to the facts of her life.

In order to reach a position where she could deploy her capacities to the full, she had to live unconventionally, to leave Coventry and set up as a journalist alone in London. If this had been all, there was nothing all that unusual – many intelligent women of her time had done as much – but George Eliot chose to link her life with that of a married man. For 25 years until his death in 1879 she lived with the scientific popularizer and scholar George Henry Lewis. Again this wouldn't have mattered if she had chosen to stay in that part of society where it did not matter, but in the more respectable intellectual social circles in which she wanted to move, it did matter, at least before her professional reputation was established. By the conventions of the time, Lewis could be received anywhere, she could not. In later years, nobody could be more readily respectable than the Lewises, as they were known and hardly anyone would be but honoured to receive George Eliot. But for her lack of respectability as well as for her plain appearance she had known many years of rejection and pain.

> Perhaps something akin to this oppressive feeling may have weighed upon you in watching this old-fashioned family life on the banks of the Floss, which even sorrow hardly suffices to lift above the level of the tragi-comic. It is a sordid life, you say, this of the Tullivers and Dodsons – irradiated by no sublime principles, no romantic visions, no active, self-renouncing faith – moved by none of those wild, uncontrollable passions which create the dark shadows of misery and crime – without that primitive rough simplicity of wants, that hard, submissive ill-paid toil, that childlike spelling-out of what nature has written, which gives its poetry to peasant life. Here one has conventional wordly notions and habits without instruction and without polish – surely the most prosaic form of human

life – proud respectability in a gig of unfashionable build, worldliness without side-dishes. Observing these people narrowly, even when the iron hand of misfortune has shaken them from their unquestioning hold on the world, one sees little trace of religion, still less of a distinctively Christian creed. Their belief in the Unseen, so far as it manifests itself at all, seems to be rather of a pagan kind; their moral notions, though held with strong tenacity, seem to have no standard beyond hereditary custom. You could not live among such people; you are stifled for want of an outlet towards something beautiful, great, or noble; you are irritated with these dull men and women, as a kind of population out of keeping with the earth on which they live – with this rich plain where the great river flows for ever onward, and links the small pulse of the old English town with the beatings of the world's mighty heart. A vigorous superstition, that lashes its gods or lashes its own back, seems to be more congruous with the mystery of the human lot than the mental condition of these emmet-like Dodsons and Tullivers.

I share with you this sense of oppressive narrowness; but it is necessary that we should feel it, if we care to understand how it acted on the lives of Tom and Maggie – how it has acted on young natures in many generations, that in the onward tendency of human things have risen above the mental level of the generation before them, to which they have been nevertheless tied by the strongest fibres of their hearts. The suffering, whether martyr or victim, which belongs to every historical advance of mankind is represented in this way in every town and by hundreds of obscure hearths. And we need not shrink from this comparison of small things with great; for does not science tell us that its highest striving is after the ascertainment of a unity which shall bind the smallest things with the greatest? In natural science, I have understood, there is nothing petty to the mind that has a large vision of relations, and to which every single object suggests a vast sum of conditions. It is surely the same with the observation of human life.

Dramatic style

Dramatic style is often the most difficult to achieve, as it can be overdone and appear melodramatic and false. Often the most effective dramatic writing is understated. On rare occasions, a truly skilful writer can use all the exigences of high drama, such as exclamation, emotive words and onomatopoeia and succeed.

Such an example is found in the powerful writing of Joseph Conrad in *The Secret Agent* where Ossipon attacks Mrs Verloc

> He leaped a foot high. Unexpectedly Mrs Verloc had desecrated the unbroken, reserved decency of her home by a shrill and terrible shriek.
> 'Help, Tom! Save me. I won't be hanged!'
> He rushed forward, groping for her mouth with a silencing hand, and the shriek died out. But in his rush he had knocked her over. He felt her now clinging round his legs, and his terror reached its culminating point, became a sort of intoxication, entertained delusions, acquired the characteristics of delirium tremens. He positively saw snakes now. He saw the woman twined round him like a snake, not to be shaken off. She was not deadly. She was death itself – the companion of life.
> Mrs Verloc, as if relieved by the outburst, was very far from behaving noisily now. She was pitiful.
> 'Tom, you can't throw me off now,' she murmured from the floor. 'Not unless you crush my head under your heel. I won't leave you.'
> 'Get up,' said Ossipon.
> His face was so pale as to be quite visible in the profound black darkness of the shop; while Mrs Verloc, veiled, had no face, almost no discernible form. The trembling of something small and white, a flower in her hat, marked her place, her movements.
> It rose in the blackness. She had got up from the floor, and Ossipon regretted not having run out at once into the street. But he perceived easily that it would not do. It would not do. She would run after him. She would pursue him shrieking till she sent every policeman within hearing in chase. And then goodness only knew what she would say of him. He was so frightened that for a moment the insane notion of strangling her in the dark passed through his mind. And he became more frightened than ever! She had him. He saw himself living in abject terror in some obscure hamlet in Spain or Italy; till some fine morning they found him dead, too, with a knife in his breast – like Mr Verloc. He sighed deeply. He dared not move. And Mrs Verloc waited in silence the good pleasure of her saviour, deriving comfort from his reflective silence.

Comic style

It is difficult to analyse what makes people laugh and what constitutes a comic style, but an

A-level student ought to be able to pick out the comic elements in a passage and say why they are humorous.

Simple humour which can stem from the childish misinterpretation of a situation is found in *Cider with Rosie* by Laurie Lee.

It is one of the most vividly drawn scenes of the novel – the village school. The writing is humorous but always quietly controlled and the ending of the passage is amusing, but understated.

> The village school at that time provided all the instruction we were likely to ask for. It was a small stone barn divided by a wooden partition into two rooms – The Infants and The Big Ones. There was one dame teacher, and perhaps a young girl assistant. Every child in the valley crowding there, remained till he was fourteen years old, then was presented to the working field or factory with nothing in his head more burdensome than a few mnemonics, a jumbled list of wars, and a dreamy image of the world's geography. It seemed enough to get by with, in any case; and was one up on our poor old grandparents.
>
> This school, when I came to it, was at its peak. Universal education and unusual fertility had packed it to the walls with pupils. Wild boys and girls from miles around – from the outlying farms and half-hidden hovels way up at the ends of the valley – swept down each day to add to our numbers, bringing with them strange oaths and odours, quaint garments and curious pies. They were my first amazed vision of any world outside the womanly warmth of my family; I didn't expect to survive it for long, and I was confronted with it at the age of four.
>
> The morning came, without any warning, when my sisters surrounded me, wrapped me in scarves, tied up my bootlaces, thrust a cap on my head, and stuffed a baked potato in my pocket.
>
> 'What's this?' I said.
>
> 'You're starting school today.'
>
> 'I ain't. I'm stopping 'ome.'
>
> 'Now, come on Loll. You're a big boy now.'
>
> 'I ain't.'
>
> 'You are.'
>
> 'Boo-hoo.'
>
> They picked me up bodily, kicking and bawling, and carried me up to the road.
>
> 'Boys who don't go to school get put into boxes, and turn into rabbits, and get chopped up Sundays.'
>
> I felt this was overdoing it rather, but I said no more after that. I arrived at the school just three feet tall and fatly wrapped in my scarves. The playground roared like a rodeo, and the potato burned through my thigh. Old boots, ragged stockings, torn trousers and skirts, went skating and skidding around me. The rabble closed in; I was encircled; grit flew in my face like shrapnel. Tall girls with frizzled hair, and huge boys with sharp elbows, began to prod me with hideous interest. They plucked at my scarves, spun me round like a top, screwed my nose, and stole my potato.
>
> I was rescued at last by a gracious lady – the sixteen-year-old junior-teacher – who boxed a few ears and dried my face and led me off to The Infants. I spent that first day picking holes in paper, then went home in a smouldering temper.
>
> 'What's the matter, Loll? Didn't he like it at school, then?'
>
> 'They never gave me the present!'
>
> 'Present? What present?'
>
> 'They said they'd give me a present.'
>
> 'Well, now, I'm sure they didn't.'
>
> 'They did! They said: "You're Laurie Lee, ain't you? Well, just you sit there for the present." I sat there all day but I never got it. I ain't going back there again!'

Another example of language being used as a source of humour is in 'the foreign visitor' episode of *Our Mutual Friend* by Charles Dickens. In this extract we have the humorous situation of lack of communication between Mr Podsnap and the foreign gentleman.

> The majority of the guests were like the plate, and included several heavy articles weighing ever so much. But there was a foreign gentleman among them: whom Mr Podsnap had invited after much debate with himself – believing the whole European continent to be in mortal alliance against the young person – and there was a droll disposition, not only on the part of Mr Podsnap, but of everybody else, to treat him as if he were a child who was hard of hearing.
>
> As a delicate concession to this unfortunately-born foreigner, Mr Podsnap, in receiving him, had presented his wife as 'Madame Podsnap'; also his daughter as 'Mademoiselle Podsnap', with some inclination to add 'ma fille', in which bold venture, however, he

checked himself. The Veneerings being at that time the only other arrivals, he had added (in a condescendingly explanatory manner), 'Monsieur Vey-nair-reeng', and had then subsided into English.

'How do you like London?' Mr Podsnap now inquired from his station of host, as if he were administering something in the nature of a powder or potion to the deaf child; 'London, Londres, London?'

The foreign gentleman admired it.

'You find it Very Large?' said Mr Podsnap, spaciously.

The foreign gentleman found it very large.

'And Very Rich?'

The foreign gentleman found it, without doubt énormément riche.

'Enormously Rich, we say,' returned Mr Podsnap, in a condescending manner. 'Our English adverbs do Not terminate in Mong, and we Pronounce the "ch" as if there were a "t" before it. We Say Ritch.'

'Reetch,' remarked the foreign gentleman.

'And Do You Find, Sir,' pursued Mr Podsnap, with dignity, 'Many Evidences that Strike You, of our British Constitution in the Streets of The World's Metropolis, London, Londres, London?'

The foreign gentleman begged to be pardoned, but did not altogether understand.

'The Constitution Britannique,' Mr Podsnap explained, as if he were teaching in an infant school. 'We Say British, But You Say Britannique, You Know' (forgivingly, as if that were not his fault). 'The Constitution, Sir.'

The foreign gentleman said, 'Mais, yees; I know eem.'

A youngish sallowish gentleman in spectacles, with a lumpy forehead, seated in a supplementary chair at a corner of the table, here caused a profound sensation by saying, in a raised voice, 'Esker,' and then stopping dead.

'Mais oui,' said the foreign gentleman, turning towards him. 'Est-ce que? Quoi donc?'

But the gentleman with the lumpy forehead having for the time delivered himself of all that he found behind his lumps, spake for the time no more.

'I Was Enquiring,' said Mr Podsnap, resuming the thread of his discourse, 'Whether You Have Observed in our Streets as We should say, Upon Our Pavvy as you would say, any Tokens –'

The foreign gentleman with patient courtesy entreated pardon; 'But what was tokenz?'

Marks,' said Mr Podsnap; 'Signs, you know, Appearances – Traces.'

'Ah! Of a Orse?' inquired the foreign gentleman.

'We call it Horse,' said Mr Podsnap, with forbearance. 'In England, Angleterre, England, We Aspirate the "H", and We Say "Horse". Only our Lower Classes Say "Orse"!'

'Pardon,' said the foreign gentleman; 'I am alwiz wrong!'

'Our Language,' said Mr Podsnap, with a gracious consciousness of being always right, 'is Difficult. Ours is a Copious Language, and Trying to Strangers. I will not Pursue my Question.'

MODEL PASSAGE AND COMMENTARY

Passage A (The end of Chapter XXXIV and the beginning of Chapter XXXV, *Tess of the D'Urbervilles*.)

'O, Angel – I am almost glad – because now you can forgive me! I have not made my confession. I have a confession, too – remember, I said so.'

'Ah, to be sure! Now then for it, wicked little one.'

'Perhaps, although you smile, it is as serious as yours, or more so.'

'It can hardly be more serious, dearest.'

'It cannot – O no, it cannot!' She jumped up joyfully at the hope. 'No, it cannot be more serious, certainly,' she cried, 'because 'tis just the same! I will tell you now.'

She sat down again.

Their hands were still joined. The ashes under the grate were lit by the fire vertically, like a torrid waste. Imagination might have beheld a Last Day luridness in this red-coaled glow, which fell on his face and hand, and on hers, peering into the loose hair about her brow, and firing the delicate skin underneath. A large shadow of her shape rose upon the wall and ceiling. She bent forward, at which each diamond on her neck gave a sinister wink like a toad's; and pressing her forehead against his temple she entered on her story of her acquaintance with Alec d'Urberville and its results, murmuring the words without flinching, and with her eyelids drooping down.

Her narrative ended; even its re-assertions and secondary explanations were done. Tess's voice throughout had hardly risen higher than its opening tone; there had been no exculpatory phrase of any kind, and she had not wept.

But the complexion even of external things seemed to suffer transmutation as her announcement progressed. The fire in the grate looked impish – demoniacally funny, as if it did not care in the least about her strait. The fender grinned idly, as if it too did not care. The light from the water-bottle was merely engaged in a chromatic problem. All material objects around announced their irresponsibility with terrible iteration. And yet nothing had changed since the moments when he had been kissing her; or rather, nothing in the substance of things. But the essence of things had changed.

When she ceased the auricular impressions from their previous endearments seemed to hustle away into the corner of their brains, repeating themselves as echoes from a time of supremely purblind foolishness.

Clare performed the irrelevant act of stirring the fire; the intelligence had not even yet got to the bottom of him. After stirring the embers he rose to his feet, all the force of her disclosure had imparted itself now. His face had withered. In the strenuousness of his concentration he treadled fitfully on the floor. He could not, by any contrivance, think closely enough; that was the meaning of his vague movement. When he spoke it was in the most inadequate, commonplace voice of the many varied tones she had heard from him.

'Tess!'

'Yes, dearest.'

'Am I to believe this? From your manner I am to take it as true. O you cannot be out of your mind! You ought to be! Yet you are not. . . . My wife, my Tess – nothing in you warrants such a supposition as that?'

'I am not out of my mind,' she said.

'And yet –' He looked vacantly at her, to resume with dazed senses: 'Why didn't you tell me before? Ah, yes, you would have told me, in a way – but I hindered you, I remember!'

These and other of his words were nothing but the perfunctory babble of the surface while the depths remained paralyzed. He turned away, and bent over a chair. Tess followed him to the middle of the room where he was, and stood there staring at him with eyes that did not weep. Presently she slid down upon her knees beside his foot, and from this position she crouched in a heap.

'In the name of our love, forgive me!' she whispered with a dry mouth. 'I have forgiven you for the same!'

Commentary on Passage A

This passage is taken from the novel, *Tess of the D'Urbervilles* by Thomas Hardy. Tess has been seduced by Alec d'Urberville, a distant relation, and she has had his child. This child has subsequently died. Tess falls in love with Angel Clare, who is undergoing practical experience of dairy farming at Talbothay's Dairy. He is the youngest son of a poor parson; he has to learn a practical skill to make his way in the world. Tess at first resists Angel's advances as she feels tainted by her relationship with d'Urberville, but because of the depth of her feelings she agrees to marry him. On their wedding night they agree to confess their past misdeeds. Clare confesses to having a sexual relationship with another woman prior to his marriage. Tess is just about to confess her relationship with Alec d'Urberville.

Tess's modest and unassuming nature is shown clearly in this passage. She uses phrases like 'forgive me', 'make my confession', as though she regards Angel as her Father Confessor and she definitely sees him as a superior being to herself. When she tells the story of Alec d'Urberville and herself she 'murmurs the words without flinching, and with her eyelids drooping down'.

Her total charm is demonstrated by descriptions of her physical beauty. The fire 'peered into the loose hair about her brow and fired the delicate skin underneath'. Her movements are light and graceful, 'she jumped joyfully up at the hope', her hesitancy and slight stumbling in her speech reflect her anxiety and her naivety. 'O, Angel – I am almost glad – because now you can forgive me! I have not made my confession, I have a confession, too – remember, I said so.'

Tess starts her confession with complete faith that Angel will forgive her. The sentence 'Their hands were still joined' shows their transitory united state which is soon to be shattered. She is so confident that she will be pardoned that she does not attempt to offer any excuses for her behaviour. 'Tess's voice throughout had hardly risen higher than its opening tone: there had been no exculpatory phrase of any kind, and she had not wept.' She does not realize until her confession is over that a double standard operates in Angel's mind over his sins and hers: his is judged as normal masculine behaviour, hers is unpardonable.

Although Angel's character has been hinted at when talking of Tess, a detailed analysis of his personality is needed in any commentary on this passage. At the beginning of the passage, he treats her confession as trivial – something which he cannot take seriously.

'Ah, to be sure! Now then for it, wicked little one?'

'Perhaps, although you smile, it is as serious as yours, or more so.'

'It can hardly be more serious, dearest.'

After she has confessed, although the surroundings are unaltered, everything will never be the same, 'the essence of things had changed'. Their previous idyllic state of happiness now seems 'supremely purblind foolishness'.

Hardy shows Angel's shocked state of mind in a series of short, staccato-like statements. His face and voice betray his complete loss of faith and feeling for his wife. 'His face had withered. In the strenuousness of his concentration he treadled fitfully on the floor. He could not, by any contrivance, think closely enough;'. . . .

'Tess!'

'Yes, dearest.'

'Am I to believe this? From your manner I am to take it to be true. O you cannot be out of your mind! You ought to be! Yet you are not. . . . My wife, my Tess – nothing in you warrants such a supposition as that?'

The melodramatic tone of his speech shows his shocked mind. He knows that she has tried to tell him before when she wrote him a letter, but the letter was lost and so this attempt failed.

Angel is an unbending character who cannot vary his opinions once they are formed, 'These and other of his words were nothing but the perfunctory babble of the surface while the depths remained paralyzed.' He is beyond any emotion and beyond any human feeling. The double standard of morality has operated against Tess and 'she stood there staring at him with eyes that did not weep'. Her last words illustrate the desperation and hopelessness of her plight –

'In the name of our love, forgive me!' she whispered with a dry mouth. 'I have forgiven you for the same!'

The main features of the style of this passage are the short, melodramatic sentence structure and the use of household objects to suggest foreboding. The melodramatic style of speech has already been discussed, but the other imagery needs further explanation. Household objects which would normally appear friendly and comforting take on a sinister appearance and seem to be conspiring against Tess. 'The ashes under the grate were lit by the fire vertically, like a torrid waste. Imagination might have beheld a Last Day luridness in this red-coaled glow.' The image evoked is one which is reminiscent of Milton's 'Paradise Lost' and the depths of hell where sinners suffer eternal damnation. The firelight makes things of beauty appear full of evil – 'A large shadow of her shape rose upon the wall and ceiling. She bent forward, at which each diamond on her neck gave a sinister wink like a toad's.'

After her story has ended, the household objects seem to gloat at her misery. 'The fire in the grate looked impish – demoniacally funny, as if it did not care in the least about her strait. The fender grinned idly. . . . The light from the water bottle was merely engaged in a chromatic problem. All material objects around announced their irresponsibility with terrible iteration.'

Hardy's pessimistic feeling that virtue and honesty go unrewarded is well shown in this passage. Tess is an innocent who suffers at the hands of a bigoted and unbending husband and when his forgiveness comes, it comes too late.

MODEL PASSAGE WITH QUESTIONS FOR PRACTICE

Passage B (Chapter XXIV, *Tess of the D'Urbervilles*)

The rains having passed the uplands were dry. The wheels of the dairyman's spring cart, as he sped home from market, licked up the pulverized surface of the highway, and were followed by white ribands of dust, as if they had set a thin powder-train on fire. The cows jumped wildly over the five-barred barton-gate, maddened by the gad-fly; Dairyman
5   Crick kept his shirt-sleeves permanently rolled up from Monday to Saturday: open windows had no effect in ventilation without open doors, and in the dairy-garden the blackbirds and thrushes crept about under the currant-bushes, rather in the manner of quadrupeds than of winged creatures. The flies in the kitchen were lazy, teasing, and familiar, crawling about in unwonted places, on the floors, into drawers, and over the
10   backs of the milkmaids' hands. Conversations were concerning sunstroke; while butter-making, and still more butter-keeping, was a despair.

They milked entirely in the meads for coolness and convenience, without driving in the cows. During the day the animals obsequiously followed the shadow of the smallest tree as it moved round the stem with the diurnal roll; and when the milkers came they
15   could hardly stand still for the flies.

On one of these afternoons four or five unmilked cows chanced to stand apart from the general herd, behind the corner of a hedge, among them being Dumpling and Old Pretty, who loved Tess's hands above those of any other maid. When she rose from her stool

20 under a finished cow Angel Clare, who had been observing her for some time, asked her if
she would take the aforesaid creatures next. She silently assented, and with her stool at
arm's length, and the pail against her knee, went round to where they stood. Soon the
sound of Old Pretty's milk fizzing into the pail came through the hedge, and then Angel
felt inclined to go round the corner also, to finish off a hard-yielding milcher who had
strayed there, he being now as capable of this as the dairyman himself.

25 All the men, and some of the women, when milking, dug their foreheads into the cows
and gazed into the pail. But a few – mainly the younger ones – rested their heads sideways.
This was Tess Durbeyfield's habit, her temple pressing the milcher's flank, her eyes fixed
on the far end of the meadow with the quiet of one lost in meditation. She was milking Old
Pretty thus, and the sun chancing to be on the milking-side it shone flat upon her pink-
30 gowned form and her white curtain-bonnet, and upon her profile, rendering it keen as a
cameo cut from the dun background of the cow.

She did not know that Clare had followed her round, and that he sat under his cow
watching her. The stillness of her head and features was remarkable: she might have been
in a trance, her eyes open, yet unseeing. Nothing in the picture moved but Old Pretty's
35 tail and Tess's pink hands, the latter so gently as to be a rhythmic pulsation only, as if they
were obeying a reflex stimulus, like a beating heart.

How very lovable her face was to him. Yet there was nothing ethereal about it; all was
real vitality, real warmth, real incarnation. And it was in her mouth that this culminated.
Eyes almost as deep and speaking he had seen before, and cheeks perhaps as fair; brows
40 as arched, a chin and throat almost as shapely; her mouth he had seen nothing to equal on
the face of the earth. To a young man with the least fire in him that little upward lift in the
middle of her red top lip was distracting, infatuating, maddening. He had never before
seen a woman's lips and teeth which forced upon his mind with such persistant iteration the
old Elizabethan simile of roses filled with snow. Perfect, he, as a lover, might have called
45 them off-hand. But no – they were not perfect. And it was the touch of the imperfect upon
the would-be perfect that gave the sweetness, because it was that which gave the humanity.

Passage B, Tess of the D'Urbervilles

Answer the following short questions on the passage and then use the information you have
written to write a commentary on the passage along the lines suggested for Passage A.

1 How does Hardy suggest the heat in the passage?

2 What do you learn of the character and appearance of Tess? Use your own words and quote
extracts from the passage.

3 What do you learn of the character and appearance of Angel Clare? Use your own words and
quote from the passage.

4 How does Hardy suggest the attractiveness of the country setting?

5 How does Hardy suggest the relationship between Tess and Angel Clare?

6 Explain the following phrases:

   (*a*) line 2 'pulverized surface of the highway'
   (*b*) line 3 'as if they had set a thin powder-train on fire'
   (*c*) line 7 'rather in the manner of quadrupeds than of winged creatures'
   (*d*) lines 13-14 'the animals obsequiously followed the shadow of the smallest tree and moved
        round the stem with the diurnal roll'
   (*e*) lines 30-31 'rendering it as a cameo cut from the dun background of the cow'
   (*f*) lines 35-36 'the latter so gently as to be a rhythmic pulsation only, as if they were obeying
        a reflex stimulus, like a beating heart.'
   (*g*) lines 37-38 'Yet there was nothing ethereal about it; all was real vitality, real warmth, real
        incarnation.'
   (*h*) lines 42-46 'He had never before seen a woman's lips and teeth which forced upon his
        mind with such persistent iteration the old Elizabethan simile of roses filled with snow.
        Perfect, he as a lover, might have called them off-hand. But no – they were not perfect.
        And it was the touch of the imperfect upon the would-be perfect that gave the sweetness,
        because it was that which gave the humanity.'

7 Comment on the sentence structure of the passage

Now, using all this information and reading the model commentary on Passage A, write your
own commentary.

Part V

English language at Advanced Level

Most A-level examinations are heavily weighted on the side of literature. The Associated Examining Board is one of the few examination boards which offers an alternative examination paper.

The AEB offers two Advanced-level papers in English. One is a 'traditional' A-level examination in English Literature with three papers: Chaucer and Shakespeare; Other Authors; and Practical Critical Appreciation. The other examination is the only A-level examination where English Language provides a substantial element and is called merely **English.** It is this paper that we shall look at in the following notes.

AEB ENGLISH (EXAMINATION NUMBER 623)

This examination consists of three papers:

Paper 1 (2 hrs 30 mins) contains an essay for which 60 marks are allocated and a précis for which 40 marks are allocated. Total 100.

Paper 2 (3 hrs) contains a prose passage with questions mainly on content but also occasionally on style and opinion, for which 40 marks are allocated. There are then two further sections each containing three set books. Candidates must answer one question from each section and a third question chosen from either of the two sections or an alternative question dealing with an aspect of language. Each of these questions is given 20 marks. Total 100.

Paper 3 (3 hrs) is literature only and is divided into two sections. Candidates must answer two questions from each section. Marks are given as 4×25. Section 1 usually contains literature pre-1800.

It is therefore possible, if the optional language question on Paper 2 is answered, to have 160 of the possible 300 marks allocated on what might be called English Language; if this question is not taken, then 140 marks are in this area; the examination is therefore on an approximately equal division between language and literature. As the literature side of A level is clearly dealt with in other parts of this book, this chapter will concentrate on papers 1 and 2 of this syllabus.

Paper 1

Essay

The Chief Examiners' Reports, issued annually by the AEB for all their examinations repay study and candidates are advised to obtain a copy of reports on recent examinations if they are able to do so. Practically all the reports over the last 12 years have commented upon the importance of basic literacy (spelling, punctuation, sentence construction) and structure (arrangements of paragraphs; logical sequence of ideas and argument; a sense of shape to the essay – beginning, middle and end).

The Essays set – usually seven or eight – are nearly always argumentative in nature, requiring some ability to organize abstract thought. They are not likely to be narrative or simple description.

For example: A likely topic might well be *Liberty or Law – is there a conflict?* rather than *A description of a town you like* or *Tell a story dealing with the detection of crime*.
This means that they need to be thought about and organized carefully.

Advice on planning and writing an essay on a controversial subject
There are two main types of controversial essay. One asks for the points for and against a particular subject; the other asks you to concentrate on one side only, either presenting a case for a particular point of view or condemning it. Whichever type of essay you attempt, find out whether you have enough facts and ideas on which to build an argument. The second stage is to mull over the facts and ideas you have and to start to organize them into some kind of plan.

Through a consideration of the material at your disposal, your own point of view should become clearer and this will help you in the organization of your material.

If your point of view is divided, you may wish to present a fair and unbiased account of the evidence on both sides, leaving the reader to make up his or her mind. You may decide that one side of the argument is stronger and gains your support and you will come out on this side in your conclusion. You must know where you stand before you start writing the essay. You cannot start a discursive essay supporting one side and then find when you are half way through that you have changed your mind.

Clarity is obviously important if a reader is to be expected to follow your point of view. State your arguments clearly and simply and make sure you leave out no essential steps in the argument. Remember a short, pithy sentence is often useful, particularly at the beginning of a paragraph, to establish a point which can be elaborated in greater detail later.

Cultivate the technique of writing persuasively. If there are arguments against your standpoint treat them fairly and balance them against your own points which, of course, you consider more important. One way of being persuasive is to give plenty of examples to support your point of view. Such examples should be pertinent and woven into the essay naturally so as to illumine the points made, not simply cited in a list and tacked on for effect.

Quotation can be used to add humour or vitality to your essay. For instance an essay on 'The Problems of an Aging Population' could include this quotation from Thackeray, 'Next to the very young, I suppose the very old are the most selfish,' whilst an essay on 'Following Trends in Fashion' could include this observation by Smollet, 'Fashion – ridiculous modes, invented by ignorance and adopted by folly'. A quotation can be used as an effective opening to your essay providing it is apt. It is a good idea to collect quotations from your general reading which might prove useful in examination essays.

Make your beginnings and endings interesting. Do not merely repeat the question or say things like 'In conclusion I would like to say' or 'To sum up, my point of view is'. These are almost certain to be boring and repetitive. Try to move on to new ground, leaving the reader with a new angle on what has already been said in the rest of the essay, and perhaps leaving him or her questioning former assumptions. You should therefore adopt a positive approach throughout your essay. Use an arresting opening and after an interesting discussion leave a good impression by ending convincingly rather than simply petering out.

General advice

1 Allow 1½ hours for the essay.

2 Read all the possible titles and choose the one where you have most information (not necessarily the one where you have the strongest views).

3 Plan your approach in **note form** (you can afford to allow about 20 mins for this). Remember you need some sense of shape – introduction: development: conclusion. Assemble arguments carefully using as many examples as illustration of your argument as possible.

4 Try to adopt a balanced approach, considering both sides of an argument rather than indulging in shrill propaganda.

5 Write careful, accurate English paying particular attention to punctuation, spelling and sentence construction – give yourself time, at the end of the examination, to check this.

Above all – practise the technique of writing this kind of essay to this length (800-900 words – 3 to 4 sides) throughout the course and do not leave it until the day of the examination. It is a very important element – 1/5 of the total marks and must not be left to chance.

You will be marked on the quality of **what you say** and **how you say it** and, of course, these two influence one another – opinions, as all politicians know, look more convincing if they are presented in an attractive way. Essays are therefore marked as a whole by examiners but a rough division of marks, which it may help candidates to keep in mind, would be content: 30, arrangement: 15, basic literacy: 15.

A summary of what Chief Examiners have singled out as faults from past papers is given below:

(a) persistent use of the comma where full-stop or semi-colon needed;

(b) poor sentence construction – e.g. no main verb;

(c) limited range of vocabulary;

(d) vocabulary frequently badly chosen and inappropriate – e.g., slang.
(Examiners do not demand a pretentious 'literary style' and welcome lively, vivid English but often candidates, trying to be off-hand and 'with-it' present views in an ugly, slip-shod and inaccurate way).

(e) lack of planning – essay becomes merely a number of thoughts as they occurred to the writer whilst in the act of writing, with no links between them and no coherent developing argument.

(f) no illustration of assertions.

(g) no link between one paragraph and the next.

(h) dullness – little evidence of any ideas at all.

In short, candidates who read sensibly, keep their eyes and ears open, and have some interest in life and some ideas of their own, who have learnt the basic structure of an English sentence and how to organize an argument clearly and effectively, score well on the essay. Mature candidates, (20+) in particular, may find that this question appeals to them, providing that they have practised the technique of writing the 900-word essay.

Suggested reading

(1) 'Quality' newspapers – *The Times, The Guardian*

(2) Sunday papers – *The Sunday Times, The Observer, The Sunday Telegraph*

(3) Weekly journals such as *New Statesman, Spectator, New Society*

The Précis

Allow 1 hour for this. Read the passage carefully several times before writing. It will be about 600 words long and you will be required to reduce it to about one-third of its length.

Don't start writing your own version before you have fully understood the original.

Don't spend great time and effort getting the piece to exactly one-third (or the number of words stipulated) but do try not to exceed the number.

Don't reproduce great chunks of the original in your own version but use your own words as far as possible. At the same time don't go to ridiculous lengths to avoid using **words** from the original – it is complete phrases and sentences you should try to avoid. It will often be necessary, for example, to use key words from the original in your own version.

Marks

The majority of marks in the précis are given for **content.** This is why **complete understanding** of the passage is necessary in order that all the points (and the relative importance of all the points to one another) are included and the balance of the whole passage is preserved. Note the sequence of points as they arise. About 28/40 marks are usually given for content so be accurate. Two marks are given for an appropriate title. This should be brief and to-the-point. Do not try to make it too much like a tabloid headline. The remaining 10 marks are given for overall impression including style and expression.

Method

Of the 60 minutes you will probably have to deal with this passage, 30 minutes – 40 minutes should be spent in reading the original and in writing a skeleton outline of the main points and of the sequence of the argument.

You must make sure that you understand the passage **as a whole** before you start to break it down. Examiners don't worry about your version being written all in the past tense and third person (old text-books often stipulate this) but they will expect it to read as a good, coherent piece of written English in its own right so give yourself a few minutes to check your version to see that it is accurately written.

Practice

You cannot expect to write a good précis in the examination if you have not written one during the course. It is a technique which is learnt by practice and experience.

Final Point

This last point is true of the Paper as a whole. Too many candidates do little preparation for this Paper. It needs as much as for the other two Papers.

Example of Précis

Write a summary of the following passage in not more than 240 words (the passage contains 701 words). Your summary, in clear connected English, should be given a brief title and the number of words used should be indicated at the end.

There is a sense, of course, in which there has always been a war of the generations among men, although it is more conspicuous in some other animals – among deer, elephants and seals. Young bucks displace old bulls. In this sense the war of generations is akin to the war of the sexes: there has always been a struggle for dominance, or for relative placings, and sheer force has not always been more important than subtlety in the process. But the war of generations has now ceased to be a private war, in herds, families or local communities. It has become war in the public arena, in which significant segments of the younger generation identify themselves as something set over against the rest of society. That they use contrasting styles as a way of sub-dividing themselves does not eclipse the fact that at least these styles have a certain relevance for each other: those of the older generation have none. And the styles are not local styles, nor the language a local argot – they are presented as appropriate for a whole generation, and only for that generation.

The agency that has provided a style appropriate to the whole youth culture is of course the entertainment industry acting through the mass-media, which are themselves increasingly devoted to entertainment. The most expensive entertainment, and hence the most prestigious, is that provided for the section of the public with the largest uncommitted incomes, which, being the young, is also the section with the least cultivated taste, and the highest vulnerability to whatever will arouse animal passions. Whereas community recreation in the past used to bring the generations together, commercial entertainment now drives them apart. We pass from a society in which we had films that were unsuitable for adolescents to one with coffee bars un-suitable for adults. The mass-media are not merely the providers of entertainment, but for the young they are also the disseminators of styles, postures and patterns of behaviour.

Television has been particularly important since, in a way that has not been true of earlier agencies of communication, it completely rejects any moral stance. Even radio, in pre-television days, had a philosophy of public responsibility, and, as an agency the goals of which were neither profit nor mere popularity ratings, its directors, conspicuously Lord Reith, saw themselves as participating in the guardianship and dissemination of particular cultural and moral values. Television, operated for profits or popularity (or both), proceeds in a completely amoral way. It has tested the market, escaped the conventions governing printed matter and the theatre and has steadily grown more daring about levels of public decency. It presents all types of attitudes and values without adopting any firm moral stance of its own. It disavows positive values and accepts the yardstick of the market, which, on moral issues, is an invitation to viewers to abandon their own standards of propriety which – because television is technical, prestigious and clearly identified with the metropolis – suddenly are made to seem provincial if not parochial. Without exerting or seeking to exert direct, didactic authority, television has managed to convey the impression that men who are outside the advanced circles of the semi-literary entertainment people who run television are somehow antiquated in their moral senses. In consequence many people, and particularly young people, who are least sure of their values, and least socialized, have aped the manners and styles of television, which is the new authority on acceptable, prestige – conferring behaviour.

Competition for audiences between channels has been the principal factor behind this development, and entertainment has been its principal genre. But this effect has also been brought about because television has adopted the impersonal, detached style of an agency that merely 'holds the ring', 'provides the facilities' for 'all points of view'. Everything is put across with the same sort of authority. An inevitable result ensues, given what is offered, given the ease with which men readily prefer to indulge gross sensations rather than engage in elevating experiences, or wrestle with subtleties. Letting things find their own level, with a mass audience is to invite the steady deterioration in standards, to let the salacious and the sensational displace or infect other material.

Bryan Wilson

Suggested answer to précis

The generation war and the media

There has always been a struggle for dominance between the generations. This struggle is most obvious in animals but also occurs in humans where cunning is as important for success as mere brute force. This conflict is now no longer fought in small groups but in large sections of society and, in particular, between the younger generation and the rest. Although there are groups within the younger generation there are enough common characteristics in attitude and behaviour to unite them.

These unifying elements are, to a large degree, in the attitudes directed at the young by the entertainments industry. The taste of the young is undeveloped and susceptible to the sensational. Entertainment can therefore influence young people's ideas and values and this, in turn, alienates them from the values of an older generation.

Although early radio was very conscious of morality, television today is largely amoral being dominated purely by commercial success and adopting an attitude which suggests its own sophisticated superiority. By suggesting that others have old-fashioned and out-dated principles, it encourages moral laxity. Young people, with unformed views, all too easily accept the authority and values of television. Therefore, because popular taste inevitably tends towards the sensational and because the mass media give no rules for guidance, traditional standards or morality are undermined and more beneficial material excluded purely because it would not be able to sustain a mass audience. Thus there is an inevitable decline of standards.

239 words

Commentary on the Précis

There is no such thing as the one perfect answer to a précis. A number of different versions can be written which can all achieve high marks. They must, however, have certain things in common:

1 Length The instructions gave 240 words as the required length. Do not become neurotic about length but do not exceed the required amount by more than ten. You may well be able to write a sound précis twenty words under; there is no need to search around for another twenty words. This version happens to be 239.

2 Information You must get all the **essential** information from the passage and render this information **in your own words** and in a **clear, concise** way. This version does contain all the important information and does not reproduce the style of the original passage by lifting out whole chunks verbatim. There is some repetition and the passage might have been pruned back even further. You might like to see where this occurs.

3 Style The précis must read as a piece of connected, coherent English **in its own right.** The reader should not be able to guess that it is a shortened version of another passage.

4 The title The title should summarize, as briefly as possible, the essential contents of the passage.

Paper 2

Question 1

As far as the language element is concerned, the comprehension test in question 1 is of a similar kind (though, of course, more difficult) to many such exercises that you will have already encountered at O Level and you are helped by the fact that the mark allocation is clearly given after each question. There will usually be a question requiring you to give your own views or develop an argument deriving your material from information in the passage – a question demanding some degree of **interpretation** of material rather than merely **explanation** of material. The interpretive question is usually heavily weighted (sometimes 10/40) and must therefore be treated appropriately. **Remember to:**

   (i) use your own words wherever possible;

  (ii) be brief;

  (iii) be accurate.

Marks are heavily weighted for **content** so be as precise in your answer as possible.

Question 2

This is always included as an essay on some aspect of language – e.g. your views on English spelling. It is **not a soft option.** You need to have **knowledge** as well as opinions; you need to be able to give **examples** to support your views. Vague, woolly waffle is no substitute.

Question 3

One or two of the books set for Section 1 will have a general, cultural or language bias rather than being works of 'literature'; Section 2 will contain (usually 20th Century) texts familiar enough in English Literature examinations – e.g., for 1981: HG Wells, *Selected Short Stories*; James Joyce, *Dubliners*; Evelyn Waugh, *A Handful of Dust*. Books in Section 1 in 1981 were Simeon Potter, *Our Language*; H Coombes, *Literature & Criticism*; Douglas Brown, *A Book of Modern Prose*.

There is little difference in technique in answering the two sections. Knowledge of contents provides the basis for opinions in both sections.

Timing Allowing 1 hour for Question 1, each of the three other questions should be given forty minutes and, as a rough guide, examiners will expect a sound answer to be between one and a half and two sides although many candidates write more and some well-organized answers are written in less. Quality, of course, is more important than length.

Advanced Level Comprehension

Read the following passage and answer the questions below it.

Study and the pursuit of knowledge is generally pleasurable. The efficient exercise of any function is normally pleasurable. If the practice of study is painful, something is almost certainly wrong – an unfortunate choice of subjects, defective methods of work, or faulty working conditions. The best results are never secured by feverish energy born of the fear of failure. Most
5 commonly, perhaps, the student is worried by the 'difficulty' of his subject; but difficulties looked at the right way up may be a source of pleasure. The sense of difficulty is by no means always to be attributed to personal limitations. In fact, all our studies should be 'difficult', full of problems, and the process of solving them the normal source of pleasure in intellectual pursuits. Perhaps the reason why students do not more frequently take their pleasures in this way is partly
10 because they are apt to be harassed by an overcrowded syllabus which leaves no time for thought, and partly because the sense of difficulty has come through faulty educational methods to be associated with a sense of subjective limitation. There are, however, intrinsically difficult subjects – subjects essentially consisting of a set of problems. These never can and never should be easy. They are inherently difficult, not only to the student but also to the teacher. If the
15 novice thinks he understands a work on the first casual reading this in itself is sufficient proof that he hasn't. He is only beginning to understand it when he finds it difficult. This applies to some parts of most subjects. It is a misunderstanding of the situation when difficulty of this kind is introjected as a sense of personal incompetence. The trouble is aggravated by the application of inappropriate standards of progress and by the pursuit of inappropriate ideals. Commonly,
20 the student expects to progress at the same rate in these subjects as in easy subjects, and failing to do so blames himself or complains of the limitations of his powers. But there is a fundamental difference between progress in 'easy' and progress in 'difficult' subjects. The characteristic of an 'easy' subject is that its facts, individually, are not difficult of comprehension. The only problem is to assimilate, organize, and apply. Under such conditions progress may be perceptibly rapid,
25 and this engenders confidence. In the 'difficult' subject (and the difficult parts of an easy subject) the facts themselves, through the abstractness of their complexity, require an effort of thought merely to be understood. The process of mere assimilation is slow and gradual. The student, obsessed by the ideal of erudition, is discouraged by his apparent lack of progress, even where progress may be all the greater by reason of being slow. In such subjects haste results in
30 vagueness, superficiality, and increasing confusion of thought, where the appropriate ideals are accuracy and clarity of mind. A difficulty should always be dealt with in a cool and deliberate way, and with an oriental disregard of time. Effort spent on difficulties should also be well distributed. These considerations apply even when the difficulty does in fact arise from individual limitations. Lack of self-assurance is perhaps the most serious emotional disability in the intel-
35 lectual life, and its roots run deep. It is perhaps almost universal. The student only slowly and imperceptibly emerges from a state in which self-depreciation is most amply justified. From birth the child is accustomed to dependence. He is more ignorant than his elders, and his

independent judgments are almost certain to be wrong. He is accustomed to be being told what he should believe, and to the arbitration of authority. What 'it says' in the book tends to be taken as final. That the book was written by some human and fallible hand is a late and devastating revelation. Apart from the special stimulus of encouragement, the measure of independence appropriate to intellectual maturity is liable to be delayed. Ultimately self-confidence requires a rational foundation. Non-rational suggestions may be useful in countering equally non-rational causes of diffidence; but in the last resort it is desirable that we should face our tasks with confidence based upon a dispassionate appreciation of attested merits. It is something gained if we at least escape the domination of inhibiting ideas. There has been a tendency in recent years to underestimate the influence of mere ideas upon the emotional life. It is true that we cannot awaken idealism merely by preaching abstract principles. Nevertheless, there are some ideas which are naturally congruent with enthusiasm, and there are some that stultify. The remedy is to make the most of powers with which we are endowed, to find rational grounds for self-confidence by doing as well as we can what we can do best. Moreover, we might be a little more exacting in our demand for proof of our own incompetence. Incidentally it may be noted that the proof of the absence of ability is always longer than the proof that it is present. If we have **once** performed a task, that is sufficient proof that we can do it. A single failure, on the other hand, is not sufficient proof that we cannot.

CA Mace   The Psychology of Study

Note Your answers should be in your own words as far as possible.

(a) Say what might lead to a 'painful' practice of study with poor results.   (5 marks)

(b) Why might some students fail to find pleasure in 'difficult' studies?   (3 marks)

(c) In what ways might a student misjudge an 'intrinsically difficult' subject?   (4 marks)

(d) Explain in your own words the writer's comments on the study of 'easy' subjects. (6 marks)

(e) What are the problems of a student faced with a 'difficult' subject?   (7 marks)

(f) What reasons are offered for lack of self-assurance in a student?   (4 marks)

(g) What remedies are suggested for a lack of confidence?   (7 marks)

(h) Give the meaning of four of the following as they appear in the passage:

    (i) inherently – (line 14)
    (ii) introjected – (line 18)
    (iii) assimilate – (line 24)
    (iv) fallible – (line 40)
    (v) stultify – (line 49)

(4 marks)
Total 40 marks

Model Answer to the Comprehension Passage

(a) There are a number of reasons why study may be painful for the student and why the results achieved may be poor. A student may have chosen the wrong subject. He may not have learnt to study most effectively or he may have to study in unsatisfactory conditions. He may worry when faced with the subject's inevitable difficulties and this may lead to panic over possible failure.

(b) Students may fail to find pleasure in difficult subjects because they are under pressure through lack of time. This is probably the main reason, but poor teaching may have contributed to a lack of confidence.

(c) A student may misjudge an 'intrinsically difficult subject' if he thinks that the difficulties are only there for him, arising from his own inadequacies. Some students may not even see that there are any difficulties and others may not focus their efforts correctly on the right targets even if they realize that there are difficulties. Other students may get confused because they are unable to judge their own progress.

(d) An 'easy' subject, according to the writer, is one where basic facts can be quickly and easily understood. These facts are quickly absorbed, ordered into a coherent pattern and then used by the student. This leads to rapid progress in the mastery of the subject and therefore to an equally rapid increase in confidence by the student.

(e) With a 'difficult subject' a student is faced with complicated facts which need to be carefully examined before they can be fully understood. It is a slow process and the effort involved can destroy confidence. It is a great temptation to become vague and imprecise or superficial and this can result in more confusion.

(f) Many students lack self-assurance because they have never had to rely on their own powers of thought. They are used to merely accepting instruction and regarding opinions in books as the final truth. They may have made mistakes when attempting to solve problems on their own.

(g) The remedies suggested by the writer for improving a student's self-confidence are mainly linked with positive encouragement. Students should learn to make the most of their own ability by looking at problems objectively, trying to understand where mistakes have been made (and realizing that these are inevitable) and, above all, ignoring the occasional failure, building on the occasional success. Any success is a proof of ability.

(h)		
	inherently	innately or naturally
	introjected	taken personally
	assimilate	absorb
	fallible	likely to make mistakes
	stultify	to deaden the mind

Commentary

1 Answers to comprehension exercises need to be as crisp and accurate as possible. They also need to be simply and clearly expressed in your own words.

2 Where a mark allocation is given, as in this case, this provides a clear guide to the number of points that you will need to make in your answer. For example, in **(a)** 5 marks are allocated and the answer gives 5 pieces of information. Check this out for yourself in the remaining points of the answer.

3 Write the answers in connected English prose. The only exception to this is in **(h)** where the one-word equivalent can be used. (For the purposes of this specimen answer all five words have been explained; a candidate, of course, should do as he is told and only give explanations for four. If all five are answered the examiner will probably only credit the first four.)

Varieties of english paper in the university of london advanced gce english examination

The Varieties of English paper was taken for the first time by 42 candidates in June 1981. This is an option in the University of London advanced Level GCE English examination as an alternative to the Comprehension and Appreciation paper on unseen literature texts, limited initially to four or five centres in a pilot scheme in June 1981 and June 1982, to be extended to more centres in June 1983 and more generally available in June 1984.

Syllabus requirements

1 The study of the forms and uses of a wide variety of different kinds of spoken and written English, both literary and non-literary
2 The understanding of the sound patterns, words and sentence structure of English with which to identify the textual features of varieties of the language
   The objectives were to gain some understanding and awareness of

(a) the nature and causes of language variety and change

(b) the sound, word and sentence patterns of present-day English

(c) factors affecting the styles and uses of English

(d) the differences between written and spoken English

(e) the difference between notions of 'correct' and 'appropriate' language

(f) how to make a simple descriptive analysis of a text

(g) how to relate linguistic features to function or context

Candidates will be required to answer questions on passages of English which may include transcripts of speech and extracts from both literary and non-literary texts and questions of a more general nature concerning the varieties of English and the language of literature.

   When this alternative paper is made generally available in the June 1984 examination, three questions will be offered. This will reduce the amount of material to be read in the examination and offer a more obvious parallel to the Comprehension and Appreciation paper.

Currently the University of London Entrance and School Examinations Council (the London GCE Board) is preparing proposals for an A-level GCE syllabus in English Language studies as a development of the successful launching of the Varieties of English Paper in 1982.

Use of criticism

INTRODUCTION

Criticism is very rarely set as prose work for examination: the exceptions are special cases which owe their presence on the syllabus to the greatness of the author (Dryden, Johnson, Wordsworth) or the special merit of the language. In the first case the criticism itself may still survive for reasons connected with the history of literature, or perhaps for its intrinsic merit, though criticism as such is normally well outdated and superseded within a few decades. Its status as an art is greatly in doubt since it exists not to exhibit itself but only to illuminate other work by the author or others' art. Consequently it is a kind of parasitic genre, at one remove from the art itself.

HOW USEFUL IS CRITICISM TO THE A-LEVEL STUDENT?

As an adjunct to the works to be studied of prose, poetry or drama, criticism may be of the highest usefulness and value to the student; unfortunately it may equally prove a great stumbling block to true appreciation. In this chapter guidance to its use will be given, with recommendations on the kind of thing that should be read, how to read it and how to make the best use of it. Equally necessary, warnings will be given on what to avoid, or what is, in Bacon's phrase, 'to be read only in parts'.

HOW TO BUILD UP A SOUND CRITICAL BACKGROUND

One of the great perplexities for students who want to obtain the best criticism, is not so much how to find it, as to know what they may safely neglect. You may find the criticism on all authors except recent ones by simply visiting the biggest library you can reach and looking up that author in the card index or display equipment. Your list of references may then be completed by obtaining a critical work which itself publishes a bibliography or list of other works available. If the book is up-to-date so will the list be. These works may all be obtained by application through the inter-library service, or borrowed from those who possess good specialized libraries, or even bought. Usually the local library or school library shelves will offer sufficient. It is normal for the main critical material on any particular work to be repeated in its essentials, though in different terms, by two or more books of criticism, and not much is missed if one central and up-to-date work is read but not the others. Normally good later critics weed out and gather together all that has gone before, so that with older classics an optimum critique is usually eventually produced.

CLASSICAL CRITICISM

Because criticism is usually dispensable, once it has served its purpose, and nearly always superseded by later work that can make use of new research or better perceptions, criticism is the one branch of letters where it is better to ignore the old and seek out the latest. The old gods of critical repute look somewhat shabby and dim when compared with the most shining specimens of possibly less learned critics who can draw on perhaps fifty years of advancing judgements. It is true there are irrational fashions, and until recently the fashion or taste has been for 'straight' expression of the language, without rhetoric of decoration – a phenomenon that CS Lewis has well described, for example, in the chapter of *A Preface to Paradise Lost* entitled 'In Defence of this Style' (i.e. the style of 'Secondary Epic').

This changing taste tends to affect criticism, especially critical enthusiasms. For example, that most responsible and perspicacious of all critics, TS Eliot, first attacked Milton as perpetrating a 'dissociation of sensibility' in the language of poetry, and later recanted more because of his own change of appreciation than any alteration in public opinion. But only Robert Browning among Victorian writers liked John Donne, whereas now thanks to Eliot and the prevailing taste all who like poetry approve him.

Occasionally older criticism is still well worth reading, especially if by an author of genius, such as Matthew Arnold, if only to give you ideas against which to place your own arguments and thoughts. Other one-time classics of criticism, for example AC Bradley on Shakespearian tragedy, are now too turgid in style to be easily read, and too biased towards one or other aspect of the work to be critically sound. No one, for example, should read Macaulay for an unbiased account of the Restoration drama, because of his blindness to its merits, nor Virginia Woolf or Lytton Strachey because of their blindness to its faults; the reaction of LC Knights and the disciples of FR Leavis to such drama should also be avoided even if understood.

AT WHAT STAGE SHOULD STUDENTS TURN TO WORKS OF CRITICISM?

If a play, for example, has to be studied, it should first if possible be seen (see p. 161), then read until understood, and then the introduction to the edition set read thoroughly until all the leads and hints have been digested and applied to one's knowledge of the text, before any other criticism is attempted. At this point there are roughly two options for further work. If any doubt about the play's meaning still lingers, which probably would arise from failure to appreciate parts, or the work as whole, then it might be advisable to work though a suitable study guide to that individual play.

STUDY AIDS ON INDIVIDUAL TEXTS

There are several versions of these and they vary in usefulness. Those designed for A-level students at least should be preferred to the more mechanical 'notes' type of study aids. A reading list is given at the end of this chapter.

Although the choice of critical works may seem wide, it is quite possible that no individual book exists for some texts; for example there is a very good study guide to TS Eliot's Selected Poems, (BC Southam, see Reading list), but not for Auden, Muir, Larkin, Graves, Dylan Thomas, Yeats, Robert Lowell; all of whose poems have been set as A-level texts, and for which only the 'Readers' Guide series' provides any detailed exegesis in some cases.

If a writer achieves lasting fame, then usually a huge critical literature accumulates around him, for example of the poets listed above there is already so much on Yeats and Eliot that the Readers' Guides which also exist would be superfluous if it were not that they are so handy. The Readers' Guides on Thomas and Auden are very useful as being the only comprehensive accounts of their poems.

BIOGRAPHICAL APPROACH

A second option, whether for play, poetry selection or novel, is better for those who need to extend their appreciation of the text, having satisfactorily understood the work itself.

This may be done in several ways. The most useful generally, though not always, is to read the last biography of the author. There is usually a 'standard' one, e.g. of Yeats by Joseph Hone; of Lawrence by Harry T. Moore; of Hardy by Robert Gittings (also the biographer of Keats); of Auden by Humphrey Carpenter; of Conrad by Jocelyn Bains; of Joyce by Richard Ellmann. In all these cases the biographies considerably illuminate the work, and provided the candidate in the examination is not tempted away from the subject of his essay into biographical irrelevances, they are quite invaluable in increasing understanding and providing additional critical material.

We include collections of the author's letters under the heading 'Biographical approach'. Often the letters of poets are actually the earliest drafts or germs of ideas for their poems, and very often they provide most illuminating guidance to them; for example, critics and people interested in literature wrote to Yeats, Joyce, Frost, Wallace Stevens and Dylan Thomas encouraging them to comment on their work, which they did to a sometimes breathtaking degree – Gerald Manley Hopkins to Bridges, and Keats to Reynolds. Indeed Keats' letters are so good, and express his ideas so well, that they are now considered to be as good in their own kind as the poetry. Similarly Dorothy Wordsworth's Journals (especially the Alfoxden and

Grasmere ones) are an almost essential supplement to the study of Wordsworth's poems, indicating the source of many of them.

HISTORICAL AND SOCIAL BACKGROUND

A study of the historical and social background of the writer is very valuable. In many papers there are actual questions on this alone, and syllabus requirements usually stipulate a reasonable knowledge of the writer's milieu. The most convenient way of discovering this is to read relevant chapters in histories of English Literature and other more generalized books (see Reading List). If the generalized accounts of background should be inadequate, there remain the admirable books of Basil Willey (see Reading list).

WARNINGS ABOUT CRITICISM

I have indicated above how to track down critical books – obviously there are too many to list here. It is in this area that students need to know what *not* to read. Many of the books are too specialized, academic or even difficult to bother with – all sixth-formers have experienced the frustration of being directed to a critical work that is harder to grasp than the text it is supposed to expound. This is a rather discouraging experience which could lead to an inhibiting of the student's own critical efforts.

If you use one of the A-level study guides to a particular author, you will find at the back a 'Selected Bibliography' which is usually rather too long. Most helpful are the editor's comments on the relative merits of the books in such bibliographies. Otherwise it would be wise to consult an expert in the subject and seek advice. Even then, the recommended book may not prove to be the most suitable, in which case it would be better to change it for another: there is no reason to struggle too far with one when there are usually several others. For authors such as Yeats there are dozens. It is often a question of reading more elementary studies first, rather than trying to tackle a bad book. But, for example, it would be inappropriate to read a large book on *The Parliament of Foules* merely in order to learn more of Chaucer's work other than *The Canterbury Tales,* unless you are preparing for a Scholarship Paper.

AUTHORS AS CRITICS

Authors of the texts set at A Level, for example TS Eliot, Auden, Coleridge, Johnson, Yeats, Lawrence, have often written much criticism themselves. It is not immediately useful to read this simply because it happens to be by 'your author'. However it should be noted that what an author writes about other writers, often applies in a subtle manner to him- or herself. It is often possible to learn valuable lessons in the author's theory of composition, themes, approval of certain styles and so on, from his or her opinion on other authors and their work. This is particularly true of Lawrence, and is worth watching for in others.

SHOULD CRITICAL SOURCES BE IDENTIFIED IN A-LEVEL ANSWERS?

Most good critics quote liberally and pointedly; their quotations are frequently worth learning by heart as anchor points for the observations for which they were quoted: both observation and quotation throw light on each other and it is a useful way of revealing good critical opinion if the quotation is memorized. Similarly, if quotation is liberal as well as being apposite, there is less need to refer back to the text, although it is axiomatic that the text is the first priority, not the critical comment. Most examiners prefer fluent and original appreciation springing directly from the actual text, rather than often painfully obvious second-hand judgements, perhaps only half understood. This may appear to be contradictory, but essay writing is an art itself, which requires well-assimilated critical reading to be reassembled and used convincingly in the expression of the writer's thought on the subject of the question he or she is answering.

For example, candidates will have learned a set of quotations from their texts, some or all attached to areas of critical judgements. Should they fire these off irrespective of the terms of the question, they are not exercising their own faculties properly. Most questions will allow a number of the quotations learned to be used relevantly, in their proper place in an essay.

When out-of-the-ordinary critical ideas are reproduced in an essay, it is better if the source is also quoted, both author and book. Some critical expressions are now well-known, and these should be credited to their authors. Furthermore, if notes are made from critical works as preparation for possible essay subjects, with the notes should also be clearly added and remembered the source-book and its author. If reference is then made to such material, its author should also be referred to as such. Some students think that more credit is given them if they pass such matter off as their own, but the opposite is true.

CRITICAL JARGON

All critical jargon should be avoided unless a technical term has to be employed for the thought: jargon should not be used to hang criticism upon, but only when absolutely necessary, to express the concept. A good explanation of terms used in poetry appreciation may be found in *A Prosody Handbook* (see reading list).

CONCLUSION – FORMING YOUR OWN CRITICAL RESERVOIR

Finally, it is a very good practice to discuss all critical matter with other students and with your teacher. In this way the ideas become sifted and tested; they may be modified in ways which make them more assimilable, more part of your own critical reservoir, and therefore to be used more naturally. If an interesting theory about a character, which you have read, is tried out and argued in class or in the seminar room, perhaps with those who are also aware of such theory, there are very good chances that it will take a more credible or healthily less credible form in the mind – at any rate not a vague idea. Others will contribute further evidence, or counter with a better-founded theory, and so on. All this helps to assimilate otherwise undigested criticism. Your own language, more natural to you, and which can be better reproduced later, is used in the process.

CRITICAL READING LIST

Classical criticism

Arnold, M, *Essays in Criticism* (Ed. Hoctor), University of Chicago Press.
Bradley, AC, *Shakespearian Tragedy,* Macmillan.

Study aids on individual texts

Casebook series, Macmillan Student Editions.
Critical Commentaries series, Macmillan.
Guides to English Literature, Hulton Educational.
Modern Masters series, Fontana.
Modern Writers series, Oliver and Boyd.
Readers' Guide series, Thames and Hudson.
Studies in English Literature, Arnold.
Writers and Critics series, Oliver and Boyd.
Writers and their Work (British Council pamphlets), Longman.
(Writers) and (their) World series, Thames and Hudson (e.g. *George Eliot and her World*).
York Notes series, Longman.
Grose, K, *Literature in Perspective,* Evans.
Mason, WH (Ed.), *Notes on English Literature,* Blackwell.
Southam, BC, *Students' Guide to the Selected Poems of TS Eliot,* Faber.

(All the books listed above are preferable to Cole's, Methuen's, Pan's (Brodie's) or Macmillan's notes, although in a few cases one of these may be the only separate aid available for a particular work.)

Biographical approach

Baines, J, *Joseph Conrad: A Critical Biography,* Greenwood Press.
Carpenter, H, *WH Auden,* Allen and Unwin.
Ellman, R, *James Joyce,* Oxford University Press.
               Yeats: The Man and the Mask, Oxford University Press.
Hone, J, *Flowers of the Forest,* Secker & Warburg.
Moore, HT, *Priest of Love: Life of DH Lawrence,* Heinemann.

Historical and social background

Cambridge History of English Literature (Ed. Ward, Sir AW and Waller AR), 15 vols, Cambridge University Press. (This is now rather out of date.)
Oxford History of English Literature, 11 vols, Oxford University Press. (The last volume deals

with eight only of the greatest writers of this century only, and largely ignores the social, political and literary scene.)

Pelican Guide to English Literature (Ed. Ford, B), 7 vols, Penguin.

Sphere History of Literature (Ed. Bergonzi, B), 7 vols, Sphere. (Like the Pelican Guide, this is very sound and succinct.)

Fraser, GS, *The Modern Writer and his World,* Penguin.
Robson, WW, *Modern English Literature,* Oxford University Press.
Swinnerton, F, *The Georgian Literary Scene,* Dent (Everyman).
Ward, AC, *Twentieth Century Literature,* London Universities Press.
Willey, B, *Seventeenth Century Background,* Routledge.
    Eighteenth Century Background, Chatto.
    Nineteenth Century Studies, Chatto.
Wilson, E, *Axel's Castle,* Fontana.

Poetry only
Alvarez, A, *The Shaping Spirit: Studies in Modern English and American Poets,* Chatto.
Deutsch, B, *This Modern Poetry,* Faber.
Press, J, *A Map of English Verse,* Oxford University Press.
Thwaite, A, *Twentieth Century English Poetry,* Heinemann.

Modern fiction only
Schorer, M (Ed.), *Modern British Fiction,* Oxford University Press.

Drama only
Nicoll, A, *British Drama,* Cambridge University Press.

Authors as critics
Eliot, TS, *Selected Prose* (ed John Hayward) Peregrine (Penguin)
Forster, EM, *Aspects of the Novel,* Penguin.

Critical terms
Shapiro, K, *A Prosody Handbook,* Harper & Row.

Useful handbooks on various genres
The Critical Idiom series, Methuen & Co.

The text in performance—external, visual and other aids to study

INTRODUCTION

Before making use of external aids in order to appreciate and understand more fully an A-level text, you should consider carefully in each case whether it is likely to be worthwhile and helpful. Such aids vary a great deal in quality, relevance and usefulness. Many are likely to be enjoyable irrespective of these considerations, so discretion is necessary. Those that may appear to be irrelevant could be worth the expenditure of time and money for the sake of your general appreciation of literature, especially if the work lies within the same period as your text. Thus the film of *The Lord of the Flies* is well worth seeing if the author's novel *The Inheritors* happens to be the set text: greater interest may be stimulated for Golding as a novelist, and valuable ideas and impressions should be gained for those questions that deal with the period in general. The Oxford Board stipulates: 'candidates are expected to show a general knowledge of the social and literary history of the period, with special reference to the works named.' The Southern Board advises: 'candidates will be well advised to read *other* works by the authors chosen for study and to interest themselves in their relevant literary and historical background.'

Two typical A-level questions along these lines may be cited here: 'With reference to any works which you have not discussed elsewhere, show some of the ways in which either Classical Mythology or the extended conceit or colloquial language is used by the writers of this period' (taken from the Oxford Board's Summer 1980 paper, the period being 1550–1680); to quote a question from the period 1896 to the present day from the same examination board and year:

'Write on the way in which any twentieth-century writer in English has experimented with literary form.' (It is noteworthy that this permits the vast reservoir of American writing to be tapped.)

It is of course necessary to check the syllabus of the Board whose papers are being taken to ascertain whether such questions will be set. It is also evident from the above specimen questions that a far more extensive knowledge of texts other than those specially set is needed than can possibly be provided by one or two visits to the theatre or cinema.

1 DRAMA

Very few plays written expressly for performance on television or radio are set at A Level as special texts. (*Under Milk Wood* by Dylan Thomas is one noteworthy exception.) Plays – and this does need emphasizing when examinations are concerned – are intended to be seen as plays on the stage, and normally (though not always) are best understood when thus seen. For students of plays at A-level standard it is particularly desirable that they should be seen performed by as good a company, whether amateur or professional, and be as well produced, as possible. For examination purposes an amateur production which does not cut too much, nor alter the text in other ways, may be more useful than many a professional performance. Shakespeare, and other dramatists of archaic language, are also better understood by the maturer student who has received some experience in understanding such language, often in the study of such plays for GCSE.

Above all twentieth-century, especially more modern, plays often have to be seen properly staged to be grasped at all: long stage directions should be seen working, and many apparent obscurities are cleared up when the play is seen, since dramatists include material that depends for its effect on live presentation. Shaffer, Pinter, Beckett and Stoppard – all of whose plays appear in the syllabuses, demonstrate this.

Failing opportunities to see good live performances, you should try to see plays on television or as films for the cinema. You should remember however that they may be greatly adapted. Losing the visual dimension, plays may be heard on the radio or record player or tape recorder – a medium much better than nothing if your study group suffers from the common lack of good readers to bring plays to life in the class or lecture room.

It is necessary, at the very earliest possible time, to begin to discover which plays are being performed, by whom and when, within a reasonable distance of your school and home. Of course, long trips to particularly worthwhile productions may also be undertaken – trips to Stratford-upon-Avon or London, for example. Apart from the better provincial theatres, Universities often mount very useful and enjoyable productions of plays students need to see.

You should write well in advance, if your teacher has not already done so, to all the likely centres of drama, for information on the season's productions. This will include helpful news not only of the plays, but also of performance times and dates, cost of seats, party rates and names of actors involved. The London scene is rich but complex and it is advisable to procure a good synopsis of all that is going on, for example the *London Theatre Guide,* obtainable from ticket agencies free, eleven of which are dotted around London, and which may be contacted by telephone. Several Shakespeare plays are performed each year, both in and around London as well as Stratford. However, you need a bit of luck to find your set play on the list for any particular year: the chances are quite good since the best plays are regularly set and these are usually precisely the ones performed. Of the London theatres, special mention should be made of: the Barbican which houses the Royal Shakespeare Company (the smaller theatre called 'The Pit' often stages very useful plays such as minor Elizabethan, Restoration or contemporary); the Donmar Warehouse near Covent Garden when the London Shakespeare Group perform; the Theatre Royal in the Haymarket which usually shows plays of good quality; the Mermaid Theatre in Blackfriars, a good little theatre whose stage has been rebuilt and extended; the National Theatre whose excellent productions are well advertised. At the National, three theatres in one building offer concurrent plays: one suitable for an open stage (the Olivier), one suitable for a proscenium-arch stage (the Lyttelton) and one for more minority audiences (the studio-like Cottesloe). Many of the plays produced in all three theatres are of the highest value for A-level students.

Finally there are several theatres that, since they customarily show more 'avant garde' and minority interest plays of a more thoughtful nature, should be mentioned as these plays are likely to throw valuable light on the contemporary drama you are studying or occasionally even show a commonly set play (e.g. by Osborne, John Arden, Shelagh Delaney, Pinter, Beckett or Stoppard). These are: the Royal Court, Sloane Square, when the Traverse Theatre Company perform; the Bloomsbury Theatre in Gordon Street; The Cafe Theatre opposite Wyndham's in

Charing Cross Road; ICA Theatre in the Mall SW1; the Lyric Theatre Hammersmith; The Studio Theatre, just off Shaftesbury Avenue (tickets and information from these may be obtained from the Fringe Box Office, 01 839 6987). Further afield, the Churchill Theatre in Bromley, The Wimbledon Theatre and the Greenwich Theatre are all well worth checking on. There are also 'fringe' theatres, for example, in Stepney (the Half Moon Theatre, 213 Mile End Road, E.1) and in Islington, the Old Red Lion, St John Street, N.1).

Outside London all the main provincial cities, and many of the larger towns, possess one or more theatres and cinemas. These are usually adequately advertised in the local press or the library, or by posters. Enquiry will always elicit leaflets or brochures with the future programmes and all necessary details.

The Guardian publishes daily a useful if limited list of provincial theatres: the Chichester Festival (0243 781312 – all numbers provided are for the Box Office) – the Liverpool Playhouse (051 709 8363); the Oldham Coliseum (061 624 2829), the Stoke-on-Trent Victoria (0782 615962), Stratford-on-Avon's Royal Shakespeare Theatre (0789 295623); the Wolsey Theatre, Ipswich (0483 53725), all have good plays advertised in the national dailies. A selection of other leading theatres would include the Theatre Royal, Norwich (0603 60955); His Majesty's Theatre, Aberdeen (0224 28080); the Aberystwyth Arts Centre, Penglais Road (0970 4277); the New Theatre in Park Place, Cardiff (0222 32466) which also has the Sherman Theatre – a film theatre (0222 30451); the ADC in Park Street, Cambridge (0223 352001) and the Arts Theatre in Pear Hill (0223 352000); the Group Theatre and Lyric Players Theatre in Belfast (0232 29685 and 660081) respectively, the Alexandra Theatre, Station Street (021 643 1231) and the Birmingham Repertory Theatre, Broad Street (021 236 4455); Birmingham also has the Centre for the Arts, University of Aston (021 359 3611 Ext. 6287) which actively sponsors various art enterprises. In Bristol there is the famous Bristol Old Vic Company, The Little Theatre, Colston Hall (0272 21182) and the New Vic at the Theatre Royal (0272 24388); at Chelmsford, the Civic Theatre in Fairfield Road (0245 61659); Colchester, the University of Essex Theatre in Wivenhoe Park (0206 862286); in Dublin the famous Abbey Theatre (Dial Operator 100 first from U.K. 744505). Not to mention the Thorndike Theatre in Leatherhead which provided many photographs for us to use. Look in your local paper for information.

The normal rule for A-level students as far as plays are concerned, is to see them as early as possible, whether in the live theatre or on television. Videos may of course help here: some schools and County Education libraries keep considerable stocks of them, and may well be prepared to lend them. Films, too, may be hired, usually from the Company that produced them; whether Rank Film Libraries (01 568 9222) or Columbia-Warner-EMI of 135 Wardour Street, W.1 who have a good stock of 16 mm films. The value of films of plays or novels is discussed below. The TV medium has the serious drawback of being cramped into 'the box' with little opportunity for observing side action or continuous parallel action. There is also a loss of the three-dimensional sense of space and the 'atmosphere' generated by the reciprocation of live audiences before live performers; enough loss indeed to cause TS Eliot, invited to see a TV performance of one of his plays, to laugh loudly at the travesty and to be urgently 'hushed' by other indignant persons present who did not recognize him.

The aural experience of the play alone, as indicated above, is a poor substitute but a good adjunct to seeing the play, especially with a view to comparing interpretations of parts and other adaptations. It can be counter-productive for students to have a fixed conception of the play based on one production, especially as in some details, even major concepts, the play seen may interpret freely the original. These ideas may be corrected by either seeing another production (perhaps too much to hope for even in two years) or hearing the same play on record or tape. But, as suggested above, because of expert performances by professional actors, as well as helpful sound effects which aid the imagination, a hearing of the play on record or tape is still desirable. A bonus of such recordings is that they are very often, because specially designed for examination candidates, much more faithful to the text than live productions, and, unlike the latter, often uncut.

Travelling companies often call on local theatres in the provinces, not only to perform 'enter-tainments' for the ordinary public but also to present known GCSE and A-level set plays, being specifically planned to complement the syllabuses. Large school parties make it worth the while of these companies to visit a particular area. Again, for this reason, the texts are respected and largely left to speak for themselves; the sets are simple and the costumes authentic (unlike so many 'gimmicky' or perhaps creative professional productions).

Some companies of this type make it their business to visit the schools themselves to mount a production in the hall or some convenient room. They may also conduct a discussion between themselves and the young audience before or after their performance. The whole thing can be informative and educational. In one such performance that took place at the Marlow Theatre, Canterbury (playing a scene in *Hamlet*) the actors discussed with the director how best to play the scene, on such matters as motive and character. This sort of thing of course can do nothing but good for prospective examination candidates. The company will occasionally recruit talented pupils to assist in playing small parts. These travelling companies naturally send advance notice of their activities to the schools they hope to visit, or near to which they intend to perform plays, and it is usually only by such notice that a student may hope to benefit by them.

An excellent method of familiarizing yourself with the dynamics and text of a play, is to become involved in a production, whether in school or in an outside amateur dramatic society. When such groups are flourishing and talented, this is the best means of all to help you appreciate your play.

As we have indicated above, professional companies are apt to modify a play, especially if the director has special purposes that do not square with the obvious design of the author. So 'contemporary' settings may be devised, ideas introduced outside those of the play, interpretations imposed not warranted by any reading, huge cuts or transpositions made, and character-representation manipulated into presentations (perhaps influenced by the type of actors taking the parts) remote from any orthodox view. John Cleese, for example, turned Petruchio in a television performance of *The Taming of the Shrew* into a character reminiscent in my view of his comic role in *Fawlty Towers*. This sort of thing if compounded may mislead the student otherwise unfamiliar with the play; after all, he is required to answer questions on the original text, unadulterated. It is the sort of thing that occurs more often with Shakespeare and the older 'classical' plays than with modern drama, where of course all the updating that the public like has been done by the author, even when his material is historical, for example in Eliot's *Murder in the Cathedral*, Brecht's *Galileo*, Bolt's *A Man For All Seasons* or Shaffer's *The Royal Hunt of the Sun*. You may be amused by crazy modifications, usually carried out in old comedies for the sake of extra laughs. For example, I once saw a college production of Beaumont and Fletcher's *Knight of the Burning Pestle* in which, among other abuses, a full-scale satire of modern drill procedure was grafted onto the equivalent scene in the play. Responsible directors who are accountable to large audiences often perpetrate similar extravaganzas. The motives behind such changes are usually worthy enough: to cut tedious or mystifying material, gain pace, directness and simplicity, clarify or broaden humour and even translate archaic language – a particularly irritating feature, but useful for the ordinary public.

In spite of all these hazards, it is important that a set play should be seen at the earliest opportunity. It may be necessary to redress any anomalies by close study and later discussions based on better knowledge. It must be emphasized that these aberrations, even if they turn out to be extensive can never outweigh the overall value of seeing the play as it was meant to be seen – on the stage. Normally, however, experienced directors and responsible companies do not overly distort a good play.

Perhaps you should be more wary of *badly done* performances of amateur groups; these can be so atrocious as to positively do more harm than good. If caught by one of these local disasters, where track suits may be worn instead of costumes, and the three witches of Macbeth played by the local boys, the only course is to forget the experience or make a point of seeing the play done properly. However, it remains true that a very great number of our local amateur and school dramatic societies possess remarkable or at worst adequate talent, and do not stage Shakespeare, Ben Jonson or Marlowe if their resources do not match the ordinary requirements of such drama. Finally, there is always the good friend's timely warning: 'Don't bother to see that one!'

There are a great many films of plays and novels, good to very bad: some books have received attention regularly, the film being remade every few years. The later versions are not necessarily the best ones, and some will surely remain as 'classics' and hardly to be improved on, as for example Olivier's *Richard III*. Other countries also produce sometimes fascinating versions of our plays: *King Lear* and *Twelfth Night* as seen by the Russians spring to mind. It seems to me that only a too flamboyant and over-emotional Malvolio mars the second and the first is entirely admirable. There is also the brilliant version of *Romeo and Juliet* from Zeffirelli, almost a 'must' for anyone studying this play. But this film also raises the question of the greater scope, together with the greater tendency for directors to alter plays to suit their purposes, and it should be said, the different requirements of a different medium. Most films escape from stage restrictions to take full advantage of the availability of realistic sets and locations, the possibility of rapid scene change and unlimited space, and the convenience of any number of supporting

Olivier's Richard III

cast: a crowd scene really can include thousands of heads. Thus although Olivier's *Othello,* which is almost wholly a domestic tragedy, is transferred almost unchanged from stage to screen, his earlier *Henry V* begins in a beautiful reconstruction of the Globe Theatre, and then, with the 'Chorus' description of the first scene travels realistically into it, and later, of course, does the Chorus's job for him in its splendid mounting of the Agincourt battle. But Zefirelli's *Romeo and Juliet* far surpasses Laurence Harvey's version (although there is a particularly lavish 'Capulet's feast' scene, with glorious and later hauntingly quoted music, in this earlier film). However, Zefirelli's film illustrates as well as any more or less blatant examples, the dangers lurking for a serious student of Shakespeare's text. Who would suppose, for example, from seeing the film alone, that Romeo does not climb up to, far less kiss Juliet, to close the 'balcony scene' nor Balthasar gallop swiftly by a slow donkey carrying Friar John and thereby beat him with false news to Romeo at Mantua. These two scenes certainly create fine visual effect, but in the case of Friar John, Shakespeare's idea is better as it sustains the 'plague' imagery and throws a better light on Friar Laurence's effort.

So long as this kind of variation is expected and corrected, it may be said that most of the better films of plays do not stray wildly from the text, and the vividness and visual energy that accrues to them make films a valuable aid to the study of a play.

2 POETRY

External aids to the fullest appreciation of poems, apart from hearing a good reader simply read them out loud, are less necessary than for drama. It is true that most poetry was and is written to be heard, but this may be accomplished merely by reading it aloud, perhaps with a tape-recorder to play back the poem. Naturally the better the reader, the better one's experience of the poem, but most students are competent enough for this. Otherwise there are plenty of recordings available of fine readers (often actors). Robert Donat and Alec Guiness have both produced good readings of poetry set in A-level examinations, particularly good I think is Guiness' reading of TS Eliot's *Four Quartets*. Companies most concerned with the production of poetry readings in many cases by the authors themselves are Argo and Caedmon. Although it is always interesting to hear a poet, especially a famous one, reading his or her or others' poems, poets do not necessarily make the ideal readers. Some are rightly nearly as famous for their readings as for the work read: Dylan Thomas, Ted Hughes, Robert Frost, Theodore Roethke and Robert Lowell are examples: others are liked by some poetry lovers but not by others. Eliot, Auden and Graves for example all have a rather flat, neutral tone. Yeats reads in a rapt, bardic sing-song which also is a matter of taste, though much of his poetry seems to call for this frankly lyrical delivery.

If you are able to hear a poetry-reading, this will be a stimulating and potentially valuable experience: there is the opportunity for questions and discussions with those best qualified to speak. It should be said that many poets detest the common reader's question 'What did you mean by this poem?' to which question they tend to answer, 'I said all that I meant in the poem', meaning that a prose explanation would say something else, which in the case of most lyrical poetry is true. Neither are poets necessarily the best explainers of their own work; they might forget as Browning did of *Sordello,* or never have known, as Dylan Thomas of *Altarwise by Owl light.* Critics are not final guides either: they are notorious for their drastic disagreements over evaluations, and even meanings of poems. For example, on Dylan Thomas's poem, *Ballad of the long-legged Bait,* the distinguished American poet, Elder Olson wrote: 'The action of the poem is a meditation . . . on the possibility of salvation through mortification of the flesh', and he rightly judges the conclusion to be 'magnificent'. Henry Treece wrote that it is 'in rough ballad form, telling what befell when a fisherman used a beautiful girl as bait.' and adds, that 'it seems at the end little more than a technical exercise'. William York Tindall, Professor of English at Columbia University, wrote (with the benefit of better research and exhaustive seminars on the subject): 'a young man goes fishing for sexual experience . . . but catches "the church and the village green".' Similar discrepancies of critical opinion occur over other great poems and the best service that visiting lecturers may render to their hearers is a stimulation of their resolution and desire to read the poems more closely and attentively for themselves.

One of the best methods of grasping modern or indeed any poems is to discuss them with other students, perhaps in sixth-form conferences with experienced leaders. Teachers of course will always be led to try to 'explain' poems and one hopes that such methods may bear some fruit. Note-taking on poets and poems will go on, and I will conclude this section by referring to some extremely able and helpful 'teachers' of poetry who also are practising poets: they are often to be found giving their services at conferences: Anthony Thwaite, Dannie Abse, Adrian Henri, Brian Jones, Vernon Scanell, DJ Enright, Patricia Beer, Seamus Heaney and many others.

3 THE NOVEL AND OTHER PROSE WORKS

We noted in (1) above the tendency of performed plays to deviate from the original text, which is all that A-level candidates have as a starting point for their answers, although they may well combine this with discussion of the various productions or even films of the play. The primary purpose of seeing the plays performed, or the films, remains that of stimulating our response to the work in order to appreciate it better and thus write more sensitively about it. This may seem heresy to those not required to sit an examination on such plays, but it is the way the emphasis must lie for the purpose of examination success.

I also noted that the deviations were likely to be exaggerated in films, and of course in some films much more than others, until we may find an extreme of absurdity in such grotesqueries (at best with regard to what Shakespeare wrote) as the Burton-Taylor *Antony and Cleopatra,* in which the greatest and most typical incident, the naval battle of Actium, is merely reported in the play when it is over. Such things are not only of minimal or merely accidental value to any student of the play (you may for example, be awakened to a sense of wonder at the historical 'romance' of the events), they could even prove to be damaging by implanting concepts and adding dialogue to the play itself, in a manner similar to the more minor deviations of good films or actual plays. When it comes to films of a novel, or occasionally also dramatizations, such as the present fashion for staged Agatha Christie novels, Waugh's *A Handful of Dust* or Hardy's *Under the Greenwood Tree,* then distortions are carried so far that we are really dealing with a different work; the change of scene from novel to drama becomes dominant; it is not a case of one thing subserving the other, merely assisting in its understanding, but an invitation to consider a new thing.

Can nothing be gained from seeing a well made, well directed and at least by intention faithful representation of a novel? The fact that a good novel may be not only the inspiration of a film but also guide its characterization, entire story line, some of its dialogue and much of its setting, makes it at least worthy of attention for examination purposes. There are a host of examples from which I will select just a few, to illustrate the strengths and weaknesses of the film as an aid to grasping a novel. Dai Bradley as 'Kes' could hardly have established that character and the whole atmosphere of Barry Hines' novel better: Peter Brooks' direction of *The Lord of the Flies* was a model of faithfulness to most of the elements of Golding's book: some of the symbolic power of images such as the staked boar's head, the cadaver in the parachute harness, and the white-uniformed naval officer of the last page, was admirably conveyed. In both these the main line of the story was presented, comedy was not spoilt by tragedy or vice

Jane Eyre

Brighton Rock

versa, the tone is firm and the world created very much the same as the original, not turning, as in such films as Peter O'Toole's *Lord Jim* into a foreign, Hollywood world.

Other useful films to lead into more enlightened readings of their novels are: *Pride and Prejudice; Wuthering Heights; Jane Eyre; The Mayor of Casterbridge; Our Mutal Friend* and other Dickens novels; *Barchester Towers; Brideshead Revisited; The History Man,* all of which were television series: and *Tom Jones, Far From the Madding Crowd, The Mill on the Floss, Tess of the D'Urbervilles, Women in Love, Brighton Rock, The Go Between* (LP Hartley) and *To Kill a Mocking Bird* (Harper Lee).

One of the merits of films such as these is that they often simplify complicated plots, or novels whose prose style is difficult for a student to grasp easily. Chapters that delay the action or effect time shifts may confuse the first-time reader, and the film helps him to grasp the whole, and better understand the function of all the parts, even when some of these have been omitted by the film. Complications begin to arise when parts are altered by the film-makers. For example, in *Lord Jim* by Joseph Conrad, the time-shifts so favoured by this author operate in the novel almost to the extent that, as for *Nostromo,* one has to read it at least twice to appreciate the structure. The film takes us blithely through the story from Jim's training-ship days to the execution.

It may be appreciated that this film is about as far as a useful aid to an understanding of the original novel can go, and it would be inadvisable to see it until after the novel has been read at least twice! Most films can really only be regarded as 'launch pads' for proper reading. But if more faithful and respectful of the original, they can simplify, clarify, provide useful period sets to help the imaginations of those ignorant of the period and historical background such as the Edwardian England of Lawrence's *Women in Love,* or the Georgian England of Jane Austen's *Pride and Prejudice.* Dialect in dialogue may be conveyed vividly and realistically, especially useful if there is a high proportion of dialogue in the novel, indeed the film transfers the material of the novel much better if the novel, for example, Fielding's *Joseph Andrews* or Hardy's *The Mayor of Casterbridge,* is constructed like a play. If a narrator is used in the film, narrative material may be conveyed in a manner close to the original method and can recapture some of its style and tone, and a novelistic shadow may be cast over the other genre: attempts have been made by mixing genres in this way in films such as *Don Quixote* and *Animal Farm* and plays such as the *Knights of the Round Table* and *Canterbury Tales,* in the former case certainly falling between the two stools.

The case against films or plays of novels for A-level purposes may be summarized thus: the novel was written to be a novel which makes it quite distinct from the play text. It is a separate genre and therefore has the characteristics of that genre only; it is not normally intended to be transferred to another genre and still retain its proper identity; if it is, inevitably distortions

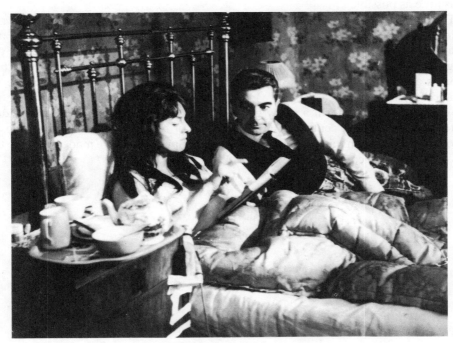

Milo O'Shea plays Leopold Bloom in Ulysses

occur as in map projections of the globe; films gain most of their impact from visual effects, novels from the imagination invoked through verbal effects such as description where a great part of one's pleasure derives from the language itself; the film's company of directors, script writer and actors have special purposes and concepts that do not necessarily square with those of the novel, and compounded with the distortions inevitable in the nature of the different genre, may well give rise to serious misconceptions about the novel, only to be corrected by very careful reading and comparative thought. Finally the greater part if not all of the novelist's distinctive style is lost, with any artistic merit such language may possess. Difference of style is also what makes one novel largely different from another, Lawrence's *The Man who Loved Islands* from Conrad's *An Outcast of the Islands* or Chariere's *Papillon* where there may, in their films, be not too much to distinguish them, but as novels, poles apart. Films are also apt to be levelled when produced by the same company, directed by the same director and their characters presented by the same actors. There was a film made of James Joyce's *Ulysses,* with Milo O'Shea as Leopold Bloom, which would sufficiently emphasize all the points I have made both for and against the film, as adjunct to the novel, and as an examination aid for the novel. All the rich complexities of the novel have been prised out, to render it akin to its own image of 'Plumtree's Potted Meat' not the real thing but more digestible for weak stomachs.

Obtaining general information

For plays the accessible theatre's seasonal programmes should be acquired, as suggested above. Travelling companies circularize schools well in advance. Libraries contain useful information, as do Information Bureaux and County Education offices. Film programmes may be similarly obtained. It is perhaps worth noting that a ticket agency in Leicester Square sells tickets at reduced prices for most London plays.

For poetry, the most useful body to which to apply for information is the Arts Council (105 Piccadilly London W1V 0AU). They produce a useful pamphlet *Writers in Schools*. This is a list of writers with their addresses and short biographies and works, who are prepared to visit schools or colleges in person to read their work and/or lecture. Subsidies on fees may be applied for from the Arts Council (50% of a minimum fee of £20); about 110 writers are available for this service.

Regional Councils should also be contacted: they also produce Directories of more local writers, and other useful information.

English club

It is essential that an English club at sixth-form level is an enjoyable activity, with little obvious connection with the academic syllabus. A democratically elected committee should decide a suitable programme of events for the term or the year. A member of staff will be needed for guidance and to keep the programme within the bounds of possibility, but he or she should intrude as little as possible.

The English club offers an ideal opportunity for members to explore their own areas of interest in English Literature and for them to read their own compositions in prose or poetry. If funds are available a visiting speaker could be booked or a film hired. Often a theatre visit can be arranged to a provincial theatre or to London or Stratford. This provides an opportunity to extend one's appreciation of drama as well as seeing both staff and pupils in more relaxed circumstances.

An excellent idea is to form a study group for a weekend. Often the County Education Committee has a residential centre which can be hired or reservations made for the cost of the accommodation. Although this can be expensive, sometimes grants are made available through the school or education committee.

Glossary

Where a word is followed by q.v. (quod vide) it is listed elsewhere in the glossary.

Aeneid An epic poem in Latin by Virgil (P. Vergilius Maro, 70–19 BC), recounting the adventures of the legendary Trojan prince Aeneas after his escape from Troy, culminating in his settlement in Italy as the ancestor of the Romans.

Aesthetics The philosophy of taste, the study of the beautiful.
> **Aesthetic** (adj.), pertaining to the above.

Agnosticism The view that man cannot know anything but the material world; especially, that he cannot prove, or disprove, the existence of God. In opposition to this,
> **Atheism** positively asserts that God does not exist. An **agnostic** (n.) professes
> **agnostic** (adj.) views.

Alexandrine In English poetry, a line of verse having six (usually iambic) feet, e.g. 'That like a wounded snake drags its slow length along' (Pope)

Alienation Effect (Ger. Verfremdungseffekt) An effect in a play intended to remind the spectator that what he is watching is not reality, but an entertainment performed by actors. As used by Bertolt Brecht (1898–1956), it is achieved by satirical songs and comments addressed directly to the audience. As a Communist, Brecht professed a contempt for the bourgeois or romantic theatre's attempt to create an illusion of reality ('the willing suspension of disbelief', as Coleridge says), and was anxious that his audience should not miss the didactic point of his plays. It is of course quite untrue that Brecht 'invented' the Alienation Effect, which older dramatists regularly achieved by the use of choruses, asides, and soliloquies. The expression is perhaps more widely used than understood.

Allegory A greatly extended metaphor, in which events are related in terms of other events, real or fictitious, and frequently at tedious length. Thus, the medieval *Roman de la Rose,* or at least that part of it translated by Chaucer, describes in some 7,700 lines the attempt of a lover to win his lady in terms of getting into a garden and trying to pluck a particular rose.
> **Allegorical** (adj.)

Alliteration Repetition of the same initial consonant sound; the basis of Old English, and of much medieval English poetry, e.g. 'In a somer sesun, whan softe was the sonne . . .' (Langland, 14th century).
> **Alliterative** (adj.)

Allusion The device of referring to characters and events in mythology, history and literature to evoke a certain atmosphere. The works of Chaucer, Shakespeare and Milton abound with allusions.

For example, this passage from Spenser's *The Faerie Queene* describes the garden of Adonis. It contains many mythological allusions derived from Plato and Aristotle.

> 'Great enimy to it, and to all the rest
> That in the Gardin of Adonis springs,
> Is wicked Tyme; who with his scythe addrest
> Does mow the flowring herbes and goodly things,
> And all their glory to the ground downe flings,
> Where they do wither, and are fowly mard:
> He flyes about, and with his flaggy winges
> Beates downe both leaves and buds without regard,
> Ne ever pitty may relent his malice hard.'
>
> Yet pitty often did the gods relent,
> To see so faire thinges mard and spoiled quight;
> And their great mother Venus did lament
> The losse of her deare brood, her deare delight;
> Her hart was pierst with pitty at the sight,
> When walking through the Gardin them she saw
> Yet no'te she find redresse for such despight:
> For all that lives is subject to that law:
> All things decay in time, and to their end doe draw.

Ambiguity Having a doubtful or double meaning. The word 'ambiguity' is also used to describe a device of style, especially of poetry, which permits two or more meanings to be kept in mind at the same time.
> **Ambiguous** (adj.)

Ambivalence Having two contrasting values or qualities.

Anachronism A mistake in dating or timing, placing an event in its wrong historical setting e.g. Shakespeare mentions doublets in *Julius Caesar*. The Elizabethan playwrights paid little attention to historical accuracy.

Analogy A likeness or comparison of a non-figurative kind, i.e., not based on simile or metaphor. 'There is an analogy between our situation and that of the Roman Empire in its last days.'

    Analagous (adj.)

Analysis An examination of a literary form in detail involving necessary division of a poem or prose into form, content, meaning, tone, diction etc. Some people see this as destructive but it is necessary for the establishment of values and is an important part in the constructive or creative process.

Anapaest In English poetry, a foot consisting of two unstressed syllables, followed by one stressed, e.g. 'The Assyrian came down like a wolf on the fold' (Byron).

    Anapaestic (adj.)

Anticlimax Arrangement of ideas in descending order of importance or power: a false climax or weak repetition, deliberately used for humorous effect, cf. bathos.

Antithesis An arrangement of words to produce an effect of balanced contrast, e.g. 'He was neither elated by the prospect of success, nor depressed by the anticipation of failure'.

    Antithetical (adj.)

Aphorism A concise observation or statement. An aphorism is distinguished from an epigram by being more solemn and less witty.

Apostrophe Breaking a speech or composition to address or appeal to a person often as part of personification, e.g.

> 'Thou, Nature, art my goddess! To thy law
> My services are bound.'
>
> Shakespeare *King Lear*
> (Edmund)

Apron stage Part of a stage projecting into the audience, beyond the line of the proscenium (q.v.)

Aristotelian Pertaining to the Greek philosopher Aristotle (384–322 BC), author of *The Poetics* (q.v.)

Art Originally, skill: hence **Artist,** a skilled artificer, e.g. 'the Tuscan artist', i.e. Galileo (Milton). Any particular skill which gives predominantly aesthetic pleasure e.g. music, poetry, painting, sculpture. Popularly, painting. **The Arts** as opposed to **The Sciences** (i.e., those studies which investigate the phenomena of the physical world). Other combinations: the **Fine Arts,** the **Liberal** (q.v.) **Arts.**

Art for Art's Sake A popular phrase thought to sum up the essence of aestheticism, namely, the view that art needs no justification but itself, and is to be judged not, for example, by its moral tendency, but solely by whether it is successful art.

Assonance Correspondence of vowel sound, an essential feature of traditional English rhyming; more generally, correspondence of sound between words and syllables.

Attitude A writer's attitude to his subject determines the tone of his writing: e.g. he may be solemn, flippant, indignant or detached.

Augustan (adj.) A word which began to be used in the early part of the 19th century to describe the early years of the 18th – the 'Age of Pope'; based on a fancied analogy between the England of Queen Anne and the Rome of Augustus, both being seen as distinguished by a high level of civilization.

Ballad A narrative poem, sometimes of folk origin, anonymous, simple and direct with historical, romantic, tragic or supernatural settings.

    Ballad Metre A four-line stanza with alternate four stress and three stress lines rhyming abcb or abab.

> 'It fell about the Martinmas,
>   When the wind blew shrill and cauld,
> Said Edom o' Gordon to his men,
>   "We maun draw to a hauld".'

Banter (n. and vb.) To make fun of someone in a good-humoured way.

Baroque (adj.) Originally a florid or extravagant style of architecture developed in Catholic countries during the 17th-18th centuries; more generally, irregular, grotesque, odd.

Bathos Descent from the serious to the ludicrous; anticlimax. Sometimes deliberate: 'Not louder shrieks to pitying Heaven are cast When husbands, or when lapdogs, breathe their last'. (Pope)
Sometimes unconscious:
'Then Montrose asked the executioner how long his body would be suspended,
Three hours was the answer, but Montrose was not the least offended'. (McGonagall)
It is a matter of taste which type is the funnier.

    Bathetic (adj.)

Blank Verse Unrhymed verse: in English, usually in iambic pentameters.

Bombast Pompous, inflated language.
  Bombastic (adj.)

Buffoonery Low jesting, clowning.
  Buffoon (n.) a low jester.

Burlesque A composition which makes it target appear ridiculous by the methods of caricature; also vb. and adj. 'Pyramus and Thisbe' in *A Midsummer Night's Dream* is a burlesque of heroic drama.

Caesura In English prosody (q.v.), a pause about the middle of a line of verse.

Caricature A character, generally exaggerated, easily recognizable and never developing. Several of Dickens' and Thackeray's characters are caricatures.

Catastrophe The change producing the final event in a play: generally, the decisive misfortune in a tragedy.

Catharsis *See* Katharsis

Chorus In ancient Greek drama, a body of performers who recited or chanted verses commenting on the action; in the modern theatre, any character, whether involved in the action or outside it, who serves as a commentator.

Ciceronian In the style of M. Tullius Cicero (106–43 BC) Roman orator; (adj.) eloquent in a stately fashion employing complex sentences (see **Periodic**).

Circumlocution A roundabout method of expression which may be a defect of style if the result does not justify the use of many words.

Classical This can have two meanings –
(1) The imitation in English of a Latin or Greek idiom. *Paradise Lost* abounds in this style.
(2) Meaning 'of the first class' – writers who lay emphasis on tradition, form and decorum, e.g. Ben Jonson, Milton, Samuel Johnson.

Cliché A trite or over-used phrase, 'at the end of the day', 'all things being equal' are two current examples of clichés.

Climax The 'building up' of a series of propositions, e.g. 'There is tears for his love; joy for his fortune; honour for his valour; and death for his ambition'. (*Julius Caesar*); generally, the culminating point of an action, especially in a play.

Comedy Originally, in the Greek theatre, referred to plays of an entertaining and satirical kind representing persons and situations in real life. In the 'Old Comedy' of Aristophanes (450–386 BC), the characters were often real personalities of the day like Socrates, represented on the stage in a ludicrous light; in the 'New Comedy' of Menander (340–292 BC), they were humorous stock types. Imitated in Latin by Plautus (254–184 BC) and Terence (190–159 BC), the New Comedy had a strong influence on Renaissance dramatists, e.g. the stock character of the 'miles gloriosus', or boastful but cowardly soldier, gave Shakespeare a hint for Pistol and Falstaff, and Jonson for Bobadill (in *Every Man in his Humour*). In the Middle Ages, just as 'tragedy' could be applied to non-dramatic works, so 'comedy' had a pretty wide application e.g. the *'Divine Comedy'* of Dante (1265–1321). This non-specific use continues down to modern times. La Comédie Française, the French National Theatre, performs tragedy and comedy alike; Balzac (1799–1850) gave the resoundingly Dantesque title of *La Comédie Humaine* to his ambitious project of a series of interlocking novels giving a wide picture of contemporary life. **Comedian** a writer of comedies, or an actor – usually in comedy, but not exclusively so in Shakespeare's day. **Comedienne,** an actress in comedies. **Comic** (adj.) **Comical** (adj.) has acquired a rather trivial everyday quality, and should be used of life's little oddities. One would hardly speak of 'Jonson's comical invention'.

Conceit A fanciful notion or far-fetched comparison, much in favour in Metaphysical Poetry. This example from Donne's *A Valediction Forbidding Mourning* is probably the most famous.

> 'If they be two, they are two so
> As stiff twin compasses are two;
> Thy soul, the fix'd foot, makes no show
> To move, but doth, if the other do.'

Context Placing a passage in its context means saying what precedes and follows it. Normally, all words and phrases have to be studied in their contexts. Often the more general context has to be studied too.

Couplet A couplet is a pair of lines rhyming together where the sense is self-contained. Pope wrote true or 'closed couplets' otherwise called 'heroic couplets'; as in:

> 'Hope springs eternal in the human breast;
> Man never is, but always to be blest.'

Elizabethan dramatists frequently use the couplet to indicate the end of a scene. Shakespeare uses the rhyming couplet to finish his sonnets.

> 'So long as men can breathe or eyes can see
> So long lives this, and this gives life to thee'.   *Sonnet XVIII*

Courtly Love The medieval view of courtly love is seen in Chaucer's poetry especially *Troilus and Criseyde* and *The Knightes Tale*. Courtly love was aristocratic, secretive, and adulterous.

Crisis A decisive turning point, especially in the action of a play.

Criticism The appraisal, particularly of art, either favourably or unfavourably, hence **Dramatic criticism, Literary criticism**: popularly, hostile comment, fault finding – perhaps because of the natural tendency of artists to consider all comment on their work as presumptuous, or proceeding from the malice and envy of the uncreative.

Critique (n.) An essay in criticism, a critical examination, usually of a work of literature or philosophy.

Culture Generally, the whole complex of factors producing a distinct way of life; in this sense one can speak of the culture of the Eskimos, or of teen-age 'pop' culture; more specifically, the possession of knowledge and taste in artistic and intellectual matters.

Dactyl In English poetry, a foot containing one stressed syllable followed by two unstressed, e.g.: 'Half a league, half a league, half a league onward' (Tennyson)

Dark Ages A vague term for the period in European history between the collapse of the Roman Empire in the West (5th century AD) and the emergence of the Frankish Empire of Charlemagne (9th century AD). In Northern Europe the 'darkness' lasted longer; but was not necessarily as total as popularly supposed.

Deism Belief in the existence of God, but rejection of the mystical and miraculous elements in, e.g. Christianity. A widespread attitude among 18th century intellectuals.
   Deist (n.), **Deistic** (adj.)

Dénouement (Fr. 'unknotting') The unravelling of the plot of a play or novel at the end.

Deus Ex Machina (Lat. 'a god from a machine') Originally refers to the practice, in some classical plays, of bringing on stage (or letting down upon it) a god in, e.g. a chariot, to bring about the dénoument; hence any unexpected person or event introduced to dispose of an apparently insoluble difficulty, especially at the end of a play. The end of Molière's *Le Tartuffe* provides a striking example.

Dialect A local variety of a standard national language.

Dialectic Argument intended to elucidate the truth; particularly the examination of contradictions, which leads to a synthesis in which all the elements of truth are brought together – a method notably employed by the German philosopher Hegel (1770–1831).
   Dialectical (adj.) **Dialectical Materialism:** the method of argument developed by Marxists, which employs Hegelian dialectic in the context of Marxist materialism (q.v.); highly esteemed by Communists as a way of arriving at conclusions known to be acceptable to the Party by methods which the Party has sanctified.

Diction Choice and arrangement of words. **Poetic Diction:** a phrase often used of the artificial style, full of elaborate periphrasis (q.v.) favoured by 18th century poets, and denounced by Wordsworth, e.g. 'the scaly tribe' for 'fish'.

Didactic (adj.) Teaching, giving instruction, usually of a morally improving kind. Bunyan's *Pilgrim's Progress* is a didactic work.

Discussion Play A phrase coined to describe a type of play in which there is little action, but much discussion of issues considered by the dramatist to be important; wrongly supposed to be characteristic of the plays of Henrik Ibsen (1828–1906), and, with more justification, of those of George Bernard Shaw (1856–1950); in both cases presumed, without any truth, to be destructive of genuine dramatic interest.

Dramatic Irony A device of style by which a character in a play is made to say something in ignorance of its full or deeper meaning. The audience, and usually the other characters, know more than the speaker and so are able to appreciate the comic or tragic irony of the speaker's situation.
   A good example of dramatic irony is in *King Lear* when Lear, having divided his kingdom between his two elder daughters, assumes they will offer hospitality to him and his hundred knights. When Goneril refuses to do this, Lear curses her and says, 'Yet have I left a daughter'. The dramatic irony here is obvious to anyone who knows the play. Regan will be as harsh as Goneril and he has rejected Cordelia, the only daughter who really loves him.

Election (theological) Choice by God of certain individuals for salvation, not because of their merits or good works, but by His own sovereign will: the only evidence of an individual's election being his own conviction that divine **Grace** (q.v.) has been extended to him. Belief in election was widely accepted by Puritans, especially followers of the teaching of the French reformer Jean Calvin (1509–1564). **The Elect:** the whole body of those so chosen.

Elegy A poem of lamentation or mourning, usually for the dead.
   Elegiac (adj.) of a grave or melancholy nature, appropriate to an elegy.

Elements The four. Earth, air, fire, and water, believed from the time of classical Greece down to the 17th Century to be the basic constituents of matter.

Ellipsis Omission of words, as in note-taking, or in the conversation of Mr. Jingle in *Pickwick Papers*.

Emotive Can be used to describe language which excites the emotions. Emotive poetry tries to move the reader with its use of language.

Empathy This is the power of entering into the experience of or understanding objects or emotions outside ourselves; the power to project oneself into the object of contemplation. In Keats' odes he enters totally the world of his poem. In Coleridge's *Rime of the Ancient Mariner* – his body beats as one with the sky and the sea.

> 'I looked upon the rotting sea,
> And drew my eyes away;
> I looked upon the rotting deck,
> And there the dead men lay.
>
> I looked to heaven, and tried to pray;
> But or ever a prayer had gusht,
> A wicked whisper came, and made
> My heart as dry as dust.
>
> I closed my lids, and kept them close,
> And the balls like pulses beat;
> For the sky and the sea, and the sea and the sky
> Lay like a load on my weary eye,
> And the dead were at my feet.'

End-stopping Composing verses so that a pause dictated by the sense of the words comes at the end of a line; not necessarily shown by punctuation.

Enjambement Continuation of the sense from one line of verse to the next without pause; running-on; the opposite of **End-stopping** (also spelt **Enjambment**).

Enlightenment, Age of A phrase used to describe particularly the early and middle years of the 18th Century, a period marked by sceptical, rational, scientific and deistic attitudes among intellectuals who wished to be as different as possible from the 'fanatics' or 'enthusiasts' of the previous age; largely inspired in England by the philosophical writings of the third Earl of Shaftesbury, and well represented in e.g. the historian Gibbon; in France, in the work of Voltaire and the Encyclopaedists; in Germany by 'die Aufklärung'.

Epic A long poem recounting in an elevated style the exploits of legendary (usually semi-divine) heroes in remote times (See *Aeneid, Iliad, Odyssey*).
    Epic (adj.) of the nature of epic poetry; pop., grand, heroic, on the largest scale.

Epic simile A long simile, worked out in elaborate detail, characteristic of epic poetry.

Epicurean A follower of the philosophical teaching of Epicurus (341–270 BC) who defined 'pleasure' as the supreme good in life; since the only kind of pleasure which most people can conceive of is that of the senses, the word has come to mean someone who lives only for sensual pleasures.
    Epicurean (adj.) 'Epicurean cooks
        Sharpen with cloyless sauce his appetite' (*Antony and Cleopatra*)

Epigram A brief but pointed statement; in modern usage, implying also the quality of wit, e.g. 'All women become like their mothers; that is their tragedy. No man does; that's his.' (*Importance of Being Earnest*).
    Epigrammatic (adj.)

Episode A coherent and substantially complete part of a longer narrative; not necessarily corresponding to Act, Scene, or Chapter.
    Episodic (adj.) consisting of episodes: often used rather disparagingly to suggest a rambling, badly-connected plot.

Epistle A letter (only humorously, in modern English); more particularly, a long discourse, didactic in purpose, addressed to a correspondent in letter form, e.g. the Epistles of St Paul, the *Epistle to Dr Arbuthnot* (Pope).

Epitaph An inscription on a tomb; hence, a composition in memory of the dead (usually short).

Erotic (adj.) Producing sexual excitement.

Eschatology (theol.) The study of the 'four last things: death, judgement, heaven and hell'.
    Eschatological (adj.)

Essay A short composition, originally of a tentative or speculative kind (e.g. Bacon's *Essays*) on any topic; today assumed to be in prose, but not in the 18th century, e.g. Pope's *Essay on Man, Essay on Criticism*.

Eulogy A composition, written or spoken, in high praise of a person or thing, e.g. Enobarbus' description of Cleopatra's appearance on the River Cydnus in *Antony and Cleopatra*.
    Eulogize (vb.)

Euphemism The expression of a distasteful idea in mild language; particularly common in connection with death, e.g. 'The deep damnation of his taking off' (*Macbeth*), 'liquidation' for 'killing'.
    Euphemistic (adj.)

Euphony Melodiousness of sound, especially in words.

Euphuism Affected, over-elaborate style (from *Euphues,* a novel by John Lyly, 1553–1606).
  Euphuistic (adj.)

Evocative 'Calling up certain feelings or memories'. Most imaginative poetry arouses evocative feelings.

Exegesis Exposition, explanation; originally of the Scriptures.

Existentialism In its modern i.e. post-Second World War, sense, the view that one can only assert one's existence, and truly be said to live, by a positive act of will or choice, even if it be absurd in the eyes of others; popular among French writers and intellectuals of the War and post-War generation, e.g. Sartre (to whom the only possible choice presented itself as active engagement in Left-wing politics), Camus, Anouilh.
  Existentialist (adj.) (n.)

Exposition With particular reference to novels and plays: the opening, considered as a setting forth of the situation and introduction of characters.

Expressionism A tendency, especially in German literature, which may be seen as beginning as a reaction against **Naturalism** (q.v.): marked by strong emotionalism ('Rausch'), aspirations towards moral and political regeneration, and a certain affinity with **Surrealism** (q.v.) in painting.
  Expressionist (adj. and n.)

Fable A short story devised to convey a useful lesson, often employing animals as symbols, e.g. Aesop's and La Fontaine's *Fables,* Orwell's *Animal Farm.*

Fancy The lighter and more playful aspect of **Imagination** (q.v.); especially when expressed through the invention of decorative imagery. Much ink was spilt by Romantic (q.v.) critics in the attempt to define the difference between Fancy and Imagination. 'Let the winged Fancy roam' (Keats).

Farce A work, especially a play, which seeks to provoke laughter by the unsubtle exhibition of ridiculous characters in absurd situations.

Figures of Speech Expressions which deviate from the strictly literal or grammatical meaning of words. These figures of speech are not meant to be ornaments; they are the total meaning and inseparable from the poem itself.

Foot A group of syllables having a fixed stress pattern (in English verse), and constituting a unit comparable in some ways with a bar in music. The names traditionally given to feet in English verse are borrowed from the terminology of classical prosody, but it should be remembered that in Greek and Latin prosody the basis is, not stress, but quantity i.e. vowel length.

Free Verse Poetical writings with no regular rhyme or rhythm.

Freudian Inspired by the work, in agreement with the ideas of Sigmund Freud (1856–1939), Austrian psychiatrist, whose exploration of the subconscious level of the mind, and particularly of the suppressed sexual motivation of much human behaviour, has had immense influence on 20th century art and thought.

Genre (n.) In painting, a style depicting common daily life; may be applied to literature which possesses a similar quality. Also means a kind or style of writing.

Georgian Belonging to the 18th century, when all the kings of England were Georges, especially in references to architecture; but also applied to a period and style of English poetry immediately before the First World War (reign of George V).

Gothic In architecture it describes the buildings of the 12th to 15th centuries. In the 18th century the word was used to describe any work of art which appeared fantastic or eerie, as opposed to the classical ideal of orderliness. The 'Gothic Novels' were those of Horace Walpole and Ann Radcliffe and were lampooned by Jane Austen in *Northanger Abbey.*

Graces Classical divinities, usually three in number, regarded as the bestowers of beauty and charm, and portrayed as women of exquisite beauty; often associated with the Muses (q.v.)

Grandiloquence Ridiculously elevated language, pomposity of style.

Hedonism The belief that pleasure is the chief good (cf. **Epicureanism**);
  Hedonist (n.)   **Hedonistic** (adj.)

Hero The chief personage in an epic poem; hence, the principal character in any play, novel, or poem.

Heroic (adj.) Of the nature of epic.

Heroi-comic(al) (adj.) Having the quality of burlesque epic, ridiculing the epic subject and manner; **Mock-heroic** (q.v.)

Heroic couplet In English poetry, the closed or end-stopped couplet of iambic pentameters, employing a witty, epigrammatic and antithetical style, employed with great success in the later 17th and 18th century by e.g. Dryden, Pope, Johnson; possibly so called because it was thought the most classical and 'correct' English metre. Pope used it for his translation of Homer.

Histrionic (from the Latin word for an actor in farce, 'histrio'). Exaggerated, overdone, 'stagey', in the manner of a 'ham' actor.
  Histrionics (n. pl.) a display of overacting, not necessarily on the stage.

Homeric In the manner of Homer (9th Century BC), supposed composer of the *Iliad* and *Odyssey* (q.v.).

Homophone A word having the same sound as another word, or words, but differing in meaning, e.g. 'soul', 'sole'; the basis of the kind of word-play known as a **Pun** (q.v.).

Horatian (adj.) In the manner of Horace (Q. Horatius Flaccus, 65–8 BC), marked by moderate epicureanism and good-humoured irony.

Horatian Ode An ode (q.v.) which possesses regularity of form and restraint of feeling, as opposed to the irregular or **Pindatic** (q.v.) ode. The most famous example in English poetry is Marvell's *Horatian Ode upon Cromwell's Return from Ireland.*

Hubris (n.) Pride, arrogance, excessive self-esteem: the quality of a tragic hero which, especially in Greek tragedy, invites divine displeasure.

Humane (adj.) Pertaining to those studies which civilize and refine; traditionally, the classics; hence 'literae humaniores' (Oxford).

Humanism The pursuit of humane studies; more particularly, the culture of the Renaissance scholar, based on 'human' as opposed to 'divine' learning, and giving preeminence to Greek and Latin over theology; (mod.) any system of thought which puts 'human' interests first; the 'religion of Humanity'; in schools today, **The Humanities** means all vaguely cultural studies.
  Humanist (n.); **Humanistic** (adj.)

Humour Originally, one of the four fluids (**The Humours**), phlegm, choler, blood and melancholy, supposed by ancient physicians to be secreted in the body, and to influence character, especially by an excess or deficiency of one in relation to the others; hence **Humorous** (adj.), behaving in the eccentric way attributed to an imbalance of the humours. On the Elizabethan stage, the 'humorous man' was a whimsical or absurd personage ('The humorous man shall end his part in peace' *Hamlet*); provoking laughter by his oddities; therefore 'humour' acquires the sense in which it is always used today: the ability to evoke, or to respond to, the comical aspects of human behaviour. Humour is generally distinguished from **Wit** (q.v.) which, in modern usage, has associations with cruel cleverness.

Humours, Comedy of Comedy of the kind particularly, though not exclusively associated with Ben Jonson (q.v.), which depends on the interaction of a group of humorous (in the Elizabethan sense) characters, usually of the most grotesque kind.

Hyperbole Rhetorical exaggeration, e.g.
> 'I lov'd Ophelia; forty thousand brothers
> Could not with all their quantity of love
> Make up my sum.'   (*Hamlet*)

Hyperbolical (adj.)

Iambus In English poetry, a foot consisting of an unstressed followed by a stressed syllable: 'The cur̆few tolls the knell of par̆ting day'.
  Iambic (adj.)

Idea (n.) Philosophically, as in **Platonism** (q.v.), an eternally existing pattern, of which the individual things we perceive in this world are imperfect copies; popularly, any concept in the mind.

Ideal (n.) (from idea) A thing conceived as perfect in its kind.
  Idealism (n.) One of the many philosophical systems deriving ultimately from Plato, and generally opposed to **Materialism** (q.v.); popularly, aspiration to lofty objectives; in literature or art, the tendency to depict character, objects, and situations, as they should be rather than as they are, represented in, e.g., the character of the Poor Parson in the Prologue to the *Canterbury Tales;* the opposite to **Realism** (q.v.)
  Idealist (n.); **Idealistic** (adj.)

Idiom A form of expression in current use. For example, 'He's easily taken in', 'I've run out of sugar'.

Idyll Originally a short poem describing a picturesque scene or incident, usually in rural life; later used to mean little more than 'episode' as in the title *Idylls of the King* (Tennyson), a series of episodes from the legend of King Arthur.
  Idyllic (adj.), generally used today to describe innocent, perfect happiness: perhaps because of the **Pastoral** (q.v.) associations of 'idyll'.

Iliad Epic poem by Homer describing an episode in the siege of Troy (Ilion): the 'wrath of Achilles' and the slaying of the Trojan hero, Hector.

Image In literary usage, a simile or metaphor; generally, any expression tending to create a 'picture in the mind'.
  Imagery (n.) The images of a poem or other composition, considered collectively; the use of images.

Imagination (n.) That mental faculty by which we create and shape, particularly in literature; invention.

'. . . imagination bodies forth
the forms of things unknown'
(*Midsummer Night's Dream*)

Generally held, especially by Romantic critics, to be a higher power than **Fancy** (q.v.).

Impressionism The name given to a style of painting which flourished, particularly in France, in the second half of the 19th century. Impressionism seeks to capture the 'feel' of a scene at a particular moment, conveying the effect of light, shape, and colour by bold brush-work, but not attempting to paint accurately observed detail; the term may be figuratively applied to literature, especially poetry, which avoids precise narration or description, and endeavours primarily to suggest atmosphere. There are affinities with **Symbolism** (q.v.).

Improvisation In speaking of drama, the making up of dialogue on the stage (apparently) on the spur of the moment; 'gagging'; particularly associated with the Italian Commedia dell' Arte of the 16th–17th centuries, in which conventional characters (Harlequin, Pantaloon) figured in predictable situations, but also a practice among Elizabethan stage clowns (and, indeed, clowns in all ages). 'Let those that play your clowns speak no more than is set down for them' (*Hamlet*). Improvisation is popular also among many modern dramatists.

Interlude A late 15th and 16th century name for a short stage entertainment of the lighter kind, originally intended to fill a gap between the performance of the parts of a **Morality** or **Mystery** cycle (q.v.).

Intrigue The **Plot** (q.v.) of a play or novel.

Intuition The immediate grasping of the truth, or what one believes to be the truth without the intervention of the reasoning process.
   Intuitional (adj.); **Intuitive** (adj.)

Invective (n.) A violent attack, denunciation; also adj.

Irony A restrained form of sarcasm or ridicule, usually taking the form of exaggerated praise, e.g. 'We were told that at Glenelg, on the seaside, we should come to a house of lime and slate and glass. This image of magnificence raised our expectation.' (Dr Johnson, *Journey to the Western Islands.*)

Jargon A form of technical language used by a small group of people. It often seems to be designed to confuse a lay audience! For example, 'one's view', 'interpersonal' and 'on-going' are used in business.

Johnsonian In the style of Dr Samuel Johnson (1709–1784), poet, critic, lexicographer, and conversationalist: expressed in a sententious, stately, periodic style; but also, on occasion, blunt and direct: 'Sir, we have done with civility; we are to be as rude as we please'.

Jonsonian In the style of Ben(jamin) Jonson (1573–1637), poet and dramatist; particularly with reference to the Comedy of Humours (q.v.).

Juvenalian In the style of Juvenal (D Junius Juvenalis, 60–140 AD) Roman satirical poet; bitter, savage.

Kafkaesque (adj.) Relating to, in the manner of, Franz Kafka (1883–1924), Czech-German–Jewish novelist. In his most famous novels, *The Trial* and *The Castle,* the protagonist grapples with incomprehensible accusations and obstacles, which he is never able to clear up, in a labyrinth of bureaucratic procedure; hence, generally, nightmarish.

Katharsis (Gk. n.) Purgation. Used by Aristotle in the **Poetics** (q.v.) to describe the purpose and effect of tragedy as 'through pity and fear effecting the proper purgation (katharsis) of these emotions.' It is not clear whether he thought that tragedy, by arousing pity and fear at the downfall of the tragic hero, purged the spectator of these ignoble emotions, or that it purged or purified those emotions of their baser elements. Often spelt **Catharsis** in English.
   K(C) athartic (adj.)

Laconic (adj.) Sparing of words, brief and pithy, as the ancient Spartans were reputed to be. (Laconia – name of the district of which Sparta was the principal city.)

Leitmotiv (Ger. n.) A musical theme associated with a character, especially in Wagnerian opera, which is introduced at appropriate moments, e.g., when the character appears on the stage; may be applied to an important idea which recurs frequently in a writer's work, e.g. the influence of heredity in Ibsen or in Zola.

Lexicographer (n.) 'A maker of dictionaries: a harmless drudge' (Dr Johnson).

Liberal (adj.) Originally, pertaining to those skills and studies considered worthy of a 'free' man, as opposed to those considered 'servile' or mechanical; a concept of immense influence, especially in education, from Renaissance times onward, the 'free' man being generally equated with the gentleman; hence such expressions as 'the liberal arts', 'a liberal education'; today generally taken to refer to the pursuit of general intellectual culture, not narrowly professional or technical.

Litotes (n.) Device of expressing something by the negative of its opposite: 'She is no shirker' (= 'She is a hard worker').

Lyric (n.) Originally, verses intended to be sung or chanted to the accompaniment of the lyre; song. Now generally applied to that kind of poetry which is felt to have the closest affinity to song; a short poem giving direct expression to personal feeling, creating an *effect* of spontaneity (though the poet has probably sweated blood over it), and employing great variety of metre and rhyme-pattern. It would be fair to say that most contemporary poetry is **Lyrical** (adj.), and that, when people think of 'poetry' (if they ever do), they have lyrical poetry in mind. The 'lyric' of a song means its words.

Machiavellianism The combination of craft and ruthlessness attributed to Niccolo Machiavelli (1469–1527), Italian statesman and writer on political subjects. His handbook for rulers, *The Prince*, was studied attentively throughout Renaissance Europe, though often publicly deplored.

> 'Though some speak openly against my books,
> Yet will they read me, and thereby attain
> To Peter's chair.'
> (*Marlow, The Jew of Malta*)

Popularly, 'Machiavel' was associated with 'Old Nick', The Devil.
    Machiavellian (adj.)

Malapropism A verbal muddle, which takes its name from Mrs Malaprop, a character in *The Rivals*, a comedy by Richard Brinsley Sheridan (1751–1816). The lady may be allowed to explain herself: 'Sure, if I reprehend any thing in this world it is the use of my oracular tongue, and a nice derangement of epitaphs'.

Mannerism (n.) Excessive addiction to a particular style in art or in literature.
    Mannered (adj.), affected; **Mannerist** (n.)

Manners With reference to epic or dramatic poetry, distinctive varieties of disposition, as revealed in behaviour.

Manners, Comedy of Term used to describe a kind of comedy which represents in a ridiculous light the speech, customs, and affectations of fashionable people; best represented in English literature by so-called **Restoration** (q.v.) comedy, and by the later plays of Sheridan (q.v.).

Masochism (n.) Sexual pleasure derived through submission to physical maltreatment; the word derives from Sacher Masock, 19th century Austrian novelist, who exploits this taste in his work.
    Masochist (n.); **Masochistic** (adj.)

Materialism Philosophically, the doctrine that nothing exists except matter, and that man, in all his aspects, is merely a form or function of matter; more generally, devotion to material interests; the opposite to **Idealism** (q.v.).
    Materialist (n.); **Materialistic** (adj.)

Medieval Belonging to the Middle Ages, a somewhat vague term for that period of time between the **Dark Ages** (q.v.) and the **Renaissance** (q.v.); approximately from the 10th–15th century.

Meiosis (Gk. n.) Understatement; a special kind of irony (q.v.) in which understatement, often negative, is employed for emphasis, e.g. Queen Victoria's celebrated 'We are not amused'; sometimes no irony is intended, and the intention is solely to add emphasis, e.g. 'Not seldom from the uproar I retired' (Wordsworth).

Melancholy (n.) 'Black bile', one of the four **Humours** (q.v.): the lowness of depression of spirits (sometimes called **melancholia**) it was supposed to produce when secreted to excess. The most prestigeful of all the humours; in Elizabethan days supposed to be a distinctive mark of the superior or intellectual man: 'I'll be more proud, and melancholy, and gentlemanlike than I have been.' (Jonson, *Every Man in his Humour*). The subject of a vast, rambling work of enormous erudition by Robert Burton (1577–1640), *The Anatomy of Melancholy;* supposed by other European nations in the 18th century and particularly in its most eccentric and suicidal forms, to be peculiarly the *English Malady*.
    Melancholy (adj.); **Melancholiac** (n.) a person afflicted with melancholy (also adj.); **Melancholic** (adj.)

Melodrama Originally, a play with songs and music, evidently devised to gratify popular taste; hence a play aiming to appeal to simple popular audiences, marked by exciting incident, strong but uncomplicated feeling, characters easily recognizable as 'good' and 'bad' characters and a happy ending; often spoken of rather condescendingly as the staple entertainment of the Victorian working class theatre, but dominates popular TV drama today.
    Melodramatic (adj.)

Metaphor A kind of image in which the qualities of one object are suggested by direct association with another, e.g. 'a *tide* of woes'. It is often helpful to consider a metaphor as a compressed **simile** (q.v.), and to explain it by converting it into a simile, e.g. (to take the example given) 'woes as overwhelming and irresistible as an incoming tide, or a tidal wave'.
    Metaphorical (adj.)

Metaphysics Originally, the world of Aristotle 'after the *Physics*'; hence, rather freely, the study of what is beyond the physical, material, or natural.

Metaphysical (adj.), pertaining to the immaterial or transcendental (q.v.); hence, popularly, far-fetched, strange. It was in this sense that Dr Johnson, in his *Life of Cowley,* bestowed on the early 17th century English poets the name of the **Metaphysical Poets,** alluding to their fondness for strained or novel images, or **Conceits** (q.v.). The word is often used to suggest cloudy impractical speculation, e.g. 'the central opacity of Kantian metaphysics' (Peacock); 'Ah, that is clearly a metaphysical speculation, and like most metaphysical speculations has little reference to the facts of real life as we know them.' (Wilde, *Importance of Being Earnest.)*

Metre Poetic rhythm divisible into regular feet.
   Metrical (adj.)

Millenium (n.) The period of a thousand years during which, according to the *Book of Revelations,* Christ is to reign on earth; hence, a period of perfect happiness.

Miltonic (adj.) In the manner of John Milton (1608–74), author of *Paradise Lost:* grand, sublime, epic, in subject and style.

Mimetic (adj.) Of, or addicted to, imitation.

Miracle Play A type of religious drama which flourished in the later Middle Ages; originally written by clerks to present stories from the Scriptures in popular dramatic form, then collected into 'cycles' and presented on movable stages by the trade guilds during religious holidays.

Mock-heroic (adj.) Same as **Heroi-comical** (q.v.).

Morality Play A late development of the **Miracle** or **Mystery Play** (q.v.) in which the scriptural story is replaced by an allegory in which the characters are personified virtues and vices. The most famous of these plays is *Everyman.*

Muses The nine goddesses attendant on Apollo, and thought of as the patronesses of the arts and sciences recognized by the Greeks. From Renaissance times down to the end of the 18th century it was customary for a poet to describe his inspiration as 'the/his Muse'; this is sometimes done today, facetiously. 'With Donne, whose Muse on dromedary trots' (Coleridge).

Mystery Play As **Miracle Play** above. The derivation from 'mister', a skilled trade ('In youthe he lerned hadde a good myster' Chaucer), is not generally supported.

Mysticism The belief that man can attain direct communion with God in an ecstatic state usually induced by solitude, fasting, and prayer; hence, any attitude, experience, or belief which is claimed to be spiritually uplifting but is beyond rational explanation or comprehension.
   Mystic (n. and adj.); **Mystical** (adj.) (The words derive ultimately from the Greek for 'a person initiated into the Mysteries', secret rites performed in honour of a variety of gods.)

Myth (n.) A traditional story expressing the religious beliefs of a people, relating its supposed origins, or offering a supernatural explanation of natural phenomena. The figures of myth are presented as gods, demi-gods, and heroes, and are frequently referred to in the epic poetry of the people concerned; popularly, a story with no foundation in fact.
   Mythical (adj.)

Mythology A body or collection of myths; more rarely, the study of myth.
   Mythological (adj.)

Nature Originally, that which is in the normal course of things. The word, and its associated adjectives, **natural** and **unnatural,** has been used in a bewildering variety of meanings, according to period and context, e.g.

1 the nature or essential property of things;
2 the 'natural' order, with its hierarchical system of beings, thought by Medieval and later theologians to be divinely established – the Great Chain of Being;
3 normal human nature, life as it is – 'o'erstep not the modesty of nature' (*Hamlet*); 'First follow Nature' (Pope);
4 the physical universe – 'Nature and Nature's laws lay hid in night' (Pope);
5 especially to the Romantic poets, the natural world unmodified by man, its appearance and forms of life, thought of as inherently beautiful and ennobling – 'Nature then . . . to me was all in all' (Wordsworth);
6 the preceding meaning personified, again by Romantics – 'Let Nature be your teacher. She has a world of ready wealth.' (Wordsworth),

Naturalism In literature, a development in the later 19th century of the **Realism** of the mid-century. Purporting to represent nature as in (3) above, it carried to an extreme the idea of the novel as a kind of documentary study, particularly of the more squalid and miserable aspects of life, and was much influenced by the idea that individuals are merely the product of heredity and environment, and cannot choose their way of life; the most celebrated **naturalist** writer is Emile Zola (1840–1902).
   Naturalistic (adj.)

Negative Capability Defined by Keats as a kind of receptive state of mind where 'a man is capable of being in uncertainties, mysteries, doubts, without any irritable reaching after fact and reason'.

Nemesis Nemesis was the Greek goddess of vengeance or retribution. In literature the word means the principle of tragic poetic justice where evil brings its own punishment. Such happenings are seen in *Macbeth*.

Neo Prefix derived from the Greek for 'new'; frequently used to describe a revival of something earlier, e.g. **neo-classicism,** to describe the culture and particularly the critical standards of the later 17th and early 18th centuries.

Neologism A newly-coined word.

Novel A prose fiction of substantial length, purporting to represent real contemporary life, which supplanted the fanciful Romance (q.v.) at the beginning of the 18th century. In English literature, Daniel Defoe (1659–1731) is often regarded as 'the father of the novel', though there are Elizabethan prototypes. Many critics associate the rapid growth of the novel with the increasing importance of the middle classes throughout the eighteenth and nineteenth centuries. In the last hundred years the novel has become the most widely-employed literary form, has shown an increasing responsiveness to general intellectual and artistic movements, is widely used as a vehicle for all kinds of propaganda, and has accommodated every kind of experiment and eccentricity. One can hardly imagine what a novelist of an earlier age would make of, e.g. a **Surrealist** (q.v.) novel like *Ulysses* (James Joyce, 1882–1941).

Nostalgia Home-sickness, longing for another place: sometimes extended in modern usage to a longing for another time.
Nostalgic (adj.)

Number Old word for **metre** (q.v.); in pl., verse, lines of verse: 'I lisp'd in numbers, for the numbers came' (Pope).

Objective (adj.) Treating a topic impartially, seeing it as it is, excluding one's own personal views and feelings – all of which is hardly possible in literature, and not always in the interpretation of what passes for scientific fact.
Objectivity (n.); Antonym, **Subjectivity** (q.v.).

Ode A lyrical poem of some length, in a dignified and serious style, often addressed to a person, or personification, or expressing a sustained meditation, e.g. *Ode on Intimations of Immortality* (Wordsworth) **Horatian** and **Pindaric odes** (q.v.) **Choric odes:** The verses assigned to the Chorus in a Greek play.

Odyssey Epic attributed to Homer, recounting the ten years' wanderings and adventures of the hero Odysseus, or Ulysses, on his return from the Trojan War.

Oedipus (literally, swollen-foot). Mythological king of Thebes, who read the riddle of the Sphinx, and, in ignorance, killed his father and married his mother; he blinded himself when his unwitting enormities came to light. The hero of probably the most celebrated Greek tragedy, the *Oedipus Rex* of Sophocles (497–405 BC).

Omniscient narrator All-knowing narrator.

Onomatopoeia The invention or use of words whose sound suggests the meaning, e.g. 'The murmur of innumerable bees' (Tennyson)
Onomatopoeic (adj.) Words like 'crash' and 'bang' are onomatopoeic.

Ottava Rima (Ital.) An eight-line stanza, consisting (in English poetry) of iambic pentameters rhyming abababcc; considered suitable for long narrative poems, and used with admirable dexterity by Byron (1788–1824) in *Don Juan*.

Ovidian In the manner of Ovid (P. Ovidius Naso, 43 BC–17 AD): ingenious, graceful, amatory – with reference to his *Art of Love*.

Oxymoron A figure of speech in which words of opposite meaning are joined together, e.g. 'A damned saint, an honourable villain' (*Romeo and Juliet*).

Palladian (adj.) Relating to, or in the style of Andrea Palladio (1518–80), Italian architect, who may be said to have initiated the neo-classical tendency in architecture by his revival of the Roman style.

Panegyric (n.) A public speech, or composition, in high praise of some person or achievement; a eulogy or encomium.

Pantheism The belief that God is everything, and everything is God; that God and the universe are one: a view that accords well with the Romantic attitude to nature, and may be found in much of Wordsworth's early poetry, e.g., in the lines beginning

'And I have felt
A presence that disturbs me with the joy
Of elevated thoughts. . . .'
(*Tintern Abbey*)

Pantheist (n.); **Pantheistic** (adj.)

Pantheon A temple dedicated to all the gods; the whole body of the gods, considered collectively.

Parable An **allegory** (q.v.) taking the form of a narrative which seeks to convey a moral or religious truth.

Paradox A statement contrary to popular opinion, apparently absurd or self-contradictory, but often containing a great deal of truth, e.g. 'It is always painful to part from people whom one has known for a very brief space of time. The absence of old friends one can endure with equanimity.' (Wilde, *Importance of Being Earnest*)

Para- (Gk. prepn.) Alongside, hence near, akin to. Therefore:

Paraphrase To paraphrase a piece of poetry or part of a Shakespeare play means to render it into simple, modern English prose. Some people may feel that this destroys the whole appeal of poetry, but it may be of great practical value for two reasons.

1 It enables the meaning which exists in most poetry to be isolated and studied.
2 The difference between the paraphrase and the original will show the beauty of the poetry of the original lines.

Pararhyme Near-rhyme: the placing in the rhyming position, at the end of lines, words whose consonants are the same, or similar, but whose vowels are different: a device particularly associated with the poetry of Wilfred Owen (1893–1918):

> 'Wearied we keep awake because the night is silent:
> Low, drooping flares confuse our memory of the salient.'
> *(Exposure)*

Parenthesis An explanatory or qualifying word, or group of words, inserted into a passage with which it has no grammatical connection, and enclosed between dashes or brackets.
Parentheses (pl.) the bracket signs; **Parenthetic(al)** (adj.)

Parody A composition which mimics the characteristic features of a writer's style and thought, in order to expose him to ridicule.

Pastoral (n.) A poem or other work which represents the life of shepherds, usually in an idealized light; extended to any work dealing with country life. Originally, i.e. in the period of the **Renaissance,** based on classical models, e.g. Spenser's *Shepheardes Calendar*, it became so much used as a ready-made form for trifling compositions, often allegorical, as to weary even those of strongly classical tastes; hence Dr Johnson's comment on Milton's pastoral elegy, *Lycidas*: 'its form is that of a pastoral; easy, vulgar, and therefore disgusting; whatever images it can supply are long ago exhausted'. (*Life of Milton*)
Pastoral (adj.)

Pathetic Fallacy A phrase invented by John Ruskin (1819–1900) to describe the tendency to credit nature with human feelings. 'All violent feelings . . . produce in us a falseness in all our impressions of external things, which I would generally characterize as the Pathetic Fallacy' (Ruskin, *Modern Painters*). It is, of course, a leading feature of the Romantic poets, e.g. Wordsworth, with whom Ruskin was by no means out of sympathy.

Pathos (Gk. n.) Suffering feeling; hence that quality in a work of art which arouses pity and sadness; in earlier times was often used to describe one of the qualities of tragedy, but has been a good deal debased in modern usage, as may be seen particularly with **pathetic** (adj.) which now usually means, in popular speech, miserable, wretched, contemptible.

Pedant (n.) In Elizabethan English, a schoolmaster or tutor: 'like a pedant that keeps a school i' the church' (*Twelfth Night*); but often, even in this period, with a pejorative suggestion of heavy learning unseasonably paraded, a quality never lacking in schoolteachers, least of all in Shakespeare's day.
Pedantic (adj.) **Pedantry** (n.) All these words are today wholly **pejorative** (q.v.).

Pejorative (adj.) (from Lat. 'peior', worse) Tending to the worse, conveying disapproval, disparaging.

Pentameter A line of verse having five feet.

Period (n.) The full stop at the end of a sentence. In **Rhetoric** (q.v.) a complete sentence, especially an elaborate one made up of many clauses. **Periodic** (adj.) used particularly to describe an ornate, stately style employing sentences of this kind, as in the historian Edmund Gibbon (1737–94), author of *The Decline and Fall of the Roman Empire*: a subject which evidently requires a majestic style.

Peripeteia (Gk. n.) A sudden change of fortune, as often in tragedy; a reversal of situation, e.g. the change in the relationship between Higgins and Eliza at the end of Bernard Shaw's *Pygmalion*.

Periphrasis (Gk. n.) Round-about expression, verbosity, circumlocution. Sometimes **periphrase** in English: (to be distinguished from **paraphrase,** (n.) expression of meaning in other words than those of the original).

Peroration (n.) The conclusion of a speech, in which the speaker usually 'gives it all he's got'.
To perorate (vb.): to declaim, speak vehemently.

Persona (n.) From the Latin for a mask of the kind used by actors in the Greek and Roman theatre; hence, the outward presentation of one's character, one's 'image', as contemporary jargon has it, in life, or as a character in a play: which need not be the same as one's 'real' personality.

Personification (n.) A kind of metaphor in which an inanimate thing or an abstract idea is treated as something living, usually a human being; a favourite device of 18th century poetry: 'Let not Ambition mock their useful toil' (Gray, *Elegy in a Country Churchyard*).

Philistine (Ger.) 'Philister', a term used derisively by German students in the 19th century of persons not members of their, or any, university; possibly by allusion to the words, 'The Philistines be upon thee, Samson' (Judges, XVI), used in altercations between students and townspeople? Hence, anyone lacking **Liberal** (q.v.) culture, devoted to **material** (q.v.) interests; much used by e.g. Matthew Arnold (1822–88), poet and critic, in deploring the **philistinism** (n.) of the British middle class.

Philosophy (n.) Literally, 'the love of wisdom'; the medieval university recognized three branches, constituting a field for advanced study leading to a Doctor's degree (hence PhD): (1) Natural, (2) Moral, and (3) Metaphysical Philosophy. (1) has become what we call 'science', (2) ethics, and (3) 'philosophy' in its accepted academic meaning, i.e. the study of 'the meaning of things', ultimate reality, first causes and principles. In Shakespeare's day, it sometimes meant knowledge acquired by the use of natural reason, as opposed to faith or revealed truth, which is why Hamlet tells Horatio

> 'There are more things in heaven and earth, Horatio,
> Than are dreamt of in your philosphy.'

In the 18th century the word often implied **scepticism** (q.v.) in religious matters, especially in France. Today, popularly, the word is used to mean no more than a general attitude to life: 'my philosophy as a greengrocer. . . .'. Since philosophers were supposed to rise above the petty concerns of other men, **philosophical** (adj) and **philosophically** (adv.) have acquired a strong suggestion of resignation or **stoicism** (q.v.) in the face of misfortune.

Picaresque (adj.) From Sp. 'picaro', a rogue; used to describe the type of novel which chronicles the adventures of a wandering rogue; popular in England especially in the 18th century. Many of the best-known novels of this period fall into this category; the hero need not always be a rogue himself, but certain features are common to all: an episodic plot, full of complications, much diversity of scene and many characters, some of whom reappear at intervals, and plenty of lively pictures of low life. Examples: any novel of Defoe's, Fielding's *Tom Jones*, Smollett's *Roderick Random*.

Pindaric (n.) An **ode** (q.v.) in the manner of Pindar (521–441 BC) Greek poet. The features of the English Pindaric, associated particularly with Abraham Cowley (1618–67), are a complex and irregular stanza, high-flown language, and a straining after intense and exalted feeling.

Plagiarize (vb.) To steal another writer's words and ideas and pass them off as one's own.
   Plagiarism (n.); **Plagiarized** (adj.); **Plagiarist** (n.); **Plagiary** (n.) hence the name of the character in Sheridan's *The Critic*, Sir Fretful Plagiary.

Platitude (n.) Flatness, commonplaceness in speech or writing; an expression having these qualities. Cf. **cliché**.

Plato Greek philospher (429–347 BC), disciple of Socrates, whose views he purported to represent in his *Dialogues*.
   Platonism (n.) the philosophy of Plato, especially in its exposition of **idealism** (q.v.): **platonist** (n.).

Platonic Pertaining to the above; particularly, with reference to purely spiritual love between the sexes, a meaning acquired in the 17th century; though originally 'amor platonicus' denoted male homosexuality.

Plot (n.) The plan of a play, novel or other work of fiction; its narrative framework. Cf. **intrigue**.

Poetaster (n.) A minor, or bad poet; a pretender to poetry. The name of a comedy by Ben Jonson ridiculing rival dramatists.

Poetic (adj.) In modern usage, extended to any prose which has the qualities of feeling, imagination, and language expected in poetry; also **Poetical** e.g. 'The most poetical account of a game of cricket I have ever read in a newspaper'.

Poetic Licence The 'right' of poets to distort language, historical and geographical truths for the sake of their art. Shakespeare, for instance, invents coastlines for countries which are landlocked as he does in *The Winter's Tale*.

Poetics, The Title of an incomplete treatise by Aristotle (q.v.), of immense influence on both criticism and the writing of plays; the part that survives deals principally with Tragedy and Epic. See also **Unities**.

Polymath (n.) One who knows many things: sometimes suggested to have been the ideal and highest type of **Renaissance** (q.v.) culture, e.g. Leonardo da Vinci.

Predestination The doctrine that God, being omniscient, has foreseen, and therefore ordained the fate of every human soul before birth; opposed by the view that God has given man Free Will to determine his salvation or damnation by his own acts.

Predestinarian (adj.) theology is particularly associated with the teaching of Calvin, but has provided a meaty bone of contention in all ages.

> 'But I ne kan nat bulte it to the bren,
> As kan the hooly doctour Augustyn,
> Or Boece, or the bisshope Bradwardyn,
> Whether that Goddes worthy forwityng
> Streyneth me nedely to doon a thyng . . .'
> (Chaucer, *Nonne Preestes Tale*)

Pre-Raphaelite (n.) A member of the 'Pre-Raphaelite Brotherhood', a group of Mid-Victorian British poets and painters (Rossetti, Millais, Morris, Burne-Jones, and others) who professed a great devotion to their concept of the Middle Ages, as opposed to the Philistinism of contemporary life. The name expressed the desire of the painters to go back to the supposedly pure, austere, and pious art of the period before Raphael of Urbino (1483–1520); they were therefore also rejecting **Renaissance** art.
    Pre-Raphaelite (adj.); **Pre-Raphaelitism.**

Prolixity Unnecessarily long and tedious expression.

Proscenium (n.) In the modern theatre, the space between the main curtain and the orchestra, or front stalls; more generally, the line dividing the stage from the audience in a 'picture-frame' stage, marked, until the development of subtler forms of stage lighting, by foot-lights.

Prose (n.) Non-metrical (though not necessarily unrhythmical) language; is not verse.

Prosody The study or analysis of **metre.**

Protagonist (n.) The chief personage in a drama, or other work of fiction; the hero or heroine: should be used as far as possible in the singular only, though pl. is permissible where there is more than one character of the first importance.

Psycho-analysis (n.) The analysis of the mind; the approach to the psychiatric treatment of mentally disturbed patients by the analysis of dreams and suppressed memories, practised notably by Freud (q.v.).

Psychology The study of the mind; popularly the understanding of human nature.

Pun A joke or piece of word-play arising from a **Homophone** (q.v.)

> 'Not on thy sole, but on thy soul, harsh Jew,
> Thou makest thy knife Keen.'

> (Shakespeare, *The Merchant of Venice*)

Puritan (n.) A reformed Protestant who wished to 'purge' or 'purify' the church of all unscriptural doctrine and Romish ritual; generally associated in the 16th–17th centuries with Calvinist theology (see **Grace, Election**), sobriety of dress and speech, and disapproval of merry-making, whether in private or in public, as at the theatre; and equally generally suspected of hypocrisy. One of the most rumbustious satires on Puritanism is the character of Zeal-of-the-Land Busy in Jonson's *Bartholomew Fair*; anyone of ostentatiously austere life.
    Puritan (adj.); **Puritanical** (adj.); **Puritanism** (n.)

Quatrain (n.) A stanza of four lines.

Quasi- (Lat. 'as if') A prefix signifying 'near', 'akin to', e.g. 'quasi-Romantic'. Cf. **Para-.**

Quibble (n.) A jest involving some verbal hair-splitting, popular in Elizabethan drama,
e.g. '*First Clown:* There is no ancient gentleman but gardeners, ditchers, and grave-makers; they hold up Adam's profession.
Sec. Clown: Was he a gentleman?
First Clown: A' was the first that ever bore arms.' (Shakespeare, *Hamlet*)

Raillery (n.) Good-humoured mockery, banter (q.v.).

Rationalism The belief that reason is man's chief or only guide, especially in what concerns religion or the supernatural; the explanation of all questions by the application of reason; (philosophically) the view that reason, rather than sense, is the foundation of knowledge.
    Rational (adj.); **Rationalist** (n.); **Rationality** (n.) the state of being reasonable.
    To Rationalize (vb.) and **Rationaliz(s)ation** (n.), connected with the idea of explaining by reason, or bringing into a 'reasonable' state by e.g. closing down redundant or profitless parts of a business, are often used today with a somewhat pejorative flavour, suggesting the finding of plausible but specious explanations for unwelcome facts.

Realism Philosophically, any system of thought opposed to **idealism;** generally, the acceptance or representation of 'things as they are'; in literature, a tendency among mid-19th century novelists (especially in France) to give a scrupulous representation of life in all its aspects, and to depict human nature as it really is, 'warts and all'; in some ways a reaction against **Romanticism** (q.v.) and a return to the attitude of 18th century novelists. *Madame Bovary* (Gustave Flaubert, 1821-80) is often cited, not altogether fairly, as the great Realist novel, and the precursor of the kind of **Naturalism** (q.v.) associated with Zola (q.v.) Naturalism may be considered as a development of Realism.

Reason, Age of A descriptive phrase used of the early and middle years of the 18th century, when **Sceptical Rationalism** (q.v.) was much in favour with intellectuals, and 'rational' was a word of high commendation. Even Chrisitanity was defended as a rational system of belief by its apologists.

Refrain Recurring phrase or line, especially at the end of a stanza. Many ballads have refrains at the end of each verse.

Regency (n. and adj.) Referring to the period at the beginning of the 19th century when, because of the madness of George III, his eldest son, later George IV, was head of state, with the title of Prince Regent; a period approximately that of the Napoleonic War and the years immediately after, and ending, technically, in 1820, with the death of George III; generally associated with frivolous and dissipated style of life among the upper classes, it was the age of Byron and 'Beau' Brummell – and also of Jane Austen: a 'Regency buck' – a man of fashion of the time, generally presented, especially by romantic lady novelists, as dashing, fascinating; also applied to styles of decoration, etc., of the time. In the history of French civilization, 'Regency' usually refers to the period (1715–23) during which the Duke of Orleans was Regent for the young Louis XV – also associated with dissipation in high life. Regencies seem to go in for this.

Renaissance (Sometimes, though not often today, **Renascence**) Literally, 'rebirth'. The name given to what must still be reckoned the greatest movement in history of European art and culture. It began in Italy towards the end of the 14th century, with a turning away from medieval art and thought, and a rebirth of interest in the art and literature of the classical civilizations. New styles of painting, architecture, and sculpture, the revived study of Greek, and a new approach to Latin, all flourished under the patronage of wealthy Italian princes and Popes. A considerable impetus was given to the movement by the fall of Constantinople to the Turks in 1453, and the consequent flight to Italy of Byzantine scholars and Greek manuscripts. The wars of the French in Italy (1494–1525) did much to accelerate the spread of Renaissance culture into France (Leonardo spent his last years in Amboise), but it did not attain its full development in England until the reign of Elizabeth. The Renaissance man, at his most fully developed, is thought of as many-sided, with a highly cultivated mind and love of art, a delight in luxury and sensual pleasure, and often a ruthless ambition and cruelty.

Repartee (n.) A smart, clever retort; especially in plays, dialogue marked by this quality, e.g.
Algernon: Come, old boy, you had much better have the thing out at once.
Jack: My dear Algy, you talk exactly as if you were a dentist. It is very vulgar to talk like a dentist when one isn't a dentist. It produces a false impression.
Algernon: Well, that is exactly what dentists always do.

(Wilde, *Importance of Being Earnest*).

Restoration (n. and adj.) In English, referring to the period beginning with the Restoration of the Monarchy in 1660, and extended, especially in such expressions as **Restoration Drama** or **Restoration Comedy,** to the end of the 17th century, and even later: it being felt that the literature of this whole extended period is essentially of the same kind.

Rhapsody (n.) Earlier, a miscellany: today, a composition, in literature or in music, extravagant or enthusiastic in feeling, but deficient in form or control: the kind of composition in which the artist gives free rein to 'the spontaneous overflow of powerful feelings'.

Rhetoric In the medieval university, the formal study of the art of speech-making, as defined in rules and typical examples of figures of speech derived from ancient authorities like Quintilian (M. Fabius Quintilianus, 35–95 AD): a basic study, one of the lower division, or 'Trivium' (hence 'trivial) of the seven liberal arts – the other two being grammar and logic. In modern usage, the art of speech-making in general, or just eloquent public speaking; but often used pejoratively, to suggest empty noise, a flow of bombastic language – 'mere rhetoric'; similarly **Rhetorical** (adj.); **Rhetorician.**

Rococo (n. and adj.) The style of, particularly French, furniture, architecture, interior decoration, in the age of Louis XIV and XV, marked by much elaborate scroll-like decoration; generally, tastelessly florid and ornate.

Roman à clef Novel in which characters are real people, disguised.

Romance (Languages) Originally, 'romanz' (O. Fr.) was the name of the vernacular tongue of Roman Gaul, as opposed to the language of the Germanic invaders; hence, generally, the name of the whole group of European languages descended from Latin – French, Italian, Spanish etc.

Romance (n.) In literature, a medieval verse tale of the kind written in a Romance language, recounting the adventures of a knightly hero, and expressing the ideals of the age of chivalry; or a later prose tale, often of great length, and containing something of the same spirit. 'Twelve vast French romances, neatly gilt', writes Pope, presumably referring to a work like *Le Grand Cyrus* by Mlle. de Scudery (1607–1701): destined to be supplanted as entertainment by the more realistic Novel. Today, a 'romance' is usually a popular sentimental love story (*True Life Romances*), the love-affair, itself, or just a tall story – a sad comedown in the world.

Romanticism The name given to the attitudes which, building up throughout the second half of the 18th century, dominated the early years of the 19th century in every aspect of life and art. Essentially it involved a turning-away from the sceptical, rational, classically-moulded culture of the 18th century, in an effort to liberate the creative imagination. The Romantic artist was no longer a craftsman, mindful of form and precedent: he saw himself as a lonely dedicated figure, often wrung by self-torture and a sense of failure, who expressed his imagination in whatever way he pleased, and felt himself charged with a prophetic mission – one of the 'unacknowledged legislators of the world', as Shelley put it. Romanticism exploited all that was felt to be mysterious, remote, or terrifying – the medieval, the supernatural, the unexplored; it cherished dreams of social regeneration which coloured the political revolutions of the age; and, perhaps most important of all, at least in England, it established an attitude to Nature discussed under **Nature** (5) and (6) which still influences us today.

   Romantic (n.); **Romantic** (adj.) at the beginning of the 18th century, was virtually synonymous with 'absurd', but in the course of a century transformed its meaning first into 'picturesque' and finally into 'grand' e.g.

> 'But oh! that deep romantic chasm which slanted
> Down the green hill athwart a cedarn cover!'
> (Coleridge, *Kubla Khan*)

Sadism (n.) Sexual pleasure derived through the infliction of physical suffering on others, as described in the novels of the Marquis de Sade (1740–1814) celebrated French madman and (unless one shares his tastes) minor writer.
   Sadist (n.); **Sadistic** (adj.)

Saga A medieval prose narrative or chronicle written in Norway or Iceland. The word is often used today as if it had some suggestion of 'epic' or 'heroic'; but, although the events related in the original sagas are often the stuff of epic (like the discovery of North America from Greenland!), their style is remarkably plain and factual.

Satire (n.) The exposure in a ridiculous light of human vice and folly, professedly to 'chasten morals with ridicule'; any work, in whatever form, which attempts this.

Scepticism Philosophically, the view that real knowledge, or truth, is unattainable generally, a doubting or disbelieving attitude, especially towards religion.

Scholasticism A general name for the theology and philosophy of the medieval university based on the writings of the Fathers of the Church and the works of Aristotle in Latin translation.

Science Originally, knowledge in general, e.g. 'Fair Science frown'd not on his humble birth' (Gray's *Elegy*); the modern meaning was usually expressed by **Natural Science** (cf. **Natural Philosophy,** q.v.), but in the course of the 19th century the modern limitation gained the upper hand.

Sciolism Pretentiously superficial knowledge.
   Sciolist (n.); **Sciolistic** (adj.)

Semantics The study of the meaning of words.

Senecan (adj.) Tragic in the manner of Seneca (L. Annaeus Seneca 4 BC–65 AD), who wrote in imitation of the Greek tragedy, but in a violently rhetorical style, and with a much greater emphasis on blood and horror. It has been questioned if his plays were intended for stage performance, but he was much admired and imitated by Elizabethan dramatists.

Sensibility (n) Power of perception through the senses, ability to feel; in the 18th and early 19th centuries, capacity for refined emotion, hence the title of Jane Austen's novel, *Sense and Sensibility*.

   Sensible (adj.) almost invariably used to mean no more than 'perceptible to the senses' in Shakespeare and contemporary writers,
e.g.
> 'Art thou not, fatal vision, sensible
> to feeling as to sight?'
> (*Macbeth*)

In the 18th century we find the modern meaning of 'possessing good, or common sense' appearing, as when Dr Johnson, having made his hearers giggle by saying 'the woman had a bottom of good sense', sternly corrected this to 'the woman was fundamentally sensible' (which is also capable of a ridiculous interpretation, though no one dared to laugh a second time). There is also the rather affected meaning of 'aware', as in 'I am very sensible of your kindness'.

Sensual Seeking, or producing, gratification of the senses through excessive indulgence. Always pejorative today, e.g. 'Free from sloth and sensual snare'.

Sensuous (adj.) Pertaining to, or affecting, the senses; readily responsive to stimulation of the senses; without the pejorative force of **Sensual** above, but used particularly of a temperament, or an effect, which is the opposite of austere. If it is desired to use a perfectly neutral word in reference to the operation of the senses, or the process of sensation, the best one is **Sensory** (adj.).

Sentimentalism In the 18th century, the provocation and indulgence of tearful emotion as a way of proving to oneself that one belonged to that superior category of mankind possessed of 'a feeling heart': as exploited by Samuel Richardson (1689–1761) in his novels, became very much of a vogue. Hundreds, perhaps thousands, of admirers of both sexes (including Dr Johnson!), both at home and abroad (particularly in Germany) wept agreeably over the distresses of his heroines, Pamela and Clarissa. For a time **sentimental** (adj.) became an almost meaningless fashionable word, signifying little more than 'chic' or 'charming'. After Richardson, **sentiment** got on to the stage in the form of the **Sentimental Comedy,** of which the most successful English practitioner was Richard Cumberland (1732–1811)

> 'Retailing nightly to the yawning pit
> The purest morals, undefiled by wit'
> (Prologue to Sheridan's *The Critic)*

There was a contemporary craze for 'comédie larmoyante' in France. But the inevitable reaction set in, largely promoted by RB Sheridan (1751–1816), who brought Cumberland himself on stage in *The Critic* as Sir Fretful Plagiary, and satirized the **Man of Sentiment** splendidly in the character of Joseph Surface, in the *School for Scandal.* Joseph is never at a loss for an improving **sentiment** – 'To pity, without the power to relieve, is still more painful than to ask and be denied' – but is really a heartless and scheming hypocrite.

   Sentimentality (n.) is today the best word to use to suggest the mawkish and excessive display of tender feeling.
   To sentimentalize (vb.)

Shavian (adj.) In the manner of George Bernard Shaw (1856–1951), witty and paradoxical.

Simile A comparison intended to bring out the qualities of something by reference to those of something else, but, unlike **metaphor,** made explicitly, e.g. 'He tore through the house like a tornado'. All similes are introduced by 'like' or 'as'.

Soliloquy (n) 'Speaking alone', speaking one's thoughts aloud, especially on the stage.
   To soliloquize (vb.)

Solipsism The view that the only person of whose existence one can be sure is oneself.
   Solipsist (n.)

Sonnet A poem of fourteen lines of iambic pentameters, of Italian origin, regularly used in English poetry from Tudor times. The Elizabethan or Shakespearean form (in which Shakespeare wrote all of his sequence of 154 sonnets) consists of three quatrains and a couplet, rhyming ababcdcdefefgg. The 'Italian' form used by most post-Elizabethan **Sonneteers,** e.g. Milton, Wordsworth, consists of a group of eight lines, or **octave,** followed by a group of six, or **sestet,** with different rhymes.

Spenserian Stanza The stanza (q.v.) invented by Edmund Spenser (1552–99) for his long allegorical poem, *The Faerie Queene:* it consists of eight iambic pentameters and a final alexandrine, rhyming ababbcbcc.

Spleen (n.) The popular old name for the milt, or melt, a large ductless gland in the stomach which controls certain blood changes; in former days its function was not understood, and it was supposed to secrete the **Melancholy Humour** (q.v.); hence the name is transferred to the humour, and becomes another word for melancholy, peevishness, lowness of spirits, throughout the 18th century.

Stanza (It. n.) A group of lines of verse arranged in a regular and recurring pattern, which fixes the number of lines (usually not less than four), the metre, and the rhyme scheme.

Stoicism from Gk. *stoa,* a porch or colonnade, and particularly the hall at Athens in which Zeno (c. 300 BC) lectured. The doctrine of Zeno that happiness was to be achieved by duty and self-denial, and that pleasure and pain were to be ignored by a virtuous man; hence, therefore, the patient uncomplaining endurance of misfortune; the opposite of **Epicureanism** (q.v.).
   Stoic (n.); **Stoical** (adj.)

Stress In English prosody, the emphatic pronunciation of certain syllables.

Style Those aspects of literature which concern form and expression rather than content: a writer's language, not his subject matter. Though the distinction between style and content is sometimes rather artificial, it is often necessary in criticism.
   Stylist (n.) particularly a writer whose style is felt to be distinctive and elegant.

Stylistics (n.) The study of style.

Subjective (adj.) Treating a question exclusively from the writer's own point of view; coloured by his own feelings and prejudices; personal, not impartial: the opposite to **objective** (q.v.).
   Subjectivity (n.)

Surrealism A movement in art and literature which may be said to have effectively begun in the early 1920's; essentially a reaction of a kind that recurs periodically in the history of culture, against what is felt to be the stifling requirements of established convention, form, logic. The early surrealists set themselves the task of liberating from the subconscious level of the mind all its freakish, unconnected images, and letting them express themselves more or less spontaneously; later, perhaps, there is more of a tendency towards the deliberate assembly of haphazard images. In this aspect of surrealism one feels the influence of the psychoanalytical writings of Freud (q.v.). Another influence was surely the feeling that civilized Europe was disintegrated in the First World War:

> 'What is the city over the mountains
> Cracks and reforms and bursts in the violet air
> Falling towers
> Jerusalem Athens Alexandria
> Vienna London'

wrote TS Eliot, in the most striking surrealist poem in English, *The Waste Land* (1922); in the novel, the greatest surrealist achievement is James Joyce's *Ulysses,* also first published in 1922. Among surrealist painters may be mentioned Dali and Picasso. It should hardly be necessary to point out that Surrealism is the direct opposite of **Realism** (q.v.).

    Surrealist (n. and adj.).

Swiftian (adj.) In the manner of Jonathan Swift (1667–1745), Dean of St Patrick's Dublin, author of *Gulliver's Travels,* etc.; bitterly satirical, misanthropic.

Symbolism The use of something to represent something else, especially the use of some material object to represent an abstract idea, e.g. the mace, or sceptre, to **symbolize** power, authority ('His (the king's) sceptre shows the force of temporal power', *Merchant of Venice*); the employment of **symbols** as a literary device. With particular reference to French poetry from about 1850, the term is used to describe a whole tendency or movement towards emotive suggestion rather than precise statement (see *Impressionism*), and the use of images as symbols of the poet's own inner state rather than as representations of the external world. The culmination of Symbolism is to be found in the poetry of Stéphane Mallarmé (1842–98).

    Symbolist (n. and adj.); **Symbolic(al)** (adj.)

Sympathy Participation, or sharing, of another's feelings; particularly, in literary criticism, the association of the reader or spectator with a character in a work of fiction, or with the author himself; a **sympathetic** character is one we find congenial, and with whom we can to some degree identify ourselves.

    To sympathize (vb.); Antonyms: Antipathy, Antipathetic.

Syntax The orderly arrangement of parts: particularly, in grammar, the orderly construction of sentences.

Tacitean (adj.) In the manner of Tacitus (Cornelius Tacitus 55–120 AD). Roman historian; brief and sententious.

Tautology Useless and repetitious verbiage, the repetition of the same idea in different words, for example,

> 'The Vase is unique and very rare'.
> 'He passed away and died'.

Theme Leading idea in a novel, play or poem. Sometimes the theme is obvious: in Hardy, the struggle of the individual against fate; in Shakespeare's plays the themes are mixed – in *Hamlet* two of the several themes are indecision and incestuous love.

Theology The study of God, divinity; a particular system of belief incorporating a God, or gods.

    Theological (adj.); **Theologian** (n.)

Tirade (n.) A violent speech, long and denunciatory: a harangue.

Tone The prevailing feeling of any work of literature. This tone can be, e.g., humorous, satirical, cynical.

Tragedy A play which represents the downfall of a great man in a serious manner, using elevated and poetical language: this is essentially Aristotle's concept, as expressed in the **Poetics** (q.v.), as well as Shakespeare's; any story which ends in disaster: this was the medieval meaning – see Chaucer's *Monk's Tale.*

    Tragic (adj.); **Tragedian** (n.) a writer of tragedy, or a performer in tragedies.

Transcendentalism A name given to any system of philosophy which is based, not on experience, but on the assumption that there exists 'something beyond', independent of man; recognizing 'eternal verities' like 'the starry heavens above, and the moral law within', as the German philospher Immanuel Kant (1724–1804) puts it; a variety of **idealism** (q.v.); rather vaguely used to signify **metaphysical** (q.v.), abstract, treating of the supernatural.

    Transcendental (adj.)

Trochee A foot of two syllables in which the stress falls on the first: the opposite to an **iambus** (q.v.) e.g.

> 'Dante once prepared to paint an angel' (Browning)

    Trochaic (adj.)

Unities, Dramatic Principles of dramatic construction elaborated from the *Poetics* (q.v.) of Aristotle. Aristotle says that the best plays observe 'unity of action', i.e., that they narrate only one coherent episode of one story; also, that tragedy 'endeavours to confine itself to a single revolution of the sun'. As interpreted by neo-Classical critics and dramatists, especially in the 17th century, this emerges as three inflexible rules of tragedy:

1 Unity of Action: no sub-plot or intermixture of 'comic staff with tragic sadness and gravity', as Milton says in his preface to *Samson Agonistes;*

2 Unity of Time: the action of the play must be confined within the supposed space of a natural day;
3 Unity of Place: the action was not to depart, except marginally, from the place where it was shown to begin. This last Unity was nowhere mentioned by Aristotle, but it is a logical complement to the others, since it cannot be supposed that the same group of characters (postulated by the Unity of Action) should in the course of a day remove from, say, Rome to Alexandria. The fact that the Unities were dogmatically asserted, and dramatists like Shakespeare roundly condemned for not understanding 'The Rules', by people who had never read a page of Aristotle, does not necessarily mean that their observance is not, in many plays, a source of dramatic strength. It is, however, true that the urgent advocates of the Unities seem to think that the dramatist's main task is to placate an imaginary spectator who goes to the theatre determined not to be taken in, and sits through the performance stop-watch in hand.

Urbane (adj.) Smooth, polished, polite; having those qualities with which **Urban** or town-dwelling man credits himself, in contrast with those of the 'rustic, ruder than Gothic'.

Verse Metrical composition, poetry; a metrical line; a group of lines arranged in a recognizable pattern, approximately the same as **stanza** (q.v.).
   Versification (n.) composition of verses.
   Versifier (n.) a maker of verses; generally with some pejorative suggestion, e.g. 'a mere versifier' as opposed to a poet; a poetaster. (q.v.)

Virgilian (adj.) Possessing the qualities associated with Virgil (see **Aeneid**) e.g. dignified eloquence, either of the epic kind or in dealing with country life, as Virgil does in the *Georgics*.

Wit (n.) Originally intelligence, intellect, reason; later, in the 17th century, high intelligence, great mental capacity, or the possessor of such qualities of mind: thus Dryden – 'Great wits are sure to madness near allied'; in the 18th century develops the meaning which is now dominant: the ability to amuse, or the quality that amuses, by brilliant and unexpected play with words and ideas. Wit is essentially a matter of cleverness, of intellect, unlike **humour** (q.v.). Wit can be cruel and stinging; it often goes with satire: humour is rarely to be found in such company.

Wordsworthian (adj.) In the manner of William Wordsworth (1770–1850) especially to suggest a reverent or mystical attitude towards Nature.

Zolaesque (adj.) In the manner of Emile Zola, French novelist. See **Naturalism.**

Index